SERIES
IN
HUMAN
RELATIONS
TRAINING

# THE
# 1981 ANNUAL
# HANDBOOK
# FOR GROUP
# FACILITATORS

(The Tenth Annual)

*Editors*

JOHN E. JONES, Ph.D.

and

J. WILLIAM PFEIFFER, Ph.D.

*Associate Editor*

MARSHALL SASHKIN, Ph.D.

UNIVERSITY ASSOCIATES, INC.
8517 Production Avenue
P.O. Box 26240
San Diego, California 92126

Reproduced from
*The 1981 Annual Handbook
for Group Facilitators*
John E. Jones and J. William Pfeiffer, Editors
San Diego, California: University Associates, Inc., 1981

*Printed in the United States of America*

*Published by*
University Associates, Inc.
8517 Production Avenue
P.O. Box 26240
San Diego, California 92126
714-578-5900

*Canadian Subsidiary*
University Associates of Canada
P.O. Box 203
Station M
Toronto, Ontario M6S 4T3
Canada

*European Subsidiary*
University Associates of Europe
P.O. Box 3
Mansfield, Notts NG19 7JH
England

# PREFACE

This is the tenth *Annual Handbook for Group Facilitators*. When we initiated the series a decade ago, we had no expectation that the *Annual* would become such a widely accepted and used part of the basic resource kit of group facilitators around the world.

Our bias in selecting articles for the *Annual* has remained constant since the first *Annual*. Stated simply, it is a bias toward *practice*—of human resource development and of organization development—based on sound theory and valid research. The *Annual* does not contain research papers; these are to be found in *Group & Organization Studies*. We are, however, careful to insist that the pieces we select for the *Annual* be based on solid research or, if the content is theoretical and unvalidated, that the limits of the piece be clearly stated. Of the relatively small number of pieces submitted to us for possible inclusion that have passed this test, we have selected those that are *useful* to the practitioner.

Our concern with usefulness and practice led us to originate a policy that is still too uncommon concerning reproduction of materials. Users may freely duplicate (as well as modify or adapt) *Annual* materials for *legitimate educational and training purposes*. Although we do not require that users obtain any special permission to do this, materials that are reproduced from the *Annual* must include the credit statement found on the copyright page. Users should, however, note that *if University Associates materials are to be reproduced in publications for sale or are intended for large-scale distribution, prior written permission is required*. The only exception to this policy pertains to materials previously copyrighted by others; to duplicate these, obviously, the user must secure permission from the original source.

In the past decade, 298 group facilitators have contributed to the *Annuals*. Since the first *Annual*, about one-quarter of the authors in each volume are "repeat" contributors. For the past five years, women have averaged about 16 percent of our contributors. Although this percentage may simply reflect the actual male-to-female proportion of group facilitators, we do want to encourage more contributions from women. Our academic/practitioner balance is just about where we always have wanted it: just under half (45 percent) of this year's contributors are in primarily academic positions. This has been true since the first *Annual*. We continue to seek well-written, quality material that passes the selection criteria discussed above, and we encourage all *Annual* users to send us their contributions (as well as their ideas, suggestions, and feedback).

Special contributions have been made to this tenth *Annual* by our editorial staff members. Rebecca Taff, managing editor, has managed to keep the *Annual's* production process closer to the planned schedule than ever before. Marshall Sashkin, senior editorial associate, contributed the section introductions as well as a theory and practice paper, and Arlette Ballew, senior editor, turned our structured-experience hopes into tightly designed realities. Most of all, we wish to express our gratitude to the authors who have participated in the *Annuals* over the past ten years, and especially to the authors represented in this *Annual*, whose creativity and willingness to share with their professional peers have made our decade-old wish a decade-long reality.

San Diego, California
December, 1980

John E. Jones
J. William Pfeiffer

## UNIVERSITY ASSOCIATES
### Publishers and Consultants

 University Associates is an organization engaged in publishing and consulting in the broad area of human relations. UA consultants are experienced group facilitators who conduct training programs (both public and private), train trainers, work with organizations and communities on developmental problems, and provide editorial direction for the publication of useful training materials.

As an organization, University Associates attempts to maintain a balance among its three major activities—publishing, consulting, and training—to ensure that each is current and that each provides a source and an outlet for practical ideas to improve human relations. Because the clients of University Associates are varied, the company's training and publications are intended to encourage the development of facilitator skills in all types of settings and institutional contexts. The international focus of UA makes it a clearinghouse for the emerging theory and technology of human relations training, organization development, and community development.

# TABLE OF CONTENTS

---

*See Structured Experience Categories, p. 7, for an explanation of numbering.

## THEORY AND PRACTICE

## RESOURCES

# GENERAL INTRODUCTION TO THE 1981 *ANNUAL*

In this tenth *Annual Handbook for Group Facilitators*, we continue the sharing of resources for human resource development and training that we initiated over a decade ago. As in the preceding nine *Annuals*, all materials presented here are new; none duplicate those found in earlier volumes of the *Annual* or in the eight volumes of *A Handbook of Structured Experiences for Human Relations Training*.

This *Annual's* format is the same as the previous volumes, with five sections: Structured Experiences, Instrumentation, Lecturettes, Theory and Practice, and Resources. Although most *Annual* users are familiar with this content division, it is worth reviewing, especially because this year does bring some change.

The *Structured Experiences* section shows the greatest change. As part of a major project that resulted in a portable kit containing all the structured experiences published in the ten *Annuals* and the eight *Handbooks*, along with selected structured experiences from other University Associates publications, a completely new structured experience categorization scheme was developed. This new system is presented in detail in the Introduction to the Structured Experiences section. That section, as usual, contains twelve new structured experiences.

In the *Instrumentation* section, we present four new paper-and-pencil instruments for use in training. None of these questionnaire-like tools is intended to be used as a "test." The purpose of each—as is the case with the thirty-six instruments published in the nine previous *Annuals*—is to be used for personal, group, and organization development with the guidance of a facilitator. The introduction to this section presents a step-by-step description of how to develop an organizational survey instrument.

Nine wide-ranging *Lecturettes* comprise the next section of the *Annual*. Each is brief, centered on a fairly specific topic, and intended to be used as the basis for concise presentations by the facilitator to the group in a lecture-like session or as "take home" handouts for training purposes. Lecturettes are specifically intended to be used in conjunction with experiential training activities, usually as a help in conceptualizing and understanding what participants have just experienced. The introduction to this section gives some guidelines on the use of humor in lecturette presentations.

*Theory and Practice* contains a diverse set of longer articles intended for the group facilitator's professional development. These pieces may be less useful as handouts but should stimulate the facilitator with ideas that are of current relevance in human relations training. In some cases the articles break new ground, while in other cases the aim is to present a solid, basic background for a specific theory or practice. In the introduction to this section, we focus—as we have in the past—on the nature of the balance between theory and practice.

In the final section of the *Annual*, *Resources*, we present four pieces: a bibliography, a list of periodicals, and two "how-to-use" articles that deal with two different types of training tools. The intent of this section is to facilitate access to tools—periodicals, research, training practices and techniques, etc. The introduction to this section contains some suggestions about how to judge the merit of such tools.

Each piece in the *Annual* includes a brief biography of its author(s). The full addresses and—when available—phone numbers of each contributor can be found at the end of this volume, listed alphabetically. The editors are interested in users' comments and feedback, but requests for further information should be directed to the author of the piece in question.

For this tenth *Annual*, we have found it both easier and more difficult to select the contents. Easier, because there is an almost constant stream of articles, structured experiences, etc., submitted by group facilitators. Difficult because this implies greater selectivity from a pool of high-quality materials.

The changes in categorizing the structured experiences (as well as the all-encompassing structured-experience-kit project) were inspired by feedback from users. We continue to desire feedback and criticism that will suggest changes and improvements, as well as new instruments, structured experiences, lecturettes, and other materials. We take pride in the belief that a decade of acceptance of the *Annuals* implies a relatively high degree of usefulness. Contributors and users alike can also take pride in the tradition of sharing resources that we initiated with the *Annual* series. We hope to continue this sharing as long as it proves useful to the community of group facilitators.

# INTRODUCTION TO THE
# STRUCTURED EXPERIENCES SECTION

For ten years, users of the *Annuals* have been asking for and suggesting changes in the way we categorize structured experiences. We avoided any major changes in the past because there was no clear consensus on any particular set of categories and because we saw no other approach that made significantly more sense (easier to use, more logical, etc.) than the empirically derived set of eleven categories that we started with.

However, the need for some better organization of the structured experiences became clearer and more strongly felt over the decade. When demands for structured experiences became so great as to justify producing a compilation of almost all UA's published structured experiences as a resource kit for group facilitators (Pfeiffer & Jones, 1980), we decided that a redefinition of our category framework was in order. After much thought and consultation we developed, in collaboration with some colleagues,[1] a completely redesigned classification system. The categories and subcategories are listed below.

### Personal

Self-Disclosure: activities that teach the ability to reveal oneself to others.

Sensory: activities that focus on personal awareness and skills through the exploration of the senses.

Feelings Awareness: experiences that focus on emotional understanding of oneself.

Feedback: activities that promote awareness of others' ability to increase one's understanding of self and that encourage acceptance of the opinions or feelings of others.

Assumptions: activities that help one to see that the assumptions he or she may make about others may significantly influence perceptions.

Values Clarification: activities that clarify the process by which one chooses, prizes, or acts.

Life/Career Planning: activities that allow one to evaluate the present and the future of one's career or life.

### Communication

Communication Awareness Experiments: activities that illustrate what happens when two people communicate, either verbally or nonverbally.

Developing Interpersonal Trust in Dyads: activities that help two people to develop a personal or work relationship.

Sexual Awareness: experiences that expand awareness of and skill at handling the sexual aspects of relationships.

Listening: skill-building activities that help people to listen actively.

Interviewing: activities to develop skills needed in the two-person-interview situation.

Assertion: activities that improve people's ability to affirm their own positions while being sensitive to the needs of others.

---

[1] We would like to acknowledge the contributions of Peter Rutherford, Wellington, New Zealand, to the conception and planning of the new category system.

## Group Characteristics

Process Observation/Awareness: activities that help develop skills for observing what is taking place in a group.

Leadership/Membership: activities that deal with issues of power, leadership style, motivation, and leaders' and members' interactions with one another.

Communication: activities that offer practice in group communication.

Values Clarification/Stereotyping: activities to illustrate the effects *on the group* of individuals' personal values and their stereotypes or prejudices.

## Group Task Behavior

Problem Solving/Awareness: activities that develop skill in and awareness of problem-solving techniques.

Generating Alternatives: activities to practice an early creative step of the problem-solving process.

Group Feedback: activities that develop awareness of and skills in group feedback.

Competition (Win-Lose): activities that involve competitive behavior by group members and explore its effect on the accomplishment of a task.

Competition and Collaboration (Win-Lose/Win-Win): activities that deal both with the competitive tendencies that emerge within groups and the appropriateness of collaborative behavior.

Collaboration (Win-Win): activities that deal with only the cooperative aspect of group task behavior.

Conflict Resolution/Values Polarization: activities that develop skills to deal with conflicts in the group because of differing values of members.

Consensus/Synergy: activities to develop the group's skills at reaching general agreement and commitment to its decisions and goals.

## Organizations

Awareness/Diagnosis: activities that help people to be aware of the forces that affect the functioning of their organizations and to learn to diagnose organizational problems.

Team Building: learning experiences to develop the effectiveness of teams within an organization.

Decision Making/Action Planning: activities that teach these necessary skills within organizations.

Conflict Resolution/Values: activities that look at values within the organizational context and at conflicts caused by differences between personal values and organizational values.

Consultation Skills: experiences that develop the skill of the internal or external consultant.

## Facilitating Learning

Getting Acquainted: activities designed for warming up a learning group that is meeting for the first time.

Forming Subgroups: activities that help a newly formed learning group break into subgroups for learning purposes.

Expectations of Learners/Facilitators: activities for use when a gap potentially exists between what the learners expect and what the facilitator is offering.

Dealing with Blocks to Learnings: activities developed to deal with situations in which learning is blocked through the interference of other dynamics, conscious or unconscious, in the group.

Building Trust: activities to create trust and a climate of openness and learning within the group.

Building Norms of Openness: activities that help participants expand their learning by being willing to give and receive feedback.

Energizers: activities that "recharge" the group when energy is low.

Evaluating Learning/Group Process: activities to help individuals evaluate what is taking place within a learning group.

Developing Group Facilitator Skills: activities designed to develop the abilities of trainers, group leaders, or group facilitators.

Closure: activities to use at the end of a training event.

The new system has fewer categories (six instead of eleven) but each category contains several areas of finer discrimination. Some subcategories appear under two major category headings; thus, values-clarification activities relating to an individual's value issues are in the "Personal" category, while structured experiences dealing with such issues in the context of groups are found in the "Group Characteristics" category. Similarly, structured experiences that probe conflict concerns with respect to group task behavior are found under the latter heading (subheading "Conflict Resolution/Values Polarization"), while those that center on organizational conflict are in the "Organizations" category.

The new category-system index appears at the end of this introduction; it replaces the old index that was included in every past *Annual*. We are certain that some users will prefer the old system; in some ways we do too, even though we believe that the new system represents a major improvement overall. What this reaffirms for us is that it is probably more important to categorize, using *some* system, than to categorize using some *particular* system. After all, almost any structured experience can be (and has been) used for several purposes. We do think that the new system is more logical and easier to use. Many *Annual* readers will recognize their own ideas and inputs in the new system, and we are grateful for receiving them.

As an organizational policy, University Associates avoids the repackaging of materials that we have already published. The *Structured Experience Kit* provided the impetus for developing the new category system and is an important exception to this rule. The *Kit* is simply a portable (if bulky) file cabinet containing 340 structured experiences in 8½" by 11" format—all those published in previous *Annuals* (Pfeiffer & Jones, 1972-1981) and in the first eight *Handbooks* (Pfeiffer & Jones, 1974-1981), plus selections from a half dozen other UA publications that incorporate structured learning activities. It is our plan to add to the contents of the *Kit* periodically, as new structured experiences appear. For many users the convenience of having everything in one easily accessible location outweighs any concern over duplication of publications. We want to emphasize, however, that with the exception of their reproduction in the *Kit*, no *Annual* or *Handbook* materials overlap or are in any way duplicative. In many cases, users will find that several similar structured experiences exist, since it is desirable that the facilitator have a variety of structured experiences to work with, in order to avoid the repeated use of one or two that then become "stale" for the facilitator and, perhaps, the group.

Structured experiences in the *Annual* are selected to be representative of the various categories, to represent current concerns of group facilitators, and to fill in "gaps" in topics not found in earlier *Annuals*. The *Annual* structured experiences are *not* chosen to be simply the "best of" those we have found, developed, or received. In every respect the standards of quality are the same for choosing structured experiences for the *Annuals*, the *Handbooks*, or for any other UA publications. However, our primary aim in the selection process, given appropriate quality, is to obtain a balance among topics, issues, types of experience, and the various dimensions just reviewed. In this way the *Annuals* and *Handbooks* are current, while retaining their usefulness in the long run.

We are pleased with the continuing flow of innovative, high-quality structured experiences, and we encourage *Annual* users to continue to send us their new ideas in order that they may be shared with professional peers.

### REFERENCES

Pfeiffer, J.W., & Jones, J.E. (Eds.). *The annual handbook for group facilitators* (1972-1981). San Diego, CA: University Associates, 1972-1981.

Pfeiffer, J.W., & Jones, J.E. (Eds.). *A handbook of structured experiences for human relations training* (Vols. I-VIII). San Diego, CA: University Associates, 1974-1981.

Pfeiffer, J.W., & Jones, J.E. (Eds.). *Structured experience kit.* San Diego, CA: University Associates, 1980.

# STRUCTURED EXPERIENCE CATEGORIES

# 281. ALLITERATIVE NAMES: A GETTING-ACQUAINTED ACTIVITY

## Goals

I. To facilitate the getting-acquainted process in a small group.

II. To promote self-disclosure in a new group.

## Group Size

Eight to sixteen participants.

## Time Required

Approximately one-half hour.

## Physical Setting

A circle of chairs.

## Process

I. All participants are seated in a circle, and the facilitator briefly discusses the goals of the activity, establishing the expectation that learning the names of group members can be fun.

II. The facilitator directs that each participant is to select an adjective that begins with the same letter as his first name, e.g., Dandy Don, Judicial Jack, or Serious Sally.

III. The participant seated to the right of the facilitator is instructed to say, "Hello, my name is ___ ___." using the alliterative name. The next person to the right then says, "Hello, may I present ___ ___ and my name is ___ ___." The third person presents the first two and himself, and so on, until the end, when the facilitator takes the last turn, presenting each of the participants (in order) and then himself. (When someone cannot remember a name, the group gives hints and any other help needed.)

IV. The facilitator leads the group in debriefing the activity. Members may wish to ask questions of others about their adjectives. The facilitator can conduct a discussion of personal meanings of names, learning/forgetting names, and how individuals wish to be perceived during the group experience.

## Variations

I. More than one adjective can be chosen, or abverb-adjective combinations can be permitted. (Examples: Energetic, Eager Ed; Terribly Tasky Trish.)

II. Members can be instructed to make the introductions in any order, not just around the circle.

III. The members can compare first impressions of each other and the adjectives chosen.

**Similar Structured Experience:** *Vol. II:* Structured Experience **42.**

———————

This structured experience is constantly re-invented; its origin is not credited to any one individual.

# 282. BIRTH SIGNS: AN ICE BREAKER

*Goals*

I. To facilitate the getting-acquainted process in a large group.

II. To alleviate participants' anxiety at the beginning of a training session.

*Group Size*

Fifteen or more participants.

*Time Required*

Approximately one-half hour.

*Materials*

A poster or sign for each birth-sign group, as follows:

| | |
|---|---|
| ARIES, the Ram<br>March 21-April 19 | LIBRA, the Balance Scales<br>September 24-October 23 |
| TAURUS, the Bull<br>April 20-May 20 | SCORPIO, the Scorpion<br>October 24-November 21 |
| GEMINI, the Twins<br>May 21-June 20 | SAGITTARIUS, the Archer<br>November 22-December 21 |
| CANCER, the Crab<br>June 21-July 22 | CAPRICORN, the Goat<br>December 22-January 19 |
| LEO, the Lion<br>July 23-August 22 | AQUARIUS, the Water Bearer<br>January 20-February 18 |
| VIRGO, the Virgin<br>August 23-September 23 | PISCES, the Fish<br>February 19-March 20 |

(These signs are posted on the walls of the room prior to the activity.)

*Physical Setting*

A room large enough for groups to meet without disrupting each other.

*Process*

I. The facilitator briefly discusses the goals of the activity, establishing the expectation that the experience will be both useful and fun.

II. The facilitator instructs the participants to mill around and find the persons whose months and days of birth are closest to theirs.

III. The members are referred to the birth-sign posters and subgroups are formed according to astrological signs. (If the total group is small, subgroups are formed according to clusters of birth signs: spring, summer, autumn, and winter; or earth, air, fire, and water.)

IV. The facilitator instructs each subgroup to discuss two topics and to prepare a one-minute report for the total group. The topics are:

1. What we have in common in addition to our sign, and

2. How we are likely to behave in this training event.

(Ten minutes.)

V. The facilitator calls for a one-minute report from each group.

VI. The facilitator leads a discussion of how participants can be sensitive to each other during the training. The danger of stereotyping each other is also pointed out.

*Variations*

I. Subgroups can be established on the basis of Chinese birth-year signs. (These can be found in any world almanac.)

II. The facilitator can hand out a description of each birth sign to focus the discussion. The group can "own" or "disown" parts of the descriptions.

III. Step II can be eliminated.

**Similiar Structured Experiences:** *Vol. I:* Structured Experience 5; *Vol. III:* **49**; *'74 Annual:* **129**; *Vol. VI:* **197**; *'80 Annual:* **269**.

**Suggested Instrument:** *'74 Annual:* "Self-Disclosure Questionnaire."

Submitted by John E. Jones.

**John E. Jones, Ph.D.**, *is the senior vice president for research and development for University Associates, Inc., San Diego, California, and vice president for academic affairs of the UA graduate school. Dr. Jones is co-editor of* Group & Organization Studies *and of the Pfeiffer and Jones Series in Human Relations Training. He consults internationally with educational, industrial, and community organizations and specializes in team development, group training, intergroup relations, organization development, and counseling.*

# 283. LOUISA'S PROBLEM: VALUE CLARIFICATION

*Goals*

I. To provide practice in clarifying issues and identifying values without passing judgment.

II. To develop awareness of some of the factors affecting one's own value judgments and those of others.

III. To provide an opportunity to exchange various points of view on a highly emotional issue.

*Group Size*

An unlimited number of groups of five or six members each.

*Time Required*

Approximately two hours.

*Materials*

I. A copy of the Louisa's Problem Work Sheet for each participant.

II. A pencil for each participant.

III. Newsprint and a felt-tipped marker for each group.

IV. Masking tape for each group.

*Physical Setting*

A room large enough to accommodate all groups.

*Process*

I. The facilitator briefly introduces the goals of the activity and divides the participants into groups of five or six members each. Each group is supplied with a sheet of newsprint, a felt-tipped marker, and masking tape.

II. The facilitator gives each participant a copy of the Louisa's Problem Work Sheet and a pencil and tells all participants to read the sheet carefully and to follow the instructions at the bottom of the page. (Ten minutes.)

III. The facilitator calls time and instructs the group members to share their lists within their small groups. As each member's list is presented, the member should give the reasons for the placement of the characters on the list. Group members may ask questions for clarification only. The facilitator makes it clear that no one is to attempt to persuade another as to the correctness or incorrectness of a decision. (Fifteen minutes.)

IV. If all members of a group agree on a particular placement for one of the characters or on a total listing of characters, a recorder is appointed to post the list on newsprint. If agreement is not reached on any aspect of the listing, no group list is posted. (Five minutes.)

V. The groups are then directed to discuss their reactions to the activity. The following items can be included in the discussion:

1. Which answers surprised you?
2. Which answers fit what you knew of the others in your group—either from your impressions about the others or from previous experiences within the group?
3. What did you learn about your own or other group members' values, based on the reasons given for the placements assigned?

(Twenty minutes.)

VI. The facilitator reconvenes the participants and allows a few minutes for general comments to be shared. New subgroups of three to four members each are formed, and group members are instructed to process their learnings from this task and their work-group discussions by identifying significant factors that influence their judgment in situations involving value conflicts. (Ten minutes.)

VII. After ten minutes the facilitator reminds subgroup members that they are to help each other clarify at least one or two of the most significant factors that influence value judgments for each of the members of the subgroup. Five to ten minutes more is allotted for this activity.

VIII. The facilitator calls time and asks to have one member from each of the subgroups report on typical factors that were identified during the processing discussion. (Ten minutes.)

IX. The facilitator summarizes the general themes or similarities among the subgroups. (Ten minutes.)

X. The participants are then instructed to spend a few minutes discussing possible applications of their personal learnings from this experience. (Ten minutes.)

*Variations*

I. A problem that is closely related to the concerns of the group can be substituted for Louisa's problem.

II. Participants can work in dyads or triads instead of small groups during steps I through VI.

III. The facilitator can give a lecturette on value clarification prior to the activity.

IV. During step V, participants can be directed to comment on the value bases that they see reflected in the behavior of each of the characters in Louisa's problem.

**Similar Structured Experience:** '*79 Annual:* Structured Experience **235.**

---

Submitted by Cassandra E. Amesley.

**Cassandra E. Amesley** *is an instructor in womens studies at the University of Washington, Seattle, Washington, and has been involved for some time in affirmative action, particularly in the area of sexism. Her training and experience include organizational theory and OD, group therapy and process, and community organizing. Ms. Amesley is also a writer and has published several articles on training, institutional change, and affirmative action.*

# LOUISA'S PROBLEM WORK SHEET

*Background:* Louisa was five months pregnant. She had delayed making a decision concerning her pregnancy because, at seventeen, she did not think she was capable of carrying out the responsibilities of motherhood alone and yet she was under pressure from her friend, Joe, who was the father, to have the child. Louisa had absolutely no desire to marry Joe; she was sure that they would be unable to live together.

Joe had previously told her that he was sterile, which proved to be untrue. When Louisa became pregnant, he offered to marry her. Joe loves children and wants a child. When Louisa finally decided to have an abortion, Joe arranged for Judge Robbins to sign a restraining order against her.

On the advice of her best friend, Anne, Louisa had the abortion anyway. It was performed by Dr. Pressley, who knowingly violated the restraining order. Joe filed charges against Louisa and the doctor. Judge Robbins fined Dr. Pressley for contempt of court but pardoned Louisa because she was a minor.

*Instructions:* Write down the names of the five people involved in this case, *in order*, from the person toward whom you feel the *most* sympathetic to the one toward whom you feel the *least* sympathetic.

When directed, share your list with your group. After everyone has presented a list, discuss each person's reasons for choosing a particular order. Notice who is admired most and least. Do not try to persuade others to your point of view; simply state it as honestly as possible. If the group comes to agreement on a particular order, appoint a member to post a sheet of newsprint on the wall and record the group list. Then advise the facilitator, who will give you further instructions.

# 284. FARMERS: INFORMATION SHARING

*Goals*

I. To demonstrate the effects of collaboration and information sharing in problem solving.

II. To explore aspects of collaboration such as verbal communication and division of labor.

*Group Size*

A maximum of four groups of seven to ten members each.

*Time Required*

Approximately two hours.

*Materials*

I. A copy of the Farmers Task-Force Instruction Sheet for each participant.

II. A copy of the Farmers Judge Sheet for each judge.

III. A copy of the Farmers Observer Sheet for each observer.

IV. A set of the Farmers Bits of Information Sheets for each group. (Each set contains six different sheets, cut apart.)

V. A pencil for each judge and each observer.

VI. Newsprint and a felt-tipped marker.

*Physical Setting*

A room in which all groups can work without disturbing each other or, preferably, a small room for each group.

*Process*

I. The facilitator leads a brief discussion of cooperation and collaboration, then introduces to the participants an opportunity to explore some aspects of collaboration through actual experience. (Five minutes.)

II. The facilitator divides the participants into approximately equal groups of at least seven members each. Six members of each group are designated as a "task force" and the seventh member as a "judge." The remaining members in each group are told that they will act as observers. (If there are only seven members in a group, the judge also serves as the observer.)

III. Each participant is given a copy of the Farmers Task-Force Instruction Sheet, and each group is assigned to a different location.

*University Associates*

IV. While the task-force members study their instructions, the judges and observers are instructed to gather around the facilitator, leaving their task forces at their separate locations. The facilitator gives each judge a copy of the Farmers Judge Sheet and a pencil and gives each observer a copy of the Farmers Observer Sheet and a pencil. Time is allowed for them to study the material and ask questions. (Ten minutes.)

V. The facilitator gives each judge a set of the Farmers Bits of Information Sheets and sends all members back to their groups.

VI. The facilitator tells the groups that they have twenty minutes in which to complete their tasks and then tells the judges to begin.

VII. When the groups have finished their tasks, or when more than twenty minutes has elapsed, the facilitator calls time and assembles all members, keeping the task forces together. The facilitator then solicits reports from the observers for each group. (Up to five minutes per report, fifteen minutes total.)

VIII. The facilitator instructs the members to discuss their reactions to the experience within their groups. (Ten minutes.)

IX. The facilitator leads a general discussion to help participants review how the various groups approached and organized the task (division of labor, emergence of leadership, exchange of information), comparing and contrasting various task-force group processes.

X. In their subgroups, participants are directed to identify helping and hindering factors that affect collaboration. (Ten minutes.)

XI. Subgroup reports are made to the total group. The facilitator helps to develop a list of principles of collaboration and cooperation based on the subgroup reports. (Ten minutes.)

XII. Each participant is instructed to develop an individual action plan to apply the principles learned from the experience to other problem-solving situations. (Five minutes.)

XIII. The action plans are shared in the large group or with one or two other participants in dyads or triads. (Ten minutes.)

*Variations*

I. If a task force is composed of only five members, the Farmers Bits of Information Sheets are cut into five pieces and distributed to the five members.

II. If task forces are composed of more than six members, the Farmers Bits of Information Sheets can be cut into *single items* and distributed among the members until all thirty bits are handed out.

III. If after ten minutes a task force appears to be unable to make any visible progress, the facilitator can offer the following clue: "Since it is forbidden to write, it becomes increasingly difficult for a single individual to remember all the necessary data as well as to process it." If after a few minutes it becomes obvious that this clue did not help, the facilitator can add another clue as follows: "It may be worthwhile to arrange yourselves physically according to the locations of the houses in the village."

**Similar Structured Experiences:** *Vol. II:* Structured Experience 31; *'72 Annual:* **80**; *Vol. IV:* **117**; *Vol. V:* **155, 156**; *'76 Annual:* **178**; *Vol. VI:* **212**.

Submitted by Aharon Kuperman.

*Aharon Kuperman, Ph.D., is the head of the teacher's workshop in creativity and design at Bezalel, Academy of Art and Design, Jerusalem, Israel, where he also conducts a faculty development program. Dr. Kuperman's background is in social psychology, T-groups, and organization development in the kibbutz, industry, government, and schools. He is currently engaged in training trainers for classroom teaching in small groups.*

# FARMERS TASK-FORCE INSTRUCTION SHEET

1. Your group's judge will tell you when and how to begin working.

2. Each member of the task force will receive written bits of information. These are *not to be shown* to others.

3. What will be required of you, and how to go about it, will become clear as you *share information* with the other members of your task force, through *verbal communication only*.

4. When you and your co-workers feel that the required tasks have been completed, call the judge to check your results.

5. If your tasks have been only *partially completed*, or if you have done *more* than what was required, the judge will consider the tasks as being totally incomplete. In that case, you will be required to keep working without the benefit of knowing which part of your task, if any, has been completed satisfactorily.

6. The following rules will be observed throughout this activity:

    a. From the moment the task force begins work, members may speak to other task-force members only.

    b. You may not show others the contents of your written bits of information.

    c. You may not *write* anything.

    d. You must obey the judge's instructions.

7. You will have fifty minutes in which to complete your task.

# FARMERS JUDGE SHEET

1. Your job is to enforce the rules and judge the task force's solution.

2. Study carefully the Farmers Task-Force Instruction Sheet. Ask the task-force members if they have read and understood their instructions and answer any questions before they begin to work.

3. When the task force is ready, give each member a separate set of items from the Farmers Bits of Information Sheets and tell the members to begin working. Record the time at which they begin.

4. Enforce the rules, e.g., do not allow the task-force members to *write* anything.

5. If the group tells you that the task has been completed, check whether or not the answers are correct:

    (a) Skinner drives (or owns) a truck.

    (b) Hull grows apples.

6. *If the answers are correct*, record the time at which the group finished the task and report to the facilitator that your task group has finished.

7. If only one of the above answers is given to you or if the group begins to recite *additional answers* (not asked for) such as "Skinner raises pigeons, grows almonds . . . ," announce that the task is incomplete and instruct the members to keep on working until they finish what was required of them or until the facilitator stops the activity.

*University Associates*

# FARMERS OBSERVER FORM

1. Your job is to observe your task force's group processes, record them, and report your observations to the entire group.

2. Do not reach conclusions or attribute intentions and feelings to others. Simply *describe* what you actually see.

3. Read the Farmers Task-Force Instruction Sheet in order to familiarize yourself with the task and the ground rules. The task force is given bits of information from which it is to determine who drives a truck and who grows apples.

4. Use the following guide, add whatever seems pertinent, and consult the solution table below as an aid for your observations.

*Individual*    a. Who initiates action, how is it done, and what is the action?

                b. Who contributes to or obstructs the task? How? Is the behavior effective?

                c. Other:

*Group*    a. Did the members know and agree on the required tasks prior to beginning the problem solving or did they start working immediately?

                b. What patterns of communication developed?

                c. What procedures to solve the problem developed?

                d. How was the data gathered and compiled?

                e. What was the climate that emerged? Were there any turning points?

                f. Other:

**Solution:**

|  | Skinner | Thorndike | Pavlov | Kohler | Hull |
|---|---|---|---|---|---|
| *Animals* | pigeons | cats | dogs | chimpanzees | Albino rats |
| *Fruit* | almonds | plums | cherries | pears | **\*apples** |
| *House* | bungalow | red brick | log cabin | cottage | ranch |
| *Location* | west | northwest | north | northeast | east |
| *Vehicle* | **\*truck** | sports car | motorcycle | station wagon | limousine |

---

*Items to be deduced by the task force.

# FARMERS BITS OF INFORMATION SHEET (A)

- The dogs' owner lives next door to the house with a plum orchard.
- Hull raises Albino rats.
- The farmer who lives in the bungalow raises pigeons.
- Only one of the village houses is located on the east side.
- The farmer who lives next to Pavlov drives a station wagon.

# FARMERS BITS OF INFORMATION SHEET (B)

- Pavlov's neighbor raises chimpanzees.
- The farmer who raises dogs also grows cherries.
- Skinner lives next to the red brick house.
- One of your group's tasks is to decide who drives a truck.
- The houses of the village are standing in a semicircle, *beside* each other.

# FARMERS BITS OF INFORMATION SHEET (C)

- Kohler grows pears.
- There is a limousine in the garage of the ranch house.
- Each farmer raises a different kind of animal.
- Farmer Thorndike lives next to farmer Skinner.
- A motorcycle stands in the back yard of the log cabin.

# FARMERS BITS OF INFORMATION SHEET (D)

- The person who raises cats lives next door, to the east, of the house with the almond trees.
- Your group has less than three tasks.
- Every week boxes of dog food are placed at the gate of the log cabin.
- Only one of the village houses is located on the west side.
- Each of the five farmers living in the village drives a different kind of vehicle.

## FARMERS BITS OF INFORMATION SHEET (E)

- The log cabin is in the most northern position in the village.
- Each farmer grows a different kind of fruit.
- The ranch house stands next to the cottage.
- Farmer Thorndike drives a sports car.
- Farmer Skinner raises pigeons.

## FARMERS BITS OF INFORMATION SHEET (F)

- Only farmer Skinner lives at the west end of the village.
- There are Albino rats in the yard of the ranch house.
- One of your group's tasks is to decide who grows apples.
- Pavlov lives in the log cabin.
- Each farmer lives in a different type of house.

# 285. ANALYTICAL OR CREATIVE?: A PROBLEM-SOLVING COMPARISON

*Goals*

I. To provide an opportunity to compare analytical and creative problem-solving approaches.

II. To increase awareness of one's own capabilities in and preferences for these two approaches to problem solving.

*Group Size*

Several groups of three to five members each.

*Time Required*

Approximately one and one-half hours.

*Materials*

I. A copy of the Analytical or Creative? Positions Problem Sheet for each participant.

II. A copy of the Analytical or Creative? Warehouse Problem Sheet for each participant.

III. A copy of the Analytical or Creative? Warehouse Problem Solution Sheet for each participant.

IV. A pencil for each participant.

V. Newsprint and a felt-tipped marker.

*Physical Setting*

A room with space for the small groups to interact separately as well as for total-group discussion.

*Process*

I. The facilitator briefly explains the goals and process of the activity.

II. The facilitator divides the participants into groups of three to five members each.

III. The facilitator distributes a copy of the Analytical or Creative? Positions Problem Sheet and a pencil to each participant. He cites a few examples of analytical problem-solving techniques and tells the members that they will have ten minutes in which to solve the problem by analytical means. (Most groups will not be able to solve it.)

IV. As soon as one group solves the problem or when the time has expired, the facilitator shows the solution (posted on newsprint) to the total group and demonstrates how the solution was reached. Then he reviews the characteristics of the analytical problem-solving approach, e.g., there usually is only one correct answer to the problem and the approach used to solve it usually involves the use of mathematics, a model, a matrix, a decision tree, or other deductive reasoning processes. (Fifteen minutes.)

V. The facilitator distributes the Analytical or Creative? Warehouse Problem Sheets and announces that ten minutes will be allowed to solve the problem by creative means. (Again, some groups will not be able to solve the problem, but the facilitator should *not* give hints or structure their efforts.)

VI. After all groups have identified a solution or when the time has expired, each group is directed to explain its solution and/or the approaches it used to solve the problem. (Three minutes each.)

VII. The facilitator gives each participant a copy of the Analytical or Creative? Warehouse Problem Solution Sheet and reviews the information on the sheet. The facilitator then reviews the characteristics of creative problem-solving processes, emphasizing the differences between the two approaches; i.e., the process of creative problem solving requires the ability to draw on experience, break down the problems in various ways, try out solutions, recombine ideas with other ideas, and use one's imagination. The facilitator adds that there usually are several acceptable answers to problems that require a creative approach to problem solving. (Ten minutes.)

VIII. The facilitator leads the participants in a discussion of which type of problem-solving approach they typically use and which type is most applicable to various kinds of problems. (Ten minutes.)

IX. Generalizations are drawn from the participants' learnings, and the group discusses applications. (Fifteen minutes.)

*Variations*

I. Groups can compete. The fastest solution for the "analytical" problem wins, and the most ingenious solution to the "creative" problem wins.

II. Groups can be given the problems to solve prior to any input on analytical or creative processes. After the problem-solving activity has been completed, participants are asked to review the process they followed to determine which approach was used in each of the subgroups. An input session contrasting the two approaches is then given.

## Solution to the Positions Problem

| | | | | | |
|---|---|---|---|---|---|
| Betty Sevald | clerk | steno | **manager** | accountant | attorney |
| Tom Arnold | clerk | steno | manager | accountant | **attorney** |
| Ed Hulbert | clerk | steno | manager | **accountant** | attorney |
| Sidney Cross | clerk | **steno** | manager | accountant | attorney |
| Ted Tucker | **clerk** | steno | manager | accountant | attorney |

1. The attorney is a male (clue 1); cross off the attorney choice for Betty Sevald.
2. Sidney Cross and Ted Tucker cannot be the manager, attorney, or accountant (clue 2); cross off those choices for them.

3. Neither Betty Sevald nor Tom Arnold is the accountant (clue 3); cross off those choices for them. This leaves only Ed Hulbert to be the accountant.
4. Ted Tucker is not the steno (clues 2 and 4), so he must be the clerk.
5. The only remaining job for Tom Arnold is the attorney.
6. Sidney Cross can only be the steno (clue 2 and process of elimination).
7. Betty Sevald must be the manager.

**Similar Structured Experiences:** *Vol. III:* Structured Experience 53; *'75 Annual:* 141; *'79 Annual:* **240.**

**Suggested Instrument:** *'78 Annual:* "Phases of Integrated Problem Solving (PIPS)."

**Lecturette Sources:** *'72 Annual:* "An Introduction to PERT . . . or . . . "; *'80 Annual:* "A Nine-Step Problem-Solving Model"; *'81 Annual:* "Creativity and Creative Problem Solving."

---

Submitted by Bruce A. McDonald.

**Bruce A. McDonald, Ed.D.,** *develops instructional materials for undergraduate vocational teacher preparation at Southern Illinois University, Carbondale, Illinois. He also trains faculty members to use these materials and teaches courses in curriculum development, teaching methods, student and program evaluation, instructional system development, and competency-based teacher education. Dr. McDonald has developed a standardized objective test of teacher competence and is refining a system of teacher preparation.*

## ANALYTICAL OR CREATIVE? POSITIONS PROBLEM SHEET

Betty Sevald, Tom Arnold, Ed Hulbert, Sidney Cross, and Ted Tucker comprise the personnel of a firm and fill the positions of clerk, stenographer, manager, accountant, and attorney, but not respectively.

1. The stenographer bandaged the attorney's finger when he cut it while using the former's nail file.
2. While the manager and the attorney were out of town, the accountant docked Tucker and Cross a half day's pay for taking an afternoon off to go to the ball game.
3. The accountant is a fine bridge player, and Arnold admires his ability.
4. Tucker invited the stenographer to lunch but his invitation was not accepted.

What position is held by each of the above people?

-----------------------------------------------------------------------------------------------

## ANALYTICAL OR CREATIVE? WAREHOUSE PROBLEM SHEET

While dealing with a rush inventory in a large warehouse, I found myself faced with the job of counting several thousand coal buckets. These buckets, which covered an area equal to several large rooms, were in stacks of twenty-four buckets each. If the stacks had been arranged in regular rows, the task would have been fairly simple. As it was, the stacks were pushed together in an irregular mass.

It was impossible to walk over the buckets to count the stacks, and there was not enough time to rehandle and restack them for counting. Yet I counted the merchandise in about half an hour without touching a single bucket.

Can you tell the method I used?

-----------------------------------------------------------------------------------------------

## ANALYTICAL OR CREATIVE? WAREHOUSE PROBLEM SOLUTION SHEET

*Example of a creative solution:*

Get above the buckets, take photos of the tops of the stacks with an instant camera, count the top buckets in the pictures, and multiply that number by twenty-four (the number of buckets in each stack).

There is more than one way to arrive at this type of answer:

1. Find an analogous problem and experiment with the problem-solving approach used for it. For example, to solve the problem posed in counting migrating waterfowl, photos are taken of flocks, the birds are counted, and estimations of migration patterns are made.
2. Break the problem into little problems and address them one at a time, working toward a solution.

# 286. GESTURES: PERCEPTIONS AND RESPONSES

*Goals*

    I. To provide an opportunity for participants to examine the perceptual biases operating in their interpretations of gestures.

    II. To increase awareness of the ambiguity inherent in various forms of nonverbal communication.

    III. To demonstrate how one gesture can elicit different feeling responses among different persons.

    IV. To examine the principle that verbal and nonverbal communication must be congruent to be effective.

*Group Size*

    An unlimited number of groups of six participants each.

*Time Required*

    Approximately one and one-half hours.

*Materials*

    I. A copy of the Gestures Response Sheet for each participant.

    II. For each group, a set of six Gestures Pictures (the pictures are to be cut apart).

    III. A pencil for each participant.

*Physical Setting*

    A room large enough for each group to converse freely in a circle, or a separate room for each group.

*Process*

    I. The facilitator gives a brief introduction, stating the goals of the activity. (Five minutes.)

    II. The large group is divided into small groups of six participants each, and the members of each group are instructed to sit in a circle, facing outward so that they will be able to concentrate more fully on their writing task. A copy of the Gestures Response Sheet and a pencil are given to each participant. A set of six Gestures Pictures is given to each group, one to each member in numerical sequence around the circle.

    III. The facilitator states that each member is to study his picture for a few seconds and then write the responses to the picture as called for on the Gestures Response Sheet. He reminds the participants that the pictures are numbered and that the responses should be entered in the appropriate numbered spaces corresponding to the picture they are viewing.

    IV. After two minutes the facilitator calls time and directs each member to pass the picture to the group member on the left. Participants are then directed to complete the appropriate responses for their second pictures.

V. After each two minutes the facilitator calls time. The pictures are rotated until each member has seen and responded to each of the six pictures.

VI. Subgroup members turn inward to form their circles. To debrief the activity, members share their perceptions of and their reactions to each of the pictures within their small groups. The members then cite cues in the pictures that guided their perceptions. Similarities or differences in perceptions of and reactions to the six pictures and to gestures are discussed. (Fifteen minutes.)

VII. The total group reassembles to discuss communication in terms of the importance of congruence between intentions and the nonverbal cues and gestures used. (Fifteen minutes.)

VIII. The participants are then asked to consider the various interpretations that may result from their own nonverbal behavior. Examples are elicited from group members. Participants are instructed to develop generalizations from the experience that could be stated as principles of good interpersonal communication. (Fifteen minutes.)

IX. The subgroups reconvene to formulate specific applications of these principles by suggesting ways in which each member's nonverbal communication can be made more congruent with his or her intent, feelings, or accompanying verbal communication. (Ten minutes.)

*Variations*

I. The individual writing aspect of the activity can be eliminated. Subgroup members then respond to each picture in turn, identifying the cues they perceive and their assumptions about the intent of the gestures. The discussion focuses on identifying gestures with high impact as an aid to congruent communication.

II. Smaller groups and more or fewer pictures can be used.

III. A variety of pictures cut from magazines can be used, providing that all members of a subgroup view the same set of pictures so that they can compare interpretations.

IV. Facilitators can use this activity to help prepare participants for role playing or other communication activities.

**Similar Structured Experiences:** *Vol. III:* Structured Experience **50**; *'72 Annual:* **75**; *'78 Annual:* **227**.

**Lecturette Source:** *'79 Annual:* "Anybody with Eyes Can See the Facts!"

---

Submitted by Stella Lybrand Norman.

**Stella Lybrand Norman,** *who holds a certificate of advanced graduate studies, is senior counselor and supervisor of the South County Office, Crossroads Drug Abuse Program, Alexandria, Virginia. She does family counseling and runs parents' groups and parents' education workshops for families with a drug abusing member and adolescent and women's groups for drug abusers. She is especially interested in family nonverbal communication and family interaction. Ms. Norman's background is in human problem solving, therapeutic community adolescent programs, communication, and adult education.*

# GESTURES RESPONSE SHEET

| Perceptions | Reactions |
|---|---|
| What is happening in this picture? How do the individuals feel? | How are you feeling as you view this picture? |
| 1. | 1. |
| 2. | 2. |
| 3. | 3. |
| 4. | 4. |
| 5. | 5. |
| 6. | 6. |

**1**

**2**

**3**

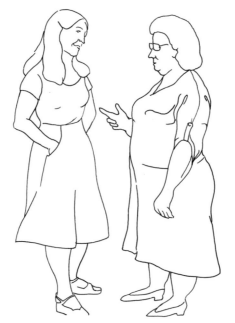

**4**

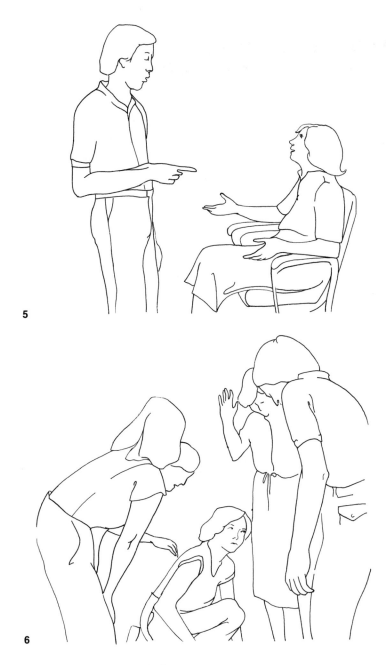

**5**

**6**

# 287. FOUR-LETTER WORDS: EXAMINING TASK-GROUP PROCESSES

*Goals*

    I.  To study the behavior of an unstructured group in accomplishing a complex task.

    II.  To heighten awareness of the importance of correct interpretation of written task instructions.

    III.  To enable group members to compare observed behavior with typical task-group behavior.

    IV.  To assist group members to better perceive and understand individual interactions within a task group.

*Group Size*

    Ten to twelve participants.

*Time Required*

    Approximately two and one-half hours.

*Materials*

    I.  One copy of the Four-Letter Words Paradox Sheet for each participant.

    II.  One copy of the Four-Letter Words Behavior Prediction Sheet for each participant.

    III.  One copy of the Four-Letter Words Observation Summary Sheet for each participant.

    IV.  A copy of the Four-Letter Words Instruction Sheet.

    V.  A copy of the Four-Letter Words Incentive Sheet.

    VI.  One large, sealed envelope bearing the instruction: *"Do Not Open this Envelope Until You Are Really Ready To Do So"* which contains a similarly sized, sealed envelope, folded in half, bearing the instruction: "If you have opened the first envelope before the required information has been given to the facilitator, you have lost $5,000 of any profit you may make. *Do Not Open this envelope until you are really ready to do so.* If you fail to observe this instruction, you will not be able to make any profit and will have incurred a further loss of $5,000."

    VII.  The inner, folded and sealed envelope should contain seven 3" x 3" cardboard squares. A different letter of the alphabet is to be printed on both sides of each of seven squares. The seven letters are: A, E, L, O, P, S, and T.

    VIII.  A pencil for each observer.

    IX.  A pencil for each member of the active group.

    X.  A wall clock, watch, or stopwatch for the timekeeper.

    XI.  Newsprint and a felt-tipped marker.

*Physical Setting*

A group-on-group arrangement in which the members of the active group are seated around a large table, with sufficient room for each observer to stand behind each seated active-group member. A separate room in which the observers can be briefed.

*Process*

I. The facilitator briefly explains the goals of the activity. (Five minutes.)

II. An "active group" (or groups) of five or six members is formed and is seated around the work table. Each member is given a copy of the Four-Letter Words Paradox Sheet. The members are directed to read the sheet thoroughly and then to discuss their reactions to the information. The group is also told that it will soon be asked to accomplish a task. No leader is designated for the group. (Twenty minutes.)

III. While the active-group members are following their instructions, the remaining participants are taken to a separate room and are told that they will act as the observer group. Each observer is given a copy of the Four-Letter Words Paradox Sheet and a copy of the Four-Letter Words Behavior Prediction Sheet and is allowed time to study them. The facilitator then clarifies any items on the Four-Letter Words Behavior Prediction Sheet and briefly explains the objectives of the task to be accomplished by the active group. (Five to ten minutes.)

IV A copy of the Four-Letter Words Observation Summary Sheet and a pencil are issued to each *observer*. Names of the active-group members are filled in. Each observer is assigned to watch one of the members of the active group or is assigned to observe for a particular type of behavior that corresponds to one of the categories on the Four-Letter Words Behavior Prediction Sheet. (Five minutes.)

V. The observers are directed to review the following guidelines (prepared on newsprint prior to the activity):

1. The observing task is to be accomplished *nonverbally*.

2. Any behavior observed after the task is begun should be indicated on the Four-Letter Words Observation Summary Sheet by an "X"—one X for each time a behavior is observed.

3. No help or suggestions, in any form, should be given to the members of the active group.

(Five minutes.)

VI. One of the observers is designated timekeeper. The timekeeper is told to record both the planning time and the working time of the active group, but to give no verbal reminders to the active group.

VII. Both groups (active and observer) are positioned in the work room. The facilitator states the time and places one copy of the Four-Letter Words Instruction Sheet, one copy of the Four-Letter Words Incentive Sheet, and the sealed envelope packet in the center of the table. The facilitator gives a pencil to each member of the active group and tells the members of the active group to begin the planning phase. The timekeeper starts timing. (Twenty-five minutes.)

VIII. When the active group gives the required information to the facilitator, the timekeeper notes the elapsed time. This information is recorded on newsprint by the facilitator.

IX. The facilitator then gives the word for the task to begin, and the timekeeper keeps track of the time until the active group gives the facilitator the number of four-letter words that has been produced. (Ten minutes.)

X. One member of the observer group is directed to check the number of words produced. (See Answer Key.) This total and the time taken to complete the task are recorded on the newsprint, and the facilitator calculates the profit/loss of the active group. (Five minutes.)

XI. Members of the active group report on their feelings about the task. (Five minutes.)

XII. A copy of the Four-Letter Words Observation Summary Sheet and a copy of the Four-Letter Words Behavior Prediction Sheet are issued to each member of the active group so that all members can review the observer's data. Observers then meet with the member of the active group whom they were observing to report on their observations. If some or all observers were assigned to observe for a particular behavior, they report on their observations to the members of the active group as a whole. (Ten to fifteen minutes.)

XIII. After both groups have debriefed the activity and observations have been discussed, the facilitator reconvenes the large group to help summarize participants' learnings from the experience. (Fifteen minutes.)

XIV. The participants are divided into small subgroups and directed to discuss the factors that increase the tendency to agree to go along with a decision that one is not convinced is appropriate or accurate. (Ten minutes.)

XV. One member from each subgroup serves as spokesperson to the total group to help generate a list of the groups' factors. The facilitator records these ideas on newsprint and summarizes the data by calling attention to recurring themes and/or key factors. (Ten minutes.)

XVI. The participants reconvene in the small discussion groups to develop applications for their learnings. (Fifteen minutes.)

*Variation*

An eighth, blank square can be included in the inner envelope. A goal then would be to explore how members follow instructions in the face of conflicting information. Groups that decide to use the blank square can be disqualified for not following the written instructions.

**Similar Structured Experiences:** *Vol. I:* Structured Experience **12**; *Vol. VI:* **200**.

**Lecturette Sources:** *'76 Annual:* "Role Functions in a Group"; *'78 Annual:* "Tolerance of Equivocality: The Bronco, Easy Rider, Blockbuster, and Nomad."

---

Submitted by Walter J. Cox.

*Walter J. Cox is a principal training officer in the department of personnel services for the Leeds, England, local government, where he specializes in management development and communication training. His background includes twenty-five years in industry, in the areas of technical management, operative training, management education, and management services.*

**Answer Key**

| A | E | L | O | P | S | T |
|---|---|---|---|---|---|---|
| ALOE | EATS | LOTS | OAST | PALI | STOP | TAPS |
| ALPS | EAST | LOST | OPAL | POTS | SPOT | TALE |
| ALSO | ELSA | LAPS | OATS | POST | SOAP | TAPE |
| ALTO | EASE | LETS | OPTS | PAST | SLOP | TEAS |
| ALES | ELSE | LEAS | OLEO | PATS | SLOT | TEAL |
| APES | ELLA | LEST | OTTO | PEST | SPAT | TAEL |
| APSE | EELS | LAST | | PALS | SLAP | TOPS |
| ATOP | ELLS | LEAP | | PEAL | SLAT | TOPE |
| ASPS | | LETO | | PETS | STEP | TOES |
| ALAS | | LOPE | | PEAS | SALE | TEST |
| | | LOSE | | PELT | SEAL | TEAT |
| | | LATE | | PEAT | SEAT | TOOT |
| | | LOPS | | PATE | SATE | TOTE |
| | | LASS | | POLE | SEPT | TOLL |
| | | LOOP | | PALÉ | SOLE | TEES |
| | | LOSS | | PLEA | SALT | TOTS |
| | | LESS | | PLAT | SEEP | TOSS |
| | | LOOT | | POET | SOOT | TOOL |
| | | LOOS | | PLOT | SEAS | TELL |
| | | LOLL | | POSE | SEES | |
| | | LEES | | PESO | SPAS | |
| | | | | POPE | SELL | |
| | | | | PAPS | SOLO | |
| | | | | PASS | SETS | |
| | | | | POOL | | |
| | | | | PEEP | | |
| | | | | POOP | | |
| | | | | POLL | | |
| | | | | PEEL | | |
| | | | | POLO | | |
| | | | | PALL | | |
| | | | | PLOP | | |

# FOUR-LETTER WORDS PARADOX SHEET

Social psychologists and group theorists[1] have studied the actions and decisons made by people in groups and compared them with actions and decisions made by people as individuals. The results may be surprising.

Frequently related to the "mob effect," the conclusions are that people will take greater risks within a group-action context than they will as individuals; that people will tend to agree to a decision that they would not make as individuals in order to achieve group consensus; and that pressure to conform to and adopt group norms exists even if the group is not actively or consciously exerting this pressure. In other words, I might not choose to eat ice cream today, but if I am with a group of friends and someone suggests going for ice cream, I will likely acquiesce, perhaps because it is something we can all do together or because I think that the *other* members of the group want to go, and I do not want to be perceived as a negative element.

This tendency to agree without really agreeing may explain not only why families squabble on the way to the seashore but also why so many unofficial strikes and other disruptive actions occur in industry and commerce.

---

[1]See, for example, the summaries of studies in D. Cartwright and A. Zander (Eds.), *Group Dynamics: Research and Theory* (3rd ed.), New York: Harper & Row, 1968; R. Brown, *Social Psychology* (Chapter 13, "Group Dynamics"), New York: The Free Press, 1965; and D.P. Cartwright and R. Lippitt, "Group Dynamics and the Individual," in L.P. Bradford (Ed.), *Group Development* (2nd ed.), San Diego, CA: University Associates, 1978.

# FOUR-LETTER WORDS BEHAVIOR PREDICTION SHEET

1. One or more members of the group will attempt to achieve a leadership position.
2. It is likely that the group will fail to fully understand the written and/or oral instructions.
3. There will be discussion about the alternative ways in which the group could organize itself.
4. There will be discussion about rules to be observed while doing the task.
5. It is likely that the group members will agree to work according to certain rules.
6. It is likely that the group members, having decided to observe certain rules, will fail to do so.
7. There will be at least one member who will try to persuade the group to plan thoroughly before taking action.
8. There will be at least one member who will be action oriented and will want to begin working on the task at once.
9. There will be at least one member who will try to persuade the group to be cautious in estimating the profit that will be made.
10. It is likely that at least one member will be primarily concerned with the time factor(s) involved.
11. Unless strong leadership emerges, it is likely that the group will lose sight of its prime objective(s) and fail to perform to the required standards.
12. It is likely that one member will indicate that he thinks the activity is stupid and not worth doing, since the reasons for doing the task are not known and the information available is incomplete.

# FOUR-LETTER WORDS OBSERVATION SUMMARY SHEET

| Prediction / Active Member | 1 | 2 | 3 | 4 | 5 | 6 | 7 | 8 | 9 | 10 | 11 | 12 | Total |
|---|---|---|---|---|---|---|---|---|---|---|---|---|---|
| | | | | | | | | | | | | | |
| | | | | | | | | | | | | | |
| | | | | | | | | | | | | | |
| | | | | | | | | | | | | | |
| | | | | | | | | | | | | | |
| | | | | | | | | | | | | | |
| Total | | | | | | | | | | | | | |

*University Associates*

# FOUR-LETTER WORDS INSTRUCTION SHEET

*Instructions:* Do not open the sealed envelope until:

1. These instructions have been read and understood,
2. The two incentive charts have been studied, and the profit motive and method of calculation are understood, and
3. The information required by the facilitator has been produced.

The sealed envelope contains seven cardboard squares. A different letter of the alphabet is printed on each square. At least one of the letters is a vowel.

As a group, your *task* is to write down as many four-letter words as possible using the seven letters. Each member of the group should make a contribution to the total number of words produced by the group. As a group your *objective*, while completing the task, is to make as large a monetary profit as possible.

*Before* beginning the task, you must give the following information to the facilitator:

1. The total number of words the group will make,
2. The time the group will take to do the task, and
3. The expected profit the group will make.

A *maximum* period of *twenty minutes* is allowed for discussion and planning before attempting the task. Any extension beyond the twenty minutes allowed will cause the imposition of an immediate $5,000 deduction from any profit made. The total number of words written down must be reported to the facilitator at the end of the time taken to do the task.

There are no further instructions. Questions may *not* be asked of either the facilitator or the observers.

# FOUR-LETTER WORDS-INCENTIVE SHEET

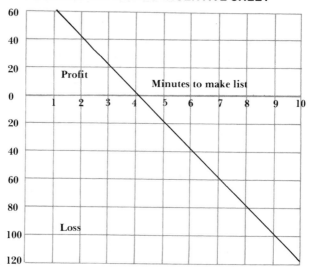

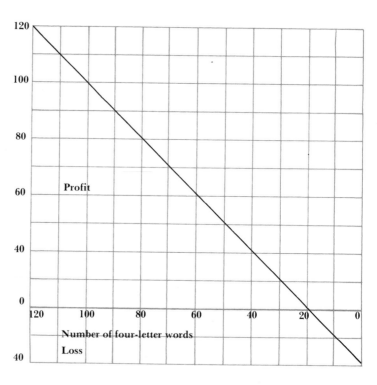

# 288. PROJECT COLOSSUS: INTRAGROUP COMPETITION

*Goals*

    I. To explore the dynamics of status, power, and special knowledge in decision making.

    II. To examine the effects of intragroup competition on team functioning.

*Group Size*

    An unlimited number of groups of five to seven members each.

*Time Required*

    One to one and one-half hours.

*Materials*

    I. One copy of the Project Colossus Information Sheet for each participant.

    II. One copy of the Project Colossus File Sheet for one member of each group.

    III. Newsprint and a felt-tipped marker for each group.

    IV. Masking tape.

*Physical Setting*

    One or more rooms so that the subgroups can deliberate in relative privacy.

*Process*

    I. The facilitator divides the participants into groups of five to seven members each.

    II. The facilitator distributes a copy of the Project Colossus Information Sheet to each participant and newsprint and a felt-tipped marker to each group.

    III. The groups are directed to move to separate locations and then to read the information sheets before beginning the task—division of the bonus money. (Five minutes.)

    IV. The facilitator circulates among the groups, giving a copy of the Project Colossus File Sheet to one person only per group.

    V. The process of decision making begins, and a time limit of twenty-five minutes is announced.

    VI. After twenty-five minutes, each group posts its plan for distribution of the bonus money for Project Colossus.

    VII. After each plan is displayed, each group, in turn, is directed to give the rationale for its solution. (Ten to fifteen minutes.)

VIII. Members are encouraged to share their reactions to the problem-solving experience. (Five minutes.)

IX. The facilitator instructs the task groups to discuss the experience in terms of one or more of the following aspects:

1. How did status or power in the group change for the person who had the "special knowledge" of the file sheet?
2. How does possession of information help a person to achieve a position of leadership in a problem-solving group?
3. What leadership styles emerged among the group members?
4. What factors increase intragroup competitiveness in this type of decision-making task? What factors decrease it?

(Fifteen minutes.)

X. The facilitator presents a lecturette on the impact of various group dynamics on the process of group decision making. (Ten minutes.)

XI. The participants are instructed to develop applications for their learnings from the experience. (Ten minutes.)

*Variations*

I. One group can engage in the problem-solving task while the other participants observe. Subgroups are then formed, the experience is processed and generalized, and applications are developed by following steps IX through XI.

II. The focus of the processing can be directed to a comparison of the rationales developed by various subgroups. The facilitator's presentation can include principles of functional and dysfunctional intragroup competition.

III. Members of the task groups can be informed of the exact amount to be distributed among project members, thereby eliminating the special-knowledge dynamic in the decision-making process.

**Similar Structured Experiences:** *'77 Annual:* Structured Experience **195;** *Vol. VII:* **260;** *'80 Annual:* **279.**

**Suggested Instruments:** *'73 Annual:* "The Involvement Inventory"; *'75 Annual:* "Decision-Style Inventory"; *'80 Annual:* "Personal Style Inventory."

**Lecturette Sources:** *'77 Annual:* "Organizational Norms"; *'80 Annual:* "Interaction Process Analysis," "Dimensions of Role Efficacy."

Submitted by James V. Fee.

*James V. Fee, Ph.D., is a professor in mass media communication at the University of Akron, Akron, Ohio. He is currently affiliated with the International Communication Association and the Central States Speech Association. Dr. Fee's background is in interpersonal communication, small-group processes, and organizational communication.*

# PROJECT COLOSSUS INFORMATION SHEET

*The Problem:* How is the bonus money for Project Colossus to be distributed among the team members?

*The Background:* You are all employed by the TT(Think Tank) Corporation. This is an organization, similar in background to the Rand Corporation, that develops economically, socially, and pragmatically feasible solutions to problems for various federal, state, and local governmental units, other private-sector corporations and organizations, and public-service organizations.

A job called Project Colossus was assigned to your team of eighteen members. This was the first project your team worked on, and it is assumed that your team members will be reassigned to various projects in the future. This may be the only project that this particular group of TT employees will work on together. Some members of your team have worked on other TT projects and may have access to file copies of budget information and/or bonus-money allocations from past projects.

*The Group Task:* The purpose of this meeting (in small work groups of five to seven members each) is to determine an equitable way to divide a substantial bonus for the Colossus project. The exact amount of the bonus has not yet been announced, but it is rumored to be the same amount as previous project bonuses. Remember that all eighteen members of your team have contributed their abilities to the completion of the project. You will have some time to examine (individually) the following descriptions of "qualities" exhibited by some of the members of the team.

Everyone on your Project Colossus team, with the exception of five members, exhibited a high level of cohesion, workmanship, conscientiousness, concern for the needs of the group, and attendance.

The following five persons had a less desirable record of performance.

1. Ms. X had some outside interests that caused her to miss two major group meetings—with good cause, she said. Her "cause" is that she edits and writes for a small local newspaper that is considered by many to be for special-interest pleading in the immediate community. The paper is in competition with the two syndicated newspapers in the area. Ms. X was a solid contributor to the major efforts of the project. Her intellect is well above average, as was indicated by her contributions.

2. Ms. Y was consistently late in arriving at group sessions. She was absent from only three major group sessions. She never offered any reason for either the tardiness or the absences. She is of average intellect. It must be kept in mind that this project is the first one she has experienced. She has had orientation training in the TT training division, but that is all.

3. Mr. A presents an interesting situation. He was chronically absent. He produced above average work when he worked in small teams. He seems to have a "sociable" life style, which he indicated was the reason for his frequent absences. It was said that he "moonlights" on other jobs in order to keep himself in the style to which he has become accustomed. He never confirmed or denied this rumor. No one doubts his ability to work, but it seems to be on his own terms and on his own time without regard for the task needs of the large team. He has worked on one other TT project.

4. Mr. B represents a rather unfortunate case. He seemed to be at a complete loss in group sessions. He did have a record of illness and family commitments during his training period. He simply did not seem able to cope with the situation and had a considerable record of absenteeism. He has indicated to supervisors that he has family and personal

problems but that they are only temporary. His intellectual capabilities were questioned by some of his co-workers. His training was relatively the same as that of all other "first timers."

5. Mr. C's situation is also interesting. He tried diligently to contribute to the tasks of the group in generating effective problem solving. He seems to possess an average intellect. He had only a few absences; he said they were because of family business that needed to be attended to. His attempts to help the group often hampered its progress, but he seemed to mean well. It would not be appropriate to say that he blocked others, but he seemed to have high authoritarian tendencies. He is a "second timer."

*Summary:* Your group's task is to find an equitable system for dividing the bonus monies for this project among the eighteen members of your task group. Merit bonuses may be in order. Demerits also may be rendered if any cases seem to demand this.

Your group will have approximately twenty-five minutes in which to reach a decision on the division of the monies. Following that time, the total group will reconvene to learn how each small group solved the problem.

When your group has reached a decision, reproduce this chart on the sheet of newsprint to show allocations:

| Name | Dollar Amount | Name | Dollar Amount |
|------|---------------|------|---------------|
| Mr. A |  | Mr. J |  |
| Mr. B |  | Mrs. P |  |
| Mr. C |  | Ms. Q |  |
| Mr. D |  | Ms. R |  |
| Mr. E |  | Ms. S |  |
| Mr. F |  | Ms. T |  |
| Mr. G |  | Ms. X |  |
| Mr. H |  | Ms. Y |  |
| Mr. I |  | Ms. Z |  |

# PROJECT COLOSSUS FILE SHEET

From past projects on which you have worked, you have information on the budget that is important to your small group's deliberation. This may give you "information status" and possibly one leadership function: focusing on what monies are available.

## Budget Information

All eighteen members earn as base salaries between $12,000 and $20,000 annually, depending on the level at which they joined TT Corporation.

Total to be disbursed: $100,000 allocated for Project Colossus in bonus salary increases.

An additional "slush" fund of $10,000 is available for meritorius contribution.

An *average* salary bonus per member would be $5,555 ($100,000 ÷ 18).

# 289. INTERGROUP CLEARING: A RELATIONSHIP-BUILDING INTERVENTION

*Goals*

    I. To "clear the air" between two work groups (departments, divisions, units, teams).

    II. To develop intergroup understanding and acceptance.

    III. To create the basis for an improved relationship between groups.

*Group Size*

    Two intact groups of fifteen or more members each.

*Time Required*

    Approximately three hours.

*Materials*

    I. Newsprint and felt-tipped markers for each group.

    II. Masking tape.

*Physical Setting*

    Separate rooms in which the two groups can meet privately and a large room for plenary sessions, with wall space for posting.

*Process*

    I. The facilitator discusses the goals of the activity and the importance to the system of improving or developing the interface between the two groups. (Fifteen to twenty minutes.)

    II. The facilitator distributes newsprint and felt-tipped markers to each group and instructs the groups to hold separate meetings in order to create the following two lists:

        1. What we think we already know about the other group.

        2. What we need to know about the other group in order to work more effectively with it.

    The groups are encouraged to develop these lists by consensus, and they are invited to use subgroups as a preliminary discussion step if they choose. Each group is instructed to select a reporter. (Five to ten minutes.)

    III. The groups meet separately and prepare their lists. (Thirty minutes.)

    IV. The two groups are brought back together to publish their lists. The facilitator warns against their forming quick, defensive reactions to each other and imposes a rule that the only reactions may be questions of clarification. The facilitator tosses a coin to determine which set of lists will be revealed and clarified first. A reporter from the first group presents its first poster and entertains questions of clarification. (Other members of the group may help to clarify the data.) Then the second list from the first group is published and clarified. (Ten minutes.)

V. The process is repeated for the second group. (Ten minutes.)

VI. The posters are exchanged across groups, and the facilitator directs the two teams to separate again and to develop responses to the data and questions generated by the other team. (Twenty minutes.)

VII. The two groups reassemble in the large room, and cross-group pairs are formed. (If groups are of unequal size, the smallest possible subgroups are formed across groups.) The facilitator instructs these pairs to share and discuss their groups' responses. (Fifteen minutes.)

VIII. The two groups meet again separately to pool the information gathered in the pairs. The facilitator instructs them to do one of two things:

1. Make a list of new questions about the other group, based on data received up to this point, or

2. Write a statement that begins with: "The best possible working relationship we can have with the other group is _____ because _____."

(Ten minutes.)

IX. In a final plenary session, the reporters from the two groups publish the results of step VIII, and the facilitator draws out reactions from the entire group. (Twenty minutes.)

X. The facilitator leads a discussion of the next steps that the two groups can take to improve their working relationship. These steps may include monitoring mechanisms. (Fifteen minutes.)

XI. The facilitator leads a discussion of the entire experience, reinforcing learnings and commitments. (Fifteen minutes.)

*Variations*

I. The facilitator can direct individuals to make the two lists prior to step III.

II. Step VIII can be carried out in a plenary session rather than in cross-group subgroups.

**Similar Structured Experiences:** *Vol. III:* Structured Experiences **67, 68.**

---

Submitted by Lawrence C. Porter.

**Lawrence C. Porter, Ed.D.,** *is a senior consultant for University Associates. He did his post-doctoral work in the applied behavioral sciences at the NTL Institute and for five years was on the NTL central staff. From 1977 to 1980, he was a member of the NTL board. In the recent past, Dr. Porter served as manager of the OD division of Lawrence Livermore Laboratory. He also is the editor of the* OD Practitioner *and is on the board of the OD Network.*

# 290. DYNASELL: HIDDEN AGENDAS AND TRUST

*Goals*

I. To demonstrate the impact of distrust on collaboration in a task group.

II. To heighten awareness of one's personal responses when the motives of others are in question.

*Group Size*

Several groups of five to seven members each.

*Time Required*

One and one-half to two hours.

*Materials*

I. A copy of the Dynasell Instruction Sheet for each participant.

II. A copy of the Dynasell Special Instruction Sheet for each participant.

III. A set of child's building blocks, five sheets of blank paper, a felt-tipped marker, a roll of cellophane tape, and a pair of scissors for each group.

*Physical Setting*

A room with enough space to provide a work area for each group.

*Process*

I. The facilitator introduces the activity but does not emphasize the element of distrust. The facilitator then divides the participants into groups of five to seven members each.

II. The facilitator distributes one copy of the Dynasell Instruction Sheet and one copy of the Dynasell Special Instruction Sheet to each participant, directing each person to follow the special instructions *only* if the appropriate block at the bottom of the page is checked. (In reality, none of the participants is assigned this role and the alternate block is checked on all sheets.) The facilitator cautions the participants not to discuss their assigned roles.

III. The facilitator directs the groups to separate locations and informs each group that it has thirty minutes in which to complete the task and that the facilitator will represent the Dynasell company in determining which city will be awarded the contract.

IV. The facilitator gives each group a set of building blocks, five sheets of blank paper, a felt-tipped marker, a roll of tape, and a pair of scissors and tells the members that they may use any or all of the materials to construct their model, but may not write on the blocks.

V. The facilitator states that if a participant is voted out of a work group during the work time, he or she is to leave the work area for the remainder of the task activity. If any workers are voted out of groups, they are joined by the facilitator and are instructed to reflect on the behaviors that triggered this response.

VI. At the end of thirty minutes, the facilitator calls time and reassembles the total group. The winning model is selected, and the basis for the choice is stated. The facilitator then informs the participants that *no one* was assigned the role of the self-seeking person.

VII. All group members, including any members who were voted out, reconvene in their work groups to discuss their reactions to the activity. The following points may serve to guide this discussion:
   1. The impact of distrust on group members' attitudes and/or behaviors,
   2. How distrust affected the group's *concern* for the task,
   3. How distrust affected the *quality* of the task accomplished,
   4. Whether some ideas, suggestions, or modifications were ignored because of group members' concern for suggester's motives,
   5. The feelings of those participants who may have been voted out of a group.
   (Thirty minutes.)

VIII. Group members are directed to discuss their learnings in terms of the effects of mistrust on their task behavior and their feelings toward the group. (Fifteen minutes.)

IX. The facilitator instructs each group to formulate a short list of things members could say or do to prevent the build-up of mistrust and the hindrance of progress in a task group. (Fifteen minutes.)

X. The large group reconvenes, and task groups report their lists of strategies. (Ten minutes.)

XI. The facilitator instructs individual participants to spend a few minutes writing notes to themselves on the implications of these learnings in terms of their back-home work groups. (Five minutes.)

**Similar Structured Experience:** *Vol. I:* Structured Experience **9**; *Vol. VI:* **218.**

**Lecturette Source:** *'74 Annual:* "Hidden Agendas."

---

Submitted by William W. Kibler.

**William W. Kibler** *is the manager of training and development for the R.J. Reynolds Tobacco Company, where he has held numerous supervisory and managerial positions for the last twenty years. In addition to being a facilitator, Mr. Kibler is a program developer, and his five-week managerial training program is currently being presented to every manufacturing and engineering manager within the organization. He has been nominated by* Who's Who in the South/Southwest *for his work in human resource development.*

# DYNASELL INSTRUCTION SHEET

*Background:* Dynasell is a young company that has grown rapidly in recent years. Dynasell manufactures and sells canned foods on a retail basis. The company is interested in building a new headquarters for its executive and clerical staff. It has narrowed its selection site to one of several cities: yours or one of the neighboring cities represented here today.

*Instructions:* You are a member of the planning and development committee for your city. The committee is composed of five members. Together you are to construct a scale model of the proposed new building. Dynasell will study your model and the neighboring cities' models. The site selected will depend on the attractiveness of the scale model of the building submitted by each of the planning and development groups. Your committee is most anxious to have the new headquarters located in your city in order to increase job opportunities, tax revenue, and so on.

You are concerned about the motives of the other members of your committee. A reliable source has given you reason to suspect that one member of your group is not committed to this project. You believe that this individual stands to benefit personally if the new Dynasell building were to be constructed in a neighboring city that is also competing for the site selection. You suspect that this person will hinder the development of the model if possible.

During the building of your model, if you have reason to suspect the identity of the saboteur based on the effects that someone's behavior is having on the work of your committee, you can attempt to have that person removed by a unanimous vote of the remaining members.

You will be instructed when to begin working on your model. Your group will have thirty minutes to complete the task.

## DYNASELL SPECIAL INSTRUCTION SHEET

If the block below designates you as the individual with the personal motive for sabotaging the project, follow this script:

For personal reasons, you are opposed to having Dynasell construct its new headquarters in your city. You have a friend in a neighboring city (which is also competing for the site selection) who has agreed to pay you $250,000 in cash *if your committee's model is not selected*.

Your objective is to hinder your committee if you can. You can do this in many ways, e.g., making improper design suggestions, delaying decisions. Make every effort to be subtle. If the other committee members become suspicious of your motives, they can vote for your dismissal from the committee, causing you great personal embarrassment and a possible loss of $250,000.

☐ You are the person.

☑ You are not the person.

# 291. I HEAR THAT YOU . . . : GIVING AND RECEIVING FEEDBACK

*Goals*

I. To establish a climate conducive to giving and receiving feedback in established work groups.

II. To practice active listening and feedback skills.

III. To help make work-group behavior more understandable by linking behavior to perceptions.

IV. To improve work-group relations and climate.

*Group Size*

An intact group of five to eight members.

*Time Required*

One and one-half to two hours.

*Materials*

I. Blank paper and a pencil for each participant.

II. Newsprint and a felt-tipped marker.

*Physical Setting*

A room with enough space for participants to speak in dyads without being overheard by other dyads.

*Process*

I. The facilitator introduces the goals of the activity. He states that it often is difficult in a group situation to spontaneously give or receive praise, constructive criticism, or negative feedback because people do not want to interfere with the group's process, to alienate others, or to be seen as troublemakers, and also because they do not know how others will respond. He says that the purpose of this activity is to provide the participants with an opportunity to pair off and exchange information about each other and to respond to the information they receive.

II. The facilitator introduces Phase I of the activity: Data Gathering. He says that each participant will pair off in rounds with every other person. During each round, partners will have three to five minutes each to exchange, in turn, "feedback" that they have for each other. The following guidelines for Phase I are posted and reviewed by the facilitator.

1. It is a good idea to begin with positive feedback and work toward more negative issues.

2. The job of the listener is to practice active listening and ask for clarification only when necessary.

3. The informers may either pass on comments they have heard from other sources (reported information) or give personal reactions to the listeners.

4. Personal feedback to the listener must be "owned," i.e., identified as such.

5. Other sources are *not* to be identified.

6. All sources are to remain confidential, i.e., during Phase II, the listener may say "I have heard that I . . . " but may *not* say "Jim told me that Fred said that I . . . ."
(Five minutes.)

III. The participants receive blank paper and pencils and are paired off. The dyads are directed to position themselves around the room so that they can converse without being overheard by other dyads. The partners are instructed to decide among themselves which one will speak first and then to begin Phase I of the activity.

IV. After three minutes the facilitator instructs the dyads to reverse roles.

V. After three more minutes, the facilitator calls time. One minute is allowed for participants to make notes on the feedback they received and then they are directed to select new partners.

VI. The feedback process continues, with partners reversing roles, until each member of the group has exchanged feedback with every other member.

VII. Participants are instructed to privately review the information they have received. (Five minutes.)

VIII. The facilitator introduces Phase II of the activity: Responding. The facilitator says that each person will have three minutes to make an input to the group in response to the cumulative data collected about himself or herself. It is stressed that this is the time to clarify issues, kill rumors, and reinforce accurate data. The members are reminded of the confidentiality of *sources*, and Phase II begins.

IX. The group discusses new perceptions of both the uses of feedback to improve the group's functioning and ways in which to best give and receive it. (Ten minutes.)

*Variations*

I. Members can be instructed to predict the feedback they expect to hear prior to the information exchange and can review this during step VII.

II. The activity can be used as a mid-course (after two or three days of interaction) intervention with "stranger" groups in a workshop setting.

III. Two or three persons can be assigned to each member of the group to give and receive feedback.

IV. Members can volunteer to receive feedback.

V. Group members can rank order other members in terms of those with whom they are most interested in giving or receiving feedback; group members then circulate at random to complete the task.

**Suggested Instruments:** *'73 Annual:* "Johari Window Self-Rating Sheet"; *Vol. IV:* "Risk-Taking Behavior in Groups Questionnaire."

**Lecturette Sources:** *'72 Annual:* "Risk-Taking and Error Protection Styles"; *'73 Annual:* "The Johari Window: A Model for Soliciting and Giving Feedback," "Conditions Which Hinder Effective Communication"; *'76 Annual:* "Making Judgments Descriptive"; *'78 Annual:* "Communication Effectiveness: Active Listening and Sending Feeling Messages," "Communicating Communication."

Based on material submitted by Drew P. Danko and Rich Cherry.


*Drew P. Danko, M.A.*, is the senior administrator of personnel and organizational research in the organizational research and development department of General Motors Corporation, Detroit, Michigan. He is currently involved in the areas of quality of work life, absenteeism, survey research, and documentation of QWL efforts. Mr. Danko's background is in industrial psychology and organization development.

*Rich Cherry, Ph.D.*, is the director of international quality of work life at General Motors Corporation, Detroit, Michigan. He is currently involved in the "internalization" of the corporation, particularly in consulting on new plant designs for locations outside the United States, and puzzling over the applicability of U.S. quality-of-work-life philosophy and value systems to other cultures in which GM is building new facilities. Dr. Cherry's background is in organization development, Gestalt group work, survey design, and team building.

# 292. DATA SURVEY: EXPLORING STEREOTYPES

*Goals*

    I. To discover how one makes judgments about others on the basis of age, race, sex, or ethnic stereotypes.

    II. To provide an opportunity to examine personal reactions to the issue of prejudice.

*Group Size*

    Unlimited.

*Time Required*

    Approximately one and one-half hours.

*Materials*

    I. A set of eight Data Survey Sheets for each participant.

    II. A pencil for each participant.

    III. Newsprint and a felt-tipped marker.

    IV. Masking tape.

*Physical Setting*

    A room large enough to allow all participants to write in relative privacy and to conduct group discussions without distracting one another.

*Process*

    I. The facilitator gives each participant a copy of Data Survey Sheets AI, RI, SI, and EI and a pencil. The participants are told to circle the choice under each item that they think is indicated by the information they have about the person being evaluated. The facilitator tells them that they have eight minutes in which to complete all four work sheets.

    II. After eight minutes, the facilitator calls time and collects all Data Survey Sheets. A second set of Data Survey Sheets (AII, RII, SII, and EII) is distributed to the participants and they are given eight minutes in which to complete the sheets.

    III. While the participants are marking their work sheets, the facilitator tabulates and summarizes the members' judgments from the first set of Data Survey Sheets (AI, RI, SI, and EI) on a previously prepared sheet of newsprint. (See the Format for the Data Survey Tabulation Summary.)

    IV. The facilitator calls time and collects the Data Survey Sheets from the participants. The facilitator divides the participants into groups of five to seven members each and directs them to share their reactions to the experience. (Ten minutes.)

    V. While the participants are engaged in group discussion, the facilitator tabulates and summarizes the responses from the second set of Data Survey Sheets on the prepared newsprint poster. He calls time, directs the participants to assemble in one group, and posts the newsprint tabulations where all can see them.

VI. The facilitator elicits comments from the group about members' reactions to the experience. (Five to ten minutes.)

VII. The facilitator directs the participants' attention to the tabulations of the confidence ratings in the two sets of Data Survey Sheets and summarizes the responses, including any contrasts in the responses from the first and second rounds. The facilitator then leads the group in a discussion of the implications of the data in the two sets of responses as they relate to the issue of stereotyping people. (Fifteen minutes.)

VIII. The participants cite examples of ways in which prejudices about age, race, sex, or ethnic background operate in their day-to-day lives, both socially and on the job. Various strategies for coping with the negative impact of prejudice are then developed by the participants and listed on newsprint by the facilitator. (Ten to fifteen minutes.)

IX. Each participant is directed to privately consider areas or situations in which he or she can apply these learnings to back-home or on-the-job situations. (Five minutes.)

X. The participants are paired off and instructed to share one situation faced by each partner and the strategy that person intends to use in coping with it. Partners also are instructed to help clarify strategies and/or coach each other. (Ten minutes.)

**Format for the Data Survey Tabulation Summary**

| AI | | | RI | | | SI | | | EI | | |
|---|---|---|---|---|---|---|---|---|---|---|---|
| Item | A | B | Item | A | B | Item | A | B | Item | A | B |
| 1. | | | 1. | | | 1. | | | 1. | | |
| 2. | | | 2. | | | 2. | | | 2. | | |
| 3. | | | 3. | | | 3. | | | 3. | | |
| 4. | | | 4. | | | 4. | | | 4. | | |
| 5. | | | 5. | | | 5. | | | 5. | | |
| Confidence* $\bar{x}$ = | | | Confidence $\bar{x}$ = | | | Confidence $\bar{x}$ = | | | Confidence $\bar{x}$ = | | |

---

*Confidence in judgments (average of all ratings submitted).

| AII | | | RII | | | SII | | | EII | | |
|---|---|---|---|---|---|---|---|---|---|---|---|
| Item | A | B | Item | A | B | Item | A | B | Item | A | B |
| 1. | | | 1. | | | 1. | | | 1. | | |
| 2. | | | 2. | | | 2. | | | 2. | | |
| 3. | | | 3. | | | 3. | | | 3. | | |
| 4. | | | 4. | | | 4. | | | 4. | | |
| 5. | | | 5. | | | 5. | | | 5. | | |
| Confidence x = | | | Confidence x = | | | Confidence x = | | | Confidence x = | | |

**Similar Structured Experiences:** *'73 Annual:* Structured Experience 94; *Vol. V:* 170; *'76 Annual:* 180; *Vol. VI:* 213, 215; *Vol. VII:* 262.

**Lecturette Source:** *'79 Annual* "Anybody with Eyes Can See the Facts!"

---

Submitted by Thomas J. Mulhern and Maureen A. Parashkevov.

**Thomas J. Mulhern, Ph.D.**, *is the director of education and training at the Letchworth Village Developmental Center, Thiells, New York. He has worked in a number of clinics and universities around the country and is now a clinical psychologist and psychology instructor. Trained as a clinical psychologist with specialization in children and mental retardation, he has approximately twenty professional publications in various aspects of psychology to his credit. His current interests are in the application of psychology to management and the utilization of biofeedback technology in staff training.*

**Maureen A. Parashkevov** *develops and presents workshops on stress management, assertiveness training, and anger control for the staff at Letchworth Village Developmental Center, Thiells, New York. She also does training in counseling, basic pharmacology, and behavior management. She previously served as a clinical instructor in the nursing division at Rockland Community College and as director of inservice education for Central St. Lawrence Health services.*

*Character:* Nurse at Letchworth Village Developmental Center named Lee Scott.
*Instructions:* For each of the items below, circle the choice that you think best describes Lee.

1. When assigned new responsibilities:

   a. catches on quickly          b. continues old patterns

2. Preference in music:

   a. classics                    b. disco

3. Political attitude:

   a. conservative                b. liberal

4. Work performance:

   a. energetic but impulsive     b. slow but thorough

5. Considers job valuable because:

   a. pension is good             b. work is challenging

Circle the number that best represents the degree of confidence you have in the above judgments.

| Little Confidence | 1 | 2 | 3 | 4 | 5 | 6 | 7 | High Degree of Confidence |
|---|---|---|---|---|---|---|---|---|

----------------------------------------------------------------------------------------------------

## DATA SURVEY SHEET

**RI**

*Character:* Twenty-eight-year-old male named Bill Rogers, resident of Minneapolis.
*Instructions:* For each of the items below, circle the choice that you think best describes Bill.

1. Favorite television program:

   a. news                         b. adventure

2. Employment:

   a. laborer                      b. accountant

3. Preference in clothing:

   a. conservative, dark colors    b. bright colors, sharp styles

4. Religious background:

   a. Episcopal                    b. Baptist

5. Sports preference:

   a. basketball                   b. tennis

Circle the number that best represents the degree of confidence you have in the above judgments.

| Little Confidence | 1 | 2 | 3 | 4 | 5 | 6 | 7 | High Degree of Confidence |
|---|---|---|---|---|---|---|---|---|

## DATA SURVEY SHEET

*Character:* Airline clerk, resident of Cleveland, named Chris Jones.

*Instructions:* For each of the items below, circle the choice that you think best describes Chris.

1. In difficult situations:
   a. acts independently          b. is dependent on others

2. Personality on day-to-day basis is characterized by:
   a. marked emotionality         b. little emotionality

3. Regarding automobiles specifically and mechanical devices in general:
   a. is skillful                 b. possesses little skill

4. Family matters at home:
   a. frequently affect work performance    b. rarely affect work performance

5. When making decisions:
   a. relies on rational methods  b. relies on intuition

Circle the number that best represents the degree of confidence you have in the above judgments.

| Little Confidence | 1 | 2 | 3 | 4 | 5 | 6 | 7 | High Degree of Confidence |
|---|---|---|---|---|---|---|---|---|

---

## DATA SURVEY SHEET

*Character:* Twenty-eight-year-old married male, resident of New York City, named Joseph.

*Instructions:* For each of the items below, circle the choice that you think best describes Joseph.

1. Preference in beverages:
   a. beer                        b. Scotch

2. Preference in recreation:
   a. boxing matches              b. opera

3. Number of children:
   a. two                         b. five

4. Occupation:
   a. teacher                     b. policeman

5. Political attitude:
   a. conservative                b. liberal

Circle the number that best represents the degree of confidence you have in the above judgments.

| Little Confidence | 1 | 2 | 3 | 4 | 5 | 6 | 7 | High Degree of Confidence |
|---|---|---|---|---|---|---|---|---|

## DATA SURVEY SHEET

*Character:* Sixty-three-year-old nurse at Letchworth Village Developmental Center named Lee Scott.

*Instructions:* For each of the items below, circle the choice that you think best describes Lee.

1. When assigned new responsibilities:

   a. catches on quickly              b. continues old patterns

2. Preference in music:

   a. classics                         b. disco

3. Political attitude:

   a. conservative                  b. liberal

4. Work performance:

   a. energetic but impulsive        b. slow but thorough

5. Considers job valuable because:

   a. pension is good              b. work is challenging

Circle the number that best represents the degree of confidence you have in the above judgments.

| Little Confidence | 1 | 2 | 3 | 4 | 5 | 6 | 7 | High Degree of Confidence |
|---|---|---|---|---|---|---|---|---|

---------------------------------------------------------------------------------------------------------------

## DATA SURVEY SHEET

*Character:* Twenty-eight-year-old black male named Bill Rogers, resident of Minneapolis.

*Instructions:* For each of the items below, circle the choice that you think best describes Bill.

1. Favorite television program:

   a. news                       b. adventure

2. Employment:

   a. laborer                    b. accountant

3. Preference in clothing:

   a. conservative, dark colors      b. bright colors, sharp styles

4. Religious background:

   a. Episcopal                 b. Baptist

5. Sports preference:

   a. basketball                b. tennis

Circle the number that best represents the degree of confidence you have in the above judgments.

| Little Confidence | 1 | 2 | 3 | 4 | 5 | 6 | 7 | High Degree of Confidence |
|---|---|---|---|---|---|---|---|---|

           *University Associates*

# DATA SURVEY SHEET SII

*Character:* Female airline clerk, resident of Cleveland, named Chris Jones.
*Instructions:* For each of the items below, circle the choice that you think best describes Chris·

1. In difficult situations:
   a. acts independently     b. is dependent on others

2. Personality on day-to-day basis is characterized by:
   a. marked emotionality     b. little emotionality

3. Regarding automobiles specifically and mechanical devices in general:
   a. is skillful     b. possesses little skill

4. Family matters at home:
   a. frequently affect work performance     b. rarely affect work performance

5. When making decisions:
   a. relies on rational methods     b. relies on intuition

Circle the number that best represents the degree of confidence you have in the above judgments.

| Little Confidence | 1 | 2 | 3 | 4 | 5 | 6 | 7 | High Degree of Confidence |

---

# DATA SURVEY SHEET EII

*Character:* Twenty-eight-year-old married male, resident of New York City, named Joseph O'Shaugnessy.
*Instructions:* For each of the items below, circle the choice that you think best describes Joseph.

1. Preference in beverages:
   a. beer     b. Scotch

2. Preference in recreation:
   a. boxing matches     b. opera

3. Number of children:
   a. two     b. five

4. Occupation:
   a. teacher     b. policeman

5. Political attitude:
   a. conservative     b. liberal

Circle the number that best represents the degree of confidence you have in the above judgments.

| Little Confidence | 1 | 2 | 3 | 4 | 5 | 6 | 7 | High Degree of Confidence |

# INTRODUCTION TO THE
# INSTRUMENTATION SECTION

## DESIGNING AND CONDUCTING ORGANIZATIONAL SURVEYS

There are many standardized instruments available for use in the applied behavioral sciences. Perhaps the single most commonly used instrument is the familiar attitude and opinion survey. Such instruments are used in group and organizational settings to measure behavioral dynamics, morale, organizational climate, leadership, and a host of other variables that describe or relate to human behavior. Some, such as Stogdill's (1979) Leader Behavior Description Questionnaire (LBDQ), are focused on a single variable while others, such as the Survey of Organizations (1980), are comprehensive instruments for use in organizational assessment and development. The Survey of Organizations (SOO), for example, often is used in conjunction with survey-guided-development (Bowers & Franklin, 1977; Franklin, Wissler, & Spencer, 1977; Hauser, Pecorella, & Wissler, 1977). When the issues of concern to a manager or group facilitator are narrowly rather than broadly defined, a full-scale organizational assessment is not needed. What is then desirable is a survey instrument designed specifically to meet the user's needs.

Everyone is familiar with the results of some survey, but how those results are obtained usually is a mystery known only to the experts—whoever they are. Actually, the development of a survey instrument is primarily a matter of care, common sense, and skill developed through practice (and based on the ability to write coherently). No set of instructions can provide basic aptitudes or the equivalent of practice, but the following guidelines can tell a neophyte surveyor how to take care, what common sense is, and where to invest efforts that amount to practice.

### Step 1: Define the Objectives

What precisely is the survey trying to find out? Can the data be obtained in some way other than a survey? If not, the objectives should be defined as precisely as possible, in writing, and should be limited to those that are really important, i.e., the reasons for doing the survey. If there are more than four or five basic issues, the survey probably will be too long and the respondents—the people who are asked to fill out the questionnaire—will not respond.

### Step 2: Identify the Population to Be Studied

The population is everyone from whom the surveyor would need to have a response in order to completely and correctly answer the basic questions. Studying managers' attitudes about worker participation is very different from studying the same attitudes of managers in the Billings Kitchen Supply Company. The populations in these two cases obviously are quite different. It is important to be precise in defining the population to be used. Although this does not mean that a list should be made of everyone in the specific population, this is the time to consider how the survey instrument will be physically brought to the people in the respondent population. For example, will the members of a group be assembled in one place? Or will the questionnaire be mailed to them at their home or business addresses?

## Step 3: Select the Survey Sample

Ideally, one would like to conduct a census, a survey that includes everyone in the population of interest. Obviously, this is not realistic if we are talking about "all managers." The researcher must settle for a sample of the population, preferably a sample that will provide the same results as if all managers had actually responded. Less obviously, the consultant helping the Billings Kitchen Supply Company may also be faced with an unrealistic task if, for example, there are 783 managers in the entire company. With limited resources, an individual consultant may find it impossible to obtain and analyze this much data. Typically, one conducts a census-type survey only when the population is relatively small or when the need for total participation is extremely great.

Sampling techniques have been developed and refined extensively over the past forty years or so, but the non-expert can generally get by with two concepts: randomness and stratification. Normally, every person in the population should have an equal chance of being picked to be in the sample. This can be accomplished by random selection. Since any number of factors can easily interfere with random selection, this step requires extreme care. Suppose, for example, that our Billings Co. consultant decided to sample 20 percent of the 783 managers by listing all 783 managers by their social security numbers and selecting 156 of them. If the consultant picked the first 156 and the list was in numerical order (low to high), the sample is not random but biased. Social security numbers are not assigned randomly, so managers from certain parts of the country or of certain ages would be excluded from the sample. If the consultant took every fifth number, the sample would be random, but the best method would be to randomly list the numbers and then select every fifth one. This procedure still may not yield a representative sample because there are different numbers of managers at each level of management and fewer high up in the hierarchy. Thus, high-level managers are less likely to be represented in the sample than lower-level managers.

To correct this problem, one must stratify the sample—in this case by managerial level. This can be done by grouping the social security numbers by management level and picking 20 percent of the people in each level. The final sample will then be random and will also accurately represent the population. One can, of course, stratify the population on any basis that logically will reduce bias or make the sample more representative.

## Step 4: Construct the Questionnaire

In order to develop a concise questionnaire, one must have some skill in writing and must also be able to endure the tedium of rewriting over and over again until the questions (or items) are as nearly perfect as possible. A typical questionnaire has at least four basic parts: the cover letter; the items; the scales; and the codes. Each of these must be prepared with maximum care in order to achieve optimum results. Each also requires skill, and such skill is attained only with much practice.

The *cover letter* should be clearly and simply written, without the use of jargon and technical words. It should speak to the respondent on at least three issues: (a) why the survey is being conducted; (b) what the benefit of the survey might be, especially with respect to the respondent; and (c) the guaranteed anonymity and security of responses. Respondents should also be thanked for their participation. The cover letter should not be long; two to three paragraphs usually is adequate. The more the letter looks like a "real" letter, the better. The use of letterhead stationery is highly desirable, and, whenever possible, each letter should be individually signed. (This usually is possible only when less than one hundred questionnaires are being used.) The more personalized attention the respondent perceives, the higher the response rate will be.

The *items* are, of course, the heart of the survey instrument, but writing the questionnaire items is surely the most tedious aspect of survey design. It is also the most important aspect. One begins with the objectives (defined in Step 1) and attempts to translate them into specific questions. Often one can receive much guidance from the efforts of others, since the topic to be examined has probably been studied before. A set of reference resources is presented in the annotated bibliography at the end of this piece. Often, one can borrow items appropriate to fairly specific needs and use them with only minor modifications. Some well-developed research questionnaires can be used or adapted freely; in other cases one must obtain written permission from the author or buy the instruments from a distributor. Obviously, one must be careful to maintain professional ethics in the use of questionnaires and questionnaire items authored by others.

There are a few clear rules about writing questionnaire items. First, each item must ask only one question and must be unambiguous and specific. It is easy to write double- and triple-barreled items such as "To what extent does your supervisor give subordinates responsible or interesting work?" There are two separate items to be considered here: "responsible" work and "interesting" work. Second, questions should be worded so as to avoid social desirability bias. That is, most people would agree or strongly agree with the statement "I support the values on which our society is based" and would disagree with the statement "Everyone should try to get as much as he can when selling a commodity." Responses to these and questions such as "To what degree do you do a good job at work?" are fairly obvious; there is little point in asking them. If the topic is important, items must be developed so that the "right" response is not obvious. For example the "get as much as you can" item could be stated this way: "To what extent do you agree that profits should be maximized?" Another example might be rephrased thusly: "Compared to others doing similar work, rate the quality of your own output." A scale of "better than anyone else"; "better than most"; "as good as most"; "not as good as most"; and "not as good as anyone else" might be used. The bias of social desirability also is avoided by avoiding "loaded" words. When objective terminology is used, people usually will respond quite honestly, even when the response is not so favorable to them personally.

The third rule is: avoid threatening the respondent. If one were trying to measure the feelings of auto workers about job security, an agree-disagree item such as "less productive workers should be laid off first" would probably threaten many people. A person who is threatened frequently will refuse to complete the survey. The threat in an item may not always be obvious; threat often is a matter of circumstances, such as the financial stability of an organization or of the economy in general. When an implicit threat is inevitable, reassurance of anonymity often helps.

Good item construction depends on common-sense writing skills: avoid leading questions, try to phrase items objectively, use common rather than obscure terms, and strive for brevity and clarity. In the long run, only practice can provide the skills needed to write good questionnaire items.

*Scaling* need not be overly technical. The most commonly used scale is called a "Likert scale" after the man who developed it, Rensis Likert (1932), the former director of the Institute for Social Research at the University of Michigan and head of the Survey Research Center. A Likert scale typically has five or seven multiple-choice alternatives, such as the following:

To what extent are you satisfied with your job?

| 1 | 2 | 3 | 4 | 5 |
|---|---|---|---|---|
| To a very great extent | To a great extent | To a moderate extent | To a little extent | To a very little extent |

Among other scale dimensions that are commonly used are "agree-disagree," "how much," "how often" (frequently-infrequently, never-always, once a day-once a year), "to what degree," and "how important." Most people are not aware that these simple scales generally make certain assumptions that render them equivalent to much more technically sophisticated scales.

There is no one best set of scale labels. "To what extent" and "agree-disagree" are probably the most used. When a questionnaire has more than twenty items, it is generally less boring for the respondent if more than one scale is used. When actual frequency of behavior is a concern, the "how often" or "never-always" sets are most relevant. When personal values or the rewards one wants from work are being examined, the "how important" scale might make the most sense. Frequently it is possible to phrase one's questions so as to use whichever scale labels one prefers.

Research shows that the "right" number of points on a scale usually is between five and nine. This is the comfortable range of discrimination for most people. Therefore, it is usually safest to use a seven-point scale, although the five-point scale does make the handling of data easier. It is important to avoid restricting the range of responses by using only two or three categories. The result of this would be meaningless data obtained at considerable cost.

Finally, we come to the matter of *coding* responses. To prepare to analyze the data, one must construct a code book. This usually is a copy of the questionnaire, marked up to indicate how each item is to be scored and how to deal with problem responses. For example, a response marked between 3 and 4 would be treated according to a general rule, explicitly stated in the code book. Other typical concerns are failure to respond to one or another item and reversed items (questions on which low scores—1 or 2—are "very good" and high scores—6 or 7—are "bad"). The latter may be coded in reverse, so as to be consistent when the data are tabulated. One must think carefully about how to score the returned questionnaires.

## Step 5: Pretest the Questionnaire

No matter how well developed the survey instrument is, there will still be minor (or sometimes major) problems that must be identified and corrected. This is the function of the pretest. A small number of instruments are prepared as mock-ups and may be typed instead of printed. Volunteers are recruited to respond to the items on the questionnaire as though they were members of the sample population. In fact, some of these pretesters should be members of the population from which respondents are to be drawn. Immediately after completing the instrument, each of these volunteers is interviewed, in order to identify flaws or errors on the form. Even if the sample of volunteers is limited to two or three, a pretest is crucial. It is almost certain that some (although, unfortunately, not always all) errors will be identified.

## Step 6: Prepare the Final Draft

After errors identified through pretesting are corrected, problems are resolved, typos are cleaned up, and an attractive, clean, final copy is prepared for reproduction, the survey form must be checked carefully; from here on errors will probably be too costly to remedy except by discarding some data, which also is a costly cure.

## Step 7: Administer the Questionnaire

Ideally, one would administer the questionnaire to everyone in the sample at the same time, perhaps in one large group meeting. Usually, this is impossible. Even the next-best situation, having several group administration sessions, is not always feasible. Quite often it is necessary to distribute questionnaires to individual respondents who complete and return them either by hand, intracompany mail, or U.S. mail. Although this can serve to increase privacy and anonymity for respondents, it also usually leads to decreased return rates. Therefore, when such a voluntary return procedure is unavoidable, the surveyor must do everything possible to boost the return rate. There are at least four ways in which this can be done.

First, *the importance of the study* must be emphasized (its intrinsic relevance, its potential usefulness—to management, for example—and the possible benefits to the respondent). These factors should be emphasized in three ways: (a) in the cover letter; (b) in informal conversation when the questionnaire is being handed to the potential respondent; and (c) by explaining that some authority (e.g., management) supports the survey (as shown by management's willingness to have it administered during work time). Telling people that they should not fill out a questionnaire during work time is, by the way, the same as saying that management thinks it is worthless and will ignore it. Most potential respondents will then ignore it too.

The second aspect to be emphasized is the *confidentiality and privacy of individual responses*. Again, this should be done in the cover letter *and* verbally. It is often wise to explain that the person affected (management, for example) will see only aggregated data—averages, percentages, etc.—not any person's or work group's data. If it is possible, the questionnaires should be returned by U.S. mail to an address other than the company's or interested party's. If people return questionnaires at the work place, a sealed box should be provided for them to drop the completed questionnaires in. Specify (on the questionnaire and verbally) that no names or identifying marks are to be put on the questionnaires.

The third aspect of administering the survey is to invest as much time and effort as possible in personal contact with potential respondents. Explain the objectives of the survey verbally. Ask if there are questions. Offer to discuss questions at any time. Promise a summary of the results. Put the questionnaire in the respondent's hand. Thank the respondent several times. In short, do everything possible to maximize personal contact. Ask the respondent when his response can be expected. Attempt to obtain a verbal commitment to a specific time frame. These investments of time and energy will be repaid amply in terms of return rate.

Finally, the questionnaire instructions must be as clear as they can possibly be. Tell the respondents to turn the page. Remind them not to omit any items. Explain how to respond each time a new type of item, scale, or topic is used.

A deadline should be set for receipt of the responses, and this date should be included on the questionnaire. Also mention it verbally to respondents. The date given should be at least one week earlier than the real deadline. Shortly before the stated deadline, all respondents should be reminded of the date by means of a letter or memorandum. An offer also could be made to provide another copy of the questionnaire if the first was misplaced. Normally one would not attempt more than two such reminders.

The actions and techniques described above are time consuming, but the more carefully they are attended to, the better will be the response rate.

### Step 8: Code the Responses

This is strictly tedious work. Accounting ledgers make good tally sheets for raw data, and there are also (more costly) forms designed for this purpose. Special forms are particularly useful when the data are to be transferred to computer cards for computer analysis (which is certainly the easiest way to analyze the data). As dull as it is, this step is very important because minor errors can have serious impact. A few of the survey questionnaires always should be checked at random to see if there are errors in coding.

### Step 9: Tabulate the Results

The aim here is to present the data so that people can understand and make interpretations from the information generated. Simple tabulations of responses for each item, using percentages (not just raw numbers), generally will suffice. This can be indicated on a "doctored" copy of the questionnaire, with percentages filled in where the check marks would go. Many results may be ignored later, but it is important to begin by tabulating everything. Table 1 is an example of a tabulation of respondents' job satisfaction.

**Table 1. Sample Tabulation of Job Satisfaction**

| Job Satisfaction % (N) | | | | | |
|---|---|---|---|---|---|
| completely | very | mostly | slightly | not at all | total |
| 61(82) | 18(25) | 10(13) | 7(10) | 4(5) | 100(135) |

The next step is cross-tabulation for items that have some important relation to one another. For example, to determine whether older workers are less satisfied than younger workers, one would cross-tabulate age by satisfaction as is exemplified in Table 2.

**Table 2. Sample Cross-Tabulation of Worker Satisfaction**

| Age | Worker Satisfaction % (N) | | | | | |
|---|---|---|---|---|---|---|
| | completely | very | mostly | slightly | not at all | total |
| under 25<br>25-30<br>31-40<br>41-50<br>over 50 | 75(15)<br>70(24)<br>60(24)<br>50(15)<br>40(4) | 20(4)<br>15(5)<br>15(6)<br>25(8)<br>20(2) | 5(1)<br>10(4)<br>10(4)<br>10(3)<br>10(1) | 0(0)<br>5(2)<br>10(4)<br>10(3)<br>10(1) | 0(0)<br>0(0)<br>5(2)<br>5(1)<br>20(2) | 100 (20)<br>100 (35)<br>100 (40)<br>100 (30)<br>100 (10) |
| overall | 61(82) | 18(25) | 10(13) | 7(10) | 4(5) | 100 (135) |

The items in parentheses are the numbers of respondents of given ages who gave specific satisfaction-level responses. For example, of the forty people between thirty-one and forty years of age, 60 percent (or twenty-four) were completely satisfied. Of the ten people over fifty in this sample, 40 percent (or 4 people) were completely satisfied. One may not know if a trend such as this is statistically significant, but might decide later that it is worth testing.

Obviously, there must be a reason for setting up cross-tabulations. If the data are to be analyzed by computer, it is quick and inexpensive to cross-tabulate everything by everything, but then one must wade through mounds of printout. So even when the calculations are easy, it is worth spending some time to decide what, if any, variables should be cross-tabulated.

Tabulating results is another important step (and can be tedious unless one uses a computer). It leads directly to data interpretation, the final output of all survey work.

## Step 10: Prepare the Report

Before preparing a final report, one must pull together all thoughts about the survey in a brief overview or summary paper. The aim is to organize these ideas and the data, not to communicate results. Based on this summary paper, the needs of the organization, and the circumstances of the survey consultation, one can then proceed with a formal, final report.

The summary paper should begin with about a page of description, highlighting what the data show and referring to the tables. It is a good idea to review the data and the tables several times, and then to review them once more, this time looking for important omissions. Then a second, more detailed summary is written. This second summary might be just a minor revision of the first, but by approaching the task this way one allows as much of a chance as possible to pull it all together without missing important findings or interpretations.

The final report will be based on the second summary, but should be tailored to the circumstances. For example, if it is clear that management is quite uninterested in doing anything with the results of the survey and would be threatened by their negative tone, it probably would be wise to prepare a brief, bland report that plays down the negative aspects. Unless there is reason to believe that some good would come of full exposure, there is little to be gained by stirring things up just for the sake of doing so. If, on the other hand, management is seriously interested in doing something with the results of the survey, the final report should be in more usable form. That exact form will, however, still depend on other circumstances. If the data will be used to work on problems, with small groups involved at all levels, the report should avoid inferences and conclusions; should contain data grouped by unit, department, or division; and should be clear to a non-expert. If top managers will work on the data to derive action plans, then more summary, charts, and recommendations are usually desirable. The guidelines for preparing the final report are to consider who will use it and to consider the purpose for which it will be used. The surveyor should prepare a report that (a) will not, in itself, do harm to the people or organization studied, (b) is targeted to the users, and (c) is in an appropriately usable form.

## Summary

This paper has discussed, in a ten-step model, professional, technical, and common-sense guidelines for planning and conducting paper-and-pencil questionnaire surveys of groups and organizations. These steps are summarized in Figure 1. The steps are, however, both abbreviated and incomplete, because the practical details involved cannot be covered in a few pages. More importantly, the skills needed to effectively design and conduct organizational surveys cannot be learned by reading but can be developed only by practice, correction, and more practice.

| | |
|---|---|
| Step 1 | Define the objectives |
| Step 2 | Identify the population to be studied |
| Step 3 | Select the survey sample |
| Step 4 | Construct the questionnaire |
| Step 5 | Pretest the questionnaire |
| Step 6 | Prepare the final draft |
| Step 7 | Administer the questionnaire |
| Step 8 | Code the responses |
| Step 9 | Tabulate the results |
| Step 10 | Prepare the report |

**Figure 1. Steps in Designing and Conducting Organizational Surveys**

## FOUR FOCUSED INSTRUMENTS

In this edition of the *Annual*, we present four highly focused, organizationally relevant instruments. Two deal with groups, one focuses on individual leadership behavior, and the last measures one aspect of organizational climate: conflict management. Although all four are most useful in organizational settings, the two group instruments may be used in almost any small-group situation to deal with group-process issues (Stokes and Tait) or, when a formal group meeting has been held, to evaluate the session (Burns and Gragg).

Although these instruments differ greatly in topic of focus, all are assessment and data-gathering tools, in addition to being teaching or learning centered. This means that Step 10 and the action steps that follow this step will be of critical importance to anyone using these instruments. For guidance in this respect, we recommend Nadler's (1977) book on feedback and OD and, especially, the *Survey-Guided Development* series (mentioned earlier) by Bowers, Franklin, and their colleagues.

### References and Annotated Bibliography of Resources in Survey Methods

Bowers, D.G., & Franklin, J.L. *Survey-guided development I: Data-based organizational change.* San Diego, CA: University Associates, 1977.

This volume presents the authors' approach to organizational surveys and the practical use of survey data for organization development through a particular group-feedback approach. It contains both the survey-feedback theory of Bowers and his associates and the conceptual rationale behind the Survey of Organizations (see Taylor & Bowers, 1972). It is a very practical, clearly written, down-to-earth text, and although it is not comprehensive in terms of describing survey feedback in general (as Nadler, 1977, is), the book is still an excellent presentation of a major approach to the use of survey questionnaires for OD.

Dunham, R.B., & Smith, F.J. *Organizational surveys: An internal assessment of organizational health.* Glenview, IL: Scott, Foresman, 1979.

Useful for morale/satisfaction measures, this book gives the impression of being comprehensive, but is deficient in many areas. It provides a basic, sound introduction to employee-morale-and-satisfaction surveys and gives three major examples.

Franklin, J.L., Wissler, A.L., & Spencer, G.J. *Survey-guided development III: A manual for concepts training.* San Diego, CA: University Associates, 1977.

A basic and well-presented text on Likert's theory of organizations as it is reflected in and measured by the Survey of Organizations (SOO). Although intended for use in a survey-guided-development program using the SOO, this text is of value to the OD practitioner who uses any survey-feedback approach. It could easily serve as a text for managers, assuming that one is comfortable with its single focus on Likert's theory.

Hausser, D.L., Pecorella, P.A., & Wissler, A.L. *Survey-guided development II: A manual for consultants.* San Diego, CA: University Associates, 1977.

This manual is for the consultant who is using the Survey of Organizations (see Taylor & Bowers, 1972) in an OD program. A very brief summary of the concepts presented in *SGD I* is given, followed by extensive practical and detailed advice for the OD consultant. Particularly useful are specific discussions of what to do when problems arise or things go wrong. Although anyone involved in organizational surveys can learn something from this book, it is of major value only to those using the SGD approach and the SOO.

Likert, R. A technique for the measurement of attitudes. *Archives of Psychology*, 1932, *140*, 1-55.

This classic article presented a new simple, straightforward method of attitude measurement.

Mahler, W.R. *Diagnostic studies.* Reading, MA: Addison-Wesley, 1974.

Excellent examples of many surveys on specific topics (such as coaching of subordinates, power conflicts, and communication) are given by an experienced, full-time consultant. An excellent resource.

Nadler, D.A. *Feedback and organization development: Using data-based methods.* Reading, MA: Addison-Wesley, 1977.

One of the volumes in the well-known Addison-Wesley OD series, this book contains the most comprehensive, yet brief, overview of survey-feedback methods used in OD. Weak on practical details—especially on how to analyze and what to do with data—the book is nonetheless a primary and essential resource.

Oppenheim, A.N. *Questionnaire design and attitude measurement.* New York: Basic Books, 1966.

This is a clear, how-to-do-it approach at a basic, detail-oriented level. It is a classic text and probably still is the best guide for the beginner on questionnaire construction.

Patchen, M. *Some questionnaire measures of employee motivation and morale.* Ann Arbor, MI: Institute for Social Research, 1965 (41).

This brief monograph contains specifically job-related measures that one must use with lower-level employees. Much technical data is included. Well-constructed and very useful indices (sets of items) on job motivation and morale also are presented.

Pfeiffer, J.W., Heslin, R., & Jones, J.E. *Instrumentation in Human Relations Training* (2nd ed.). San Diego, CA: University Associates, 1976.

This book presents detailed reviews of ninety-two instruments, with data on where to obtain them and evaluations of each. The first part of the book is a discussion of how to use instruments. The second part lists the instruments by focus. A valuable resource.

Robinson, J.P., Athanasiou, R., & Head, K.B. *Measures of occupational attitudes and occupational characteristics.* Ann Arbor, MI: Institute for Social Research, 1969.

A catalog of questionnaires, this is an extremely useful basic reference. It gives some evaluative and descriptive background on seventy-seven major questionnaire instruments, all relating to work and work-related attitudes and behaviors.

Shaw, M.E., & Wright, J.M. *Scales for the measurement of social attitudes.* New York: McGraw-Hill, 1967.

Some excellent examples are included, but this is not a basic-level text. Some sophistication is needed before one can use this book effectively.

Stogdill, R.M. *Manual for the Leader Behavior Description Questionnaire* (form XII). Columbus, OH: Ohio State University Press. (Mimeo).

For a detailed review of this instrument see "Instrumentation" in *Group & Organization Studies: The International Journal for Group Facilitators,* 1979, *4*(2), 247-250.

*The Survey of Organizations* (SOO). Ann Arbor, MI: Institute for Social Research, The University of Michigan and Rensis Likert Associates, Inc., 1980. (Available from University Associates.)

A new verison of the SOO, derived from the 1974 form. The questionnaire is designed to assess critical organizational dimensions.

Taylor, J.C., & Bowers, D.G. *The Survey of Organizations: A machine-scored standardized questionnaire instrument.* Ann Arbor, MI: Institute for Social Research, 1972.

Both technical and pragmatic, this book describes the development of a standardized organizational-assessment survey instrument, the SOO, based on Likert's System 4 theory of organizations. It is a necessary resource for anyone planning or conducting organizational surveys.

# THE GROUP INCIDENTS QUESTIONNAIRE (GIQ): A MEASURE OF SKILL IN GROUP FACILITATION

## Joseph P. Stokes and Raymond C. Tait

Group-oriented therapy has become increasingly popular with many health service providers because it provides a means by which a relatively small number of counselors can see a large number of clients. The advantages of group counseling for the client include the presence of peer support and peer pressure, an opportunity to practice interaction skills, and a chance to learn that personal problems are shared by others. Unfortunately, the trend toward group counseling has been bolstered by the misconception that an unskillful counselor can get by in a group because the group members will take care of themselves.

Training of group leaders traditionally has occurred at the professional level and has consisted of reading relevant theoretical material (e.g.,Yalom, 1975) and co-facilitating a group. As paraprofessionals become increasingly responsible for the delivery of health and welfare services, they may be thrust into the role of counselor with little or no experience in group treatment. Because facilitating a group's process is difficult and involves a number of skills (Banet, 1974; Conyne, 1975), an untrained leader can impede the group's progress and have a negative effect on its members (Lieberman, Yalom, & Miles, 1973).

In order to assess the competence of group leaders and in order to evaluate programs that are designed to train potential leaders, an instrument that measures skills in group facilitation is needed. Both Wile (1972) and Arbes (1972) have developed instruments to measure leadership styles, but these instruments are nonevaluative; they provide feedback without evaluating the effectiveness of the various leadership styles. They are not useful, therefore, in measuring competence or in evaluating training procedures.

The Group Incidents Questionnaire (GIQ) is a fifteen-item instrument designed to measure skill in leading process groups, including the ability to identify and respond to issues in an ongoing group. An assumption underlying the GIQ is that the greatest therapeutic value in groups derives from attending to how members interact within the group context (Yalom, 1975); thus, effective leader interventions focus on the "here and now" of the group interaction and encourage members to be responsible for the movement of the group.

The instrument consists of fifteen descriptions of critical incidents that might occur in groups. Each description is followed by three interventions that the leader might make. The respondents are instructed to rank the three interventions according to which intervention they like the most and which they like the least.

## Reliability and Validity

The reliability of the GIQ is satisfactory, both in terms of internal consistency (coefficient alpha = .80) and test-retest reliability ($r$ = .76 with a two-week retest interval). Evidence for the validity of the GIQ includes its ability to discriminate professional group leaders from undergraduate students in psychology. The professionals had a mean score of 52.6 (SD = 3.1) on the GIQ; the undergraduates scored an average of 36.9 (SD = 7.1). More complete information about the development and psychometric properties of the GIQ can be found in Stokes and Tait (1979).

## Scoring

To score the GIQ, the rank orders chosen by the respondents are compared with the "correct" rankings. Each response to each item is assigned a value: one, for the least appropriate response; two, for the intermediate response; or three, for the most appropriate response. A respondent's score for each item is determined by subtracting the value of the response ranked least appropriate from the value of the response ranked most appropriate. Thus, if a respondent completely agrees with the a priori rankings on an item, the score on that item is 2 (3-1 = 2). Scores of 1, -1, and -2 also are possible. A respondent's total score is determined by summing the fifteen scores and adding a constant of 30 to eliminate negative scores.

## Suggested Uses

The GIQ can be used to assess an individual's competency to lead process groups or it can help to evaluate training programs that are designed to impart skills in leading process groups. The instrument also can be used to instruct people who are being trained as group leaders by discussing the various situations and the possible responses to them. Finally, the GIQ may be useful in the selection of group leaders, since it is likely that high scorers would respond more positively to training in group facilitation skills.

### REFERENCES

Arbes, B.H. Intervention style survey. In J.W. Pfeiffer & J.E. Jones (Eds.), *The 1972 annual handbook for group facilitators.* San Diego, CA: University Associates, 1972.

Banet, A.G., Jr. Therapeutic intervention and the perception of process. In J.W. Pfeiffer & J.E. Jones (Eds.), *The 1974 annual handbook for group facilitators.* San Diego, CA: University Associates, 1974.

Conyne, K. Training components for group facilitators. In J.E. Jones & J.W. Pfeiffer (Eds.), *The 1975 annual handbook for group facilitators.* San Diego, CA: University Associates, 1975.

Lieberman, M.A. Problems in integrating traditional group therapies with new group forms. *International Journal of Group Psychotherapy,* 1977, *27,* 19-32.

Lieberman, M.A., Yalom, I.D., & Miles M. *Encounter groups: First facts.* New York: Basic Books, 1973.

Stokes, J.P., & Tait, R.C. The group incidents questionnaire: A measure of skill in group facilitation. *Journal of Counseling Psychology,* 1979, *26,* 250-254.

Wile, D.B. Nonresearch uses of the group leadership questionnaire (GTQ-C). In J.W. Pfeiffer & J.E. Jones (Eds.), *The 1972 annual handbook for group facilitators.* San Diego, CA: University Associates, 1972.

Yalom, I. *The theory and practice of group psychotherapy.* New York: Basic Books, 1975.

*Joseph P. Stokes, Ph.D., is an assistant professor of psychology at the University of Illinois at Chicago Circle. His professional activities include design and evaluation of training in interpersonal skills and group process as well as research in small-group development and self-disclosure.*

*Raymond C. Tait is a graduate student in clinical and social psychology at the University of Illinois at Chicago Circle, and recently completed a clinical psychology internship at the University of Virginia Medical Center, where he is now employed. His interests center on group psychotherapy, especially the influence of imposed structure on cohesion and risk taking in groups.*

# GROUP INCIDENTS QUESTIONNAIRE
## Joseph P. Stokes and Raymond C. Tait

*Instructions:* On the following pages, a number of group incidents are described. Following each situation are three interventions (comments) the group leader might make. Read each intervention and decide which one you think is best (most appropriate for the group process). Put a plus (+) beside the best one. Put a minus (-) beside the intervention you think is the worst, or least facilitative. So for each situation you will put a plus (+) by the intervention you like the best, put a minus (-) by the one you like the least, and leave one intervention blank.

1. As the members of this group have begun to get to know each other, hostility seems to have developed between Ned and Tom. This has been shown in a number of ways. Usually, they ignore each other. At times, when one of them speaks, the other responds in a sarcastic way. Occasionally, they belittle each other's accomplishments openly. These behaviors have been mentioned by other members, but Ned and Tom have ignored them.

During the current meeting, Ned is speaking of problems he has in relating to women, and Tom responds with a laugh: "I'm not surprised. You have trouble relating to the group, too." Ned looks furious and stops talking.

*Interventions:*

_____A. "Tom, you seem to be intent on teasing Ned. I feel irritated when you do that. I bet it gets you into trouble a lot."

_____B. "There you guys go again. You're always cutting each other up. If you can't grow up, I'm going to have to consider dropping you from the group."

_____C. "There seems to be something going on between Ned and Tom. Ned, since Tom made that remark, how are you feeling about him?"

2. Elaine is an intelligent young woman who is afraid of being rejected. During the last two meetings she has spent much of the time exploring her problems and has been frustrated at her apparent inability to change. After forty-five minutes of the third session, Elaine still seems to be stuck. Frustrated, she wonders out loud whether she should keep talking, since she has been dominating the group. She also says: "I'm afraid that people in the group will be mad at me for taking up so much time."

*Interventions:*

_____A. "Elaine, you are wondering whether the people in the group are angry. Why don't you check it out with them?"

_____B. "Elaine, it seems to me that you are making this awfully tough for yourself. Didn't you join the group to work on your problems?"

_____C. "Elaine, you shouldn't feel that way. Don't worry about being rejected; just go ahead and tell us about your problems."

**3.** By the eleventh meeting of this group, all the members except Joan have shared personal material with the group. Joan, who is withdrawn and fidgety, has not spoken at all during this session. The other group members seem to be frustrated and stuck at this point, waiting for Joan to join in. Jim says: "I'd like to help Joan but I can't until I find out what is going on with her." Sue echoes the same feelings. Helen expresses some anger at Joan. Bob says: "I can't feel comfortable talking about myself with people I don't know." Throughout these comments, Joan sits silently and bites her nails.

*Interventions:*

_____A. "The group seems eager to have Joan aboard, but Joan doesn't seem to feel secure enough to share some things yet. Joan, is there anything you can share with us that will help us to know you better?"

_____B. "Since Joan doesn't seem to feel like talking, I wonder if we could change the subject to something we can talk about."

_____C. "Joan, you *have* been quiet. I have the feeling that you are afraid to say anything. You know, you have to take some chances if you are going to make progress in here."

**4.** This is the third meeting of a newly formed group. The first two meetings were a little tense, and people spent a lot of time talking about general topics and getting to know one another. So far, this session has been an awkward one. There were long silences at the beginning, and attempts to initiate general discussions failed. Finally, Gail turns to you and says, "We don't seem to be going anywhere. I thought that you were trained to guide us through tough spots like this. What should we talk about?"

*Interventions:*

_____A. "You seem to be feeling uncertain about your direction now. Why don't people talk about how it feels to be uncertain about where they want to go?"

_____B. "It is early in the group and I'm willing to give you some help now, but once you get started, I want you to know that I'm not going to be here for you to lean on. Why don't people talk about some of the things that brought them into the group?"

_____C. "I understand that you feel uncertain about where to go, but I feel uncomfortable in being asked to tell people in the group what they should talk about. I think people have to decide for themselves where they want to go."

**5.** Stan is a nineteen-year-old member of an established group. He has been silent during many of the meetings. On the few occasions on which he has talked, he has indicated that he is facing some very difficult issues with his parents, who are separated. At the opening of this session, Stan says that he is feeling depressed and anxious about some of the incidents that have occurred with his parents. Jane, Al, and Sue all express interest in hearing more from Stan. Stan continues in general terms, speaking of "how hard it is to figure out what to do" and "how painful it is to think of the things that have happened." Silence follows these vague statements, and the group continues to look at Stan.

_____A. "Stan, I feel pretty irritated at you; you seem to be holding back from the group. How do other group members feel?"

_____B. "Stan, you're being pretty vague. I get the feeling that you want to talk but that you also want to set it up so that we come looking for you. How does this check out?"

_____C. "Stan doesn't really want to talk. As I've said before, we'll be back next week, so Stan can pick his time. Who else has something to say that we *can* talk about?"

**6.** In an established group, Jan and Lisa rush into the meeting ten minutes late, laughing and giggling. George, Harold, and Ed had been talking comfortably with each other but became silent when Jan and Lisa burst in and explained that they had just been to a party for a friend and apologized for being late.

For the past five minutes, Jan and Lisa have been talking about the party and how they are happy to know each other outside the group. The other members of the group have said nothing during this time.

*Interventions:*

_____A. "Since Jan and Lisa have arrived, the rest of you have not said anything. I wonder what other people are thinking."

_____B. "So you feel that you know each other better now that you are doing things together outside the group. Could you tell us a little more about that?"

_____C. "Jan and Lisa, you two seem to be leaving the rest of the group behind. How are other people feeling?"

**7.** During the last few sessions, several members have taken risks and have shared some problems with the group. Two weeks ago, Jim, a thirty-one-year-old married man, spoke of a homosexual incident he had experienced in his early twenties; he said that it still bothers him a lot. Keith and Mark seemed to be uncomfortable with the discussion, but the rest of the group members seemed to handle the topic well. Today, when Jim mentioned his difficulties in asserting himself, Keith responded, "Well, no wonder you can't assert yourself. After all, you're a faggot!" A few uncomfortable laughs and some shifting around in chairs have followed this comment.

*Interventions:*

_____A. "I wonder if other people have difficulty in asserting themselves in certain situations. I know that I do."

_____B. "Jim, I wonder if you can tell us how you react to Keith's comment."

_____C. "Keith, that's a pretty mean thing to say. Jim has been sharing information with us, and now you attack him for it."

8. Helen is an attractive woman who desperately wants people, especially men, to like her. In the past, she was hurt in several relationships that she entered against the advice of her friends. Since the beginning of the group, she and Barry have seemed to get along well. They have come into the group together, sat together, and expressed support for each other in times of stress. For the last two weeks, Barry has spent time discussing problems in his marriage and Helen has responded by blaming his wife. During this meeting, when Barry opens the discussion with a story about another fight with his wife, Helen asks, "How can you live with that woman? I know I couldn't." Barry smiles and asks, "Do you have a place for me to stay?" Helen giggles and blushes.

*Interventions:*

_____A. "As Helen says, Barry seems to be in a tough spot. What suggestions do other people want to give him? Has anyone else had similar problems?"

_____B. "Helen has made a lot of comments about your marriage, Barry. How do you respond to what she has been saying?"

_____C. "Barry, you seem to be joking, but I wonder if part of that comment was serious."

9. Ellen has been a very active member of the group. From the start, she has not hesitated to express her opinions or to question other group members about their reactions. In particular, her aggressive questioning has made her a powerful figure in the group and has kept other people from focusing on her. You know that outside the group she keeps people away with her dominating manner and has lost several jobs as a result of "personality conflicts."

In this session, Harry, one of the more withdrawn members, has been speaking of problems he has in socializing with people. Ellen has been questioning him about what situations he is talking about, whether he dates, what his past experiences with women were like, and other topics. After ten minutes of this, Harry says, "I'm tired of your constant questions, Ellen. I feel as though I am being cross-examined. Situations like this scare me. I wish I hadn't said anything." Ellen replies, "Why are you afraid?" Then Joe cuts in and says, "Harry has a point. Ellen is always asking us questions and never giving anything herself." Other members nod their heads and look at Ellen, who looks anxious.

*Interventions:*

_____A. "Often experiences in the group reflect events that take place outside the group. Ellen, have you had any experiences similar to this in other situations?"

_____B. "The group seems to have moved away from Harry. Ellen has been active in the group from the beginning, so we can always go back to her."

_____C. "People in the group seem to feel a little distant from you, Ellen, and also a little angry. How do you react to that?"

**10.** Steve walks into the sixth meeting of the group looking very angry. The group, aware that he is upset, becomes silent. Eventually, Kathy asks Steve what is bothering him. When he shakes his head, you encourage him to talk. At this point Steve says, "Why should I talk? Last week I shared some things with the group, and it wasn't easy, but I did it. How do you think I felt when my friend Hank stopped me at the lab today and gave me a hard time about problems I have with my folks. Hey, nobody knows about that except the people here! If I can't trust people not to gossip about me, I'm not going to say a word!" As Steve finishes, the other group members look uneasily at each other.

*Interventions:*

_____A. "Steve, I can understand that you are really angry about that. Other people seem to be upset about it, too. How do people feel about what Steve has just said?"

_____B. "You think that someone has talked outside the group about what you said. Are you absolutely sure that Hank couldn't have found out from someone else? Could someone in your family have told him?"

_____C. "You're angry about the gossip and so am I. We agreed at the beginning not to talk outside the group about things that go on in here. It would be a nice gesture if the person who gossiped would leave the group, but that won't happen. Let's try to go on as if nothing has happened."

**11.** The members of the group have begun to talk about what it means to share feelings and problems with others in the group. Mark says that he feels very uncomfortable revealing anything to the group. Most other members nod their heads in agreement. When Linda says that she feels tense just talking about the issue, Mark and most of the others agree. Susan, however, says that talking in the group is easy for her and that once she starts to talk she has a hard time stopping. Then Susan launches into a long discussion of the unsolvable difficulties she now is facing. The other group members seem to be relieved because Susan has taken the focus off them. They encourage Susan to talk by asking her numerous questions.

*Interventions:*

_____A. "Susan, I wonder if you could tell us more about your problems. I'm interested in your relationship with your husband."

_____B. "There seems to be lots of interest in the group in Susan's problems. Could people tell us what they are feeling about her right now? It would probably be wise for Susan to get some feedback about that."

_____C. "I wonder if Susan's willingness to talk isn't being used by the group members to avoid some of our own issues."

12. Hank is a thirty-eight-year-old man who has avoided talking about his feelings throughout the group's history. As the other members have shared their feelings with each other, he has become more and more isolated. In this meeting, he is speaking of feeling "turned off" in his visits to a doctor's office because they treated him like a "hunk of meat without feelings." After he says this, Shirley turns to him and says, "Hank, even though you talk in here about some things that happen to you, I don't feel like I know you as well as I know the others. I have a feeling that you want to keep me away, and I'm hurt by that." Hank tenses up and responds, "I've participated as much as anyone. If that's the way that you feel, I can't help it." Other group members react angrily and begin to agree with Shirley.

*Interventions:*

_____A. "I can see both sides of this. Hank has talked a lot but he hasn't told us much about how he feels. How do you react to that, Hank?"

_____B. "I don't understand why people are so upset. After all, Hank has just shared with us some of his feelings about being at the doctor's office. It seems to me that Hank has been participating as much as anyone today. What else might be going on that people are angry about?"

_____C. "Hank, people seem to be angry with you for not sharing your feelings with the group. You say that you're not willing to change this. Has this ever happened to you before?"

13. In an established group, Harry, Linda, and Sue have been working on certain issues and seem to be making progress. Betty, Steve, and Al initially were more reluctant to talk, but have been more open recently. Pairings have occurred in the group along the lines of early participation, so that Harry, Linda, and Sue generally speak to each other and Betty, Steve, and Al talk chiefly within their own subgroup. At the end of last week's meeting, several members expressed dissatisfaction with the group's progress. Today, people seem to be tense. The discussion has followed the usual patterns for the first ten minutes and now has begun to fade. The members are looking at each other uneasily.

*Interventions:*

_____A. "I have a hunch that a split among members of the group is causing much of the discomfort I sense here today. How does that check out with people?"

_____B. "I wonder what this silence means."

_____C. "We seem to be pretty quiet today. Something must have happened in the past week that someone wants to talk about. Sue, Steve, how about you. What's going on?"

14. Alice has been talking about problems that she is having with her husband. She has told the group about the fights that they have, how they cannot talk with each other without arguing, and how she has begun to look outside the marriage for gratification. As she talks, her voice starts to tremble and her eyes fill with tears. When Paul remarks on how miserable Alice seems, Alice breaks into tears and says, "I *am* miserable and there's nothing the group can do about it. Just leave me alone for a few minutes." As she continues to cry, John says, "I'd like to talk about some problems I'm having with my boss."

*Interventions:*

_____A. "You're still having troubles with your boss, John? Could you tell us what kinds of things have happened? I thought that you and she had worked things out."

_____B. "Alice, I understand that you are in a difficult situation, but trying to ignore it won't help. Tell us more about your problems with your husband."

_____C. "John, I sense that you are responding to Alice's request. Alice is feeling bad enough to cry. How do other people in the group feel about that?"

15. Tom has been in several groups prior to this one, but the other members have not had that experience. Consequently, Tom has assumed a position of some power. Recently, people in the group have been sharing many personal issues. Tom has attended these sessions irregularly, but no one has mentioned this to him. Last week's session was a very good one, but Tom missed it, leading Dan to comment at the end: "I wonder what's happened to Tom. He doesn't seem to be too interested in us because he's never here."

The beginning of this week's group meeting has been awkward. Tom tries to start things up by asking: "Hey, what happened last week? I had some things to do and couldn't make it." Anita mumbles a few words, and then silence follows.

*Interventions:*

_____A. "Tom, I want to remind you that when we started this group, we agreed to attend all the meetings possible. You have missed a lot of them lately. I want you to be aware of that."

_____B. "Tom, I'm irritated at you for missing our meeting last week and I suspect that other people are too. What was going on that was so much more important than the group meeting?"

_____C. "Lots of things were shared last week that Tom missed, and it seems hard to summarize them. How do people feel about Tom's missing a lot of that?"

# GROUP INCIDENTS QUESTIONNAIRE SCORING SHEET

1. Indicate your plus and minus responses for each item on the scoring table below.
2. Calculate your score for each item by subtracting the value given to your minus (-) response from the value given to your plus (+) response. (Item scores will be either 2, 1, -1, or -2.)
3. Add all the item scores together and enter the total in the space marked "Total of item scores."
4. Add 30 to your total of item scores. This number is your score for the GIQ.

| Item | Response A | Response B | Response C | Item Score |
|------|-----------|-----------|-----------|-----------|
| 1 | ____2 | ____1 | ____3 | |
| 2 | ____3 | ____2 | ____1 | |
| 3 | ____3 | ____1 | ____2 | |
| 4 | ____2 | ____1 | ____3 | |
| 5 | ____2 | ____3 | ____1 | |
| 6 | ____3 | ____1 | ____2 | |
| 7 | ____1 | ____3 | ____2 | |
| 8 | ____1 | ____2 | ____3 | |
| 9 | ____2 | ____1 | ____3 | |
| 10 | ____3 | ____2 | ____1 | |
| 11 | ____1 | ____2 | ____3 | |
| 12 | ____3 | ____1 | ____2 | |
| 13 | ____3 | ____2 | ____1 | |
| 14 | ____1 | ____2 | ____3 | |
| 15 | ____1 | ____2 | ____3 | |

**Total of item scores** _____

+ 30 _____

**GIQ** score _____

*University Associates*

# GROUP INCIDENTS QUESTIONNAIRE NORMS AND INTERPRETATION SHEET

*Instructions:* The facilitator will develop a set of norms for your group. Copy these frequencies onto the table below.

| Tally of Group Scores | |
|:---:|:---:|
| Score | Number |
| 55+ | _____ |
| 50-54 | _____ |
| 45-49 | _____ |
| 40-44 | _____ |
| 35-39 | _____ |
| 30-34 | _____ |
| 25-29 | _____ |
| 20-24 | _____ |
| 15-19 | _____ |
| 10-14 | _____ |
| 5- 9 | _____ |
| 0- 4 | _____ |

Interpretation suggestions:
1. Compare your score with the scores of other members of your group.
2. Isolate items on which you scored low and study the situations again in the light of the "correct" answers.
3. Study the rationales that follow to find ways to plan more effective interventions in your own groups.

## The Underlying Model

A basic assumption underlying the development of the Group Incidents Questionnaire is that the greatest value in groups comes from attending to how members interact within the immediate group context. Thus, the developers of the GIQ assume that an effective group leader will focus largely on the processes that occur during the group sessions. Yalom (1975) has argued strongly for the adoption of such a process focus in therapy groups. In a study of encounter groups, Lieberman, Yalom, and Miles (1973) identified four functions performed by group leaders; all are concerned primarily with how the actions of the leader impact a group's current functioning. Furthermore, Lieberman (1977) has described a trend among traditional group psychotherapists toward a process orientation. Finally, other people writing on the subject of training group leaders have recommended that potential leaders learn skills relevant to leading process groups (Banet, 1974; Conyne, 1975).

The model underlying the GIQ describes leader interventions in a group along three dimensions:
1. *Focus.* This dimension refers to the number of group members addressed by an intervention; e.g., an individual member, a subset of members, or the entire group.
2. *Immediacy.* This refers to the extent to which an intervention focuses on the here-and-now process in the group as opposed to there-and-then content topics.

3. *Responsibility*. Responsibility refers to the locus of control in the group—at one extreme, the leader directs the group's activities; at the other extreme, the group members make decisions about what happens in the group.

Although these dimensions are descriptive—and can be applied easily to most process interventions—there also is an evaluative component to the immediacy and responsibility dimensions. Interventions aimed at here-and-now issues are considered superior to those directed at there-and-then material. Interventions that place responsibility for group movement on the members rather than on the leader also are considered preferable.

Interventions that focus on what is going on in the group are desirable for several reasons: (a) members learn to attend to ongoing feelings and events and see that conflicts can be resolved if they are attended to; (b) keeping the focus on immediate material helps group members to work through issues together and helps to increase the cohesiveness of the group; (c) members act out their problems, rather than merely talking about them; and (d) the participants become entangled with one another, and much of the learning that takes place is experiential.

Helping the group to be responsible for its own activities fosters member-to-member interactions. This prevents the group meetings from becoming a sequence of one-to-one counseling sessions in which most interactions are member-to-leader. If the group members feel responsible for their actions, increased solidarity and involvement result. Members relate personally to one another, which facilitates communication and interaction within the group. Finally, as the group develops a sense of potency and cohesion, individuals feel that they belong to the group and learn that the group can be effective.

**REFERENCES**

Banet, A.G., Jr. Therapeutic intervention and the perception of process. In J.W. Pfeiffer & J.E. Jones (Eds.), *The 1974 annual handbook for group facilitators*. San Diego, CA: University Associates, 1974.

Conyne, K. Training components for group facilitators. In J.E. Jones & J.W. Pfeiffer (Eds.), *The 1975 annual handbook for group facilitators*. San Diego, CA: University Associates, 1975.

Lieberman, M.A. Problems in integrating traditional group therapies with new group forms. *International Journal of Group Psychotherapy*, 1977, 27, 19-32.

Lieberman, M.A., Yalom, I.D., & Miles M. *Encounter groups: First facts*. New York: Basic Books, 1973.

Yalom, I. *The theory and practice of group psychotherapy*. New York: Basic Books, 1975.

# BRIEF DIAGNOSTIC INSTRUMENTS

## Frank Burns and Robert L. Gragg

Four examples of scales that have been constructed for various types of measurement situations are included here. These are intended to be not only immediately useful but also instructive about how to create other similar scales. Each of these instruments can be easily edited to fit a given assessment need, since the format is both standard and simple. The examples and their possible uses are as follows:

| Scale | Uses |
| --- | --- |
| Meeting-Evaluation Scale | Evaluation of meetings |
| | Critiquing of process during meetings |
| | Action research on meeting quality |
| | Meeting planning |
| Work-Group-Effectiveness Inventory | Team building |
| | Organization survey |
| | Team self-assessment |
| Organizational-Process Survey | Organization survey |
| | Team building with executives |
| | Management development |
| Learning-Group Process Scale | Group self-assessment |
| | Clarification of expectations |
| | Comparative study of groups |

These instruments are brief; their reliabilities across time would, consequently, be unimpressive. They are best used as "here-and-now" snapshots of what is happening and must be validated by the group in question. If they serve to focus attention on processes that can be managed toward more effectiveness, they can be considered valid. The instruments in this section have models that are implicit within them. The scales selected provide respondents with an easy method of describing their experience. The number of items written depends on the amount of time available for the assessment and processing.

Other inventories of this sort can be constructed easily by using variations of the Likert scale, using the following guidelines:

1. Construct a model of the process to be assessed.
2. Select a Likert-type scale.
3. Write items from the model.
4. Try out the instrument and modify it based on its use.

The following are variations on the basic attitude-measurement scale published by Likert in 1932.[1] Sometimes more than one version can be incorporated into one inventory.

| | | |
|---|---|---|
| Strongly agree | Strongly approve | To a very great extent[2] |
| Agree | Approve | To a great extent |
| Undecided or uncertain | Undecided | To some extent |
| Disagree | Disapprove | To a little extent |
| Strongly disagree | Strongly disapprove | To a very little extent |
| | | |
| Very satisfied[2] | Little or no influence[3] | Very ineffective |
| Fairly satisfied | Some | Ineffective |
| Neither satisfied nor dissatisfied | Quite a bit | Undecided |
| Somewhat dissatisfied | A great deal | Effective |
| Very dissatisfied | A very great deal of influence | Very effective |

---

[1] R.A. Likert. A technique for the measurement of attitudes. *Archives of Psychology*, 1932, No. 140, pp. 1-55.

[2] J.C. Taylors and D.G. Bowers. *Survey of Organizations*. Ann Arbor, MI: Center for Research on Utilization of Scientific Knowledge, Institute for Social Research, The University of Michigan, 1972.

[3] *Survey of Organizations*. San Diego, CA: University Associates, 1980.

**Frank Burns** *is a senior organizational effectiveness consultant in the Office of the Chief of Staff at the Department of the Army Headquarters at the Pentagon, Washington, D.C. His interests center on neurology, linguistics, consciousness, cybernetics, operations research, and systems theory and on the application of recent breakthroughs in these fields to the co-development of individuals and human systems. He currently specializes in discrete consultation and training in subtle influence, high-performance programming, metasystems design, and executive counseling.*

**Robert L. Gragg** *is the chief of organizational effectiveness, U.S. Army Development and Readiness Command, Alexandria, Virginia. He has been a behavioral science instructor and management consultant at the U.S. Army Command and General Staff College and has provided consulting services to all levels of military organizations, academic departments, and heads of complex systems.*

# MEETING-EVALUATION SCALE
## Frank Burns and Robert L. Gragg

Meeting: _____

Date: _____

Time: _____ to _____

Circle one number for each statement.

*Strongly Disagree* | *Disagree* | *Undecided* | *Agree* | *Strongly Agree*

1.  I was notified of this meeting in sufficient time to prepare for it.

    1    2    3    4    5

2.  I understood why this meeting was being held (e.g., information sharing, planning, problem solving, decision making, open discussion, etc.) and what specific outcomes were expected.

    1    2    3    4    5

3.  I understood what was expected of me as a participant and what was expected of the other participants (including the leader, coordinator, chairperson, facilitator, etc.).

    1    2    3    4    5

4.  I understood how the meeting was intended to flow (e.g., agenda, schedule, design, etc.) and when it would terminate.

    1    2    3    4    5

5.  Most participants listened carefully to each other.

    1    2    3    4    5

6.  Most participants expressed themselves openly, honestly, and directly.

    1    2    3    4    5

7.  Agreements were explicit and clear, and conflicts were openly explored and constructively managed.

    1    2    3    4    5

8.  The meeting generally proceeded as intended (e.g., the agenda was followed, it ended on time) and achieved its intended purpose.

    1    2    3    4    5

9.  My participation contributed to the outcomes achieved by the meeting.

    1    2    3    4    5

10. Overall, I am satisfied with this meeting and I feel my time here has been well spent.

    1    2    3    4    5

11. At the start of this meeting, I understood its purpose and agenda.

    1    2    3    4    5

# WORK-GROUP-EFFECTIVENESS INVENTORY
## Frank Burns and Robert L. Gragg

Work Group: _____

Date: _____

Circle one number for each statement.

*Strongly Disagree — Disagree — Undecided — Agree — Strongly Agree*

1. I have been speaking frankly here about the things that have been uppermost in my mind.  1  2  3  4  5

2. The other members of this team have been speaking frankly about the things that have been uppermost in their minds.  1  2  3  4  5

3. I have been careful to speak directly and to the point.  1  2  3  4  5

4. The other members of this team have been speaking directly and to the point.  1  2  3  4  5

5. I have been listening carefully to the other members of this team, and I have been paying special attention to those who have expressed strong agreement or disagreement.  1  2  3  4  5

6. The other members of this team have been listening carefully to me and to each other, and they have been paying special attention to strongly expressed views.  1  2  3  4  5

7. I have been asking for and receiving constructive feedback regarding my influence on the team.  1  2  3  4  5

8. I have been providing constructive feedback to those who have requested it—to help them keep track of their influence on me and the other team members.  1  2  3  4  5

9. Decisions regarding our team's operating procedures and organization have been flexible, and they have been changed rapidly whenever more useful structures or procedures have been discovered.  1  2  3  4  5

10. Everyone on the team has been helping the team keep track of its effectiveness.  1  2  3  4  5

11. Members of this team have been listening carefully to each other, and we have been paying special attention to strongly expressed values.  1  2  3  4  5

*University Associates*

12. We have been speaking frankly to each other about the things that have been uppermost in our minds.  1  2  3  4  5

13. We have been speaking directly and to the point.  1  2  3  4  5

14. We have been helping our team keep track of its own effectiveness.  1  2  3  4  5

15. Our team's internal organization and procedures have been adjusted when necessary to keep pace with changing conditions or new requirements.  1  2  3  4  5

16. All members of this team understand the team's goals.  1  2  3  4  5

17. Each member of our team understands how he or she can contribute to the team's effectiveness in reaching its goals.  1  2  3  4  5

18. Each of us is aware of the potential contribution of each of the other team members.  1  2  3  4  5

19. We recognize each other's problems and help each other to make a maximum contribution.  1  2  3  4  5

20. As a team, we pay attention to our own decision-making and problem-solving processes.  1  2  3  4  5

# ORGANIZATIONAL-PROCESS SURVEY
## Frank Burns and Robert L. Gragg

Circle one number for each item to indicate how effective you believe each of the following organizational processes is here.

|  | Very Ineffective | Ineffective | Undecided | Effective | Very Effective |
|---|:---:|:---:|:---:|:---:|:---:|
| 1. *Communications:* The content and flow of information between and among the senior leaders in this organizaiton. | 1 | 2 | 3 | 4 | 5 |
| 2. *Leadership:* The individual behavior and procedures senior leaders use to accomplish tasks and attain goals. | 1 | 2 | 3 | 4 | 5 |
| 3. *Decisions:* The manner in which senior leaders identify and solve problems and the level at which decisions are made. (How effective is the balance between centralized and decentralized decision making?) | 1 | 2 | 3 | 4 | 5 |
| 4. *Coordination:* The degree and quality of coordination and cooperation among the senior leaders. | 1 | 2 | 3 | 4 | 5 |
| 5. *Planning:* The procedures used to anticipate the future, set realistic goals, and develop plans. | 1 | 2 | 3 | 4 | 5 |
| 6. *Responsiveness:* The manner of reacting to unforeseen events and unanticipated requirements. | 1 | 2 | 3 | 4 | 5 |
| 7 *Control and Influence:* The procedures used to assess, guide, and provide feedback on individual actions and unit activities. | 1 | 2 | 3 | 4 | 5 |
| 8. *Motivation:* The manner in which senior leaders influence the conditions that encourage or discourage effective individual and unit performance, morale, and esprit de corps. | 1 | 2 | 3 | 4 | 5 |
| 9. *Conflict Management:* The methods used to surface and resolve conflict between and among senior management personnel and their organizational elements. | 1 | 2 | 3 | 4 | 5 |

| | Very Ineffective | Ineffective | Undecided | Effective | Very Effective |
|---|---|---|---|---|---|

10. *Training and Development:* The methods used in individual training and team development to enhance the effectiveness of all the above processes.

    ⇩    ⇩    ⇩    ⇩    ⇩

    1    2    3    4    5

# LEARNING-GROUP PROCESS SCALE
## Frank Burns and Robert L. Gragg

Learning Group:_____

Date:            _____

Circle one number for each statement.

*Strongly Disagree*   *Disagree*   *Undecided*   *Agree*   *Strongly Agree*

| | | Strongly Disagree | Disagree | Undecided | Agree | Strongly Agree |
|---|---|---|---|---|---|---|
| 1. | Members of this learning group know each other well enough to understand the potential contribution of each of the other members. | 1 | 2 | 3 | 4 | 5 |
| 2. | We have been listening carefully to each other, and we have been paying special attention to strongly expressed views. | 1 | 2 | 3 | 4 | 5 |
| 3. | Each of us has been speaking frankly about the things that have been uppermost in our minds, and we have been speaking directly and to the point. | 1 | 2 | 3 | 4 | 5 |
| 4. | The learning goals of this group have been clearly specified and understood. | 1 | 2 | 3 | 4 | 5 |
| 5. | I understand what activities and procedures are planned for this learning group. | 1 | 2 | 3 | 4 | 5 |
| 6. | I expect these planned activities and procedures to contribute to the group's effectiveness in reaching its learning goals. | 1 | 2 | 3 | 4 | 5 |
| 7 . | I understand what contribution is expected of me for each of the planned activities and procedures. | 1 | 2 | 3 | 4 | 5 |
| 8 | I anticipated that the group's planned activities and procedures will contribute to my achievement of my personal learning objectives. | 1 | 2 | 3 | 4 | 5 |
| 9. | So far, I am satisfied with this learning group, and I feel that my time in the group has been well spent. | 1 | 2 | 3 | 4 | 5 |
| 10. | Overall, I am committed to this learning group, and I look to our future activities with interest and enthusiasm. | 1 | 2 | 3 | 4 | 5 |

*University Associates*

# PATTERNS OF EFFECTIVE SUPERVISORY BEHAVIOR

**Henry P. Sims, Jr.**

The purpose of the Supervisory Behavior Questionnaire is to identify patterns of leader behavior and to describe them in terms of an operant theory of leadership (Mawhinney & Ford, 1977; Scott, 1977; Sims, 1977). This introduction to the instrument will present a conceptual approach to leadership theory that is different from the traditional approaches of consideration/initiating structure, managerial grid, and/or contingency theory.

## Theory Underlying the Instrument

The instrument assumes a theory of leadership based on operant, or reinforcement, principles (Skinner, 1969). According to this theory, behavior within organizations is controlled by "contingencies of reinforcement." Figure 1 represents a positive reinforcement contingency, which consists of three parts. The first part is a discriminative stimulus ($S^D$), which is an environmental cue that provides an individual with information about how behavior will be reinforced. A discriminitive stimulus is environmental information that comes *before* individual behavior. The second is the response or behavior of the individual. The behavior is followed by the administration of a reinforcer. A positive reinforcer (the third part) is a reward that is administered following a desired behavior; it has the effect of increasing the frequency of the behavior.

Reinforcers are frequently thought of as material benefits, i.e., pay or some extrinsic incentive. In the supervisor-subordinate relationship, however, interpersonal reinforcers frequently are more potent (at least in the short term). Compliments or statements of recognition that are contingent on desirable behavior at work can have reinforcing effects that serve to increase future performance.

Another type of reinforcement contingency is punishment[1]—the administration of an aversive stimulus contingent on a specific response. In leadership practice, punishment typically is used to decrease the frequency of an undesirable behavior. In work situations, leaders typically use oral reprimands or undesirable job assignments in an attempt to eliminate behavior that is undesirable or detrimental to job performance.

$S^D$ = discriminative stimulus
R = response behavior
$S^+$ = positive consequence

**Figure 1. Contingency of Positive Reinforcement**

---

[1]"Punishment" is technically distinct from "negative reinforcement," which involves the *removal* of an aversive stimulus in order to *increase* a target behavior. However, punishment and negative reinforcement are both aversive control techniques.

Both positive reinforcement and punishment are actions of the leader that *follow* subordinate behavior. Obviously, the behavior of the leader also can have a substantial impact on the subordinate's successive performance. Frequently, the type of behavior that occurs *before* subordinate behavior can be considered a discriminative stimulus ($S^D$)—a cue that informs the subordinate of what behavior is expected in order to be reinforced. An example of this is a goal or objective.

These three types of leader behavior (positive reinforcement, punishment, and discriminative stimulus or goal specification) are basic elements in a leader's behavioral repertoire. Although these classes of behavior are not exhaustive, they form the key foci for any operant-based theory of leadership.

## Purpose of the Instrument

The Supervisory Behavior Questionnaire[2] was developed for training purposes. The instrument is designed to direct the participants' attention to three types of leader behavior: goal specification behavior (scale A), positive reward behavior (scale B), and punitive reward behavior (scale C).

The instrument is self-scored, and most participants can determine their own scores and derive a profile of the three scores with little or no assistance.

## Procedure for Administering the Instrument

Participants are instructed to think about a job they now hold or have held in the past (and, more specifically, about the supervisor on that job) and then to complete the questionnaire. Participants may need to be reminded that the questions refer to the supervisor.

After completing the questionnaire, the participants are directed to complete the self-scoring procedure and then to draw a profile of the scores of all three scales on the graph.

## Debriefing and Discussion

The facilitator begins the debriefing by initiating a process to name the three scales and, after this is done, reads the descriptive name most often used to designate the characteristics that were measured. These are: supervisory goals and expectations (scale A), supervisory positive reward behavior (scale B), and supervisory punitive behavior (scale C).

A few volunteers go to the board and write the names of the jobs they described and their scores for scales A, B, and C, for both the most effective and least effective supervisors. The facilitator directs each participant to briefly describe the aspects of the supervisor that prompted the scores reported (e.g., "He tells me what I will be doing next"). The facilitator then attempts to develop patterns of differentiation of scores between highly effective and highly ineffective supervisors and between conditions leading to highly satisfied and highly unsatisfied workers. The facilitator can calculate mean scores for both the most effective and the least effective supervisors.

Finally, the facilitator presents a lecturette on the theory underlying the instrument. Material from the literature of supervisory development can be assigned as back-up reading or used as handouts (Hammer, 1974; Jablonsky & DeVries, 1972; Luthans & Kreitner, 1975; Mawhinney, 1975; Mawhinney & Ford, 1977; Nord, 1969; Scott, 1977; Sims, 1977; Skinner, 1969).

## Variation

An alternative way to use the instrument is to direct the participants to provide two scores for

---

[2]The roots of this instrument can be traced to a leadership instrument originated by Ronald Johnson, William E. Scott, and Joseph Reitz, and originally published in Johnson (1973). Other research using similar scales has been reported by Greene (1975), Reitz (1971), Sims (1977), and Sims and Szilagyi (1975). In general, these scales have been found to possess acceptable construct validity and reliability. Individuals wishing to use these scales for research should *not* use the version reported here, which is intended to be a classroom exercise, but should consult the sources listed above.

each question: one for the supervisor and the second for how the participant *would behave* as a supervisor. This variation provides a self-description component.

## Value of the Instrument

This instrument provides an experiential introduction to leadership theory and allows the participants to examine leadership behaviors from the perspective of *their own* past experiences. This personal aspect induces substantially greater interest and involvement and longer retention of the underlying theory. In addition, several opportunities exist during the debriefing phase to describe the underlying theoretical principles in terms of actual past behaviors. If accompanied by significant exposure to principles of behavior modification (Brown & Presbie, 1976; Luthans & Kreitner, 1975), the instrument offers a unique opportunity to demonstrate how leadership theory can be put into practice.

### REFERENCES

Brown, P.L., & Presbie, R.J. *Behavior modification in business, industry, and government.* New Paltz, NY: Behavior Improvement Associates, 1976.

Greene, C. Contingent relationships between instrumental leader behavior and subordinate satisfaction and performance. *Proceedings of the American Institute for Decision Sciences,* 1975.

Hamner, W.C. Reinforcement theory and contingency management in organization settings. In H.L. Tosi & W.C. Hamner (Eds.), *Organizational behavior and management: A contingency approach.* Chicago: St. Clair Press, 1974.

Jablonsky, S.F., & DeVries, D.L. Operant conditioning principles extrapolated to the theory of management. *Organizational Behavior and Human Performance,* 1972, 7, 340-358.

Johnson, R.D. *An investigation of the interaction effects of ability and motivational variables on task performance.* Unpublished doctoral dissertation, Indiana University, 1973.

Luthans, F., & Kreitner, R. *Organizational behavior modification.* Glenview, IL: Scott, Foresman, 1975.

Mawhinney, T.C. Operant terms and concepts in the description of individual work behavior: Some problems of interpretation, application, and evaluation. *Journal of Applied Psychology,* 1975, 60, 704-714.

Mawhinney, T.C., & Ford, J.C. The path goal theory of leader effectiveness: An operant interpretation. *Academy of Management Review,* 1977, 2, 398-411.

Nord, W.R. Beyond the teaching machine: The neglected area of operant conditioning in the theory and practice of management. *Organizational Behavior and Human Performance,* 1969, 4, 375-401.

Reitz, H.J. Managerial attitudes and perceived contingencies between performance and organizational response. *Proceedings of the 31st Annual Meeting of the Academy of Management,* 1971, 227-238.

Scott, W.G. Leadership: A functional analysis. In J.G. Hunt & L. Larson (Eds.), *Leadership: The cutting edge.* Carbondale, IL: Southern Illinois University Press, 1977.

Sims, H.P. The leader as a manager of reinforcement contingencies: An empirical example and a model. In J.G. Hunt & L. Larson (Eds.), *Leadership: The cutting edge.* Carbondale, IL: Southern Illinois University Press, 1977.

Sims, H.P., & Szilagyi, A.D. Leader reward behavior and subordinate satisfaction and performance. *Organizational Behavior and Human Performance,* 1975, 14, 426-438.

Skinner, B.F. *The contingencies of reinforcement: A theoretical analysis.* New York: Appleton-Century-Crofts, 1969.

*Henry P. Sims, Jr., Ph.D., is an associate professor of organizational behavior and academic director of the Human Resources Management Program at The Pennsylvania State University, University Park, Pennsylvania. Dr. Sims has served in a variety of academic and organizational positions. His research efforts currently focus on the use of behavioral modeling for managerial and supervisory leadership training, the leadership of self-managed work groups, and long-range planning for human resource systems.*

# SUPERVISORY BEHAVIOR QUESTIONNAIRE
## Henry P. Sims, Jr.

*Instructions:* This questionnaire is part of an activity designed to explore supervisory behaviors. It is not a test; there are no right or wrong answers.

Think about supervisors (managers) you have known or know now, and then select the *most effective* supervisor and the *least effective* supervisor (effective is defined as being able to substantially influence the effort and performance of subordinates).

Read each of the following statements carefully. For the *most effective* supervisor, place an X over the number indicating how true or how untrue you believe the statement to be. For the *least effective* supervisor, place a circle around the number indicating how true you believe the statement to be.

Most effective . . . . . X

Least effective . . . . . O

| | Definitely Not True | Slightly Not True | Not True | Slightly Not True | Uncertain | Slightly True | True | Definitely True |
|---|---|---|---|---|---|---|---|---|
| 1. My supervisor would compliment me if I did outstanding work. | 1 | 2 | | 3 | 4 | 5 | 6 | 7 |
| 2. My supervisor maintains definite standards of performance. | 1 | 2 | | 3 | 4 | 5 | 6 | 7 |
| 3. My supervisor would reprimand me if my work was consistently below standards. | 1 | 2 | | 3 | 4 | 5 | 6 | 7 |
| 4. My supervisor defines clear goals and objectives for my job. | 1 | 2 | | 3 | 4 | 5 | 6 | 7 |
| 5 My supervisor would give me special recognition if my work performance was especially good. | 1 | 2 | | 3 | 4 | 5 | 6 | 7 |
| 6. My supervisor would "get on me" if my work were not as good as he or she thinks it should be. | 1 | 2 | | 3 | 4 | 5 | 6 | 7 |
| 7. My supervisor would tell me if my work were outstanding. | 1 | 2 | | 3 | 4 | 5 | 6 | 7 |
| 8. My supervisor establishes clear performance guidelines. | 1 | 2 | | 3 | 4 | 5 | 6 | 7 |
| 9. My supervisor would reprimand me if I were not making progress in my work. | 1 | 2 | | 3 | 4 | 5 | 6 | 7 |

*University Associates*

# SUPERVISORY BEHAVIOR QUESTIONNAIRE SCORING SHEET

*Instructions:* For each of the three scales (A, B, and C), compute a *total score* by summing the answers to the appropriate questions and then subtracting the number 12. Compute a score for both the most effective and the least effective supervisors.

| Question Number | Most Effective | Least Effective | Question Number | Most Effective | Least Effective | Question Number | Most Effective | Least Effective |
|---|---|---|---|---|---|---|---|---|
| 2. | + ( ) | +( ) | 1. | + ( ) | +( ) | 3. | + ( ) | +( ) |
| 4. | + ( ) | +( ) | 5. | + ( ) | +( ) | 6. | + ( ) | +( ) |
| 8. | + ( ) | +( ) | 7. | + ( ) | +( ) | 9. | + ( ) | +( ) |

| | | | | | | | | |
|---|---|---|---|---|---|---|---|---|
| Subtotal | | | Subtotal | | | Subtotal | | |
| ( ) - 12 | ( ) - 12 | | ( ) - 12 | ( ) - 12 | | ( ) - 12 | ( ) - 12 | |
| Total Score ___ A | ___ A | | Total Score ___ B | ___ B | | Total Score ___ C | ___ C | |

Next, on the following graph, write in a large "X" to indicate the total score for scales A, B, and C for the most effective supervisor. Use a large "O" to indicate the scores for the least effective supervisor.

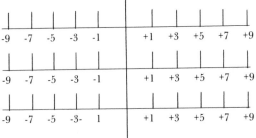

A. _____

B. _____

C. _____

# DIAGNOSING ORGANIZATIONAL CONFLICT-MANAGEMENT CLIMATES

## Bob Crosby and John J. Scherer

There are factors in the "climate" of any organization that can help or hinder third-party efforts to address and manage conflict. Although these climate conditions do not themselves create or resolve conflict, they can be powerful variables in determining how effective an intervention will be. When these factors are favorable, even a moderately skilled third-party consultant, working with moderately skilled participants, can be effective. When they are not favorable, even a highly skilled consultant, working with highly skilled individual participants, is likely to be frustrated.

### Uses of the Instrument

Because these climate conditions are so critical, it may be impossible to help a given organization unless the climate conditions are first adjusted. For this reason, it is imperative that these factors be identified and analyzed in terms of the organization in question *before* a commitment is made to a method of third-party intervention. The Conflict-Management Climate Index presented here is useful in the following initial steps of the consulting process:

1. *Deciding Whether to Accept the Conflict-Management Assignment.* By collecting a sampling of opinion (using the instrument presented here) from organizational members regarding these climate factors, the consultant can generate very useful data to be used in establishing expectations with the client. Whether or not the consultant decides to accept the job, in sharing the instrument data with the client, he can provide a great deal of useful information to the organization. This information frequently will indicate a need for deeper, long-term organization development work, beyond the particular crisis intervention.

2. *Sensing Interviews.* The instrument can be used in the sensing-interview stage to collect and organize attitudes of organizational members prior to the introduction of any conflict-management intervention and is an excellent method of gathering data in a new or "cold" group.

3. *Diagnosis of Needs.* Once the data have been collected, the categories themselves become self-explanatory diagnostic guides, thus enabling the third-party consultant to focus on factors that need attention during initial discussions with key members of the client system.

4. *Training Intervention.* The instrument also can be used as a teaching device to introduce the concept of conflict-management climate to members of an organization in such a way that they can learn something about conflict management at the same time that they are diagnosing the organization. This is a very powerful combination of input and output and increases the value of both.

5. *OD Program.* Obviously, the particular crisis for which the third-party consultation is needed can be a symptom of larger, more profound issues in the organization. It is possible for the consultant to use the data generated by the instrument to explain to decision makers why these crises may continue unless something is done about the climate to make it more supportive of effective conflict management.

Thus, when asked to "come and do something on conflict management" for an organization, the consultant can use the instrument to elicit data that will help to determine the significant issues that need to be addressed and the best interventions by which to address them.

## A Few Notes on Scoring

The lower the score on this instrument, the less likely conflict-management efforts will be to succeed, unless some climate-changing activities are first carried out. It generally would not be advisable to engage in conflict-resolution projects in organizations in which average scores on this instrument were lower than 30, without clear and strong commitment on the part of top management to attempt to understand and change the climate factors operating within the organization.

Many of the items on the instrument are derived from Richard Walton's work in the field (Walton, 1969), and the authors recommend his book as a companion piece to the use of this measurement device.

### REFERENCE

Walton, R.L., & Dutton, J.M. The management of interdepartmental conflict: A model and review. *Administrative Science Quarterly*, 1969, *14*, 73-84.

**Bob Crosby** *is the president of Concern for Corporate Fitness and is on the faculty of the Whitworth/LIOS graduate program at Whitworth College in Spokane, Washington. Mr. Crosby has specialized in citizen participation, youth work, sex education, and organization development. He has recently published an article on the role of the applied social scientist in the future, which reflects one of his current interests.*

**John J. Scherer** *is the associate director of the Whitworth/LIOS Center for Applied Studies at Whitworth College, Spokane, Washington, where he is a core faculty member for the Master of Arts in Applied Behavioral Science program. He is also executive vice president of Concern for Corporate Fitness and has co-edited a manual for applied-behavioral-science practitioners.*

# CONFLICT-MANAGEMENT CLIMATE INDEX
## Bob Crosby and John J. Scherer

Your Name _____

Organizational Unit Assessed _____

*Instructions:* The purpose of this index is to permit you to assess your organization with regard to its conflict-management climate. On each of the following rating scales, indicate how you see your organization as it actually is right now, not how you think it should be or how you believe others would see it. Circle the number that indicates your sense of where the organization is on each dimension of the Conflict-Management Climate Index.

1. **Balance of Power**

   1 _____ 2 _____ 3 _____ 4 _____ 5 _____ 6

   Power is massed
   either at the top or at
   the bottom of the organization.

   Power is distributed
   evenly and appropriately
   throughout the organization.

2. **Expression of Feelings**

   1 _____ 2 _____ 3 _____ 4 _____ 5 _____ 6

   Expressing strong
   feelings is costly
   and not accepted.

   Expressing strong
   feelings is valued and
   easy to do.

3. **Conflict-Management Procedures**

   1 _____ 2 _____ 3 _____ 4 _____ 5 _____ 6

   There are no clear
   conflict-resolution
   procedures that
   many people use.

   Everyone knows about,
   and many people use,
   a conflict-resolution
   procedure.

4. **Attitudes Toward Open Disagreement**

   1 _____ 2 _____ 3 _____ 4 _____ 5 _____ 6

   People here do not openly
   disagree very much.
   "Going along to get
   along" is the motto.

   People feel free to
   disagree openly on
   important issues without
   fear of consequences.

5. **Use of Third Parties**

   1 _____ 2 _____ 3 _____ 4 _____ 5 _____ 6

   No one here uses
   third parties to
   help resolve conflicts.

   Third parties are
   used frequently to help
   resolve conflicts.

6. **Power of Third Parties**

| 1 | 2 | 3 | 4 | 5 | 6 |
|---|---|---|---|---|---|

Third parties
are usually superiors
in the organization.

Third parties
are always people of
equal or lower rank.

7. **Neutrality of Third Parties**

| 1 | 2 | 3 | 4 | 5 | 6 |
|---|---|---|---|---|---|

Third parties are
never neutral, but serve as
advocates for a certain
outcome.

Third parties are
always neutral as to
substantive issues and
conflict-resolution
methods used.

8. **Your Leader's Conflict-Resolution Style**

| 1 | 2 | 3 | 4 | 5 | 6 |
|---|---|---|---|---|---|

The leader does not deal
openly with conflict but
works behind the scenes
to resolve it.

The leader confronts conflicts
directly and works openly with
those involved
to resolve them.

9. **How Your Leader Receives Negative Feedback**

| 1 | 2 | 3 | 4 | 5 | 6 |
|---|---|---|---|---|---|

The leader is defensive and/or
closed and seeks vengeance
on those who criticize
him/her.

The leader receives criticism
easily and even seeks it
as an opportunity to
grow and learn.

10. **Follow-Up**

| 1 | 2 | 3 | 4 | 5 | 6 |
|---|---|---|---|---|---|

Agreements always fall
through the cracks;
the same problems must be
solved again and again.

Accountability is
built into every
conflict-resolution
agreement.

11. **Feedback Procedures**

| 1 | 2 | 3 | 4 | 5 | 6 |
|---|---|---|---|---|---|

No effort is made
to solicit and understand
reactions to
decisions.

Feedback channels for
soliciting reactions
to all major decisions
are known and used.

12. **Communication Skills**

| 1 | 2 | 3 | 4 | 5 | 6 |
|---|---|---|---|---|---|

Few, if any, people possess basic communication skills or at least do not practice them.

Everyone in the organization possesses and uses good communication skills.

13. **Track Record**

| 1 | 2 | 3 | 4 | 5 | 6 |
|---|---|---|---|---|---|

Very few, if any, successful conflict-resolution experiences have occurred in the recent past.

Many stories are available of successful conflict-resolution experiences in the recent past.

# CONFLICT-MANAGEMENT CLIMATE INDEX
## SCORING AND INTERPRETATION SHEET

*Instructions:* To arrive at your overall Conflict-Management Climate Index, total the ratings that you assigned to the thirteen separate scales. The highest possible score is 78 and the lowest is 13.

Then compare your score with the following conflict-resolution-readiness index range.

| Index Range | Indication |
|---|---|
| 60-78 | Ready to work on conflict with little or no work on climate. |
| 31-59 | Possible with some commitment to work on climate. |
| 13-30 | Very risky without unanimous commitment to work on climate issues. |

Find your lowest ratings and study the following descriptions or interpretations of the thirteen separate dimensions. As you read the descriptions, think about what specifically might be done (or changed) in other activities described, in order to increase your organization's readiness to manage conflict more effectively.

## CLIMATE FACTORS AFFECTING CONFLICT MANAGEMENT IN ORGANIZATIONS

1. *Balance of Power.* Simply stated, is power spread appropriately and realistically throughout the organization, or is it massed at either the top or bottom levels? The ideal is not for everyone to have equal power, but for a general feeling among most members of the organization that they have sufficient influence over the most significant aspects of their work lives. This may include the power to obtain a fair hearing and a realistic response from someone in authority.

This factor is important because it reflects the extent to which communication is likely to be distorted. Research evidence (Mulder, 1960; Solomon, 1960) seems to indicate that when two people perceive their levels of power to be different, they are likely to mistrust any communication that takes place between them. People who perceive themselves as being less powerful than the other party tend to perceive communication from that person as being manipulative or condescending. Those who see themselves as being more powerful experience communication from the less powerful as being devious or manipulative. Ironically, these more powerful persons also perceive collaborative behavior as an indication of weakness on the part of those whom they see as less powerful. These perceptions can make effective conflict resolution all but impossible.

In organizations in which power is massed at the top, it is extremely difficult for the third-party consultant to achieve the neutrality necessary to be effective without appearing to "take sides" with someone at the less powerful end of the organization. In organizations in which power is massed at the bottom, there is frequently so much disrespect for—or even disgust with—top management that it is difficult for the third-party consultant to encourage the more powerful workers to respect or even attend to any collaborative actions that top management may take.

Because an appropriate balance of power within an organization is relatively rare, the third party and the participants involved in the conflict will need to collaboratively seek ways to create a balance of power within the limits of the conflict-resolution episode. The two persons or parties in conflict must understand that the more powerful member is to lend some skills or status to the weaker member for the duration of the intervention and also that the more powerful member may not use that power to punish the subordinate, regardless of the outcome of the conflict-resolution process.

The purpose of this balancing of power between the two parties in conflict is to facilitate the process of discussion and mediation, not to create institutional equals. When the consultation process is finished, the parties involved will return to their usual roles (e.g., the boss will still be the boss and the subordinate will still be the subordinate), and it is essential that everyone involved understand this.

2. *Expression of Feelings.* Conflict management is much easier to achieve in a climate in which open expression of members' feelings—especially when those feelings are strongly negative—is valued. In many organizations, a person will find the expression of strong emotions a costly experience and may be either subtly or openly ostracized or reprimanded for such conduct.

It is easy to see why conflict management is more likely to be successful in a climate in which feelings are valued. In the first phases of any conflict resolution, the expression of feelings on the part of the parties in conflict is extremely important; in fact, the success of the next two steps in the conflict-resolution process, differentiation and integration, is directly related to whether complete and honest communication of emotions has occurred.

3. *Conflict-Management Procedures.* In organizations in which there are clearly defined procedures or channels for conflict resolution, the work of a third-party consultant—whether internal or external to the organization—is obviously much easier. In a system in which there are no clearly defined ways to resolve conflict, and in which people do not know what to expect or what to do when conflict arises, the work of the third party is made extremely difficult. When people feel safe in using conflict-resolution procedures, they are more likely to have confidence in the outcome. Conversely, if people in conflict feel that they are fumbling through it, they are not likely to put much faith in either the acceptability or the reliability of the procedure they have chosen to use. If top management seriously wants to support effective conflict management, then specific procedures must be made known to and accepted by members at all levels of

4. *Attitudes Toward Open Disagreements.* This factor reflects the attitudes of members of the organization about open disagreement over proposals or issues. Janis' book *Victims of Groupthink* (1972) vividly describes decision making at the national level and shows how unexpressed reservations can lead to apparently consensual policy decisions with which few of the decision makers are in actual agreement.

In a system in which open disagreement about issues is viewed as disloyalty or insubordination, effective third-party conflict mediation is almost impossible. In such organizations, participants may pretend to agree or to work out differences of opinion without actually allowing themselves to find out how very far apart their views or positions are. Where differentiation is insufficient, integration or long-term conflict resolution is simply not possible.

Organizations that require creativity, such as advertising firms and think tanks, solicit and encourage differences of opinion because the discussions that result make possible insights and solutions that might never be thought of in a climate in which everyone agreed with the first idea suggested.

5. *Use of Third Parties.* A healthy conflict-management climate will encourage people to ask others in the system to act as third-party consultants when conflicts arise. Most organizations have, at least tacitly, established the norm that conflict must be kept "in the family" and not "aired in public." This makes the work of the person who is called in to help extremely difficult. One of the first concerns then is to confront the reservations and resistances that people have about working with a third party. In particular, it should be made clear that the use of a third party is not a sign of weakness on the part of the persons in conflict. This can be reinforced merely by using third parties effectively.

6. *Power of Third Parties.* As Walton (1969) points out, it is difficult for someone with hierarchical power to be an effective third party. When subordinates feel that anything they say may later be used against them, it is highly likely that crucial information will not be shared during the confrontation episode. However, these data frequently are the keys to unlocking conflict situations. In a healthy conflict-management climate, a supervisor would encourage subordinates to seek third-party help from someone on their level or even lower in the organization. It is hard for most managers to do this, because they want to be seen as helpful and caring and also because they want to have some control over potentially explosive situations.

7. *Neutrality of Third Parties.* Third parties from within the organization must remain neutral about substantive outcomes, or at least suppress their biases sufficiently to be effective. When third parties are unskilled and biased about what the outcome of the conflict-resolution process should be, one of the people in conflict is likely to feel "ganged up on" and the person who wins may feel a little bit guilty. Such a "conflict-resolution" process may result in a defusing of the issue but also is likely to cause the significant feelings of the people involved to be submerged, to increase mistrust of management, and to make participants feel a lack of ownership of a solution which they may feel was imposed on them.

In addition, past experience with a biased third party makes it difficult for members of the organization to trust the process in the future. Therefore, the third-party consultant may need to spend a great deal of time and energy in establishing his or her neutrality and credibility with the persons involved.

8. *Your Leader's Conflict-Resolution Style.* The senior people in any organization greatly influence the climate. Walton and Dutton (1969) showed that it is possible to characterize a general style of conflict management in an organization and that the people at the top of the organization set that style by their own behavior. In their "contingency theory" of organization, Lawrence and Lorsch (1969) found that not only could they characterize the way people generally approached conflict but also showed that one particular approach, "confrontation," worked best and was associated with organizational effectiveness. In other words, these researcher/consultants found that the way people approach conflict is not a contingency factor, but that there was a "best way": confrontation. It means that conflict is openly recognized when it occurs and the people involved proceed to deal directly with the conflict problem. It means *not* running away, *not* trying to "smooth over" real and important differences, *not* immediately trying to "split the difference," and *not* fighting a win-lose battle. Confrontation implies creative problem solving. When superiors confront conflicts they are seen as strong and their behavior encourages others to deal directly with problems of conflict.

The model set by those in positions of power has effects on all sorts of subordinate behavior, but especially influences how subordinates relate to each other when dealing with conflicts. Even when the supervisor's nonconfrontational style is successfully applied to solve a particular problem, it still weakens the organization's problem-solving and conflict-resolution capacity.

9. *How Your Leader Receives Negative Feedback.* In a conflict situation there is always great potential for the expression of negative feelings. It is rare, even when conflict is dealt with very effectively, for no negative comments to have been expressed. Such comments may concern the content of the conflict ("I think your approach is unlikely to increase sales as much as mine would") or may relate to how the parties feel on an emotional level ("Your attempts to dominate our ad campaigns are signs of your inflated ego"). Grossly ineffective handling of conflict is associated with an inability to deal with either of these types of negative feedback. Even worse is when the leader or person in authority acts against the other party at a later date, thus gaining "vengeance." This kind of behavior is associated with other nonfunctional ways of handling conflict, such as not letting the other party know one's true feelings, never letting disagreements get out in the open, and trying to deal with conflict "behind the scenes." The type of persons

using these strategies avoid showing anger or any expression at all. Their motto might be "Don't get mad, get even."

No healthy person actually enjoys negative feedback, on either the content or interpersonal level, but effective leaders are able to ignore or fail to respond in kind to personal attacks—while often openly recognizing the feelings expressed by the other party—and are likely to look at content criticism more objectively, to determine whether there really is a sound point to the critique. At our best we may relatively quickly transfer the kernel of truth in a negative item into positive corrective action. A conflict, for example, over the leader's daily "check-up" on a delegated project might lead this leader to examine and correct the tendency to avoid really "letting go" of an important project.

10. *Follow-Up.* Follow-up procedures and methods of accountability should be built into all conflict-resolution decisions. It is possible to have a highly successful confrontation dialog between two people, to have them reach intelligent resolutions, and then to have those resolutions disappear between the "cracks" in the relationship or in the organization's busy work schedule. It is extremely important that the last step in the conflict-resolution process specifies:

1. What has been decided?
2. What will be done next and by whom?
3. What checks are there on how and whether it is carried out?
4. What are the expected consequences?
5. How, when, and by whom will the effectiveness of these decisions be evaluated?

When people are used to making sure that planned outcomes are implemented, the work of a third party is made much easier. In places in which problems historically must be solved over and over again, it is necessary for the third-party consultant to train people in follow-up procedures before beginning the conflict dialog.

11. *Feedback Procedures.* When communication channels exist that can be used to surface disagreements and conflicts, it is obvious that more conflict resolution is possible. This does not guarantee that conflicts are generally resolved effectively, but it *is* a prerequisite if such effective action is to take place at all. There are many ways by which organization members can be given access to and encouraged to use channels for feedback. When upper levels or those in power are responsive to feedback that indicates conflict problems, then even relatively simple "mechanistic" feedback approaches, such as the old-fashioned suggestion box, can work well. Some years ago New England Bell Telephone Company instituted an "open lines" program whereby people at lower levels could raise problems by telephoning an anonymous executive ombudsman, with their own anonymity guaranteed. Certainly a situation in which the parties feel free to directly approach one another is the most preferable, but when the overall climate cannot support this, a mechanistic approach, if used responsively, can be a useful and productive step toward changing the conflict-management climate.

One commonly touted action that may not work is the so-called "open-door policy." When lower level or less powerful individuals actually try to use the open door, they find that the policy exists in name but not in fact: that it is not so easy to get through the door at all, and, when done, the response is overtly or covertly a turn off or "cooling out" process. Furthermore, one is observed in the process and the person using the open door may be labelled as a tell-tale, a spy, someone who cannot handle his or her own problems, etc. All of these negative factors are characteristic of organizations with poor conflict-management climates, and would not, of course, apply to organizations with good climates: open expression of feelings and disagreements, clear procedures for dealing with conflict, effective use of third parties, etc. As it happens, it is the former type of organization in which a so-called open-door policy is likely to succeed, while such a policy would be laughably unnecessary in the latter type of organization.

12. *Communication Skills.* If people in an organization are accustomed to blaming, criticizing, projecting their own issues onto other people, and scapegoating, if they do not know how to make "I" statements (Gordon, 1970) that clearly communicate how to listen to their own positions, or if they cannot listen empathically (Milnes & Bertcher, 1980; Rogers & Farson, 1977) without forming opinions, then it probably will be necessary to prepare them for confrontation dialogs by training them in communicating and listening in high-stress situations. Of course, it is easier to do conflict-management work in an organization in which the members have received training in communication skills. In that case the role of the third party is to help the participants to stay "on track" and to coach them in maintaining open communication.

13. *Track Record.* How successful were past attempts to resolve conflict equitably? If there is a history of people being reprimanded or fired for initiating an attempt to resolve a conflict, the third-party consultation may be perceived as "window dressing." On the other hand, nothing succeeds like success, and nothing helps the conflict-management consultant more than an organization with a history of useful and lasting involvement in dealing with conflict.

## CONCLUSION

The conflict-management climate in organizations functions a great deal like the weather. When the weather is good, you can do many more things more enjoyably than when the weather is bad. In the middle of a storm, you can still do many of the things you could do when the weather was good, but it requires much more energy, and the risks of failure are increased. We believe that one of the major skill focuses of consultants to organizations trying to learn to manage conflict is in collaborating with top management in seeking innovative ways to change the weather in the organizations along the dimensions charted in the Conflict-Management Climate Index.

### REFERENCES

Gordon, T. *Parent effectiveness training.* New York: Wyden, 1970.

Harriman, B. Up and down the communications ladder. *Harvard Business Review*, 1974, *52*(5), 143-151.

Janis, J.L. *Victims of groupthink.* Boston: Houghton-Mifflin, 1972.

Lawrence, P.R., & Lorsch, J.W. *Organization and environment.* Homewood, IL: Richard Irwin, 1969.

Milnes, J., & Bertcher, H. *Communicating empathy.* San Diego, CA: University Associates, 1980.

Mulder, M. The power variable in communication experiments. *Human Relations*, 1960, *13*, 241-256.

Rogers, C.R., & Farson, R.E. Active listening. In R.C. Huseman, C.M. Logue, and D.L. Freshley (Eds.), *Readings in interpersonal and organizational communication* (3rd. ed.). Boston: Holbrook Press, 1977.

Solomon, L. The influence of some types of power relationships and game strategies upon the development of interpersonal trust. *Journal of Abnormal and Social Psychology*, 1960, *61*, 223-230.

Walton, R.L., & Dutton, J.M. The management of interdepartmental conflict: A model and review. *Administrative Science Quarterly*, 1969, *14*, 73-84.

# INTRODUCTION TO THE
# LECTURETTES SECTION

When we began to look for and prepare materials for the first *Annual*, friends and colleagues, somewhat to our surprise, kept referring to the need for brief, clear concept statements focusing on a particular topic, issue, or theory. We soon realized the falsehood of the myth that group facilitators "think with their guts." Most facilitators need and use conceptual pieces in appropriate contexts. And, like us, most had struggled with old college or seminar notes, outlined text chapters or articles, and had tried in a variety of ways to turn these materials into brief lecture inputs. Since few materials existed in forms appropriate to these needs, we included a "Lecturettes" section in the first *Annual*.

We have now published well over one hundred lecturettes, on topics ranging across the field of applied behavioral science. One of the greatest benefits of the *Annuals*, for our own training activities as well as for readers, has been the easy access to a variety of lecturettes that can be used as starting points in the designing of training sessions, as starting points for our own thinking about specific issues, as back-ups for other types of presentations, and as handouts for participants. We have sometimes wondered how many thousands of copies of various lecturettes have been distributed over the years. Thus, we would appreciate notes from users of the *Annuals*, telling us which lecturettes they use most and suggesting new topics.

## Lectures and Lecturettes

Although the lecturette is based on the lecture method, there are differences, as well as similarities, between the two methods. Both the lecture and the lecturette format have a clear content focus, a theme or topic, and, in both cases, structure, order, and clarity in presentation are necessary. Both, of course, involve an audience, and, more importantly, the lecturer and facilitator both want to gain the acceptance of the audience for the ideas they are presenting.

Aside from the most obvious difference, that of length, there are several significant ways in which lectures and lecturettes differ. Lectures tend to have greater depth and detail, while lecturettes are more often imprecise outlines and are more simplified in content. Lecturettes, however, tend to generate a much greater degree of rapport between the facilitator and the participants than that which exists between the lecturer and the audience. Perhaps the most important difference of all is in the basic purpose. A lecture is intended to transmit knowledge and to intellectually enlighten the audience. A lecturette is most often aimed at helping participants to make a connection between their experiences and what those experiences mean; to understand why it might be desirable to change their behavior; and to make enlightened choices about such changes.

## Using Humor in Lecturettes

Good public speakers and lecturers learn quickly how useful humor can be in maintaining audience interest. In the most serious of situations, humor becomes all the more useful in serving to reduce tension so that people can focus on the task instead of on their own anxieties. In less than crisis situations, one of the strongest audience turnoffs is an overly serious demeanor.

Using humor appropriately is a skill. It is not enough to memorize and correctly retell a good joke; in order to "grab" one's audience, one must use humor in context, with reference to specific topics and situations with which the listeners are concerned (or are, at least, able to identify).

There are at least four rich sources of appropriate humor material. First, there is the "Bob Hope" vein of humor: current events. Local or national news that can somehow be turned toward the topic being presented provides good humor potential. Second, and perhaps easier, are the many available "joke books" that catalog humor, by topic, from "one-liners" to long anecdotes. Used carefully, often with personal touches, such resources can be a worthwhile investment (many such books are available in paperback form). Third, and safest, is humor focused on oneself. Such jokes are unlikely to offend others. They also expose the teller to the audience, and this is often desirable both for building rapport between the facilitator and the participants and also as a behavioral model of self-disclosure. Everyone has some humorous stories based on personal experience. The challenge is to relate them to the topics of concern to the participants. Fourth, and probably most difficult for most people, is the use of puns and "shaggy dog" stories. Although skill in presenting such humor can be cultivated, it is best left to those people who seem to have a particular talent for it. A good pun can be memorized, but it is often difficult to fit one into a lecturette. Because this type of humor is so often based on the immediate situation, the person with a natural talent for it can best and most easily exploit such an opportunity.

As a general rule, the facilitator should remember that the objective of humor is to increase involvement and participation. Jokes that alienate or make fun of people are not likely to aid in developing rapport. Other than the obvious problem of offending participants, humor can backfire in several ways. First, the joke may "fizzle." This is relatively harmless and can even be used to humorous advantage. What is worse is the case in which participants' attention is focused on some point that is different from the content that the facilitator was using the joke to emphasize. Or participants may remember the joke but forget the message. This is less likely to occur if the joke is appropriately related to the topic; a totally "off-the-wall" joke may draw laughter but also may reduce the facilitator's effectiveness in communicating the major points of the lecturette. A final pitfall also concerns the focus of the participants' attention: a joke that aims *at* the facilitator can draw attention to the person at the expense of the lecturette content.

The best type of humor is that which flows naturally and spontaneously out of the situation. Overplanning or inappropriate use can result in no laughing matter.

## Developing Skills in Using Humor

There are a variety of approaches to developing skills in using humor. Most people can learn to tell a simple joke and can easily practice on friends, family, and colleagues. As part of a more programmatic effort, one can work with a co-facilitator and contract for help with humor. This can work very well if the other person is skilled in humor. It is important to find safe situations for practice; one might volunteer for informal presentations in classes or staff meetings, or one might join a club such as the Toastmasters, which is organized for the development of public-speaking skills. Finally, the local college, extension, or community college may offer classes that deal with or focus on the use of humor.

Practice and effort will not make a bore into a raconteur, but such efforts are very likely to provide one with the skills adequate for the effective use of occasional humor in delivering lecturettes.

# DEFENSIVE AND SUPPORTIVE COMMUNICATION

## Gary W. Combs

Much of our time as teachers, parents, and workers is devoted to social influence. We attempt to modify the views of others and move them to action; others attempt to do the same with us. The quality and effectiveness of our efforts to influence one another depend on our style of interaction.

A variety of prescriptions have been suggested for communicating effectively: speak clearly and thoughtfully, avoid stereotyping, maintain an attentive posture, be honest and timely, listen carefully, and repeat for emphasis and retention. These principles are important and useful for improving our skills of expression and listening, but *climate* is more fundamental to successful communication. *Supportive* climates promote understanding and problem solving; *defensive* climates impede them.

### DEFENSIVE COMMUNICATION

As with weather climates, communication climates represent more forces than we can readily see. The dominant motive behind defensive communication climates is *control*. Although control can take many forms, it is often manifested by communication designed to persuade. The speaker may be friendly, patient, and courteous; the goal, nevertheless, is to *convince* the listener.

The speaker's conscious or unconscious desire to prevail in the situation elicits a characteristic set of results: *evaluation, strategy, superiority,* and *certainty* (Gibb, 1961). As the interaction continues, these behaviors become increasingly pronounced. Each party becomes less able to hear the other or to accurately perceive the other's motives, values, and emotions. In short, communication breaks down. An example of defensive communication follows:

> Nancy Russell, director of administrative services, is talking with Bob Wheeler, director of finance. Wheeler asks Russell to prepare an additional weekly report summarizing selected financial data. Wheeler balks at Russell's request and lists several reasons why an additional summary is unnecessary. Russell, who is determined that such a report be prepared, patiently answers Wheeler by explaining why she needs the supplementary data. Wheeler responds by defending his position.

What is likely to happen?

### Evaluation

If Wheeler continues to question the validity of Russell's request, one or both of them will inwardly or outwardly become critical of the other. Their dialog may appear calm and friendly and they may or may not be aware of their own judgmental feelings, but these feelings will be obvious. The longer the conversation goes on, the greater their frustration will become until each begins to evaluate the other as stubborn, unreasonable, or downright stupid.

---

This lecturette is based on the work of C.R. Rogers and F.J. Roethlisberger, Barriers and gateways to communications, *Harvard Business Review*, 1952, *30*, 46-52 and J.R. Gibb, Defensive communication, *Journal of Communications*, 1961, *11*, 141-148.

## Strategy

As the conversation progresses, each will strategize and prepare rebuttals while the other is speaking. Energy will be focused on winning and overcoming rather than on listening and problem solving.

## Superiority

One or both of the speakers will begin to feel superior to the other. Inwardly or outwardly each will start to question why the other cannot see the logic or "correctness" of his or her views and begin to think of the other as being inferior in intelligence and savvy.

## Certainty

The energy of their arguments will lock the opponents into the correctness of their original views. Any feeling of tentativeness either may have had about his or her position gradually will be replaced with convictions of certainty.

We can predict that eventually one of the parties will withdraw or capitulate, that a compromise will be negotiated, or that the individuals involved will leave in anger. Regardless of the outcome, their feelings about each other are likely to be negative, and commitment to following through with agreed-on action will be low. In all likelihood, their feelings about each other will be manifest in future encounters. The "loser" will admit to having lost the battle, but not the war.

## SUPPORTIVE COMMUNICATION

The dominant goal underlying supportive communication climates is *understanding*. Supportive communication climates often facilitate a synergistic resolution to conflict. *Synergy* describes outcomes that combine elements of contrasting positions into a new and meaningful solution that satisfies the needs of both (a win-win situation). It differs from *compromise* wherein each receives only part of what is desired (a lose-lose strategy), because the emphasis is on integration. The speakers seek to establish a dialog, to listen, and to appreciate and explore differences of opinion.

The results characteristic of such communication are *empathy, spontaneity, problem solving*, and *synergy*. As each speaker listens to and attempts to understand the other's position, he or she, in turn, becomes free to fully hear and appreciate the first speaker's views of a particular situation. A supportive climate allows both to seek a creative resolution of their differences. A supportive communication climate could be illustrated by the earlier example, except that Russell could choose to explore Wheeler's objections. What is likely to happen now?

## Empathy

If Russell listens and discusses Wheeler's reasons for not doing an additional report, she naturally will come to understand his position better. Her willingness to talk about their differences will convey to Wheeler her respect for his thoughts and her evaluation of his importance. If Wheeler feels understood and respected, his need to defend himself will diminish and he will feel free to hear what Russell has to say. The net result will be that each party will gain an appreciation of the other's point of view.

## Spontaneity

If Russell is open and responsive, less energy will be focused on strategic rebuttal. Both will be able to concentrate on what is being said, and each will feel free to express his or her own thoughts and feelings.

## Problem Solving

Russell's willingness to explore their differences will imply that she is open to collaborative resolution, and Wheeler will respond in kind. Once both are less concerned with winning, they will be more inclined to tolerate each other's perspectives and to settle the conflict in a way that is mutually satisfying.

## Synergy

There is a good chance that Russell and Wheeler will find a way to satisfy Russell's concern for additional data and Wheeler's desire to keep down the number of reports produced, if they communicate in a way that allows them to appreciate, scrutinize, and fuse their respective—and respected—views into a new whole that is pleasing to both (Jones, 1973).

## BARRIERS TO CREATING SUPPORTIVE COMMUNICATION CLIMATES

Supportive communication seems simple, but it is very difficult for those who are not in the habit of developing supportive climates. Our cultural training is a major barrier to creating such climates. We are often rewarded for developing skills of argument and persuasion. Little or no time is given to teaching us the attitudes and skills of listening and understanding. Therefore, it is necessary for us to practice the skills of supportive communication until they become second nature.

Lack of time and energy is also a barrier to supportive communication. Creating a positive milieu takes work! At least one speaker must assume responsibility for developing an atmosphere that permits both to understand and to respond to what is actually being said. It is often more convenient to respond superficially or inappropriately.

Supportive communication also involves risk. If we permit ourselves to know reality as others perceive it, we run the risk of being changed ourselves (Rogers & Roethlisberger, 1952). But such risks must be taken if we are to share our thoughts and feelings with one another authentically.

Additionally, it is difficult to give positive support to another person when we are feeling angry and hostile. Our inclination under these circumstances is to attack and hurt. Yet it is at such times that empathic communication can be most helpful. Sharing the other person's perspective defuses otherwise hostile environments and increases our appreciation for each other's points of view.

## FACILITATING SUPPORTIVE COMMUNICATION

A genuine desire to define situations through interaction with others is the most important ingredient for supportive communication. If this desire is not genuine and a pretense of openness is made, it will be easily detected, others will no longer feel free to express themselves openly, and communication will break down.

Active listening is also essential to supportive communication. We must try to grasp the full meaning—both fact and feeling—of what others say and test our understanding by clarifying and checking.

We must also share our perspectives with others and, when there is conflict, search for an end result that will satisfy both our own and our partner's objectives. This requires a shift of thinking from "me versus you" to "how we can both gain in this situation." Pragmatically, supportive communication means moving from thinking in terms of preconceived answers to thinking in terms of the end results that we want to accomplish and then seeking solutions that satisfy those ends (Filley, 1975).

## CONCLUSION

Supportive communication requires a sharing and understanding attitude. When speaking and listening supportively, people become less defensive and more open to their experiences and the experiences of others. They become more ready to integrate other points of view and seek solutions to conflict that satisfy the needs of both parties.

## SUGGESTED ACTIVITY

See Structured Experience 238, "Defensive and Supportive Communication: A Dyadic Role Play" in the Structured Experiences section of the 1979 *Annual.*

### REFERENCES

Filley, A.C. *Interpersonal conflict resolution.* Glenview, IL: Scott, Foresman, 1975.

Gibb, J.R. Defensive communication. *Journal of Communication,* 1961, *11,* 141-148.

Jones, J.E. Synergy and consensus-seeking. In J.E. Jones & J.W. Pfeiffer (Eds.), *The 1973 annual handbook for group facilitators.* San Diego, CA: University Associates, 1973.

Rogers, C.R., & Roethlisberger, F.J. Barriers and gateways to communication. *Harvard Business Review,* 1952, *30,* 46-52.

*Gary W. Combs, Ph.D., is an associate professor of administration at Sangamon State University, Springfield, Illinois. He teaches courses in human-services administration, quality of work life, life-career planning, and human relations. Dr. Combs' background is in public administration and organization development, with special interest in the application of organization-development strategies to human-service organizations.*

# THINKING ABOUT FEELINGS

## Walton C. Boshear

Those aspects of the helping professions that attempt to deal with feelings are the most subjective, tenuous, and hard to express because thinking and talking about feelings is difficult. There is no doubt that feelings influence behavior—and the stronger the feeling, the more it influences behavior. But exactly how feelings and behavior are related is difficult to say. To paraphrase Freud, we may someday be able to predict the behavior that will result from a known feeling, but we may never be able to deduce the feeling by observing the behavior because the same apparent behavior can result from many different feelings.

A framework for thinking about some of the aspects of feelings and a common vocabulary are needed to communicate with individuals and groups. The empirical model presented here was stimulated by a model developed by Albrecht (Boshear & Albrecht, 1977) to explore how people accommodate their strong feelings.

## A BASIC MODEL OF FEELINGS

At the most basic level, feelings have two characteristics, *intensity* and *duration*. By using intensity and time as intersecting axes on a graph, we can plot an emotional episode as shown in Figure 1. The episode is initiated at $t_0$ when the person perceives an event, which provokes an emotional reaction—feelings about the event. Between $t_0$ and $t_1$, the reaction period, emotional intensity increases to a peak. Between $t_1$ and $t_2$, the recovery period, the intensity of feelings lessens. The duration of the emotional episode is the entire period from $t_0$, the perception of the event, to $t_2$, the return to the base level of feelings. This is the *primary* episode, provoked by the actual event. Following the primary episode, *secondary* episodes may occur as the person recalls the event. These recurring secondary episodes will have the same basic characteristics as the primary episode, but will be of successively lesser intensity until at some future time the event will be recalled with no perceptible emotional reaction.[1]

Behavior varies depending on the peak level of intensity of an emotional episode. The intensity of the emotion can be thought of as the range between a hypothetical base of no emotion and some ultimate limit of the human system to tolerate the emotion. The intensity of an emotion does not seem to be on a continuum. As intensity increases, it seems to pass through certain tolerance limits. As each limit is passed, there is a definite change in the person's state of awareness and type of behavior the feelings provoke. These tolerance limits and the characteristic regions of awareness and behavior are shown in Figure 2.

The first limit, the upper boundary of a Region of No Perceptible Behavior, can be called the Natural Tolerance Limit. If his or her feelings are below this limit, the person is not aware of any unusual emotion and will exhibit no observable behavior change. Feelings within this range do not seem at all unusual.

Beyond the Natural Tolerance Limit is a Controlled Tolerance Limit. Between these two is a Region of Involuntary Behavior. If his or her emotions are within this region, the person will

---

[1]Under hypnosis people have relived the primary episode with essentially the same intensity of feelings. This, however, is an entirely different phenomenon from simply recalling an emotion-provoking event.

be aware of an unusual emotional intensity but will be in control and will not deliberately react. Involuntary reactions, such as tensed muscles, nervous gestures, or flushed face, may be evident as the person attempts to control behavior. The Controlled Tolerance Limit seems to be established in part by conscious decision and partly by a person's unconscious reactions to the situation, social norms, personal values, and self-image. Conscious control of the Controlled Tolerance Limit is most evident in specific situations. A person may lower the limit to express joy at a ball game, but raise it to control the same behavior in church. The reverse may be true with respect to behavior provoked by grief.

The final threshold would appear to be an Absolute Tolerance Limit, setting the upper boundary of a Region of Deliberate Behavior. If an event provokes an emotional response within this region, the person will take some deliberate and overt action. The behavior will be deliberate in the sense that it is justified by the intensity of the emotion. It may not always be planned or the result of a strategy. It may well be impulsive.

Beyond the Absolute Tolerance Limit, a person is unable to rationalize behavioral responses to emotion. He or she may react compulsively or may be immobilized by the intensity of feelings. In this Region of Compulsive Behavior there may be an apparent disconnection between cause and effect. The person may exhibit behavior that he or she does not understand and cannot later rationalize. There is a suspension of intellect when the peak of the emotional episode is in this region.

## IMPACT OF VARIED REACTION TIMES

The simplified curve shown in Figure 1 implies an even rate of reaction to and recovery from an emotional episode. This is not representative of real life. People react and recover at different rates. Some people react instantly and reach an emotional peak quickly. Others may reach the same emotional peak in reaction to the same event, but over a longer period of time. The same can be said of recovery times. Some people will recover from an emotional peak very quickly; others may take a long time. Figure 3 illustrates the extreme cases of this phenomenon, showing the characteristic curve for each reaction/recovery type.

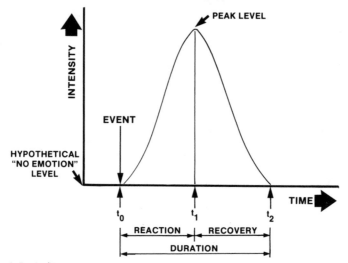

Figure 1. Basic Characteristics of Feelings

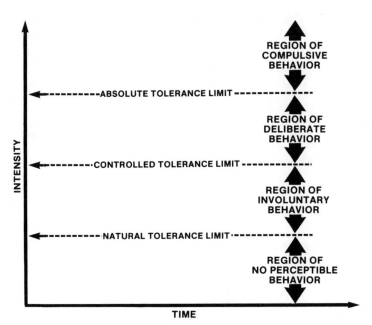

Figure 2. Emotional Tolerance Limits and Behavioral Regions

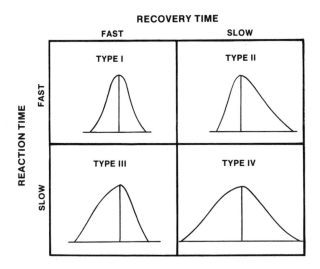

Figure 3. Comparative Reaction/Recovery Times

There are strong implications of this difference in reaction and recovery times when people communicate about an experience that they have apparently shared. Figure 4 illustrates the problems that may occur between Joe, a Type I, and Mary, a Type IV. An emotion-provoking event occurs at $t_0$. Joe, a quick reactor, feels the full intensity of his emotions at $t_1$. Mary, who is slow to react, is still low on her reaction curve. If they attempt to communicate at $t_1$, they will not appear to share the same feelings about the event. At $t_2$, Mary will be at the peak of her emotional response, but Joe will have fully recovered. The discrepancy is even greater at $t_2$. If Mary brings up the subject at $t_2$ she could provoke a secondary episode for Joe, who would recall the event and experience a recurrence of emotion, but a lower intensity. Because of Joe's fast reaction/recovery style, he may recover a second time while Mary is still in the recovery mode from her primary episode. At $t_3$ both Joe and Mary are fully recovered and appear to be on a common emotional basis. At no point between $t_0$ and $t_3$ have Joe and Mary been able to communicate from the same experience base, even though both perceived the event at the same time and reacted to it with the same intensity of feelings. Communication at $t_3$ and beyond may still be complicated by the fact that Joe has had two emotional experiences, one provoked by the primary event, the other provoked by Mary's delayed reaction to the primary event.

## IMPACT OF TOLERANCE LIMITS

The conceptual framework presented here is useful for exploring another important aspect of feelings. When emotion-provoking events occur at close intervals, a person's emotional intensity may be sustained at a high level for extended periods of time. If a second event occurs before the person has made a full recovery from a prior episode, the intensity of emotion may remain at, or even exceed, the level of the first episode. If the circumstances of a person's life are such that he or she is exposed to a series of emotion-provoking events, spaced closely together, then a *situational base level* may be established and maintained considerably above the hypothetical base level of no emotion. Figure 5 and the following example illustrate this concept.

A forest ranger may have a situational base level of anxiety that is below his Natural Tolerance Limit. He will not be aware of any anxiety. A harried executive, on the other hand, may live in a daily environment with recurring crises that sustain his situational base level much

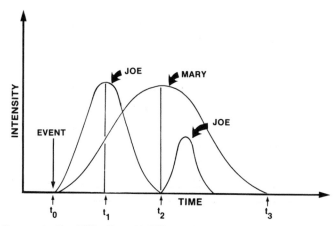

**Figure 4. Communication Difficulties with Different Reaction/Recovery Styles**

higher, perhaps just below his Controlled Tolerance Limit. He is constantly aware that he is experiencing anxiety but does not deliberately take any action to relieve this anxiety. If the forest ranger and the harried executive have an accident at an intersection, they share an anxiety-provoking event and react to it with the same *relative* increase in intensity of their anxiety. As shown in Figure 5, the forest ranger will become aware of an unusual amount of anxiety, but will be able to control his behavior. He may show signs of involuntary behavior such as nervousness, but will attempt to approach the problem logically. The harried executive, however, may appear to be reacting quite inappropriately to the incident. He may swear at the ranger or kick his car. The ranger and the executive will have difficulty talking about their different reactions to the same event. Even after they have both recovered from that particular episode, they may still have difficulty because of the discrepancy between their situational base levels of anxiety.

It is generally accepted that a sustained high level of emotion can be physically harmful. Because the human mind is highly adaptable and can accommodate a wide range of circumstances, a potentially dangerous situation can develop. If a person's environment contains a high level of emotional stimulation, e.g., in the Region of Involuntary Behavior, the person may become so accustomed to this level that he or she adapts to it mentally. In a sense, the Natural Tolerance Limit is raised to encompass the higher level and the person will cease to be motivated to seek any resolution to his or her life situation. In spite of the fact that emotional stimulation is higher and puts more strain on the body, the person will no longer perceive a problem.

## APPLICATIONS FOR THE MODEL

Practitioners in the helping professions may be able to develop better methods for recognizing and assessing the severity of this "problem of no problem" and discover ways to help clients learn to lower their Natural Tolerance Limits.

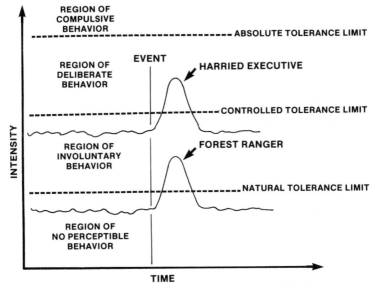

**Figure 5. Different Reactions to Emotional Episode of Same Relative Intensity**

The phrase used most often to describe the process of inhibiting overt feeling behavior is "suppressing emotions." This may be an unfortunate choice of words. To "suppress" an emotion implies that it is reduced in intensity. The conceptual framework we have developed here suggests that a more accurate description of the process may be "raising the Controlled Tolerance Limit"; the level of emotional intensity remains the same. Thinking in this way may lead to some entirely different strategies for learning to relieve negative tension through overt behavior. The old approach suggests that in order to get feelings out in the open to be acted on, they must be relived or raised in intensity into the Region of Deliberate Behavior. In fact, some practitioners use the technique of prodding at hidden emotions until the intensity level is raised to the point at which the client reacts overtly. This may work in some situations, but may lead to another problem. The person may be forced to misperceive events in order to realize a stronger emotional reaction to justify overt behavior. The inability to act out intense feelings is indicative of a high Controlled Tolerance Limit. If the limit remains high and the client is encouraged to use different strategies that raise emotional intensity until it is experienced in the Region of Deliberate Behavior, the strategies may become habitual.

Because the Controlled Tolerance Limit is "positioned" partly by conscious decision and partly by pressures of social norms, personal values, and self-image, an alternate strategy may be to tackle the source of these pressures so that people can exercise more conscious control over their limits. To exercise that control, people must recognize the mechanisms by which they respond to social norms, develop their values, or assess their self-images. In this way, people can learn how to maintain a lower level of feelings rather than increasing the level.

People can become more aware of their own limits and learn to manipulate deliberately the limit levels to meet their functional needs. With practice, people may be able to position their tolerance limits at the most functional levels for their current circumstances.

Another application of the conceptual framework presented here is to clarify communication about different responses by different people to the same event. People react with differing intensities to the same event as a function of their perceptions of the event and its relevance to them. For example, if the remark is made that "Fat people are clumsy," a person of average weight will barely be aware of the emotional potential of the remark. Someone who is slightly overweight may feel hurt but not respond. However, a person who is considerably overweight and who has just failed miserably in attempts to diet may react very strongly.

People often feel guilty or inadequate if they act, or fail to act, on their feelings. When an event provokes an emotional response with a peak intensity at or near the Controlled Tolerance Limit, the person will feel some ambiguity about responding overtly. If the peak intensity is just below the limit, the person feels a pressure to act, but the intensity is not quite sufficient to elicit an overt response. The recovery period, and the emotional episode, may be extended because of the person's inability to reconcile his or her failure to act with personal values, the pressure of social norms, and his or her self-image.

On the other hand, when the emotional intensity is barely sufficient to cause an overt response, as the person enters the recovery period and feelings are reduced in intensity, he or she wonders whether there was really sufficient cause to act. It is difficult to fully justify the reaction. In this case, too, the person's recovery period may be extended by anxiety over the possible consequences of the behavior.

The implications and inferences of the conceptual model presented here for thinking about feelings are numerous. The possible avenues for refinement and application are many. It is extremely useful for understanding and communicating about some of the more difficult aspects of feelings and how we deal with them.

## REFERENCES

Boshear, W.C., & Albrecht, K.G., *Understanding people: Models and concepts.* San Diego, CA: University Associates, 1977.

*Walton C. Boshear is the president of Solutions, a consulting firm in Rancho Santa Fe, California. He is the creator of the on-line team-building approach to organization development and is active in organizational problem solving in both the systems and behavioral sciences. Mr. Boshear also conducts personal growth programs and writes monthly columns on behavioral science and real estate for various magazines.*

# KENEPATHY

## Michele Stimac

The importance of understanding feelings and emotions in the communication process or in a helping relationship has been stressed so often that there is no question but that affect is as important as cognitive data for human expression and understanding. Human relations trainers have stressed the importance of "catching feelings" (empathy) and have emphasized the importance of discerning feelings in order to understand an individual's inner being. But training manuals filled with structured activities too often concentrate on affective understanding to the exclusion of cognitive understanding. This concentration on the affective dimension has created an imbalance in our skill training as egregious as the previous concentration on cognitive communication. Human beings function continually at several levels, and true understanding requires listening to them at all levels.

Individuals trained to listen to others must "kenepathize," i.e., hear the verbal message, see the nonverbal behavior, and grasp what the speaker's thoughts and perceptions are as well as what that person is feeling and experiencing at the moment. The term "kenepathy" supplements the term "empathy." We have come to associate empathy almost exclusively with "catching feelings" or understanding affect, so the term kenepathy has been coined to convey a more all-inclusive understanding. The prefix *ken*, borrowed from the archaic Scottish word meaning to know or understand, has been joined to the root *pathy*, from the Greek *pathos* or feelings. Kenepathy, as defined here, means to understand cognitive as well as affective data—to grasp another's thoughts, perceptions, and feelings.

The "bucket" model developed here is useful in human relations or leadership training to convey the complexity of the human being and the need for a confluent grasp of feelings, thoughts, perceptions, and actions.

## THE BUCKET MODEL

Human beings are so complex that their behavior is not easy to understand, a fact Lewin (1951) attempted to explain with his concept of "life space." According to Lewin, behavior is a function of each person's life space and to understand it requires that we understand the dynamics in that person's space—a challenge even the most proficient listener finds difficult to meet. The bucket model illustrates the complexity of life space and helps us perceive the monumental task involved in listening for true understanding. The model is explicated below.

### Here-and-Now Level: The Conscious

Each of us is like a bucket (Figure 1) containing several dimensions. At the surface is our here-and-now (conscious) life space, which includes current behavior, both verbal and nonverbal. This facet is most accessible to anyone else who attempts to listen and understand.

Also included in our here-and-now space at the surface are our current thoughts and perceptions. These are apparent to others if we choose to disclose them directly or indirectly. Because we generally have been encouraged through schooling and societal conditioning, most of us readily exchange thoughts and ideas unless we find ourselves in inhibiting climates.

Finally, also at the here-and-now level, are our current feelings and what we are experiencing at the moment. Our feelings are often not very accessible, especially if we are adept at hiding them. Societal conditioning has typically not encouraged their expression, although the human relations movement has helped to modify this conditioning by pointing out that feelings are essential data that listeners must have if they are to really understand what we are like.

### There-and-Then Level: Preconscious

Kenepathizing requires more than understanding thoughts, perceptions, and feelings, however, because there are other levels in our "buckets." As each moment passes, the here-and-now becomes past data that fill "mini-buckets" in the there-and-then (preconscious) area of our larger buckets (Figure 2).

While receding into the there-and-then area, data are either posited so that they influence our current behavior, thoughts, and feelings or so that they are comparatively insignificant in our lives.

Through memory we can recall a great deal of this data, but some is virtually lost forever. Much of what we have done, thought, and felt has the potential to dynamically influence us at some later time in our lives. The data remain to be recalled and perhaps serve as a modifier of our current (here-and-now) behavior, thoughts and perceptions, feelings and experience. Sometimes harmoniously, sometimes not, the past and present interrelate. Lewin (1951) might call these data the "facts" in our life space—memories that force their way into the current situation where they stir old feelings and thoughts and modify current perceptions and behavior. To kenepathize with us, others must understand the influences of the intruding mini-buckets that act as catalysts at the present moment.

### There-and-Then Level: Unconscious

Even more remote and inaccessible is the unconscious area of our bucket—the most inscrutable of all (Figure 3). This area contains miniature buckets that represent what we have repressed throughout our lives. Experiences too painful to deal with have been pushed into the unconscious. Like experiences stored in our preconscious, they often thrust their way into the present and influence our behavior—albeit in ways incomprehensible to us except through analysis.

The bottom of the bucket in some sense remains bottomless. There is no way for behavioral scientists to make definitive statements concerning the unconscious. It is important to remember, however, that these forces influence our current behavior. Total kenepathy—in the sense of understanding the facts in our unconscious and how they influence our behavior—we leave to the psychotherapist.

Unlike the neatly placed miniature buckets in Figures 2 and 3, the pieces of data that the miniature buckets represent are often in collision and disharmony with one another. This very conflict is another source of our feelings, thoughts, and behavior.

### MINI-BUCKETS MODIFY THE HERE-AND-NOW

The bucket model depicts the combination of here-and-now and there-and-then cognitive and affective data that must in some measure be understood by anyone who tries to understand another person. If Person B, for example, attempts to understand Person A (Figure 4), B must learn A's frame of reference, which includes facts from both cognitive and affective levels. As B kenepathizes with A, B must try to understand some of what is in A's there-and-then, especially if

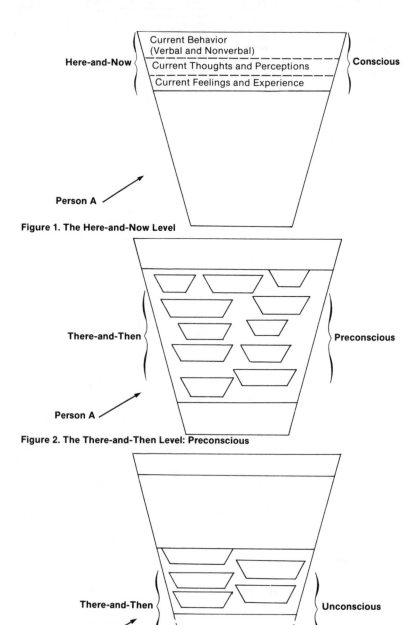

**Here-and-Now** { Current Behavior (Verbal and Nonverbal) / Current Thoughts and Perceptions / Current Feelings and Experience } **Conscious**

Person A

**Figure 1. The Here-and-Now Level**

**There-and-Then** { } **Preconscious**

Person A

**Figure 2. The There-and-Then Level: Preconscious**

**There-and-Then** { } **Unconscious**

Person A

**Figure 3. The There-and-Then Level: Unconscious**

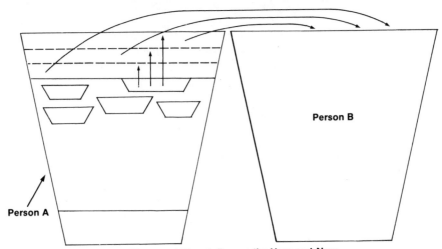

**Figure 4. Mini-Buckets from There-and-Then Influence the Here-and-Now**

one or more of A's mini-buckets greatly influence A's here-and-now. This defies the general rule that group members must stay exclusively in the here-and-now when exchanging information. A better rule might be to remain in the here-and-now when functional, but to be alert to when there-and-then data that need to be expressed and understood invade and alter present experience.

For example, if Person A has recently quarreled with a spouse, the residue of that quarrel will undoubtedly affect his interaction with Person B. The experience of the quarrel, a mini-bucket in A's there-and-then, will probably intrude on the current moment, so B must attempt to pick up on the experience of the quarrel also. The residue of the quarrel is probably mostly affect, so to kenepathize B must respond to A's feelings about it.

On the other hand, A may have just come from a stimulating brainstorming session with colleagues. In this instance, his mini-bucket contains a great deal of cognitive as well as affective material. In this case, it is essential for B to understand A's thoughts as well as A's feelings, especially if they modify his current behavior.

The examples are endless that illustrate the demand on the listener for confluent attention and understanding; as shown here, to grasp only affect may be as remiss as to grasp only cognitive material.

Of course, the disposition of B, the listener, further complicates the process of communication. If her bucket were accurately analyzed, it would be apparent what mini-buckets impose their dynamics into the here-and-now surface of her conversation. She may fail to perceive accurately what is being communicated to her because of her own preconscious or unconscious data.

The complexity of life space—the bucket each of us possesses—is enormous and the phenomenon of communication commands respect, even awe, when its intricacies and complexities are assessed. It is no wonder that so much miscommunication occurs.

## SAMPLE ACTIVITIES CONTAINING COGNITIVE AND AFFECTIVE DATA

The bucket model reflects the multifaceted nature of the human being and illustrates the necessity for kenepathy, i.e., simultaneously reacting to multiple levels of personality when communicating. The model is learned most effectively when reinforced with activities designed to develop discriminating yet comprehensive listening techniques. A few sample communications are cited below. After reading each, consider your own kenepathic response before reading the sample response.

At a meeting with the principal, a teacher suggests:

> I really believe now that we should try to get our teachers to teach for mastery learning. We talked a lot about mastery learning in our departmental meetings this past month, and now I'm sold on it. I think it's the way to go.

This teacher is functioning mostly at the cognitive level, so the principal could respond kenepathically as follows:

> You've had an insight that's changed your opinion of how to teach. You think we should move from our current method of giving students one chance to learn the material to a method that gives them as much time as it takes to learn the material.

This response obviously catches the teacher's thoughts on the subject and adequately lets her know that she is understood. Another example of an exercise in kenepathy follows:

A coordinator speaks to his manager:

> Ms. Coronoa is really making a mess of that job I gave her last week.

If the listener reflects this statement with "You feel that she's not doing a good job"—a typical empathic response—the message has not been captured adequately. It is more accurate for the respondent to leave the statement at the cognitive level and respond with "You disapprove of her performance." A judgment, not a feeling, was expressed. If the listener detects affect also, he might add "and that makes you feel disappointed." But the speaker's statement alone, without accompanying body language or innuendo, is a cognitive statement.

Other examples of the intermix between affective and cognitive data can be generated easily. Examples rife with feeling are quickly available in training manuals. Practicing responses to both types helps us to see the importance of simultaneous discrimination of both dimensions. It exercises our skill at detecting ideas, preconceptions, and perceptions as well as feelings. It teaches us to listen to nonverbal and verbal cues in behavior. It helps us verify that human beings think and feel simultaneously—a fact that we all experience in everyday life. In order to understand an individual, we must be in tune with as much of that person's bucket as possible. Being able to kenepathize means getting in touch with every aspect of another individual. The bucket model and the concept of kenepathy can be helpful tools to facilitate an understanding of the complexity of human beings and to develop comprehensive listening skills.

## REFERENCES

Brammer, L., *The helping relationship*. Englewood Cliffs, NJ: Prentice-Hall, 1973.

Carkhuff, R.R. *Helping and human relations* (Vols. I & II). New York: Holt, Rinehart and Winston, 1969.

Egan, G. A two-phase approach to human relations training. In J.E. Jones & J.W. Pfeiffer (Eds.), *The 1973 annual handbook for group facilitators*, San Diego, CA: University Associates, 1973.

Egan, G. *The skilled helper: A model for systematic helping and interpersonal relating*. Monterey, CA: Brooks Cole, 1975.

Gazda, G.M., Asbury, F.R., Balzer, F.J., Childers, W.C., & Walters, R.P. *Human relations development: A manual for educators*. Boston: Allyn and Bacon, 1975.

Lewin, K. *Field theory in social science: Selected theoretical papers*. (D. Cartwright, Ed.) New York: Harper, 1951.

*Michele Stimac, Ed.D., is a professor and doctoral-program counselor at Pepperdine University, Los Angeles, California. For doctoral programs in institutional management and community college administration, she teaches management of human endeavor and leadership. At the master's level, she teaches courses in educational psychology, group dynamics, and career development. She has published in the areas of human relations, leadership, humanism, and career development.*

# CREATIVITY AND CREATIVE PROBLEM SOLVING

## Martin B. Ross

Creativity and creative problem solving are much researched but little understood processes (Stievater, 1973a, 1973b). The topics studied include creative personality, creative problem formulation, the creative process, creative products or outcomes, the creative climate or environment, and the relationships among creativity, intelligence, and mental health, but no one factor, or combination of factors, explains the accomplishments of a Leonardo da Vinci, a Thomas Edison, or a Ludwig von Beethoven.

Creativity is an intriguing and controversial topic. The controversy and the absence of a unified theory do not mean that research efforts have been fruitless. Studies have revealed that there are certain *factors that block the creative process* and that a conscious effort to avoid or overcome these blocks can enhance creativity. In addition, laboratory and empirical research have produced *techniques that facilitate creative problem solving*.

## BARRIERS TO CREATIVITY

Barriers to creativity have been described as "mental walls which block the problem-solver from correctly perceiving a problem or conceiving its solution" (Adams, 1974, p. 11). These walls, which exist for all of us but vary in quantity and intensity, are of two types: structural and process. The common structural barriers include psychological, cultural, and environmental blocks. Process barriers result from our choice of thinking language, our functional fixedness, and our tendency habitually to visualize things in the same way. An expanded awareness and understanding of these impediments is a first step toward more creative problem solving. The framework used here to describe these blocks is based on the work of Adams (1974).

### Psychological Barriers

A variety of psychological factors serve to block individual creativity by inhibiting the freedom with which we explore and transform ideas, impeding our conceptual abilities, and blocking communication. The more common psychological blocks to creativity include our preference for the predictable and orderly and, conversely, our intolerance of the unknown or ambiguous; our high achievement motivation and quick success orientation and, conversely, our inability to allow ideas to incubate and develop; our tendency to value our sensory perceptions (that which is) to the exclusion of our intuitive perceptions (the possibilities); and our fear of failure.

These common psychological barriers exist because we are generally educated and socialized with an overriding emphasis on situations and learning experiences for which there is only one correct answer. Rarely is attention paid to and reward offered for the creative process itself. Because we seek to be liked and respected by others, searching for and "selling" unique, creative ideas or solutions involves risks—the risks of making a mistake, failing, being ridiculed, losing money, losing respect, or losing friends.

The psychological barriers to creativity are the most deep rooted and, hence, most difficult to overcome. The first step is to recognize their existence and seek self-awareness. By identifying which psychological factors impede our own creativity, we can determine the techniques available to overcome the barriers.

## Cultural Barriers

Certain aspects of our culture promote creativity and others impede it. We acquire from our parents, peers, teachers, and society at large a set of values, attitudes, beliefs, and behaviors. The high value placed on individuality and competition, for example, may promote the risk-taking behavior required for creative problem solving in certain situations. Conversely, the high value placed on reason, logic, numbers, and practicality may impede solutions requiring feeling, intuition, and qualitative judgments. Because fantasy, reflection, and playfulness are proscribed behaviors for adults, creativity is impeded in situations that may benefit from these behaviors. The prescription that problem-solving behavior be serious and humorless may also block creativity. Recognizing how aspects of our culture may inhibit creativity is an important first step in overcoming blocks to creativity.

## Environmental Barriers

Some aspects of our social and physical environments also act as blocks to creativity. Social blocks are illustrated by work or school settings in which the boss or teacher is threatened by new ideas, fails to act on new ideas, or fails to reward innovative thinking. Overcoming social blocks requires that teachers, bosses, peers, and colleagues recognize their roles in facilitating or impeding creativity and seek to design creative environments and engage in supportive behaviors.

Physical blocks are generally more obvious and more easily overcome than are social blocks. For some, a ringing telephone, a barking dog, or a blaring stereo impedes creativity. Others may find silence an impediment. By looking for the situations in which we seem most creative and productive, we can define our personal supportive physical environments and can seek them out when confronted with problems and opportunities requiring creativity.

## Thinking Language Blocks

We have at our command a variety of languages with which to think about solutions to problems. Verbal, mathematical, visual, and other sensory languages are available individually and in combination. Selecting the correct thinking language may result in the most creative solution.

Adams (1974) offers an example of how the selection of thinking language affects problem solving. Picture a large piece of ordinary paper. In your imagination, fold it once (now it has two layers), fold it once more (into four layers), and continue folding it for 50 times. How thick is the folded paper? A mathematical approach would quickly reveal that the first fold results in a stack two times the original thickness. Extending the answer, the result is $2^{50}$ times the original thickness of the paper. Had we selected a visual or verbal approach, we undoubtedly would never arrive at the correct value.

Early in childhood we display preferences for different ways of thinking. We tend to use the processes we prefer, develop skill in using them, and thereby reinforce our preferences. Our preferred thinking patterns may promote creativity in certain situations and block it in others.

When confronted with a problem, we should consciously consider the various thought languages available and attempt to use whichever is most appropriate. When the problem-solving process becomes bogged down, it may be time to step back and examine which thinking language is being employed and consider the use of an alternative.

## Functional Fixedness

Functional fixedness results from our tendency to use tools, people, and techniques in only one way. Raudseep and Haugh (1977) illustrate functional fixedness. Imagine that you are standing in the middle of a room. You have been given the task of holding the ends of two strings suspended from the ceiling. The strings are located so that you cannot reach one string with your outstretched arm while holding the second. The room is bare except for a pair of pliers and a screwdriver. When presented with this problem, many people fail to think of using a belt or some other article of clothing to extend the length of one string so that they can reach the other. They also fail to consider tying the pliers or screwdriver to the end of one string, swinging it, and catching it, thereby solving the problem. These solutions involve overcoming our tendencies to use common items in a conventional manner only—overcoming functional fixedness.

## Habitual Ways of Visualizing

Our tendency to develop habitual ways of looking at things is a block to creativity best defined and illustrated by example. Let us say that there are four volumes of Shakespeare's collected works on the shelf. The pages of each volume are exactly two inches thick. Each cover is one sixth of an inch thick. If a bookworm starts eating at page one of volume one and eats through to the last page of volume four, how far does it travel? The answer typically provided is nine inches. Rarely is the proper answer, five inches, given. People attempting to solve this problem are blocked by their habitual ways of visualizing books—facing them, with the first page near the left-hand cover and last page near the right-hand cover. This is the way we prepare to open books to read them, not the way they typically sit on a shelf with the order of pages reversed (Raudseep & Haugh, 1977).

There is a maxim in problem solving that the more familiar the object, the harder it is to see it in another context. Creativity can be enhanced, particularly in problems involving the familiar, if we seek to visualize them from new and different angles and in new and different ways.

## TECHNIQUES THAT STIMULATE CREATIVITY

As the previous discussion indicates, avoiding and overcoming the common barriers to creativity is best achieved by altering thought and behavioral processes, even though these are among the most difficult changes to achieve. Fortunately, research on creativity has resulted in problem-solving and decision-making techniques to promote creativity in both individuals and groups. Creative problem finding, analogies, morphological analysis, a questioning attitude, and a creative climate promote creativity for individuals and groups. Brainstorming, "odd man in," and designing a creative climate are techniques specifically designed to promote group creativity. These techniques, which have proven useful in overcoming barriers to and otherwise promoting creativity, are described in the following paragraphs.

## Creative Problem Solving

Obviously, the problem itself is important for initiating solution-oriented thought, but little is known about how problems are discovered and formulated. The way in which a problem is stated or defined may determine the difference between a poorly solved or unsolved problem and a creative solution. Albert Einstein (Getzels, 1975, p. 12) stated that "The formulation of a problem is often more essential than its solution, which may be merely a matter of mathematical or experimental skill. To raise new questions, new possibilities, to regard old questions from a new angle, requires creative imagination." The following example illustrates the importance of creative problem finding.

An automobile traveling on a deserted road blows a tire. The occupants discover that there is no jack in the trunk. They define the problem as "finding a jack" and decide to walk to a station for a jack. Another automobile on the same road also blows a tire. The occupants also discover that there is no jack. They define the problem as "raising the automobile." They see an old barn with a pulley for lifting bails of hay to the loft, push the car to the barn, raise it on the pulley, change the tire, and drive off while the occupants of the first car are still trudging toward the service station. One might comment, "What a clever solution." "What a creative problem statement" is a more accurate observation. The occupants of the second car ignored the obvious and formulated the problem in an unusual and fruitful way (Getzels, 1975).

Creative problem finding means not settling on the obvious problem, seeking to think divergently rather than convergently, raising new questions and new possibilities from new angles, and using one's imagination.

## Use of Analogy

Using personal analogies to move information stored in the subconscious to a conscious level and thereby making it available for problem solving is an effective technique for promoting creativity. For example, in dealing with a problem related to water pollution, one might attempt to imagine how it would feel to be a polluted river. This technique expands creativity by allowing one to "get inside" the problem and view it from a different angle. Direct analogy, which often relies on biological or natural analogies, provides creative insight. Fantasy analogy is useful for overcoming cultural blocks to creativity. This technique encourages one to suspend natural laws and create a universe in which anything is possible. Faced with the problem of having to move water up a hill, it might be interesting to suspend the laws of gravity and create a fantasy whereby water can flow uphill. It has been suggested that the divining rod and modern metal detectors originated from fantasies of magic wands (Wilson, Greer, & Johnson, 1973).

## Morphological Analysis

Morphological analysis involves breaking a complex problem into components, listing as many alternatives as possible for each component, and then recombining the alternatives to create new variations. Consider the complex problem of creating a new mode of human transportation. Using morphological analysis, the problem can be broken into its component parts and alternatives can be listed. Component 1 might be defined as the carrier or support for the human being, and alternatives might be a cart, a chair, a sling, and a bed. Component 2 might be the medium of support for the carrier, with surface, water, air, rollers, rails, and oil as alternatives, and so on. Once the major components and alternatives are identified, they can be put into combinations, for example, adding another component to make an *electric* rolling chair. It is obvious that a variety of potential modes of transportation—some feasible and others absurd—can be generated. A variety of possibilities that would not have been identified without morphological analysis now exist. One may be a creative solution to the problem (Parnes & Harding, 1962).

## Questioning Attitude

Through probing and questioning, alternatives are generated and the possibility of discovering creative solutions is enhanced. Anyone who has spent time in the presence of young children has been the recipient of such questions as "Why is the ocean salty?" or "Where does the sun go at night?" A probing attitude appears to be almost instinctual in children. Unfortunately, this characteristic diminishes as they mature to adulthood because adults discourage their questions. Older children avoid asking questions because they have learned that it is good to be smart and bad to be dumb, and silence does not reveal ignorance. But remaining silent removes a powerful weapon from one's learning arsenal. A questioning attitude is a useful technique for expanding one's creativity, and all one needs to do to develop a questioning attitude is ask questions (Adams, 1974).

## Brainstorming

The best known group technique for expanding creativity is brainstorming, used for complex problem solving in groups ranging in size from two to seven. Brainstorming frees people from many of the previously described inhibitions and blocks to creativity. A cooperative group-problem-solving process, it is constrained by four basic rules.

1. Evaluation of any kind is not permitted; adverse or favorable judgments must be withheld. By withholding judgment, people avoid the tendency to defend their ideas and concentrate on generating ideas. This rule is particularly important when defining the problem and generating ideas and alternative solutions.
2. Freewheeling is encouraged and welcomed. The group seeks to include all possibilities, even the absurd, which can always be weeded out later.
3. As many ideas as possible are sought, the rationale being that the larger the number of ideas, the higher the probability that good ideas will be generated.
4. Combinations of, elaboration on, and improvements of ideas are encouraged to produce better, more creative solutions.

## Odd Man In

The "odd-man-in" technique involves including in a problem-solving group one or more individuals who have little or no background or relationship to the problem at hand. This technique was developed because research has found that individuals have difficulty being creative about familiar things. The U.S. Navy employs this technique. For example, a home economist was included along with medical and naval experts in a group attempting to determine whether physician staffing on a nuclear submarine should be reduced. The "odd-man-in" technique can expand creativity directly by offering a unique perspective and indirectly by knocking group members out of their persistent ruts of thinking.

## Creative Climate

Creating a physical, psychological, and social climate conducive to creativity is the final group technique for expanding creativity. Group members must avoid blocks to creativity and employ techniques that promote creative problem solving. They should themselves, and encourage others to, communicate freely, offer risk-taking opinions, probe and question, discuss, compare, and elaborate on ideas, engage in divergent rather than convergent thinking, avoid win-lose competition, and engage in freewheeling and fantasy. Group members should also seek and maintain physical environments that are conducive to creativity.

From a social standpoint, they must attempt to minimize the enforcement of behavior norms that may block creativity. Emphasis should be placed on problem solving, working through conflict, and avoiding dysfunctional interpersonal conflict.

Finally, group members must learn to see themselves as a part of the group climate and promote creativity by ensuring that they are a model to others in heeding the above advice, avoiding barriers to creativity, and using special techniques to overcome creative blocks.

## CONCLUSION

Research on creativity showing ways it is inhibited and facilitated dispels the popular belief that creativity stems from inherited traits. On the contrary, each individual has a capacity for creativity which, for a variety of reasons, is significantly underutilized. Understanding the nature of the barriers to creativity and practicing techniques to overcome them can be extremely beneficial to all of us. The key to promoting creativity is to expand our awareness and consciousness, to force ourselves to see the familiar in new and different ways—to make the familiar strange and the strange familiar (Bennis, 1975). The knowledge and techniques presented here can be useful in tapping the latent wellsprings of creativity in us all.

## REFERENCES

Adams, J.L. *Conceptual blockbusting.* San Francisco: W.H. Freemond, 1974.

Bennis, W.G. *The unconscious conspiracy.* New York: AMACOM, 1975.

Getzels, J.W. Problem-finding and the inventiveness of solutions. *Journal of Creative Behavior,* 1975, 9(1), 12-18.

Kneller, G.F. *The art and science of creativity.* New York: Holt, Rinehart and Winston, 1965.

Parnes, S.J., & Harding, H.F. (Eds.). *A source book for creative thinking.* New York: Charles Scribner's Sons, 1962.

Raudsepp, E., & Haugh, G.P. The so you think you're creative quiz. *Playboy,* November 1977, pp. 177; 210-215.

Stievater, S.M. Bibliography of recent books on creativity and problem solving: Supplement IV. *Journal of Creative Behavior,* 1973, 7(3), 208-213. (a)

Stievater, S.M. Bibliography of recent theses on creativity and problem solving: Supplement II. *Journal of Creative Behavior,* 1973, 7(3), 214-222. (b)

Wilson, S.H., Greer, J.F., & Johnson, R.M. Synectics: A creative problem-solving technique for the gifted. *Gifted Child Quarterly,* 1973, 17(4), 260-267.

*Martin B. Ross, Dr., Ph.,* is an assistant professor and associate director of the Program in Health Services Management, School of Public Health, University of California at Los Angeles. He is also the founder and senior partner of Pointer-Ross and Associates, a management training and consulting firm for health services organizations. Dr. Ross's specialty is in management and organization development in health services organizations.

# COPING WITH ANARCHY IN ORGANIZATIONS

## Michael A. Berger

Any discussion on the management of change includes a claim of the universality of the change strategies across organizations. In most theoretical and empirical papers, the assumption is that all the change agent needs to do is apply the change strategy in the proper manner for constructive change to result. Although this may be true, organizational characteristics vary, and, consequently, the implications are different for the management of change.

## THE RATIONAL MODEL

A rather simplistic theory, labeled the "rational model" of management (Cyert & March, 1963; March & Simon, 1958), underlies much of the discussion on the behavior of organizations:

1. It is possible to establish clear, prioritized goals.
2. The most effective means (technologies) to accomplish the goals can be selected.
3. Once the means are applied, the organization's managers can evaluate whether successful goal achievement has occurred.
4. When problems occur, managers will make rational decisions on the way goals and/or the technologies should be modified to correct the gap between what is desired and what is occurring.

## IMPLICATIONS FOR MANAGING CHANGE

Given these assumptions, it follows that change agents should direct their energies toward facilitating the establishment of clear, prioritized goals. Presumably, an MBO strategy would be helpful (Thomson, 1972). However, sometimes the goals of the organization are relatively clear, but the commitment of the organization's participants is problematic. In these cases, change strategies such as rational-empirical, normative-re-educative, and power-coercive (Chin & Benne, 1969) may be appropriate.

In practical terms, the fundamental objective of these change strategies is to find goals and/or means that can be evaluated easily and to which the participants can commit themselves. It is assumed that if relevant information is gathered to define the problem properly and if the resistance of recalcitrant parties is overcome, then a decision can be made that will correct any problems. In this view, a fairly stable group of decision makers who agree on goals and technology is managing change.

## THE ORGANIZED ANARCHY MODEL

In contrast, some organizations do not exhibit the close link between goals and means, the ease in evaluation, or the stability of decision makers assumed in the rational model. Known as organized anarchies (Cohen & March, 1975; March & Olsen, 1976), these organizations are characterized by ambiguous goals, unclear and contested technologies, strong norms against evaluation, and unstable participation by decision makers.[1]

---

[1]March and his colleagues conceived the notion of organized anarchies to describe educational organizations. Their description, however, can be generalized to all human service organizations with a professionalized component, e.g., hospitals, community mental health centers, correctional institutions, and social welfare agencies.

In organized anarchies, the measurable goals are not widely accepted; if the goal priorities *are* accepted, they are usually not operational (e.g., "quality health care"). Technologies in these types of organizations are also turbulent. Either the technology is constantly changing—as in the shift in mental health treatment from mileau therapy to behavioral therapy to drug therapy—or the technology is strongly contested within the management group.

Evaluation of outcomes is also difficult in anarchic organizations. Professionals typically resist administrative scrutiny of their performance, saying that professionals alone must evaluate performance. Even if evaluation were possible, it is unclear what would be evaluated. There simply is no rational way to evaluate the degree to which such goals as quality health care have been realized. Decisions on anything except political considerations are extremely rare, although those involved may think that their choices are made on a rational basis.

The process of decision making also varies in anarchic organizations. It is assumed that people inside and outside the organization have limited time and energy resources for most of the issues. Often, solutions vaguely resemble the problems that spawned them; decision makers come and go (March calls it "fluid participation"); and issues keep resurfacing. Under these conditions, decision making resembles a "garbage-can process" in which loosely coupled components such as problems, solutions looking for problems, participants, and choice opportunities are mixed together in a less than rational manner (March & Olsen, 1976).

## IMPLICATIONS FOR MANAGING CHANGE

It is apparent that change in organized anarchies does not come from a group of managers that makes decisions in a rational fashion but from various factions that make choices based only partially on rational criteria. The following tactics may be useful under these highly complex circumstances (Baldridge, 1975).

1. *Concentrate Efforts.* Because people in organized anarchies do not care about most issues and tend to wander in and out of the decision-making process, the change agent may have a greater chance of success if he or she focuses on one or two critical problems.

2. *Learn the History.* The wise change agent attempts to learn when the issue came up previously, who took what position, who won, and who lost. He or she also weighs carefully whether the time is right to make a fight for the issue or whether to wait until the issue comes up again.

3. *Build a Coalition.* Because the anarchic theory assumes the presence of powerful internal and external constituencies who can apply pressure to the decision-making process, the wise change agent mobilizes the support of these various elements to help influence the "garbage-can" processes.

4. *Use the Formal and Informal Systems.* Committee membership, doing one's homework, and being ready to "fill the garbage can" with distracting issues are all viable change strategies, but the model also emphasizes the use of the informal system. For example, a committee will often simply ratify what has already been agreed to informally (Goffman, 1959). Bargains among professionals are often facilitated not by "face-to-face" confrontations, as some rational change strategies suggest (Harrison, 1972), but in the "face-saving" processes of informal discussions and mediation. Furthermore, these are instances when change can take place informally with no formal action at all. Managers simply agree on a new set of understandings and operate as if these were formalized into the system.

## CONCLUSION

Although these change strategies are not exhaustive and may not be appropriate in all settings, they do illustrate that the management of change varies depending on the character of the organization. This insight is not new, but in reaffirming our understanding of these differences, we not only specify how organizations differ, we also sharpen our understanding of the various tools needed to manage change. We simply cannot assume that our favorite change strategies have universal application.

## REFERENCES

Baldridge, J.V. Rules for a Machiavellian change agent: Transforming the entrenched professional organizations. In J.V. Baldridge & T.E. Deal (Eds.), *Managing change in educational organizations.* Berkeley, CA: McCutchan, 1975.

Chin, R., & Benne, K. Strategies of change. In W. Bennis, K. Benne, & R. Chin (Eds.), *Planning of change.* New York: Holt, Rinehart and Winston, 1969.

Cohen, M., & March, J.G. *Leadership and ambiguity: The American college president.* New York: McGraw-Hill, 1975.

Cyert, R., & March, J.G. *A behavioral theory of firm.* Englewood Cliffs, NJ: Doubleday, 1959.

Goffman, E. *Presentation of self in everyday life.* Garden City, NY: Doubleday, 1959.

Harrison, R. Role negotiation: A tough minded approach to team development. In W.W. Burke & H.A. Hornstein (Eds.), *The social technology of organization development.* San Diego, CA: University Associates, 1972.

March, J., & Olsen, J. (Eds.), *Ambiguity and choice in organizations.* Bergen, Norway: University Press, 1976.

March, J., & Simon, H. *Organizations.* New York: John Wiley, 1958.

Thomson, T. Management by objectives. In J.W. Pfeiffer & J.E. Jones (Eds.), *The 1972 annual handbook for group facilitators.* San Diego, CA: University Associates, 1972.

**Michael A. Berger, Ph.D.,** *is an assistant professor of education at Peabody College of Vanderbilt University, Nashville, Tennessee. He teaches a graduate program to train counselors and coordinators of human service organizations. Dr. Berger's background is in organizational sociology, management development, and consultation to human service organizations.*

# STRESS-MANAGEMENT SKILLS: SELF-MODIFICATION FOR PERSONAL ADJUSTMENT TO STRESS

**L. Phillip K. Le Gras**

## STRESS, STRESSORS, AND STRESS REACTIONS

Stress can be understood best as a state of imbalance between demands made on us from outside sources and our capabilities to meet those demands when the expected consequences from meeting or not meeting the demands are significantly different. Stress describes a hypothetical state caused by events, called "stressors," that result in behavioral outcomes, called "stress reactions." A stressor can be any physical event, other people's behavior, social situations, our own behavior, feelings, thoughts, or anything that results in heightened physiological awareness. Pain, anger, fear, depression, and ecstasy are examples of stress reactions.

All people do not react to stressors in the same way, nor do individuals always react the same way to a particular stressor. Some people handle stress better than others; in fact, some people suffer from overstress while others are stress seekers. Individual differences in our reactions to stress are not as important as learning how to manage the stress we do feel. Through learning certain stress-management skills, we can develop self-control when stressful events occur.

The way we feel and behave under stress is determined by what we think (self-statements or private speech) in a given situation. The stress reaction involves two major elements: (1) heightened physical arousal, e.g., increased heart rate, sweaty palms, rapid breathing, or muscular tension, and (2) anxious thoughts, e.g., a sense of helplessness, panic at being overwhelmed, or a desire to run away. Because behavior and emotions are controlled by inner thoughts, the best way to exert control over them is by acquiring skills that change these thoughts.

## CONTROLLING PHYSICAL AROUSAL

One method is as follows: Sit in a comfortable position in a quiet place with no distractions; close your eyes and pay no attention to the outside world, concentrate on your breathing, slowly inhaling and exhaling; softly say "relax" when each breath has been exhaled completely. This should be a gentle, passive process—a relaxing experience. Eventually the word "relax" will be associated with a sense of physical calm and just saying it in a stressful situation will induce a sense of peace.

Another simple, effective way to induce relaxation is through tension release. The general idea is to first tense a set of muscles and then to relax them so that they will be more relaxed than they were before they were tensed. Each muscle group is practiced separately, but the ultimate goal is to relax all groups simultaneously to achieve total body relaxation. For each muscle group, in turn, tense the muscles, hold them for five seconds, then relax them. Repeat the tension-release sequence three times for each group of muscles. Next, tense all the muscles together for five seconds, then release them, take a slow deep breath, and say "relax" softly to yourself as you breathe out. This sequence is also repeated three times. To incorporate this technique into everyday life, notice your bodily tension, identify the tense muscle groups, and then relax them while saying "relax" inwardly.

Total relaxation can also be obtained through exercise, either aerobic or Yoga type. The relaxation experience can be extended into daily life through personal fitness programs in conjunction with inner messages to "relax." With practice we have the capability to call up the relaxation response whenever it is needed.

## CONTROL OF THOUGHTS

Flexibility in thinking about situations is necessary to manage stress effectively. We must take alternative views and keep from attaching exaggerated importance to events. By taking a problem-solving approach, we can learn not to take things personally. Adverse events should not be seen as personal affronts or as threats to our egos. By taking a task orientation, we can focus on desired outcomes and implement a behavioral strategy that results in those outcomes.

A very effective mental intervention for stress management consists of talking to ourselves to guide thoughts, feelings, and behavior in order to cope. The control of stress through self-instruction is accomplished by considering a stress experience as a series of phases. The phases and some examples of coping statements are as follows:

1. *Preparing for a Stressor.* What do I have to do? I can develop a plan to handle it. I have to think about this and not panic. Don't be negative. Think logically. Be rational. Don't worry. Maybe the tension I'm feeling is just eagerness to confront the situation.

2. *Confronting and Handling a Stressor.* I can do it. Stay relevant. I can psyche myself up to handle this. I can meet the challenge. This tension is a cue to use my stress-management skills. Relax, I'm in control. Take a slow breath.

3. *Coping with the Feeling of Being Overwhelmed.* I must concentrate on what I have to do right now. I can't eliminate my fear completely, but I can try to keep it under control. When the fear is overwhelming, I'll just pause for a minute.

4. *Reinforcing Self-Statements.* Well done. I did it! It worked. I wasn't successful this time but I'm getting better. It almost worked. Next time I can do it. When I control my thoughts I control my fear.

We must become aware of and monitor anxiety that causes self-defeating statements in stressful situations, e.g., "I'm going to fail" or "I can't do this." We must listen to what we say to ourselves with a "third ear." The occurrence of such thoughts is a cue to substitute coping self-statements. We can cope with many stressors by employing relaxation methods and coping self-statements, but at critical moments when the stress reaction is exceptionally intense and seemingly beyond our ability to cope, we can extend self-control by applying whichever of the following techniques is compatible with our needs in the particular situation:

1. *Distraction.* Focus on something outside the stressful experience (e.g., mental arithmetic, sexual fantasy);

2. *Somatization.* Focus on body processes and sensations (e.g., closely observe and analyze physiological responses at the time);

3. *Image Manipulation.* Manipulate stress experiences by creating complex, detailed images that reinterpret, ignore, or change the context of the experience (e.g., putting the experience of pain into a fantasy of being tortured by a sadistic Third World spy).

## SUMMARY

Several useful skills have been presented for use in managing stress. Each of us should consider stressful situations he or she has experienced in the past and will face in the future, then practice stress-management skills to cope with these stressors in the future. The more we practice the skills, the greater our ability to effectively adjust to stress will be. Deep breathing, the tension-release technique, aerobic activities, and Yoga-type exercises permit us to relax physically simply by saying softly "relax." Using a problem-solving approach and using thought control to develop a repertoire of coping self-statements incompatible with self-defeating thoughts will help us to cope with stress.

## REFERENCES

Cooper, K.H. *The new aerobics.* Toronto, Ontario: Bantam, 1970.

Couch, J. The perfect post-run stretching routine. *Runner's World,* April 1979, pp. 84-89.

Mahoney, M.J., & Thorensen, C.E. *Self-control: Power to the person.* Monterey, CA: Brooks/Cole, 1974.

Meichenbaum, D. *Cognitive-behavior modification: An integrative approach.* New York: Plenum, 1977.

Thorensen, C.E., & Mahoney, M.J. *Behavioral self-control.* Toronto, Ontario: Holt, Rinehart and Winston, 1974.

Watson, D.L., & Tharp, R.G. *Self-directed behavior: Self-modification for personal adjustment* (2nd ed.). Monterey, CA: Brooks/Cole, 1977.

Zastrow, C., & Chang, D.H. *The personal problem solver.* Englewood Cliffs, NJ: Prentice-Hall, 1977.

**L. Phillip K. Le Gras** *is an assistant professor, Department of Military Leadership and Management, Royal Military College of Canada, and teaching master, Business Department, St. Lawrence College, Kingston Campus. He serves as an applied behavioral science consultant to industrial and public-service organizations. He is pursuing his doctoral degree in industrial and organizational psychology at the University of Waterloo. Mr. Le Gras' background is in personnel selection and placement, management/leadership development, organization development, stress, and self-control.*

# INTRAPERSONAL CONFLICT RESOLUTION

## Hugh Pates

With the development of psychology has come a recognition of the conflicting needs, values, and attitudes inside many persons. These intrapersonal conflicts are now recognized as a major source of personal problems; the person frequently becomes antagonistic toward himself and then transfers, or projects, his turmoil and discontent to his associates, and to relationships or systems of which he is a part.

An individual can discover these inner conflicts by identifying the "shoulds" that he has internalized. Parental criticism, the implication that one will not be loved or accepted if one does not do as he "should," and the *anger* that results from this situation are crucial issues in personal development. Inability to measure up to one's internalized standards creates feelings of guilt and a lack of personal acceptance. This lecturette focuses on the recognition of one's own strengths and the acceptance of one's own limitations—in effect, a process of coming to terms with oneself.

One must accept oneself before one can truly accept, or expect to be accepted by, other people. A major step in achieving this is through the development of a sense of personal power.

## DEVELOPING A PERSONAL POWER BASE

The first step in self-acceptance is the recognition of those "shoulds" that are unnecessary or unrealistic, as well as a realization that people *punish* themselves for failing to live up to their own standards. When a person feels that he has not been, or done, what was expected of him, he translates this into "I don't deserve to feel happy (energetic, rested, content, etc.)" and, thus, may experience depression, insomnia, irritation, restlessness, or lack of energy. As long as the inner conflict continues, the guilt, punishment, and discontent will occur. Figure 1 illustrates this cycle.

In childhood, the fourth stage of the cycle occurred when the punishment had "paid one's debt" and one's sense of "goodness" was restored (until the next infraction). In self-punishment, however, there is no sense of relief. The person's sense of strength and purpose becomes diminished and he begins to feel that he deserves all the bad things that happen to him— partially as a result of his own weakness. He is depressed because he is "bad," and only when he is "good" is he allowed to be happy or successful.

## Breaking the Cycle

The first step in breaking the cycle is to identify the "shoulds" and "shouldn'ts" and where they come from. Often the first discovery is that these come from *outside* oneself, that they are, in fact, the values or rules of one's parents or of a particular influence from one's childhood. These edicts are often "swallowed whole" without being examined; they are called "introjected" values.

The second step is to ask "Is this 'should' really something that I want to do? What do I want to do?" Identification of one's own needs, responses, and purposes helps to restore personal

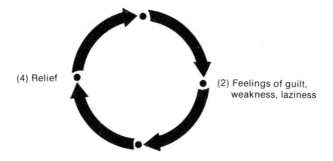

(1) Shoulds or shouldn'ts
ought tos, had betters, etc.

(4) Relief

(2) Feelings of guilt,
weakness, laziness

(3) Punishment (irritability, sleeplessness,
depression, restlessness)

**Figure 1. Personal Conflict Cycle (Punishment Cycle)**

power. It is important in this phase to distinguish between what one *wishes* he could do and what he sincerely *wants* to do. Wishing leads to daydreaming and continued conflict. Authentic wanting leads directly to a specific behavior.

One way to distinguish between wishes and wants, or actual intentions, is to test the person's commitment to action. For example, consider the following dialog:

A: "I want to get together with you to discuss it."
B: "How about tomorrow?"
A: "No, tomorrow's not good; I'm pretty busy."
B: "Well, how about next week?"
A: "Oh, next week is worse."
B: "O.K., let's set a date for two weeks from now."
A: "I never plan that far ahead, but I do want to talk to you."

At this point, person B probably doubts A's intent. Although this example is simple, the same test is true for dieting, working overtime, getting in shape, taking a trip, or whatever.

The third step, then, is to ask "What is keeping me from doing it?" People usually do what they want to do, so if a behavior is contrary to a stated want, the next question may be "Do you want to give that up or do you want to accept yourself as you are?" The last question is "What changes will you make from the way you now behave to the way you want to behave?" A stated want is probably more functional as a wish if the date of its implementation is repeatedly delayed. This can be all right if the person can accept that realization, enjoy the wish, and not feel guilty about not implementing it.

Implementation of a plan, on the other hand, resolves the conflicts about avoiding it and—assuming that the results of the action are not disastrous—reinforces the person. He feels that he has taken charge of himself and may even *feel* a surge of power.

So the ultimate goal of breaking the conflict cycle is to create a sense of personal power, of being able to analyze, choose, and act on one's *own* challenges. This power base increases the chance that the person will not punish himself unnecessarily in the future.

## ASSUMING RESPONSIBILITY

It is important to realize that people generally give themselves permission to do what they really want to do. Some situations or people may make it easier to give oneself permission; for example, being more open with someone one knows well, or having a banana split with a group of friends who also are ordering ice cream. However, ultimately it is the individual who allows himself to act or denies himself that freedom.

The most crucial step in developing self-acceptance is to assume responsibility for oneself. A person who assumes responsibility in any situation probably feels strong; in the case of personal responsibility, the act contributes to the feeling of strength. Like physical exercise, the more one does it, the easier it seems.

When a person refuses to grant himself permission to do something, he frequently says "I can't do it." The question then is "Who is keeping you from doing it?"—not "what," but "who." The answer usually is that the person really means "I *don't want* to do that." When he admits this, he accepts the responsibility for the *decision*. At the same time, by realizing that he has made a choice, he assumes responsibility for whatever *action* he chooses.

Another answer that may be used to forestall a decision or action is "I don't know." The next question here is "What do you want to do with your lack of knowledge?" (Do you want to explore possibilities or alternatives? Do you want me to ask you questions?) If the answer repeatedly is "I don't know," the person clearly is avoiding responsibility. The same is true of "I'm confused." If this is said repeatedly, or after a clear explanation, the person probably chooses to be confused. Some progress can be made here if the person is willing to take responsibility at least for the decision to remain confused in order to avoid further responsibility.

A third tactic used to avoid responsibility is to ask a question when one really has a statement to make. An example is when one says "Where do you want to go next weekend?" when one actually means "I want to go to the races next weekend." The *intra*personal conflict here is between the desire and the failure to assume responsibility for it. In addition, *inter*personal conflict is likely to result because one appears to be offering an option when that really is not the case at all.

An indication that a person is going to assume responsibility is the phase "I *am* going to . . . ." Likewise, it is likely that choice is exercised when a person says "I won't" or "I do not want."

## BEHAVIOR IS BELIEVABLE

The proof of, and most critical step in, any conflict resolution is *behavior*. The sequence is to be aware, for oneself, of what one wants to do and gives oneself permission to do (or not do); to assume responsibility for the decision or choice; to assume responsibility for and *do* the action. The behavior then becomes part of oneself, and the experience strengthens one's base of personal power. In this way, the person is more able to avoid the personal conflict cycle and to make decisions based on personal evaluation, in effect, to manage his own life.

*Hugh Pates, Ph.D., is a senior consultant for University Associates and a counseling psychologist at the University of California at San Diego. He has been the director of counseling at UCSD, has been an associate professor in business administration at National University, and is president of Programs in Communication, a nationwide consulting firm. Dr. Pates has served as a consultant to many large organizations. His major interests are in the areas of interpersonal communication, managerial effectiveness, and conflict management.*

# INTRODUCTION TO THE
# THEORY AND PRACTICE SECTION

In some ways theory and practice, at least in the field of human relations, are analogous to science and art. In both relationships each element serves to stimulate the other, but the relationship between science and art is sometimes less than happy because of their inherent differences. Science involves development of a theory, objective observation of phenomena, and assessment, evaluation, and modification of the theory. The ultimate result of this process is "truth." Art, on the other hand, involves style, judgment, and values; it can be said to be an *expression* of "truth." Another interesting difference is that in science one's theory or model must *always* work; when it does not, one must then determine exactly why. Such a determination is always possible, and the theory is then modified and made more perfect. In art, however, one often hears the artist—or critic—say that something "works" or does not work, but one rarely, if ever, finds out why.

Such uncertainty is also characteristic of the behavioral sciences in general and of human relations training in particular. It is typically seen as a problem and is sometimes stated as the "reason" why behavioral science is not truly a science. Behavioral scientists have tried to cope with this problem by building more complex models, since "science" seems to demand theoretically perfect predictability from models. When cause and effect are not clear (as is often true in the behavioral sciences), we construct models that contain more variables, with more indirect connections. (B follows A only when X is present; when Y occurs—rather than X—the effect is C, rather than B.)

$$\text{Condition } X \qquad\qquad \text{Condition } Y$$
$$A \longrightarrow B \qquad\qquad\qquad A \longrightarrow C$$

If we identify enough conditions, we can, of course, "explain" anything. Unfortunately, this is often said to be a result of random errors of measurement. (If we had measured A perfectly and had identified all the components of condition X, then it would be obvious why the result was D and not B in a particular case.)

One might argue that it is not valid to make an analogy between behavioral science and physical science. The question then is whether the former is actually art rather than science or whether some of our beliefs about the basic definition of "science" are incorrect.

Freud and Einstein shared at least one very important scientific premise: both insisted on the absolute validity of the model: *if* A takes place, *then* B must follow. B does not follow A half the time or part of the time, but *all* the time. If it happens that B does not follow A, then we have measured one or both incorrectly or some important condition is missing from the model. The premise allows for no other possibilities. Einstein, an atheist, expressed this view well when he said, "God does not play dice with the universe." The theories of Freud, too, are based on certain cause-and-effect assumptions. In fact, Freud saw human behavior (effect) as not merely fitting this model and therefore being determined by specific (past) causes, but as being overdetermined; that is, a variety of causes could all lead to the same behaviors or consequences.

Modern physics has moved away from Einstein's deterministic beliefs toward the more uncertain "probabilistic" theory pioneered by Nils Bohr, who invented quantum physics. To put it simplistically, Bohr asserted that the fact that a particular electron may or may not "behave" in a certain way is not a measurement error but, rather, is random chance. Although Einstein could not accept this, most new evidence supports Bohr. In the "hard" sciences, therefore, scientists are less certain about what causes what, and are even suggesting that sometimes—on a subatomic level—"cause" and "effect" may be interchangeable terms.

This may suggest that it is time to re-evaluate the analogy between physical science and behavioral science—not to assert that they are different, but to select a new, probabilistic model. This would distress many people; first, because it would suggest that case studies tell little about cause and effect and that any situation could have a random-chance outcome. The implication is that there always will be failures, no matter what one does, no matter how good a practitioner or change agent one is. For people who require certainty in their lives, this premise is difficult to accept. Many "hard-line," cause-and-effect behavioral scientists also would not approve of a probabilistic model for the social sciences. Like those physical scientists—and there are many— who still insist that Einstein was correct and that God does not gamble with the universe, traditional behavioral scientists will not find it easy to accept a random-chance basis for social and psychological processes. The individually centered social scientist also is likely to oppose a probabilistic approach, because it implies that one cannot learn about psychological or social processes from individual cases. This implication is not really true; Piaget has shown that one can extract basic processes from individual studies; the error is in trying to turn them into certain, cause-and-effect *laws*.

If one gives up the theoretical approach that says "If you engage in OD intervention A in organization type X under conditions H, K, and L, then a variety of positive results (B, C, D, etc.) will occur," how does one plan for results based on certain actions? The answer is that randomness is at the individual level, not at the aggregate level. One may well be able to specify exactly what proportion of OD efforts will succeed that are based on a certain type of intervention in a certain type of organization. It is conceivable that interventions with high success rates, in given situations, could be identified. In fact, some applied social scientists have begun to take just such an approach (Bowers, 1973), and that approach may be the means by which the link is found between the science of behavior and the art of practicing behavioral science.

### Reference

Bowers, D.G. OD techniques and their results in 23 organizations: The Michigan ICL study. *Journal of Applied Behavioral Science*, 1973, *9*, 21-43.

# LEARNING CYCLES: MODELS
# OF BEHAVIORAL CHANGE

## Albert B. Palmer

Learners move through a number of stages as they acquire new information or skills. A model that describes these stages is of interest to theorists, facilitators, and teachers since it can be used to assess where a given learner or group of learners is focused and to guide further learning. This paper summarizes several models that describe the learning process, presents a synthesis or general model, and concludes with some observations generated by the study.

Not all of the models to be presented were initally viewed as examples of a learning cycle. Newell, Shaw, and Simon (1960), Miller, Galanter, and Pribram (1960), and Pounds (1969) were concerned with the development of problem-solving models. On the other hand, Kolb, Rubin, and McIntyre (1971), Jones and Pfeiffer (1975), and Argyris (1976) specifically describe their concepts as indicators of learning cycles. In spite of the different labels, each theorist uses a series of concepts to describe how an individual develops and ultimately manifests a change in behavior.

It should be noted that all these processes are associated with *changes* in behavior. *Learning* has occurred when individuals adjust or modify their behavior; this differs from *understanding*, wherein awareness may occur but behavior remains the same. Although understanding is a part of learning, the learning process is completed only when the individual actually produces new behavior either in an unfamiliar situation or in a situation that was previously experienced as unsatisfying.

## SIX THEORIES

Figure 1 includes each of the theories summarized in this paper. They are arranged in order of publication and their components appear in the order specified in each theory and in approximate relationship to each other. The models are discussed in this paper in chronological order.

Newell, Shaw, and Simon (1960) studied complex analytical processes and formulated an early, three-step model of decision making. Step one, *intelligence*, wherein alternative actions are developed and defined, is followed by *design*, the process of evaluating the alternatives. The third step, *choice*, involves selecting an action from those available.

Parallel concepts more related to cognitive psychology were developed by Miller, Galanter, and Pribram (1960). *Image*, referring to the internal nature of the process, involves the generation of alternatives. *Test*, like design, is the evaluation of the consequences of various alternatives prior to actual action. *Operate* is the term for carrying out the choice.

Pounds (1969) divided the decision-making process into two separate but interrelated procedures: *problem finding* and *problem solving*. He analyzed each procedure and described how individuals move through each in a series of steps. One begins, according to Pounds, by *selecting a model*—some standard for performance. It defines what ought to be. The model is then *compared to reality* and *differences are identified*. These two processes provide the data— the range of problems to be tackled. Problem finding ends when a specific *difference is selected* for action.

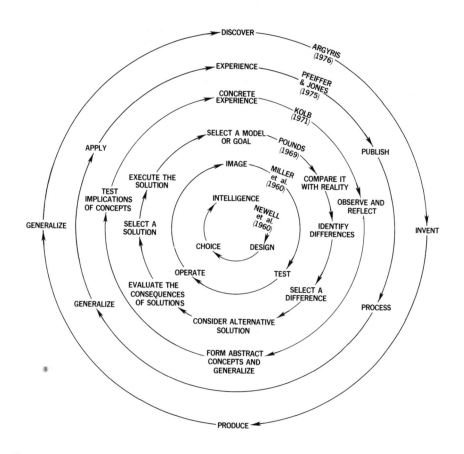

**Figure 1. Learning Cycle Models for Behavioral Change**

Problem solving begins with the *consideration of alternative solutions* followed by *evaluation of the consequences of those solutions,* i.e., outcomes are predicted for each possibility. The final steps are *selection of a solution* and its *execution.*

Computer science had a strong influence on Newell et al., Miller et al., and Pounds. Their writing is heavy with such terms as operator and input and output variables, and the relationships between the terms are portrayed in flow charts. Little attention is paid to expediting the change process or to the facilitator as an agent of change.

Kolb, Rubin, and McIntyre (1971) changed this emphasis from enumerating the skills necessary for successful management to one of investigating how the manager learns, i.e., how one adapts to changes in the environment and the job. Kolb et al. developed the *experiential learning model* to describe this adaptive learning process. The real world, with its demands, dilemmas, and disappointments, serves as the basis for *concrete experience,* a frequent stimulant to learning. Internal or cognitive processes are the mechanisms for reducing experiences to more manageable form, so we observe, and then *reflect* on experiences. Once internalized, the observations and reflections lead to the *formulation of abstract concepts and generalizations.* Such personal theory building leads to application, which Kolb et al. defined as *testing the implications of concepts in new situations.*

In the previous model, the learner must have some expertise in each of the steps for learning to be effective. This is made more difficult by the fact that some of the skills seem to be mutually exclusive. For example, individuals who are highly skilled in observing and reflecting on the world around them may be reluctant to intervene and take action. Kolb et al. described the process as two-dimensional, with the concrete experiencing of events and abstract conceptualization at the poles of one dimension and active experimentation and reflective observation at the poles of the other.

Jones and Pfeiffer (1975) present experiential learning as a five-step cyclical process in which each step is dependent on the completion of the previous step. Behavior associated with involvement in the world, *experiencing*, is the most common (and most effective) impetus for learning. The second step, *publication*, is the process of making public or sharing observations, feelings, or other reactions generated by the experience. This learning process is a group, rather than a solitary, activity. The involvement of more than one person obviously leads to a range of reactions. *Processing* is a systematic examination of patterns and dynamics that emerged during the sharing stage. This essential step gives some meanings to the experienced event. The next stage, *generalizing*, relates those meanings to life. Implications and principles—the "so what?" of the learning—are stated. Finally, these principles are *applied* to actual situations and the learner states how he or she will apply the new learning or behavior. The experiential process is not complete until the new learning is tested behaviorally. The cyclical nature of the process becomes apparent now, since testing the new behavior is in fact a new experience.

The most succinct explanation of this process can be found in the introduction to the structured experiences section in the last *Annual* (Pfeiffer & Jones, 1980), and ways to facilitate the process are presented by Gaw (1979).

Argyris (1976) utilizes the concept of learning cycles to explain the changes noted in individuals who have examined their organizational behavior. When people are given the opportunity to compare their actual behavior and its consequences with their intentions, more often than not they *discover* inconsistencies or incongruities between intentions and actual outcomes. This discovery is the basis for the *invention* of new behavior to reduce or eliminate the inconsistencies and accomplish what was intended. Argyris separates the invention (design) of new behavior from its *production*—actually carrying out the behavior. Finally, the discoveries and new behaviors are *generalized* from the situation that spawned them (usually the laboratory or consulting experience) to other situations. While discovery is a convenient starting place, Argyris notes that in reality learning can begin at any point in the sequence.

Each of the learning cycles described here is an abstraction, a model applied to observed behavior. Kolb suggests that we have predispositions or preferences for learning styles and that those preferences shape our learning effectiveness. Argyris, on the other hand, says that skill in all phases of the cycle is required for effective learning. He suggests that most people do not know how to learn effectively and therefore must be taught (in a workshop or other setting) how to learn.

The answer for Argyris is to use the learning cycle in teaching the learning-cycle model. Thus, participants need to discover, invent, produce, and generalize about the discovery phase of the learning cycle. They also need to discover, invent, produce, and generalize about invention, production, and generalization. We often take for granted the ability of participants to profit from their experiences, especially if those experiences occurred under our leadership. Learning to learn may be as fundamental to the success of an intervention as anything else that is done.

Learning-cycle models have evolved in a way that mirrors changes in the technology of organization development. Each new learning cycle has been more elaborate than the one preceding, with greater and greater emphasis on the participant as a complex entity. The cycles have moved from mechanistic and computer-influenced technologies to those that stress change as a process influenced as much by the affect, or emotions, of the learner as by rational thought. We now understand that change requires much more than data or manipulation of situational variables in a learner.

## A GENERAL MODEL

Although the theorists discussed in this article have not approached the problem in the same manner, it seems clear that they would agree that learners move through a series of steps as they acquire new skills. Those steps may or may not be followed in sequence, but the success of the learning experience probably is related directly to whether or not each step occurs. Although the labels applied to the steps may differ, the theorists seem to be trying to describe an experience observed by all; thus, those experiences common to all learners provide the basis for a general model of the learning cycle.

The Argyris model seems to come closest to qualifying as a universal model—one that accounts for most of the behavior we see. Nevertheless, concepts from the other models are consistent with and can enhance the learning cycle described by Argyris. It is all part of the process that Argyris calls "decomposition," the breaking down of the learning process into smaller, more manageable units.

The general model that follows focuses on the common actions of learners and the similarities and connections between descriptions of those actions. Issues in the application of the concept of learning cycles are also noted.

### Phase One: Discovering

The word *discover* means "to perceive or see" and "to gain knowledge or understanding"; both of these occur in the early stages of the learning process. Each process is a source of data.

Most participants in human relations workshops are there to learn about dynamics that pertain to one or more of the following:

1. The behavior of another person or persons.
2. The intentions of another person or persons. (Participants often are not aware of the difference between intentions and behavior, and treat them synonomously. The discovery that one's behavior is in response to an intention attributed to another person, not what that person actually does, can be a powerful motivation for learning.)
3. His/her own behavior.
4. His/her own intentions. (Many workshop participants are aware of this dilemma, but still have difficulty in differentiating between their intentions and how they actually behave.)

During the discovery process, a participant will define goals, standards, or ideals as well as the way things actually are. These data will come from observations of others and oneself as well as reflections on internal processes and personal behavior. The trainer can facilitate discovery by:

1. Providing opportunities for participants to focus on their own behavior or the behavior of significant other people in their lives.

2. Helping the participants to express their observations. (Most people find it especially difficult to express feelings.)

3. Identifying and working with the group dynamics that influence risk taking.

Discovery is promoted by observing and thinking about one's experiences and then sharing those thoughts and feelings with others who have had the same or parallel experiences. The sharing focuses on perceptions of the events, the dynamics of the sharing process itself, and the formulation of explanatory ideas or concepts. Ideally, discovery would lead the learners to formulate and attempt new or alternative behavior.

The way in which individuals make discoveries about themselves and their behavior can influence the remainder of the learning cycle. Discovery for understanding is different from discovery for change. The task of the facilitator is to promote discovery for change (action) either by involving participants in specific events that lead to this type of discovery or by providing the opportunity for them to express and work with discoveries made outside the training event. Lewin's (1958) theory of change explains it as a three-step sequence: unfreezing current patterns of behavior, moving to new behavior patterns, and freezing the new patterns into place. The "unfreezing" sequence can generate anxiety but it also provides the motivation to continue the learning process as well as the experientially derived data that are needed in order to learn.

Several techniques can be used to unfreeze participants. Obviously, the one selected must be congruent with the needs of the group and the skill and preferences of the facilitator. Structured experiences can be used to promote discovery (see earlier reference to Pfeiffer & Jones, 1980); role playing is an excellent discovery process (Shaw, Corsini, Blake, & Mouton, 1980); and Argyris (1976) prefers to have participants write scenarios of their interactions.

### Phase Two: Formulating New Behavior

One of the persistent dilemmas in psychology is the role of insight in behavioral change. Few of the learning-cycle theorists present a clear statement about this relationship. Most seem to treat thinking about behavior and actually behaving as the same process. Because learners frequently work out alternative behaviors verbally before actually attempting them, the learning model presented here encourages facilitators to focus on and encourage the development of new behavior at a verbal level before it is put into action.

The verbal expression of what needs to be done and how it can be done allows refinement of the plan. Other group members can say how the new behavior would affect them to provide the learner with unexpected consequences of or confirmation for the behavior.

Ideas about new behavior generally are:

1. Self-generated. Participants often know how they *should* behave and can be encouraged to explore alternatives. New behavior may be consistent with previously articulated principles or related only to the current task.

2. Leader generated. Leaders may suggest or model alternative ways of behaving in a situation. Leader behavior usually is based on a theoretical "should," i.e., certain behaviors are more effective. Such principles should be shared with the learner.

3. Member generated. Other members of the learning group also serve as sources of new behavior.

When helping participants learn to formulate new behavior, the trainer must be aware of dynamics within the learning group that could interfere with such creative activity. Exploring these dynamics often becomes a discovery process in itself and can lead a group off in other directions. The dynamics may be perceived as resistances to learning. The response "It wouldn't make sense to tell you what I'd do because no one here understands my problem" is loaded with information about dynamics and resistance.

The transition from discovery to formulation is not abrupt; the two phases often flow back and forth. Participants discover inconsistencies between what they hoped to accomplish in a given interaction and the actual outcome. They share their dilemmas and describe what they wish they had done. Other participants respond, perhaps by sharing their own reactions to the original learner's behavior or by offering alternatives or similar experiences. These responses allow the original participant to refine discoveries and new behaviors. This process should lead to some clearly formulated behavior that would reduce or eliminate the dilemma.

## Phase Three: Producing New Behavior

Discovering inconsistencies and describing desired behavior are significant steps in learning. However, for learning to be complete, it is important that people translate their formulations of new behavior into actual behavior. Theorists have used expressions such as "execute the solution," "operate," and "apply" to denote the implementation of the results of the discovery and formulation processes. Argyris includes the idea of producing the new behavior under moderate stress, noting that behavior in the real world (as opposed to the world of the training event) will probably be produced under such conditions.

The dynamics of the learning group are critical factors in the production of new behavior. Facilitators may need to:

1. Ensure that there is a situational demand for the new behavior. It is hard for individuals to produce meaningful new behavior without some stimulation. Role playing is a common technique for providing such stimulation.

2. See that the setting is conducive to risk taking. An atmosphere of acceptance within the learning group is critical during the process.

3. Provide feedback for the learner. Knowing how new behavior was perceived by others is necessary for growth and change. Encouraging such sharing in ways that promote rather than stifle growth is often a challenge to the leader.

The learning group provides an excellent arena for the practice of new behavior. In short, intensive workshops, the value of practice in the acquisition of human relations skills must not be underestimated. It is readily acknowledged that the development of a fluid golf swing requires hours of concentrated practice in controlling the body and club. The acquisition of complex relationship skills requires the same effort if fundamental changes in behavior are to become integrated and automatic.

## Phase Four: Generalizing to the Real World

Theorists and facilitators recognize the necessity for a transition from the laboratory into the real world. A section of each training event commonly is devoted to back-home application and/or re-entry. Inclusion of a specific phase devoted to generalizing learnings from the training event to the outside world provides a basis for what Lewin termed "refreezing." Workshop participants return to an environment that has not changed significantly. A participant may have made valuable discoveries about behavior, systems, group dynamics, etc., but may not have acquired enough competence to be able to influence or change the outside system in any significant way. Thus, as Schein (1972) has noted, many good ideas and useful behaviors are lost because they never become integrated into the environment. Weekend or other short-term workshops preclude any real refreezing of participants' behavior since useful generalization probably requires that the participants return to the workshop environment with examples of the application of their "new" behaviors. These experiences then become the bases for new discoveries and new learning cycles. So although there is value in encouraging participants to talk about how they plan to behave when they leave the training setting, how others will respond to their new behaviors, and how they expect to deal with these responses, such discussion is not a substitute for using real-world applications as the basis for new learning. Some factors can positively reinforce new back-home behavior. These are:

1. Support in the back-home environment. Consultation or the creation of an ongoing support group can provide continued help for the learner. Development of such a group requires significant effort on the part of the trainer.

2. Consistency between workshop design and the real world. Topics, learnings, and structures in training events ought to be compatible with what the learner will face back home or on the job.

3. The learning group as a resource. Ideally, learners would be able to return to the learning group with their new discoveries. One technique is to have pairs from the learning group agree to communicate with each other for a specified period of time. Norms for this interaction should be established during the training event.

## A FINAL CONSIDERATION

Although the phases of the change process have been presented as discrete events, it is clear that the interaction between them (and within them) is complex. No learner goes through these phases step by step, and it would not be desirable to do so. Such a strategy too easily allows the members to become diverted. The danger always exists that participants might become fixed at one level because changing one's behavior is frightening or emotionally demanding. Another danger is that a participant might engage in what seems to be whimsical behavior because he or she fails to see how the training is related to issues or dilemmas in his or her own life.

If there is a major shortcoming in the area of change agentry, it lies in the realm of generalizing. The economics of time and money have discouraged the development of programs that might result in more integrated and long-term behavioral change. All too often one is seduced by the exhilaration of the discovery and formulation phases of the learning cycle and finds generalization and application hurriedly relegated to the last hour of the last day. Thus, while the concept of learning cycles can be a valuable tool, it also reminds us of some pertinent issues. The criticism that has been applied to other parts of our society—namely, that technology has exceeded our ability to manage it and that important values related to technology have gone unattended—may often be applied to the work of the human relations trainer. Audiovisual technology has made it possible to package an exciting learning experience in a format that is easily presented. Jargon proliferates and the "science" in behavioral science is everywhere. Yet we all know people who have left workshops full of good intentions but have soon returned to their old ways of behaving. When long-term change in individuals and/or organizations eludes us, we may begin to blame it on the participants rather than examine the training design.

Perhaps the decade of the Eighties will be the time to examine the ethical dilemmas posed by the learning-cycle concept. Is it "right" in the name of a learning experience to offer a short workshop that emphasizes discovery and is clearly lacking in generalization and application? How long can we facilitate the discovery process in people without facilitating the actual production of new behavior in those situations that brought people to the workshop in the first place? How long can we continue to deal with resistances to learning while at the same time accepting (at face value) a client's assertion that he or she cannot afford a longer, more substantial workshop? These issues may have as much impact on the credibility of our profession as will the creation of sophisticated scientific technology.

### REFERENCES

Argyris, C. *Increasing leadership effectiveness.* New York: John Wiley, 1976.

Gaw, B.A. Processing questions: An aid to completing the learning cycle. In J.E. Jones & J.W. Pfeiffer (Eds.), *The 1979 annual handbook for group facilitators.* San Diego, CA: University Associates, 1979.

Jones, J.E., & Pfeiffer, J.W. *The 1975 annual handbook for group facilitators.* San Diego, CA: University Associates, 1975.

Jones, J.E., & Pfeiffer, J.W. Role playing. In J.E. Jones & J.W. Pfeiffer (Eds.), *The 1979 annual handbook for group facilitators.* San Diego, CA: University Associates, 1979.

Kolb, D., Rubin, I.M., & McIntyre, J.M. *Organizational psychology: A book of readings.* Englewood Cliffs, NJ: Prentice-Hall, 1971.

Lewin, K. Group dynamics and social change. In E.E. Maccoby, T.M. Newcomb, & E.L. Hartley (Eds.), *Readings in social psychology* (3rd. ed.). New York: Holt, Rinehart and Winston, 1958.

Miller, G.A., Galanter, E., & Pribram, K.H. *Plans and the structure of behavior.* New York: Henry Holt, 1960.

Newell, A., Shaw, J.C., & Simon, H.A. A general problem-solving program for the computer. *Computers and Automation,* 1960, *8,* 7-10.

Pfeiffer, J.W., & Jones, J.E. *The 1980 annual handbook for group facilitators.* San Diego, CA: University Associates, 1980.

Pounds, W.F. The process of problem finding. *IMR,* 1969, *11,* 1-20.

Schein, E. *Professional education.* New York: McGraw-Hill, 1972.

Shaw, M.E., Corsini, R.J., Blake, R.R., & Mouton, J.S. *Role playing: A practical manual for group facilitators.* San Diego, CA: University Associates, 1980.

***Albert B. Palmer, Ph.D.,*** *is a professor of psychology at the University of Toledo, Toledo, Ohio, where he teaches graduate and undergraduate courses in clinical psychology. He also is an instructor in Thomas Gordon's Leadership and Parent Effectiveness Training programs. Dr. Palmer serves as a change agent and human relations facilitator for a variety of organizations. His particular interest is in studying the impact of court mandates on human service organizations.*

# THE ORGANIZATIONAL UNIVERSE

## John E. Jones

Most human organizations are complex; they consist of individuals, informal and/or formal groups, divisions, and so on. They have operational characteristics, implicit or explicit objectives and philosophies, and various levels of morale. In addition, they function within settings that sometimes contain conflicting pressures. It is necessary to separate and identify the systems that constitute the organization before one can choose what to observe and where to place emphasis in managing change within the organization. The Organizational Universe model[1] provides a basis for looking through the whole to those structures and processes that need to be monitored before change can be managed effectively.

## VALUES

At the core of any human organization is a set of values, an underlying philosophy that defines the reason for the existence of the organization, the purpose for which it is established. So long as there is consensus on values among persons in positions of power and influence within the organization, the work activity is likely to be marked by cooperation and coordination. Priorities are generally obvious, because the commitment to a commonly held set of values usually motivates people to work together in flexible ways.

VALUES

(Reason for existence, philosophy, purpose)

Unfortunately, the values on which the organization was originally based frequently become lost in the shuffle of everyday work. One nonprofit association was created to provide low-cost insurance for members of a religious group. When it began to amass profits, it provided grants to the religious group for various projects. Its function then was changed; it became a political force within the system it was founded to serve. Other nonprofit organizations may find that obtaining funding has attained a higher priority than providing service.

Organizational values affect purpose and management philosophy. When these values are not held in common, the lack of consensus creates a tension that can preclude organizational effectiveness. Managers may engage in empire building in order to further their careers at the expense of the coordinated functioning of the entire system. Thus, managers may need to consider values that are internal to the organization in addition to the traditional ones of making a profit and/or providing quality services. These internal organizational values include:

| | |
|---|---|
| Cooperation | Functional impersonal conflict |
| Strategic openness | Acceptance of interdependence |
| Achievement of objectives | Respect and dignity in the |
| Clarity | treatment of people |

[1]An earlier version of this model was developed with Anthony J. Reilly at a University Associates workshop on organization development skills.

| Acceptance of responsibility | Commitment to studying the functioning |
|---|---|
| Thoroughness | of human systems |
| Systematic problem solving | Expressions of feelings as well |
| Confrontation | as points of view |
| Providing and soliciting | Autonomy for individuals and groups |
| feedback | *Pro*action, rather than *rea*ction |
| Concreteness | Experimentation |
| Authenticity | |

Factors that affect organizational values are often covert and difficult to manage. Influential insiders and the prevailing reward system can sometimes "shape" the value system of the organization. The stability of the work force and the focus of recruitment can influence the dominant set of values adhered to by the system. Crises, successes, and failures also can lead to values shifts, as can the almost inexorable processes of hierarchy, routine, and standardization. The permeability of the organization—its susceptibility to outside intrusion—can be a determinant of the stability of its core values. The value changes that result from these factors generally lead to institutionalization, rigidity, looseness, pluralism, or chaos. Managers need to be aware of the status of the value system underlying the operation of the organization in order to ensure that at least a moderate amount of consensus exists regarding the basic purpose of the organization.

To maintain organizational values, a manager must monitor the extent to which people espouse a common set of assumptions, philosophies, and purposes, and—more importantly— must exhibit value-oriented managerial behavior. The following are some things that managers can do to focus attention on values.

1. Keep organizational values explicit whenever possible.
2. Share your own values with your subordinates.
3. Support and model commitment to organizational values.
4. Assess the "fit" between organizational values and those of workers.
5. Make value considerations a valid part of the agenda at meetings.
6. In problem solving, question values as well as facts and procedures.
7. Look for value differences ("shoulds" and "oughts") underneath conflict situations.
8. Avoid win-lose arguments about values.
9. Update the organization's statement of purpose.
10. Set goals that are consistent with organizational values.

## GOALS

Organizational goals can be thought of as articulated values. For example, the goal statement "to increase our market share by 6 percent in the next twelve months" implies that attaining business growth is valuable. The goal "to develop and publicize a family-counseling service by October 1" similarly may imply a value placed on expansion. Goals, then, are operational statements of underlying values.

GOALS

VALUES

(Articulated values)

Perhaps the most common organizational failings are in the areas of goals, roles, and communication. The latter two are both affected adversely by a lack of commitment to common goals. Lack of clarity with regard to goals can lead to disorganization, inefficiency, and ineffectiveness.

The goal-setting process needs to be made explicit whenever possible, and members of the organization need to be part of the process if they are expected to be committed to its outcomes. The managerial implication is to pay attention to participation in goal setting. Meaningful participation leads to a sense of involvement; this evokes a feeling of influence that generates psychological ownership, which leads to *commitment*. There is no shortcut to commitment; it evolves within individuals as a result of their perception of themselves as influential.

Objectives are goals that have been made more specific. For example, the goal "to improve the order-processing system" may generate several objectives such as "in the next quarter, to reduce the data-processing time on an average order by thirty seconds." When objectives are highly specific, they can be monitored more easily, but the individuals who implement them may lose sight of and commitment to the overall goal and value perspectives beneath them. Management by objectives (MBO) programs fail more often than they succeed, usually for a combination of reasons: (a) they are imposed; (b) they inadvertently encourage individual objectives at the expense of group and system aims; (c) the initial enthusiasm for the program is not maintained; (d) the goal-setting process does not extend to lower level employees; (e) people work on the more visible objectives; and (f) the programs are poorly implemented. As McConkie (1979, p. 472) concludes from an extensive review of evidence regarding MBO, "Properly implemented and maintained, MBO will do what it is designed to do. It is the practice, not the theory, of MBO that is frequently faulty . . . .The most serious faults in MBO applications center around inadequate training for those implementing MBO and the lack of follow-up."

In managing change it is important to relate desired outcomes both to organizational values and to the means available for attaining objectives. It may be useful to think about organizational change as having implications that range along a continuum from general to specific:

| General | Value |
|---------|-------|
| ↑ | Goal |
| | Objective |
| | Strategy |
| ↓ | Tactic |
| Specific | Technique |

Managers must foster consciousness of the interrelationship between all these aspects of change if those persons who implement change are to have a proper perspective.

The major managerial implications of this approach are:

1. Provide training in goal and objective setting for all personnel.
2. Model the process. (One school superintendent initiated an MBO process for school principals by making a large poster of her objectives and displaying it in her reception area. People began to see its value and asked for assistance in setting objectives for themselves.)
3. Create mechanisms by which all employees participate in goal setting.
4. Advocate organizational values during goal setting.
5. Assess the clarity of goals in all work-oriented encounters.
6. Test commitment to organizational goals.

Because individual goals often override organizational ones, it is incumbent on leaders to make certain that the objectives of the system reflect both the wants of the organization and the needs of its members.

## STRUCTURE

Most people think of the organizational chart when they consider structure, but there are many other structures and systems within an organization in addition to the reporting relationships. In establishing an organization, one must consider not only its purpose and philosophy (values) and aims (goals) but also how those goals will be implemented or made operational. One must establish a system of boss-subordinate relationships, methods of communication, procedures for making decisions and solving system problems, rules or guidelines for the conduct of organization members, ways of accounting for the outcomes of the organization's behavior, and a system for rewarding goal attainment. All these systems constitute the organization's structure.

Each of the six major aspects of the structure of the organization begins as a formal system, but its operation almost inevitably generates a parallel informal system. Often these informal systems become more powerful in shaping behavior than the formal systems that spawned them. Reporting relationships comprise a formal system of status and authority (a hierarchy or a matrix, for example). Everyone knows, however, that there is often discrepancy between the organizational chart and the dispersion of power within the system. A chart showing the relative power and influence of individuals by means of different size boxes would reveal the potency of the informal system.

Most formal communication systems within organizations create more problems than they solve. Typical systems are meetings, reports, management-information systems, memoranda, and publications. Organization development practitioners have learned to be particularly alert to difficulties in this aspect of organizational structure because so many people problems relate to failures to communicate effectively. The fault usually is that the formal systems create communication patterns that are top-down, one-way, document-focused (as opposed to being focused on the transfer of meaning), unclear, and subject to competing interpretations. Therefore, an informal system arises in the forms of rumors, in-group sharing, speculation, and networks. These ways of obtaining and disseminating information are coping mechanisms;

they encourage the tendency to screen information to serve individual needs. Much miscommunication within organizations stems from the tension between the formal and informal systems. Disaffected and alienated organization members will believe rumors or gossip more readily than official pronouncements.

The decision-making procedures within the organizational structure are the formal and informal ways that problems are solved within the system. Often there are regulations and precedents that govern how choices are to be made within the organization. For example, a supervisor believes that the overtime policy is unfair and ineffective. The formal decision-making policies dictate how that supervisor is *supposed to* initiate a reconsideration of the policy and how his or her request is *supposed to* be handled. Since these formal procedures are often frustrating to individuals, informal ways to influence decisions are developed. Individuals resort to political behavior in order to obtain decisions that are satisfactory to them, and tension develops between the formal and informal systems. For example, the existence of an "old-boy network" that systematically excludes some classes of people (notably women and minorities) from participation in decision making invites the development of a competing formal system. This often results in a lose-lose situation, and organizational problem solving suffers as a result.

Norms are expected behaviors. They are both formal and informal, and often the informal ones are the more powerful. Formal norms are explicit rules of conduct, governing such things as eating or smoking in offices, punctuality in reporting for work, safety, dress codes, etc.; informal norms (e.g., politeness, collusion not to confront each other, deference to authority, working for no pay on Saturday, etc.) are developed within a peer-influence system. In consciously creating formal norms, managers can expect resistance that may produce more potent informal interpersonal expectations. For example, in one unit of the United States Navy the officers attempted to enforce a strict code regarding facial hair; the men retaliated by agreeing among themselves to begin wearing nonregulation black shoes.

The formal accountability system usually consists of the annual performance review, methods for measuring results of the behavior of individuals and groups, and a financial accounting model. Unfortunately, informal accountability systems also appear. Managers may hold individuals personally accountable for certain outcomes or may "get on the case" of a given department for a while. Formal methods of accountability usually suffer from problems of measurement (as in education) and inadequate confrontation. Consequently, in some organizations there are many places to hide, and people collude not to confront incompetence. Instead of demoting or firing a loyal employee who has been over-promoted, an organization may create a new position: vice president for rare events. An organization cannot withhold evaluative feedback, both positive and negative, and expect individual and group effectiveness in the absence of accountability.

The reward system is probably the most powerful determinant of individual and group behavior. Formal rewards usually include compensation, benefits ("perks"), and recognition programs (e.g., "employee of the month"). Informal rewards are often motivating factors, however. Such rewards as having a private office with more than one window and a carpet, getting more salaried lines on one's budget, and being "stroked" in a meeting of an important group are very influential in shaping the behavior of individuals and groups. Expectancy theory (Nadler & Lawler, 1980) states that people will behave in ways that they expect will produce outcomes that they value. The pay system may have less saliency for some individuals than the opportunity for promotion, recognition for a job well done, or the broadening of one's task responsibilities.

The organization structure consists of interdependent systems, each of which has both formal and informal components. This is the proper locus of organizational change, since it is the operating core of the organizational universe. Problems that arise among the units of the organization can be traced to deficiencies in these six systems. Vertical intergroup problems (e.g., top versus middle management) often stem from difficulties in reporting relationships and communication patterns. Horizontal intergroup conflict (e.g., manufacturing versus warehousing/shipping) can arise when there are ineffective accountability and reward systems. When decision-making procedures and norms are detrimental to specific classes of people, diagonal intergroup relations (e.g., black-white, male-female) became strained. Managers must not only monitor the effectiveness of all aspects of the structure but must also assess their joint effects. Some guidelines to this approach are:

1. Study how power is distributed within the organization. (One method is to use the PODIA instrument [Sashkin & Jones, 1979].)
2. Institute critiques of process in all meetings. (How are we doing in this meeting?)
3. Set up feedback loops so that information flows up the organization as well as down.
4. Establish procedures for correcting the deleterious effects of rumors. (For example, in a crisis, create a rumor control center to provide accurate information.)
5. Experiment with consultative and consensus methods of decision making.
6. Conduct an assessment and diagnosis of organizational norms. (See, for example, the Organizational Norms Opinionnaire [Alexander, 1978].)
7. Provide training for managers in conducting performance reviews. (See, for example, Maier's [1976] interview-skills course.)
8. Confront inadequate performance in a problem-solving way.
9. Develop employee participation in evaluating the pay-and-benefits system.
10. Look for informal ways to reward individuals.
11. Schedule team-building sessions for groups that are in conflict with each other before staging an intergroup confrontation.

Managing the structure of the organization requires diligence, both because it is the essential core of the system and also because so many of its aspects are covert. This requires a commitment to continuous assessment of the organization.

## CLIMATE

The functioning of the organizational structure creates an emotional "wash." The climate of the organization is the psychological atmosphere that results from and surrounds the operation of the structure; consequently, it is both a result of and a determinant of the behavior of individuals and groups within the structure. Gibb (1978) emphasizes the assessment of the organization's trust level as a beginning point in managing change. Others emphasize different aspects of the climate, such as morale or stress. But although elaborate techniques have been developed to survey employee attitudes, the explanation of job satisfaction remains elusive.

It is important for managers to recognize that the organizational climate and the attitudes of others cannot be controlled or changed directly. Attitudes can be thought of as rationalizations for behavior; if you change the behavior (through the reward system, for example), the attitudes will ultimately "catch up." Problems in the organizational climate are likely to have roots in the structure. Consequently, organizational improvements are targeted within the structure. To improve the climate, one must make changes in the ways work gets done. For example, talking about trust does not generate trust and may produce the opposite. Trust results from achieving success in shoulder-to-shoulder work toward common goals. The primary action steps indicated by this approach to managing organizational climate are:

1. Monitor attitudes and morale as well as organizational functioning.
2. Focus on problem identification and problem solving in:
   a. Reporting relationships (role expectations, reorganization),

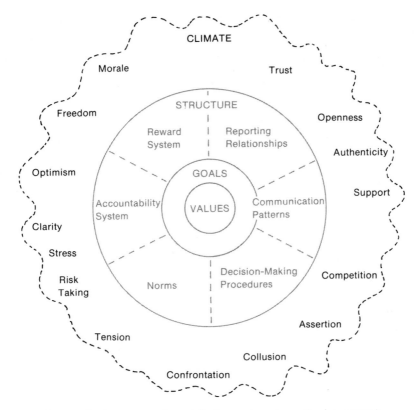

b. Communication patterns (especially in meetings; try outlawing memos),

c. Decision-making procedures (initiate more consultation with subordinates; experiment with consensus seeking in meetings),

d. Norms (rules, pressures for group conformity),

e. Accountability system (put some punch into the performance review; establish criteria for success),

f. Reward system (initiate a multilevel task force to investigate salary administration; publish criteria for promotions and transfers).

3. Include the disaffected as well as those who are satisfied when diagnosing the causes of climate problems.

4. Push for *visible* results.

The organizational climate can produce a drag on the productivity and goal attainment of the system. Managers need to be sensitive to the effects of their behavior on the climate, and they should examine the structure to find ways to ameliorate conditions.

## ENVIRONMENT

The organization exists in a milieu with which it must interact in order to accomplish its goals. Although this environment is somewhat different for each organization, organizations share some global considerations; e.g., the availability of energy affects almost all human organizations. We tend to think of organizations as closed systems, but they are all open in the sense that each has a permeable boundary. In the organizational universe model this characteristic of permeability is depicted by the uneven line surrounding the climate dimension.

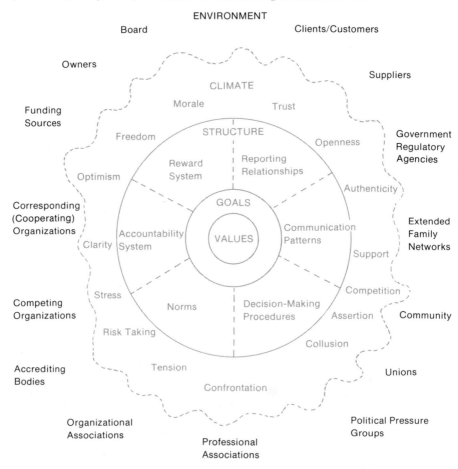

Satisfactory transactions with the environment require that the internal structure be flexible enough to cope with the unexpected. If the organization becomes excessively bureaucratic, its members become more oriented to internal rather than external realities. Consequently, they may lose their sensitivity to the environment, and the organization may become vulnerable. The reverse situation—in which forces in the environment are permitted to upset internal priorities—promotes disorganization. For example, a consulting firm may embrace the dictum "the client is king." The problem is that any client could create havoc within the system at any time, and the resultant scramble could affect schedules, priorities, and innumerable other operations.

Organizations in our culture have become increasingly permeable. The intrusions, in some cases, have affected the core values around which organizations have been built. Governmental regulations dealing with safety standards and with creating job and promotion opportunities for women and minorities have struck at the heart of many organizations. A system created to manufacture widgets does not necessarily function with similar effectiveness when it is asked to solve social problems. It may respond with resentment, resistance, and minimum compliance. The organization is, in effect, being told: "You are no longer only in the business of making products for a profit; you now have to make a contribution to the improvement of the community." In legal terms, this represents a "piercing of the corporate veil"; it requires the organization to shift its values, philosophy, and purpose.

The organizational boundary often is ambiguous. Just as there are degrees of being "inside," there are degrees of being "outside" as well, because most individuals are members of more than one organization. Family and political ties can contaminate the workings of the organizational structure, for better or for worse. In addition, what is a primary environment for one organization may be a secondary one for another. The larger, macroeconomic environment that impinges on virtually all organizations is described by an increasing number of observers as turbulent (see Emery & Trist, 1978). Environmental disturbances can create challenges in almost all facets of the organization's operations: leaders find it more difficult to manage relations with and among relevant environmental components in their areas; the organization's niche in the marketplace becomes increasingly precarious. Some ways that managers can prepare to deal with this environmental change are:

1. Monitor the organization's speed of response to changes in the environment.
2. Assess the costs of the degree of permeability that the organization is presently experiencing.
3. Establish clear policies regarding transactions with components of the environment.
4. Be proactive in setting goals rather than simply reacting to outside pressures.

## SUMMARY

At the core of human organizations there is a set of values, a *raison d'etre*, an implicit or explicit, dynamic system of shared beliefs. When consensus about values is not maintained within the organization, members work in parallel at best and at cross-purposes at worst. Organizational goals are best understood in terms of the values on which they are based. Objectives are targets that are extrapolated from the goals of the organization. Conflicts about goals can result from poorly articulated values; and human disorganization can be defined as a lack of functional consensus on objectives and values. The structure for implementing goals within an organization consists not only of the organizational chart but also of the *communication patterns, decision-making procedures, norms, accountability systems,* and *reward systems* that support and lend substance to the *reporting relationships* depicted on the chart. Within each of these six aspects of the organizational structure there is both a formal and an informal element, a technical and a social component. For example, formal rules of conduct and informal social pressures toward conformity both constitute norms. The tension between the informal social system and the formal technical system creates a psychological atmosphere that surrounds and influences work. This climate is both a result (or symptom) of the functioning structure and a mediator of the productivity of the system. Furthermore, the organization exists within a larger environment. In order to interact effectively with its environment, it must resolve the conflicting demands that are made on it from the outside and must be sufficiently integrated internally to deal effectively with such intrusion. Intervention into the organization in order to improve its functioning is best focused on its values, goals, and structure. Similarly, changes in the organizational climate follow from changes made in the ways people are treated within the structure.

**REFERENCES**

Alexander, M. Organizational norms opinionnaire. In J.W. Pfeiffer & J.E. Jones (Eds.), *The 1978 annual handbook for group facilitators*. San Diego, CA: University Associates, 1978.

Emery, F.E., & Trist, E.L. The causal texture of organizational environments. In W.A. Pasmore & J.J. Sherwood (Eds.), *Sociotechnical systems: A sourcebook*. San Diego, CA: University Associates, 1978.

Gibb, J.R. *Trust: A new view of personal and organizational development*. Los Angeles: Guild of Tutors Press, 1978.

Maier, N.R.F. *Appraising performance: An interview skills course*. San Diego, CA: University Associates, 1976.

McConkie, M.L. Classifying and reviewing the empirical work on MBO: Some implications. *Group & Organization Studies*, 1979, *4*(4), 461-475.

Nadler, D.A., & Lawler, E.E. III. Motivation: A diagnostic approach. In W.B. Eddy & W.W. Burke (Eds.), *Behavioral science and the manager's role* (2nd ed.). San Diego, CA: University Associates, 1980.

Sashkin, M., & Jones, J.E. Power and OD intervention analysis (PODIA). In J.E. Jones & J.W. Pfeiffer (Eds.), *The 1979 annual handbook for group facilitators*. San Diego, CA: University Associates, 1979.

*John E. Jones, Ph.D.*, is the senior vice president for research and development for University Associates, Inc., San Diego, California, and vice president for academic affairs of the UA graduate school. Dr. Jones is co-editor of Group & Organization Studies and of the Pfeiffer and Jones Series in Human Relations Training. He consults internationally with educational, industrial, and community organizations and specializes in team development, group training, intergroup relations, organization development, and counseling.

# DEVELOPING COLLABORATION
# IN ORGANIZATIONS

## Udai Pareek

Collaboration can be defined as one or more persons working with other persons toward the attainment of a common or agreed-on goal. The literature of experimental research on the subject of collaboration is growing. In such studies collaboration, or cooperation, usually is contrasted with competition. Competition can be defined as one or more persons working against other persons for the attainment of mutually exclusive goals. The basic difference between collaborative and competitive behavior is the perception of the goal. If the goal is seen as sharable, collaborative behavior, i.e., working with other persons for the attainment of the goal, generally results. If the goal is seen as unsharable, e.g., a situation in which only one person can "win," rivalry—or competitive behavior—generally results.

### FUNCTIONAL AND DYSFUNCTIONAL FORMS OF COOPERATION AND COMPETITION

Both collaboration (or cooperation) and competition can fall into two categories: one functional (or effective, or positive) and the other dysfunctional (or ineffective, or negative). We will use the terms Coll (+) and Coll (-), and Comp (+) and Comp (-) to indicate functional and dysfunctional, or positive and negative, collaboration and competition.

Comp (+) can be defined as a rivalry between two or more persons for the attainment of a desired goal. If such competition is used to achieve excellence and to search for or create further challenges for oneself, it is functional or positive competition—Comp (+). Such competition contributes to development of the sense of self-worth.

When a person focuses on a competitor and how the competitor can be prevented from attaining a goal, the interaction becomes negative—Comp (-). As Likert (1967) has often noted, if competition reduces a person's feeling of self-worth, it is dysfunctional. Likert also gives the example of some sales people who were motivated by this kind of competition. These salesmen withheld information about better methods of sales, new markets, and new sales strategies from their colleagues.

Similarly, collaboration can be either functional or dysfunctional. Functional collaboration, or Coll (+), can be defined as the tendency to contribute to the joint effort for faster and more effective goal attainment, resulting in mutual trust, respect, and concern. Such collaboration increases self-worth and contributes to the development of other desirable characteristics.

Coll (-) is the tendency to conform to others' demands in order to ingratiate oneself with them or to avoid or escape task stress or task demands. When a person collaborates with another person because the latter is more powerful, or in order to please the latter, it is also dysfunctional collaboration.

Both competition and collaboration are important and can be conceived as complementary qualities. However, they perform different functions. Figure 1 shows these various functions.

### THE ROLE OF COMPETITION

The main function of competition in an organization is to help an individual to develop and attain his own identity. In this regard, competition serves the following purposes:

## Developing a Sense of Identity

In order to be effective a person must develop his own identity and function as an individual. The development of identity occurs as one realizes his own uniqueness, strengths, capabilities, and weaknesses by testing them in the environment with other people.

## Developing a Sense of Responsibility

Unless a sense of responsibility is developed, a person's general competence and task involvement will be low. Responsibility includes a realistic assessment of how much one has contributed to a success or has been responsible for a failure. Competition helps to develop a sense of responsibility because it isolates a person to face the consequences of his own actions. If he succeeds in a competitive situation, he attributes his success to his own efforts and abilities. Similarly, if he fails he analyzes and takes responsibility for his failure.

## Developing Internal Standards of Behavior

When a person takes responsibility for the consequences of his actions, he develops his own standards for evaluating what is done well and what needs to be done better. A person who engages in collaboration merely for the sake of conformity will place little value on the outcome, since the decision to cooperate was not based on his own values or standards of behavior. Competition, however, helps to develop such internal standards. Successful competitive experiences help a person in learning to assess what he wants to do, why he wants to do it, and how he views the outcome. This increases his autonomy in setting goals and taking necessary steps for their attainment.

## Developing Excellence

The most important result of competition is the development of a concern for excellence, or what has been called achievement motivation. The success one achieves in relation to other persons produces a desire for even greater success. This occurs not only in relation to the standards set by others but also in relation to the individual's own standards or past performance. There is a continuous process of self-competition. One who has done very well in the past often wants to excel even more and is, in fact, competing with himself. Generally, the word competition is used in the context of relations with others. But the sense of competition that a person acquires from "outside" may also be internalized, and it promotes achievement motivation in which competition exists not only in relation to others but also in relation to one's own past behavior. When competition is used properly, it can develop a concern for excellence instead of a desire to pull another person down.

*Competition Develops*

A sense of identity
A sense of responsibility
Internal standards
Excellence
Individual creativity
Individual autonomy

*Collaboration Develops*

Mutuality
Alternative ideas and solutions
Mutual support and reinforcement
Synergy
Collective action
Supplementary expertise

**Figure 1. Functions of Competition and Collaboration**

## Developing Individual Creativity

Individual identity and a concern for excellence create a desire in the individual to find his own new and unconventional ways of solving problems, of looking at things, and of acting on decisions. Positive competition often encourages the development of such individual creativity.

## Developing Autonomy

Competition helps an individual to develop his own ways of looking at problems and finding solutions. It helps him to be original, think on his own, and develop his own framework and his own way of doing things. Developing autonomy does not conflict with relating to others or with working for a larger cause. Because autonomy helps to maintain the identity of an individual, if properly used it can help people to respect each others' identities. Thus, individual autonomy can be maintained in a larger context in which individuals have to surrender their autonomy on some matters in order to work for a common goal. This leads us to the issue of how competition emerges in collaboration and the role of collaboration.

## THE ROLE OF COLLABORATION

Competition by itself is a very important instrument in the development of the individual, but it should complement and supplement collaboration. Likewise, collaboration supplements the learnings of competition and allows further personal development.

## Building Mutuality

Collaboration helps to build relationships based on mutuality—recognizing the strengths of others and the contributions that other people can make and accepting these contributions. Such a relationship helps the individuals in an organization to develop respect for each other and to accept each other in a work situation. It also helps them to encourage the strengths of other persons, to utilize them, and to contribute to the further development of others.

## Generating Ideas and Alternatives

In a collaborative relationship, people stimulate each other in thinking about problems and alternatives and generating ideas, approaches, and solutions. Because several people may be involved, more ideas are generated than one single individual could produce.

## Building Mutual Support and Reinforcement

The collaborative relationship plays a significant emotional role by reinforcing members' efforts toward mutual support. In a collaborative situation, individuals receive immediate feedback from their colleagues, and this helps them both to use this feedback as well as to give feedback to the others. In this continuous process of feedback and support, successes are reinforced and the team is strengthened.

## Developing Synergy

A collaborative relationship produces synergy, the multiplication of talents and resources available in the group. Through continuous stimulation of each other, the members achieve results beyond the total of all individual resources. This generation of more potent resources in the group has an effect of multiplying resources in an organization.

## Developing Collective Action

When people work together in a group or team, their commitment to the goal is likely to be high and their courage to stand by that goal and take necessary action is much higher. The difference in the behavior of an individual in isolation and his behavior as a member of a team is evident in the case of trade unions, representative committees, and delegations. People act with more of a sense of power when they have several people behind them than they do when they present only their own points of view. This generates courage. The secret of success of a trade union in an organization lies in the strength of collective action that it is able to generate. The higher the level of collaboration, the greater the strength the group will have for collective action.

### Supplementing Expertise

The greatest advantage of collaboration is that individuals go beyond their own limitations, and one person's lack of expertise in a particular area does not keep the group from achieving its goals. The group's pool of strengths and expertise supplements the various individual contributions; as a result the collaborative group is able to generate multidimensional solutions and is not limited by a single individual's approach to the problem.

## COMPARING COMPETITION AND COLLABORATION

The discussion so far has shown the respective roles that collaboration and competition play in the organization. One is not always "better" than the other because in some instances competition is more functional while in others collaboration is called for. Much work in an organization is done in groups. These groups may be departments, interdepartmental committees, vertical role groups, or horizontal role groups such as the managers on a particular level. In many cases there may be informal collaborative groups in which two or more persons work together on a problem. In most cases, most of the time, people work with other people and, therefore, are continuously interacting in either a competitive or collaborative framework. In most such situations the collaborative framework is much more functional than the competitive one because these situations deal with organizations and problems: setting standards, searching for alternatives, etc. Collaboration is therefore an extremely important dimension in organizational life; if an organization has a low level of collaboration, the possibility of solving multidimensional problems within the organization is rather low.

Many researchers—and those who have worked in the field of management—have reported that on the whole collaboration contributes to better development and has better side effects than competition. Likert (1967), analyzing various studies done with sales people, reported that the most successful sales managers were discovering and demonstrating that when a sense of personal worth and importance was used to create competitive motivational forces, the level of productivity and sales performance was not as high as was expected. It was very high, on the other hand, when motivational forces to cooperate rather than to compete with one's peers and colleagues were used. The latter results included better performance, lower cost, highest levels of earnings, and much higher employee satisfaction. Likert concluded on this basis that collaboration releases motivational forces that develop people and contribute to the achievement of targets more effectively. Cartwright and Zander (1968), summarizing most of the research done since the famous research by Deutsch (1949) on cooperation and competition, reported that the basic conclusions drawn by Deutsch (that cooperation has a much higher payoff to the organization than does competition) were true in most of the studies surveyed. Collaboration contributes to better communication, coordination of efforts, an increased climate of friendliness, and pride in one's own group. Cartwright and Zander concluded that these were important qualities for group effectiveness.

Because people increasingly are called to work together to solve multidimensional organizational problems, collaboration becomes very relevant. This study will examine how collaboration takes place and how it can be further developed in the organization. The first question, therefore, is why and how people collaborate. Once this is answered, we can proceed to the next issue: how collaboration should be managed.

## BASES OF COLLABORATION

A great deal of research has been done on cooperation and collaboration. Experimental social psychologists have devised ways to study group relationships involving cooperation or collaboration. A frequent vehicle for study is an activity called "Prisoners Dilemma" (Pfeiffer & Jones, 1974c), in which team members are required to make a move demonstrating either cooperation or competition with another team. If both teams make a cooperative move, they score equally. If one "tricks" the other, it gains points and the other loses points. But if both teams attempt to trick each other, they both lose points. The object is to compare chance scores resulting from competition with the slow but consistent gains resulting from collaboration. A number of studies (Pareek, 1977a) have been done on this structured interaction, and some of this research is significant for understanding the bases of collaboration, some of the factors that contribute to collaboration, and the reasons why people collaborate.

### Collaborative Motivation

There is a basic need in most human beings, called *extension motivation,* to relate to other people and to be helpful to them. This need is reflected not only in concern for another individual but also in concern for larger groups, including the organization to which one belongs and the society at large. Extension motivation is the basis of collaboration. Individuals who have high extension motivation will collaborate more than others. Extension motivation or any other motivation is not innate or inborn. It is a product of many forces, and other factors can contribute to raise or reduce the level of extension motivation. Most of these factors interact with each other; many reinforce others or have implications for others. If extension motivation operates, and if there is reciprocal motivation within the group (if the members of the group have concern for each other and are also concerned about the performance of the total group), the individual's motivation is further reinforced. On the other hand, if other members do not demonstrate extension motivation, it will be reduced in individual members.

### Group Norms

The norms that prevail in a group have a strong influence on the behavior of the members and can raise or lower motivation. A member with low extension motivation may have a tendency to compete. However, if the collaborative norms in the group are high, this individual's extension motivation will also increase in time. Norms are informally evolved; members implicitly agree with them, agree to conform to these standards of behavior, and expect others to conform to them.

### Higher Payoff

Generally, an individual's behavior is dictated by perceived rewards. If one type of behavior is rewarded more (or has higher payoff), the individual will repeat that behavior. It is worthwhile, therefore, to examine whether collaborative behavior is rewarded in an organization.

Pareek and Banerjee (1977) have found that competition is not highly correlated with achievement motivation. In the past, achievement motivation (concern for individual excellence and competition) was thought to have a high correlation with competitive behavior. The reason why this has not proved to be true seems to lie in the perceived payoff for competition. A person with high achievement motivation is interested in results. If he perceives that by collaborating he can get better results, he is likely to collaborate; if he perceives that the results are better from competition, he is likely to compete. Even those who have a tendency to compete are likely to collaborate if collaborative behavior has a higher payoff. Collaborative behavior, for example, can lead to recognition, a chance to develop one's abilities, increased creativity, increased influence in the system, or perception of one's role as useful or contributing to a cause that is greater than individual interests. Such psychological payoff, in terms of motivation or role efficacy (Pareek, 1980), especially if it supplements a monetary or material payoff, is likely to reinforce collaborative behavior.

## Superordinate Goals

Several factors contribute to the development of a *superordinate* goal. First, the goal should be attractive to the various members; it should be seen as desirable by all concerned.

Second, the goal should be seen as sharable (all persons, or groups, concerned can share it). If the perception is that one party can achieve a goal at the expense of the other party and that the nature of the goal is such that it cannot be achieved jointly by both parties, it is called zero-sum game, because the sum of the payoff to both parties is zero. All traditional sports are zero-sum games. In a football or hockey match the goals secured by one team are the positive payoff; the team losing the game has a negative payoff. Adding the payoffs of both teams results in zero. However, within the same team, members play a nonzero-sum game. The gain by different players within the same team contributes to the higher gain by all members. The sum total of payoff to the different members of the team can be on the plus or the minus side.

Third, if the situation is such that the goal cannot be achieved by a single individual or a single group without working with others, it becomes a superordinate goal. In traditional sports, a team that is competing with other teams has the superordinate goal of getting a higher score than the other team. Within the team itself, members play a collaborative game because they perceive the superordinate goal. To all members the goal of achieving victory is attractive; they see this as sharable and as nonzero-sum, and each member realizes that this cannot be achieved individually—they have to work together to achieve the goal.

When persons involved in a situation see a goal as having all three elements described above, it becomes a superordinate goal.

Sherif and Sherif (1953) have described some interesting experiments that demonstrate the value of superordinate goals and have contributed significantly to the understanding of cooperation. Experimental conflict and competition were first created in two groups of adolescents who were taken on a camping trip for several days. Situations were created in which the problems faced by both groups could not be solved by either group alone. It was found that the perception of the superordinate goals by both the groups (involved at first in conflict and competition with each other) changed their behavior and they later engaged in the maximum possible collaboration.

## Perceived Power

Another condition that contributes to the development of collaboration in a group is the perception of power. Power can be of two kinds: reward and punishment. Punishment may take the form of depriving another person of reward. Everyone in the system has at least the negative power of depriving another person of something that is desirable to him. This may be done by holding back information, by misleading the other person, and so on. Even a person at the lowest level in the organization can use his negative power to create annoying situations, delay matters, hold back information, or give information that creates misunderstandings. Every person in the system has some kind of power. If people in the system perceive clearly that they have power that is positive in nature—that they may be able to contribute to and use their influence for the attainment of certain goals—they usually will use their power positively.

Similarly, it is important for people to realize that others who are involved in the situation also have power, both positive and negative. Such power should not only be perceived, it should also be demonstrated. If people do not perceive the power of others, they are likely to use their own power in a competitive or exploitative manner. Pareek (1977a) has reported that unconditional cooperation does not lead to the development of collaboration. Unconditional cooperation by one party may communicate lack of power. If this happens, the other party will find it more and more difficult to enter into a collaborative relationship. For effective collaboration the perception of power of both (equality) is essential. This was dramatically demonstrated in one experiment in which the author was involved with four groups composed of educators from six Asian countries. These groups engaged in a structured activity called "Win As Much As You Can" (Pfeiffer & Jones, 1974c). The activity consisted of ten moves. One of the four groups consistently made cooperative moves and—as was revealed in the later interview and discussion—was fully convinced that, looking at the nature of the game and the implicit rules, only cooperative behavior could help all the groups to maximize their gains. However, the unconditional cooperation by this group blocked the emergence of cooperation among the other groups, and the first group was exploited by the others. The final result was that the cooperating group stopped communication with the other three groups, and the other groups also refused to negotiate, since they saw themselves in a powerful and advantageous position that could be threatened by negotiation. Other research has shown that cooperation emerges after some competitive moves by the groups concerned; in this process the various parties or individuals demonstrate to each other the power they have and their ability to use power. Research also has shown that a competitive move or a stalemate in a relationship can result in collaboration, particularly in situations in which the parties are competitive by nature. In situations in which the parties are collaborative by nature, a stalemate in negotiation or relationship works against collaboration. The implications of these findings seem to be that when there are highly competitive or noncooperative parties or individuals, demonstration of their power to each other helps to loosen the situation, and a stalemate may encourage the possibility of collaborating for mutual benefit.

## Mutual Trust

Along with the perception of power, it is important that the parties concerned also perceive that the power that the other party has will not be used against them. This is trust. Trust is indicative of high probability that the power of the other party will not be used in a malevolent way. Some degree of mutual trust is likely to lead to cooperation.

As shown in Figure 2, collaboration results from a combination of perceived power of both parties and a minimum amount of trust in each other. In a no-trust condition there may be coercion and exploitation if the other party is seen as weak, or submission or compliance if the other is seen as having power. If the perception is that neither has power, there may be indifference to each other; perception that both have power may lead to either competition or individualistic behavior. High-trust perception of the partner having *low* power may lead to nurturance (paternalistic behavior), perception that the other *has* power may result in dependency, and perception that *neither* has power may generate mutual sympathy. It is only when trust exists and both parties perceive, as well as clearly demonstrate, that both have power that collaboration emerges.

Figure 3 shows that collaboration results from three main factors: the perception that the goal is sharable, the perception that both (or all) involved have power, and a minimum level of trust prevailing among those involved in the task. Absence of these may result in low (or absence of) cooperation. We thus see that trust interacts with both power and superordinate goal.

**Perceived Power (Who Has Power?)**

| | Only I | Only He | Neither | Both |
|---|---|---|---|---|
| **Low** | Coercion Exploitation | Submission Compliance | Indifference | Competition or Individualistic Task |
| **High** | Nurturance | Dependence | Mutual Sympathy | Cooperation |

**Trust** (label at left, spanning Low and High rows)

**Figure 2. Cooperation as a Function of Perceived Power and Trust**

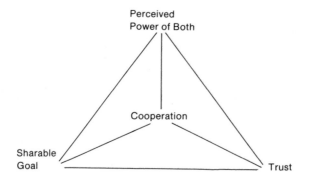

**Figure 3. Cooperation as a Function of Sharable Goal, Perceived Power, and Trust**

## Communication

Another factor contributing to the development of collaboration is communication between parties involved in the situation. Pareek and Dixit (1977) have reported the results of experiments conducted on adult groups to show the role of communication in the development of collaboration. These and various other experiments have demonstrated that when groups or representatives of the groups have an opportunity to communicate with each other, the chances of collaboration increase. Communication also helps the groups to share their perceptions of each other's power and to discover that the power they have can be turned into a positive force for the benefit of all concerned. The experiments showed that communication tends to produce repentant behavior in those who have been exploiting or using power against others. Communication also helps in the development of trust. When groups communicate through representatives, it is important that the groups trust their representatives and that the representatives are sure that their commitments be honored by the group. Again, experiments have shown that when the group has trust and confidence in its representatives and honors the commitments made by them, collaboration becomes easier.

### Fait Accompli

If groups or individuals live together and share certain norms, they begin to see good points in each other and collaboration begins to emerge. Various experiments aimed at reduction of conflict have employed this technique. People may be prejudiced against each other or have incorrect notions about each other when they do not work together or live together, but through sharing experiences they evolve common norms. When the individuals work together, it should be in a larger context so that they become members of a larger group. As part of a larger group to which they contribute, they develop new norms that encourage the development of better relationships. When competing groups or individuals become part of the same group, they slowly lose their identity as individuals or groups in a narrow sense and develop a new identity or sense of belonging to the larger group. This helps in the emergence of collaboration.

## Risk Taking

In the final analysis, cooperation results from an initiative taken by one party to cooperate. This is a risk-taking behavior and it makes that party vulnerable to some degree. In a nonzero-sum game the individual or group that makes the cooperative move runs the risk of losing a great deal and of having a lower payoff. This risk, the initiative, demonstrating the courage to lose initially for the benefit of all concerned, is the key to the development of cooperation. However, it is only after mutual trust has been achieved and mutual power has been demonstrated that such risk taking is effective. At that point, the fact that one person or group takes the initiative to become vulnerable starts the process of change toward collaboration. The strength that enabled the person or group to make such a move helps to support the collaborative relationship. This is shown in Figure 4.

## INTERVENTIONS TO BUILD COLLABORATION IN ORGANIZATIONS

Several interventions can be used to help raise the level of collaboration in organizations. The interventions discussed here can be classified as *process interventions* and *structural interventions*.

Process interventions focus on the basic processes that contribute to collaboration. They help to demonstrate the effects of collaboration. When people experience some dramatic effects of collaboration in a laboratory situation, they frequently are motivated to collaborate more effectively. Process interventions also help to increase awareness that collaboration is a complex phenomenon and that many conditions and processes promote it. Process interventions help people to become aware of and recognize such conditions, so that they may be able to take

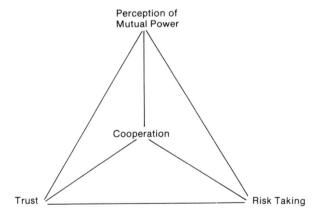

Figure 4. Cooperation as a Function of Individual Risk Taking

appropriate actions. Finally, process interventions help people to look at themselves in a self-confrontive manner. If an individual analyzes his own motivation and realizes that he has a tendency either to use collaboration in a minimum way or to use a dysfunctional type of collaboration, he may be concerned enough to work toward developing collaborative motivation. In this way process interventions provide opportunities for individuals to experiment with new behavior, to explore what methods they can adopt for collaboration, and to see how collaboration helps in a particular situation. Such experiencing and experimenting is the basic approach to behavioral change.

While the main role of a process intervention is to create motivation and release the process of collaboration, the main role of a structural intervention is to consolidate such change, make it a part of the organizational life, and ensure that the collaborative motivation that has been released is designed into the system and is sustained in the regular life of the organization. Structural interventions serve several functions. In the first place, they provide opportunities for people to actually collaborate in real-life situations. When their motivation for collaboration is high, structural interventions provide people opportunities to collaborate in order to sustain that motivation. Secondly, if collaboration is encouraged and rewarded, there will be a greater tendency for people to collaborate, so structural interventions create higher payoffs for collaboration in various forms, continuously reinforcing collaborative efforts. In the third place, these interventions legitimize collaboration because they do not leave it to informal arrangements. By formalizing the ways in which people collaborate, the organization recognizes and communicates the value of collaboration, and this process of legitimization helps to make it a regular part of organizational life. Finally, structural interventions help to establish norms of collaboration, making it clear that the organization expects people to collaborate. We have already said that such norms are important determinants of behavior; influencing behavior is an important role of structural interventions.

Figure 5 summarizes the various interventions that will be discussed here.

## Motivation-Development Interventions

In order to develop collaborative motivation it is useful to pay attention to the extension motive, which is characterized by concern for other persons and a general feeling that one should be of some use to others. Two interventions can be used to develop extension motivation: a laboratory approach and a simulation activity.

### Motivation-Development Laboratory

A laboratory of about one week's duration would be based primarily on the propositions suggested by McClelland and Winter (1969) for building motivation. An extension motivation lab also can be organized along the lines suggested for a power motivation lab (McClelland & Burnham, 1976). The design for such a lab would include (a) helping participants to analyze their levels of extension motivation and whether they are satisfied with them, (b) helping them to analyze various aspects of their jobs and to what extent these jobs provide opportunities to use their extension motivation, (c) helping them to diagnose the organizational culture again to see what elements in the culture contribute to or work against extension motivation and collaboration, (d) helping them to analyze the norms prevailing in the organization to determine which norms promote collaboration and which work against it, (e) helping them to share their apprehensions about the consequences of cooperation, and (f) helping them to deal practically with such apprehensions and to see that collaboration can be a strength rather than a means of giving up some powers. Collaboration eventually should be perceived as, and should in effect contribute to, the development of influence or power in individuals. Of course, this influence or power is of a particular nature; in the laboratory model, stage 4 of McClelland's (1975) concept of power should be used (Pareek, 1977b; Rao, 1976).

| Bases of Collaboration | Related Interventions |
|---|---|
| Motivation | Motivation Development Laboratory<br>Simulation Activities |
| Norms | Norm-Setting Exercises<br>Developing Norms of Sharing<br>Temporary Systems |
| Reinforcement | The Appraisal System<br>Rewarding Collaboration |
| Superordinate Goals | Joint Goal Setting<br>Redesigning Work<br>Organization Building |
| Power | Simulation Activities<br>Open Sharing of Feelings<br>Role Negotiation<br>Role Erosion |
| Trust | Training Groups or Process Groups<br>Nonverbal Exercises<br>Simulation Activities |
| Communication | Simulation Activities<br>Feedback System |
| Team Development | Team-Building Laboratories<br>Data Feedback<br>Sharing of Feelings<br>Image Sharing<br>Role Linkage<br>Joint Problem-Solving Groups |
| Initiative | Process Analysis of Simulation Experiences<br>Recognizing and Rewarding Initiative |

**Figure 5. Bases of Collaboration and Related Interventions**

## Simulation Activities

Simulations or structured activities also can be used to develop motivation for collaboration. One example is the activity "Win As Much As You Can" (Pfeiffer & Jones, 1974b), described earlier.

### Norm-Building Interventions

Interventions can be used to develop norms of collaboration within the organization. Such behavioral standards sustain collaboration in the long run. The following three strategies are suggested in this regard.

## Norm-Setting Exercises

De la Porte (1974) has suggested the development of group norms for team building. The interventions de la Porte has suggested include building new norms by examining old norms, i.e., creating understanding and appreciation of the significance of norms, establishing positive norm codes through cooperative action, determining the best aspects of norms for the company, establishing normative change priorities, developing a systematic change strategy by examining and modifying ten crucial areas that relate to norm setting, implementing the change strategy, providing follow-up and maintenance, and providing for continuous evaluation of the change strategy.

## Developing Norms of Sharing

If people in an organization continuously, openly, and jointly share various problems that they face, discuss ideas about solutions, and develop strategies for action, norms for collaboration will develop. Such activities may be conducted both within departments and across departments. Norms cannot develop in an organization unless particular behaviors are established as desirable. Therefore, steps must be taken to establish such norms and to reinforce them, if collaboration is to result.

## Temporary Systems

In solving various organizational problems or in working on specific tasks, it may be useful to use temporary systems such as task groups, special problem-solving groups, or data-collection groups. Such groups are created for a specific purpose and as soon as that purpose is achieved the groups are dissolved. Usually such groups are comprised of people from different departments, sections, or functions. The advantage of an interdisciplinary group is that members share concerns and thereby establish the norm of collaboration on common tasks. The more often such groups are used, the more the norm of collaboration will pervade the organization.

## Reinforcing Interventions

Interventions can be used to reinforce collaborative behavior. When behavior is rewarded, it tends to be repeated. Two main interventions are suggested for this purpose.

## The Appraisal System

Appraisal of employee performance and potential can be used to strengthen collaboration in an organization. One of the items to be appraised should be the individual's contribution to team building and collaboration in the organization. When such an item is pinpointed, the individual realizes that value is placed on such behavior and it becomes legitimized. This results in greater effort on the part of the individual employees to consciously collaborate and contribute to team work. In due course, this helps to develop skills of, and eventually motivation for, collaboration. Similarly, while appraising the potential of an individual for higher jobs, the employee's ability to develop a collaborative spirit to contribute to the development of subordinates may also be assessed.

## Rewarding Collaboration

Some method of rewarding collaboration in an organization is helpful. The reward may be merely special mention or recognition. For example, if a team consisting of people from several departments or sections has achieved something remarkable, it can be mentioned at board meetings, in the company newsletter, or in a special bulletin issued to describe successful collaborative efforts. Prizes can be given for remarkable work done by teams of workers in relation to specific tasks, when collaboration is a part of such efforts.

## Creating Superordinate Goals

As has been discussed, a superordinate goal should be attractive, should be seen as sharable, and should be seen as achievable only through collaborative effort. The following interventions may be used to establish superordinate goals.

### Joint Goal Setting

If persons from various departments and teams are involved in setting goals, the results are likely to be superordinate goals. In the joint goal-setting process it is important that the goals be defined jointly by the members and seen as worthwhile, attractive, and challenging by all concerned. Resources necessary to attain the goals may also be discussed during such meetings. This frequently occurs in the top levels of organizations; however, at the lower levels the process could be used much more frequently.

### Redesigning Work

De (1977) has described this intervention in detail. The intervention essentially consists of redesigning work in which several skilled workers are involved. The redesign is achieved by creating autonomous work teams consisting of members with various skills. They set their own goals, they use their own resources, and they are responsible for their overall production. In this process they learn each other's skills and replace one another whenever necessary. They take over the task of managing the entire production process in their own group. As De has explained, this certainly leads to new problems and dimensions, but more creative ways of managing problems also emerge. For example, as a result of such collaboration the role of the supervisor must be redesigned. Although there are several repercussions from such work redesign, it is an effective intervention for creating superordinate goals.

### Organization Building

Several models of organization building are available. Although these could be called organization development (OD) efforts, they are more elaborate than usual, and therefore the term "organization building" will be used. Two major interventions of this nature are those by Blake and Mouton (1964) and Likert (1961, 1967). These two major theories of organization design have been widely used, and the results have been reported from numerous organizations and countries.

Blake and Mouton developed the now famous managerial grid, in which several attempts are made to build an organization on the basis of collaborative effort. The major interventions in the grid approach relate to team building. Teams are built in the organization structure vertically, horizontally, and diagonally. For example, teams from various levels within the same department meet to collaborate on problems. This is the vertical slice. In the horizontal slice people at the same level from different departments come together to work on problems; in the diagonal slice people from different departments and different levels meet together to build a team. These team-building efforts eventually lead to goal-setting processes and a reshaping of the organization, resulting in a collaborative effort throughout the organization.

Likert proposes a theory of four types of organizations, which he calls type 1, type 2, type 3, and type 4. These types, broadly speaking, can be labeled authoritarian-exploitative, authoritarian-benevolent, consultative, and participative. The main characteristics of the type-4 organization (the participative or ideal organization)relate to collaborative relationships. In a more recent book Likert and Likert (1976) report new findings confirming that type-4 organizations can be built through emphasis on collaboration and team building. Out of ten items used to measure human organizational variables, six relate directly to collaboration.

## Power-Related Interventions

Unless the individuals or groups involved in the relationship perceive that all concerned in the situation have power, collaboration cannot emerge. Several interventions can be used to create conditions in which people both perceive and increasingly have power in the system.

### Simulation Activities

Several simulation activities or structured experiences such as "Win As Much As You Can" (Pfeiffer & Jones, 1974b) or "Broken Squares" (Pfeiffer & Jones, 1974a) involve power, since participants can withhold any help they can provide to the group, and even a small piece withheld prevents the group from achieving the task. Such negative power can be converted into positive power for the attainment of a goal. This and other activities used to simulate competitive and collaborative behavior demonstrate the importance of power very dramatically.

### Open Sharing of Feelings

One useful intervention to use in connection with a sense of loss of power or of not having enough power in the system is to allow and encourage people to openly share their feelings about being powerless. Sharing such concerns may help people to become aware that they do, in fact, have some power, and it is important that they recognize the areas in which they do have power. In most cases this perception is very important. Also, the open sharing of concerns and feelings may help to set norms of sharing in the group.

### Role Negotiation

Two important interventions relate to roles. Harrison's (1971) intervention called "role negotiation" is very useful. In the role-negotiation intervention, people negotiate their roles on the basis of mutuality. The basic concept of role negotiation is that people have equal power in the system, and they can make demands in exchange for promises of help. Role negotiation effectively utilizes the fact that people have power of different kinds, can use their power positively by helping others, and in turn can demand functional help themselves.

### Role Erosion

Another role-related intervention that can be used to increase power within various roles is called "role erosion" (Pareek, 1975, 1976). This activity helps those who feel that they do not have power in the system or that their power has been eroded as a result of reorganization or redesign of roles. The role occupants meet together and prepare maps to indicate in which areas their power has been eroded; they also identify areas of vacuum. After identifying specific areas in which their power seems to be less, they discuss how more power can be built into their roles or how some hidden power that the role occupant is not able to see may exist in the role. This exercise may lead to role negotiation for building more power.

All interventions that deal with power proceed on the basis that power is not a limited quantum. The more power is shared, the more it increases in the organization. It should be regarded as a multiplying entity. The main question is: How much power is needed in what areas by which role in order to be effective?

## Trust-Building Interventions

With the increasing application of the behavioral sciences to organizational matters, trust-building interventions have been more widely used, both with stranger groups and with organizational groups. The basic assumption behind trust-building interventions is that if the individual is helped to find out why he trusts or does not trust people, he will be able both to learn to trust and to generate trust in others. Three main interventions are worth mentioning in this area.

## Training Groups or Process Groups

In the training group—or T-group as it is more widely known—individuals sit without any agenda and explore issues that may be predominant in the group. Through this they explore their own personal and interpersonal orientations and help each other to look at their personal and interpersonal effectiveness as well as to plan to improve such effectiveness. The T-group explores the various dimensions of trust building and helps members to test how trust can be built in the group. T-groups generally comprise part of a stronger laboratory setting. If the culture of the organization is fairly closed, the use of the T-group may create problems. But T-groups or process groups have been used effectively to create more trust among members and to build norms of trusting behavior within the organization.

## Nonverbal Exercises

More recently, nonverbal exercises have been widely used for building trust. One such exercise is what is called a "trust walk." Half the members of a group are blindfolded, and each blindfolded person forms a pair with one who is not blindfolded. The latter accompanies the former for several hours and in some cases for the whole day. He helps him to go for lunch and attend to various other necessities; he also helps his partner to explore the environment and leads him around. Sometimes this experience is very dramatic and has a tremendous impact on people in building trust. Some prework on personal relationships and interpersonal dimensions may need to be done before such a nonverbal exercise is used.

## Simulation Activities

Several simulation activities have been used for building trust, especially the "Prisoners Dilemma" (Pfeiffer & Jones, 1974c). This and "Win As Much As You Can" (Pfeiffer & Jones, 1974b) are both discussed previously.

## Communication Interventions

Collaboration increases when communication channels are open. In an emotionally charged situation when there is some kind of stalemate as a result of negative competition, if communication becomes blocked the relationship degenerates into a lose-lose situation. At such a point communication becomes extremely important. Two interventions are useful in establishing helpful communication.

## Simulation Activities

Simulation activities dramatically bring out the usefulness of communication, as mentioned earlier.

## Feedback System

Another important way to keep communication open is to encourage giving and receiving negative feedback. In a face-to-face situation, if such feedback is allowed and encouraged, communication channels will continue to remain open. This can be done by legitimizing process review and feedback in a collaborative project from time to time. For example, an hour or so per week can be set aside for sharing feelings and other concerns that various group members have in relation to the work being done.

## Team-Development Interventions

Team building is most important because it leads directly to collaboration. A variety of structural and process interventions have been used for this purpose.

### Team-Building Laboratories

Special programs for team building are often developed for specific organizations. Alban and Pollitt (1973), for example, have developed what they call a "team-building group." They contrast the team-building group with the T-group mainly on the basis that team building is done in the organization with members who will work continuously with each other and that more structured activities are used. Although the team-building program is more structured in nature, process data are analyzed. Various simulation activities, theoretical inputs, and task work are used in a four-to-five-day program. The authors report effective changes as a result of such team-building activity.

Several team-building laboratories have been reported by other authors. All of these, whether they emphasize process or rely more on structured material, aim at creating teams of people who have respect for each other and who emerge with strengthened collaborative relationships.

### Data Feedback

Team building can also be promoted when data collected by an outside consultant from interviews with various organizational members are used as the basis for team-building activities. This intervention has been found to be especially useful for top team building. The consultant interviews each individual who will participate in the team-building program and then writes all the data anonymously on large sheets of paper. These are posted on the walls before the meeting starts. This feedback from the interviews helps to stimulate discussions about the problems faced by the group and deliberations about how the team building could be attempted.

### Sharing of Feelings

Team building is facilitated if people are allowed to share their feelings about what happens in their groups or in the organization. Even when role negotiation has taken place, there may be residual, unexpressed feelings. Legitimizing discussions of the dimensions generated by sharing of such feelings helps in promoting team building and should be practiced regularly whenever special teams are working on projects.

### Image Sharing

This intervention was originally suggested by Blake, Shepard, and Mouton (1964) for increasing role effectiveness. Essentially, the members generate images they have of the other groups or other members and predict what image the groups or members have about them. These images are shared. The rationale behind this intervention is that the negatives images that people have of each other get in the way of working together. So before mutuality can be established and teamwork can be developed, it is necessary that these images be both shared and cleared.

### Role Linkage

One very effective team-building intervention is role linkage (Pareek, 1975). Various role occupants come together to determine the amount of linkage existing among their roles. By analyzing such role linkages (an instrument can also be used for this purpose), members become aware of where role linkages are weak and can then work to improve the linkages, leading to team development.

## Joint Problem-Solving Groups

Another effective intervention is to set up groups that have joint responsibility for solving certain problems. The organizational problems should be urgent and most of the members should be concerned about them.

### Initiative-Promoting Interventions

As has been discussed, collaboration develops when someone takes the initiative and the risk to cooperate and opens a way to establish a collaborative relationship. This can be promoted in various ways.

## Process Analysis of Simulation Experiences

Simulation activities provide data that can lead to understanding why there was a change toward collaboration, e.g., some individuals took the initiative to turn the situation in a positive direction. This kind of process analysis generally can be done with good results.

## Recognizing and Rewarding Initiative

It is also important that the initiative taken by a member or a group to establish collaboration is both recognized and rewarded. This will help to set norms of recognizing collaboration as well as to set examples that others can follow.

## CONCLUSION

In conclusion, we can say that to build collaboration in organizations it may be useful to treat collaboration and competition as complementary phenomena and work toward the development of functional (positive) forms of both. Understanding the bases of collaboration (why people collaborate) may help in designing both structural and process interventions in an organization. The interventions suggested here can be applied in a wide range of organizations.

### REFERENCES

Alban, B.T., & Pollitt, L.I. Team building. In T.H. Patten (Ed.), *OD: Emerging dimensions and concepts.* New York: American Society for Training and Development, 1973.

Blake, R.R., & Mouton, J.S. *The managerial grid.* Houston, TX: Gulf, 1964.

Blake, R.R., Shepard, H.A., & Mouton, J.S. *Managing intergroup conflict in industry.* Houston, TX: Gulf, 1964.

Cartwright, D.P., & Zander, A.F. (Eds.). *Group dynamics: Research and theory.* New York: Harper & Row, 1968.

De, N. *New forms of work organisation in India.* New Delhi: National Labour Institute, 1977. (Mimeograph)

de la Porte, P.C.A. Group norms: Key to building a team. *Personnel,* 1974, *51*(5), 60-67.

Deutsch, M. A theory of cooperation and competition. *Human Relations,* 1949, *2*, 129-152.

Harrison, R. Role negotiation: A tough minded approach to team development. In W.W. Burke & H.A. Hornstein (Eds.), *The social technology of organization development.* San Diego, CA: University Associates, 1971.

Likert, R. *New patterns of management.* New York: McGraw-Hill, 1961.

Likert, R. *The human organization: Its management and values.* New York: McGraw-Hill, 1967.

Likert, R., & Likert, J.G. *New ways of managing conflict.* New York: McGraw-Hill, 1976.

McClelland, D.C. *Power: The inner experience.* New York: Irvington, 1975.

McClelland, D.C., & Burnham, D.H. Power is the great motivator. *Harvard Business Review,* 1976, *54*(2), 100-110.

McClelland, D.C., & Winter, D.C. *Motivating economic achievement.* New York: The Free Press, 1969.

Pareek, U. *Role effectiveness exercises*. New Delhi: Learning Systems, 1975.

Pareek, U. Interrole exploration. In J.W. Pfeiffer & J.E. Jones (Eds.), *The 1976 annual handbook for group facilitators*. San Diego, CA: University Associates, 1976.

Pareek, U. *Share or fight: Dynamics of cooperative and competitive behaviour*. Ahmedabad: Indian Institute of Management, 1977. (a) (Mimeograph)

Pareek, U. Some new trends in personnel and OD areas. *Administrative Change*, 1977, 5(1), 26-33. (b)

Pareek, U. Dimensions of role efficacy. In J.W. Pfeiffer & J.E. Jones (Eds.), *1980 annual handbook for group facilitators*. San Diego, CA: University Associates, 1980.

Pareek, D. Achievement motive and competitive behaviour. *Manas*, 1976, 23(1), 9-15.

Pareek, U., & Dixit, N. Effect of partner's response and communication on competitive and cooperative game behaviour. *Psychologia*, 1977, 21, 38-48.

Pfeiffer, J.W., & Jones, J.E. (Eds.). *A handbook of structured experiences for human relations training* (Vol. I). San Diego, CA: University Associates, 1974. (a)

Pfeiffer, J.W., & Jones, J.E. (Eds.). *A handbook of structured experiences for human relations training* (Vol. II). San Diego, CA: University Associates, 1974. (b)

Pfeiffer, J.W., & Jones, J.E. (Eds.). *A handbook of structured experiences for human relations training* (Vol. III). San Diego, CA: University Associates, 1974. (c)

Rao, T.V. *Stewart Maturity Scale*. New Delhi: Mtnasayan, 1976.

Sherif, M., & Sherif, C.W. *Groups in harmony and tension*. New York: Harper, 1953.

**Udai Pareek, Ph.D.**, is Larsen & Toubro professor of organizational behavior at the Indian Institute of Management, Ahmedabad, Gujarat, India. Dr. Pareek's background is in organization development, human resource development, organizational design, and change in persons and systems. He has consulted with industrial and nonindustrial systems in various countries and with many international organizations.

# MEETING MANAGEMENT

## David R. Nicoll

A conservative estimate would indicate that most of us who work spend four hours per week attending meetings. At this rate, each of us can anticipate sitting through more than eight thousand hours of meetings in a lifetime of work. This time is valuable, both to us and to our organizations. A *productive* meeting of fifteen top managers can cost an organization from one thousand to four thousand dollars per hour; an *unproductive* meeting during which problems are not solved and intelligent decisons are not made can cost much more.

Most of us have learned how to run meetings by osmosis—by watching another person, who, in turn, learned by watching someone else. This method of learning would be valid if the observed processes worked. But what is usually learned is a weak version of Roberts' Rules of Order, which may have worked for the House of Lords in the nineteenth century but is grossly inadequate for twentieth century meetings.

Fortunately, behavioral scientists have developed various methods for running meetings that work for thousands of individuals in all kinds of organizations across the country. The purpose of this piece is to convey a few of the concepts that have been developed and a number of suggestions that will help foster the effective management of meetings.

## TYPES OF MEETINGS

In productive organizations, meetings are of distinctive types. All meetings have specific purposes for being held and specific tasks to be performed by the participants. These meetings are effective only when the participants clearly understand the type of meeting they are holding and then make sure they accomplish the tasks associated with that type of meeting. The different types of meetings conducted in organizations are as follows:

*Informational.* The purpose of this type of meeting is to disseminate data and facts as well as decisions and policies made by people or groups in the organization senior to those holding the meeting. Three subtypes of informational meetings exist: *from supervisor to subordinates*, in which the former conveys information; *from subordinates to supervisor*, in which the subordinates convey information; and *interactional*, in which the supervisor and subordinates share information.

*Validational.* This type of meeting is held to announce a previously made decision to the employees affected so that the supervisor can obtain their assent to the decision's implementation. The desired outcome of a validational meeting is the participants' agreement to the wisdom, appropriateness, or logic of the decision. The informational flow here is primarily from top to bottom.

*Planning/Strategizing.* The purpose of the planning/strategizing meeting is the generation of long-range (one- to ten-year) action plans for the work group in attendance. Involved is an effort to define how the group would like to see its future evolve. Often the outcome of such a meeting is a description of both an ideal state and the sequence of action needed to achieve it. The conversational flow is generally from peer to peer.

*Problem Solving/Decision Making.* The objective of this type of meeting is also the generation of action plans, but the time factor considered is short (one day to six months), and the focus is on day-to-day business rather than on long-range planning. The conversational flow is from peer to peer or interactional.

*Staff Conferences.* This type of meeting is held to ensure the progress of action plans generated in planning and problem-solving meetings. Progress reports are provided, a full expression of opinions is solicited, and coordination of disparate actions is achieved. The flow of conversation is from peer to peer and interactional.

*Feedback/Evaluation.* The purpose of the feedback/evaluation meeting is to assess progress in accordance with the schedules set forth in previous planning and/or problem-solving meetings. Organizational and/or personal performance is the focus. The informational flow is often from supervisor to subordinates, occasionally from peer to peer. Generally, it should be from implementing subordinates to supervisor.

*Training.* This type of meeting is held to educate the staff. The goal is to expand the knowledge, improve the skill, or change the behavior/attitudes of the participants so that they will perform in their jobs more effectively. The informational flow is downward and interactional.

*Celebrational.* The celebrational meeting is held so that the participants can enjoy being together, relax, and have a good time. The conversational flow is in all directions.

For each type of meeting, Figure 1 lists the kinds of tasks to be performed and those who should perform them.

## CONVENER/MANAGER RESPONSIBILITIES

The meeting convener or manager has two primary responsibilities. The first is to declare the type of meeting being held. Ideally, this announcement is made before the meeting is convened and is repeated at the start of the meeting to focus the participants on the objectives. The second convener responsibility is to declare his or her function in the meeting and that of the participants as well. The choices of function are limited to decision maker, participant, resource expert, facilitator, and data recorder. It is important for all concerned to know what parts they are to play, and unfortunately these parts are not always obvious.

## PACING CUES

The concept of "pacing cues" suggests that every successful meeting, regardless of type, has a definite and distinctive pace. It follows, then, that each type of meeting also has cues or signals governing movement toward a satisfactory conclusion. The distinct phases of a meeting are as follows:

- Definition of the task;
- Application of energy to the task;
- Consolidation; and
- Closure.

Three kinds of cues signal that a meeting is ready to move from one phase to another:

- Quick repetitions of the same points by different people;
- Successive lulls in the dialog; and
- A feeling of confusion on the participants' part, often vocalized in terms of statements such as "What are we doing now?"

When these cues are noted, someone should take responsibility for suggesting that the meeting is ready to move to the next phase of the process.

184

| Meeting Type | Tasks | Task Performer |
|---|---|---|
| Informational | Disseminating information | Information holder |
| | Listening | Participants |
| | Questioning for clarification | Participants |
| Validational | Disseminating decisions | Decision maker or a representative of the decision maker |
| | Listening | Participants |
| | Presenting action assignments | Supervisor |
| | Assenting/dissenting | Participants |
| Planning/Strategizing and Problem Solving/ Decision Making | Identifying the problem/issue | Decision maker |
| | Developing data | Participants |
| | Generating alternatives | Participants |
| | Selecting a solution | Decision maker |
| | Planning action | Participants |
| | Presenting action assignments | Supervisor |
| Staff Conference | Developing data | Participants |
| | Identifying progress | Decision maker/participants |
| | Identifying the problem/issue | Decision maker |
| | Generating alternatives | Participants |
| | Selecting a course of action | Decision maker |
| | Planning action | Participants |
| | Presenting action assignments | Supervisor |
| Feedback/Evaluation | Developing data | Participants |
| | Identifying the problem/issue | Decision maker |
| | Generating alternatives | Participants |
| | Selecting a solution | Decision maker |
| | Planning action | Participants |
| | Presenting action assignments | Supervisor |
| Training | Presenting the concept | Trainer |
| | Listening | Participants |
| | Experimenting | Participants |
| Celebrational | (As appropriate) | Participants |

**Figure 1. Tasks to Be Completed in Meetings**

Another cue worth noting is the tempo of successful meetings. Each meeting type is listed below along with its characteristic pace.

| Meeting Type | Pace |
|---|---|
| Informational | Crisp, quick |
| Validational | Episodic (ebb and flow) |
| Planning/Strategizing | Slow, deliberate |
| Problem Solving/Decision Making | Meandering |
| Staff Conference | Repetitive (long-then-short cycles) |
| Feedback/Evaluation | Slow, contemplative |
| Training | Smooth, flowing |
| Celebrational | Rambling |

*Advance Preparation*

1. *Set the agenda and post a meeting notice.*
   a. Designate the meeting topic.
   b. Designate the meeting type and the attendees.
   c. Specify expectations.
      • Set the activity-level standards.
      • Decide on the attendees' responsibility regarding functional role.
      • Identify resource people.
2. *Assign any necessary prework.*
3. *Establish and secure a base of information.*
4. *Make the logistic arrangements.*
   a. Space
   b. Time
   c. Seating
   d. Materials (audiovisual equipment, etc.)

*Meeting Dynamics*

1. *Opening Phase—Defining the Task*
   a. Convene the meeting.
   b. Introduce the participants (if necessary).
   c. Reinforce/change expectations.
   d. Reinforce participation and norms of representation.
   e. Introduce the resource experts.
   f. Identify the problems/issues that will *not* be dealt with during the meeting.
   g. Present the time schedule.
2. *Middle Phases—Application of Energy and Consolidation*
   a. Test issue formation and understanding.
   b. Reiterate the decisions that are made.
   c. Monitor pace.
3. *Closing Phase*
   a. Evaluate the progress that has been made.
   b. Assign tasks.
   c. Establish a means for dealing with unfinished business (such as including it in the agenda for the next meeting).

*Follow-Up Documents to Be Produced*

1. Minutes
2. Action-plan summaries
3. Individual action-assignment sheets
4. Action-review reminders
5. Completion reminders
6. Appreciation/recognition notes

**Figure 2. Meeting-Management Check List**

Pacing cues should be used as indicators as to whether the meeting is moving toward a successful conclusion. The meeting manager should monitor the tempo of the meeting and alter the pace when necessary.

## CONCLUSION

Meetings are microcosmic organizations, and as such they should be structured and designed carefully. The check list in Figure 2 provides a means by which the meeting manager can plan and execute a well-designed, properly structured meeting.

**David R. Nicoll, Ph.D.**, is an organization consultant for Kaiser Permanente Medical Center in San Diego, California. His areas of consultation include organization design, strategy, long-range planning, and traditional organization development. Dr. Nicoll is also a private consultant and serves as co-director of Confluent Systems, an OD consulting firm, and as a consultant to the Life Meanings Center, which offers career and life-planning workshops and consultation.

# HUMAN RESOURCE DEVELOPMENT: WHAT IT IS AND HOW TO BECOME INVOLVED

## John E. Jones

Within the broad field of human relations, such diverse terms as sensitivity training, leadership development, laboratory methods, experiential education, organization development, socio-technical systems, and quality of work life are defined, redefined, and finally settled into the professional argot. When a new concept is introduced the question is where, or how, it fits within the already defined framework. To many, the term human resource development is synonymous with training (see Donnelson & Scannell, 1978). The purpose of this paper is to attempt a more concise definition of human resource development (HRD), to explore the major components of this emerging field of professional activity, and to point out some ways in which trainers can become involved in this field.

There is a need for clarity in professional terminology because we have to communicate with our clients and potential clients in order to establish proper expectations for our work if we are to develop appropriate contracts. The lack of clarity about what constitutes HRD has resulted in what we believe to be an underemployment of group facilitators within organizational systems. It is our view that trainers, consultants, and group facilitators need to be aware of and relate effectively to the various activities that we believe constitute HRD in order to develop a more well-rounded perspective of the part that training and development play in the array of programs that focus on the people aspect of an organization.

### Defining HRD

Although it may be presumptuous to attempt to define an emerging activity, we believe that HRD is describable as a set of activities. The following definition, while not the result of a consensus of practicing professionals, represents our view of how HRD can be thought of productively by practitioners:

> Human resource development is an approach to the systematic expansion of people's work-related abilities, focused on the attainment of both organizational and personal goals.

A number of elements of this definition bear some comment. First, human resource development focuses on people. The human aspect of the organization or system is the one to which group facilitators can most productively be oriented. We are, in a sense, the champions of human values, human dignity, human concerns, and the human implications of organizational change. People are seen as having skills, having potential, and having the ability to grow, change, and develop; HRD focuses on increasing the talents and abilities of the people in the system. Of course, people learn and grow within organizations without formal programs and opportunities. HRD, however, is sytematic in that it is comprised of a number of activities that are individually designed to focus on the pool of people who constitute the human organization. The term resource implies that the individuals or groups of people within the organization are considered to be resources rather than problems. The term development is ambiguous in the literature of training and development as well as in the literature of organizational behavior. In this context it implies an emphasis on the discovery and nurturing of human resources.

The programs and practices of HRD focus not only systematically on the development of people but also on the system as a unit. So HRD can also be thought of as systemic. The emphasis is on the possibilities for the enhancement of the total human system. Expansion implies growth, and all HRD activities are focused toward learning and behavior change—toward increased effectiveness. Theoretically there are many untapped human abilities that can be made available to the organization and to individuals within the organization. The focus here is on goal attainment. The "bottom line" is the accomplishment of the objectives of both the organization and the individuals in it. HRD activities, when they are coordinated with each other, offer the promise of making the relationship between the individual and the organization more effective by focusing on the development of people and of people's systems.

## HRD Components

Five major areas of activity can be utilized by organizations to improve human systems and to develop people within those systems. These five professional activities are training, organization development, education, system change, and human-systems programs. The traditional view of HRD would include only training and organization development, but it is our view that numerous other activities designed to ameliorate human systems, support the smooth functioning of human systems, and develop members of the system are legitimate ones to be engaged in by HRD personnel.

Figure 1 is a categorization of the major activities that comprise HRD. What these efforts have in common is that each has a human aspect, a people dimension. It is clear from this listing that there are myriad programs that affect individuals and groups within an organization. Some of these activities could be classified in more than one category, but this listing represents our judgment of the primary focus of each component.

*Training.* Within the training function are numerous programs that are typically carried out by HRD personnel. In each of the enumerated activities the main emphasis is on the development of individual persons with regard to skills, knowledge, and attitudes. This area is the core of many HRD practitioners' work; it presents opportunities to reach and influence almost all the influential people within the organization. Conducting effective training is one of the best ways for the HRD person to establish credibility with managers. In addition, training provides a foundation of knowledge and skills on which other HRD programs can be built. For example, for MBO to succeed there must be adequate training of individuals as well as system planning.

*Organization Development.* In this area of activity the emphasis is not on individual people but on people systems. Common to all these program components is attention to process, i.e., consulting with groups of people on the processes through which work gets done in a social context. The role played by the HRD practitioner is that of a helper to the human system in learning about its own functioning in order to increase the effectiveness of that system.

*Education.* In educational programs the emphasis is on providing assistance to the individual as a person, not as a worker. The rationale is that fully functioning people are more productive. The career-development center is an offshoot of the traditional assessment center; it differs from the latter in that the focus is on development rather than selection.

*System Change.* Large-scale redevelopment of organizations has innumerable effects on people. New plant start-ups and internal reorganizations both are new designs for human systems as well as for operational systems. Numerous efforts are made inside organizations to minimize the effects on people of large, pervasive change. When organizations are decentralizing or centralizing, merging with other organizations, or expanding in dramatic ways, the HRD practitioner can be enormously helpful to planners in working through the process of planning as well as consulting on the human aspects of such system change.

*Human-Systems Programs.* Other programs and activities in organizations attempt to help the human system function more effectively. These include the wide array of HRD components that regulate and maintain the people system. HRD personnel need to be thoroughly conversant with these activities and find ways to become involved in them.

These categories of HRD components are neither discrete nor mutually exclusive. Their overlap provides opportunities for HRD practitioners to cross boundaries and provide services to managers in assuring that the organization's social and technical systems are compatible and mutually beneficial.

## Entry Strategies

Persons involved in training inside organizations often seem unaware of the system effects of what they are doing. When the training department and the organization development group are separate, the trainer may inadvertently work against the integrity of the organization as a system unless the training is carried out with proper regard for goals and priorities. Conversely, organization development personnel often tend to see all organizational problems as people problems, communication problems, conflict problems, or examples of the need for redistribution of power. Both sides can benefit from an overview that puts their work into a matrix of activities that are designed to benefit both people and the organization. Getting involved in the broad spectrum of HRD activities can provide that perspective.

Since we believe that persons involved in "traditional" training and development might beneficially become active in other HRD activities, we want to spell out what we believe to be a set of strategies by which the HRD practitioner might maximize his or her impact. Many of the programs enumerated are technical specialties for many consultants.

**Training**
Executive development
Management development
Supervisory development
Sales training
Technical skills training
Personal-growth programs
Stress-management programs
Time-management programs
Pre-retirement planning

**Education**
Career-development centers
New-employee orientation
Physical fitness programs
Employee-assistance
  programs
Personal counseling
Life/career planning
Tuition-assistance programs

**Organization Development**
Organization Assessment
Team building
Resolving interunit conflict
Third-party consultation
Coaching
Process consultation
Job design/enrichment
Work simplification
Quality-of-work-life
  programs
Sociotechnical-systems
  interventions

**System Change**
Transition planning
Centralization/
  decentralization
Mergers
Organization design
  (e.g., sociotechnical-
  systems interventions)

**Human-Systems Programs**
Performance appraisal
Manpower planning
Succession planning
Assessment centers
Compensation (wage/
  salary administration)
Job analysis
Job classification
Recruitment/exist
  interviewing
Personnel-policies
  planning (including
  benefits and rewards)
Labor/employee relations
Scanlon plan
Affirmative action/equal
  employment opportun-
  ity programs
MBO programs
Occupational-health-
  and-safety-standards
  compliance

**Figure 1. Human Resource Development Components**

The HRD practitioner can adopt the major strategy of becoming a clearinghouse, the person who familiarizes outside experts with the training and development activities going on inside the organization, works with the experts, and becomes the recipient of referrals from the technical specialists when they encounter training and development implications in their specialty work. This means that the HRD practitioner must, in effect, set up a referral resource system for managers within the organization and do research on the credible experts in the community who might be brought in to work on the development of particular systems.

The HRD practitioner can become involved in activities that are not thought of as training or organization development in three ways. First, most of these activities can benefit from process consultation; the HRD person should be equipped to provide that service. Second, many group facilitators can function easily as experts on applications of behavioral science to organizational planning and problem solving. Third, HRD practitioners can enter these activities as advocates of humanistic values. People in HRD have, we believe, a responsibility to help the organization manage what often is a lack of attention to the people aspects of organizational decisions. There always is creative tension between the development of the human system as a system and the development of individuals as private, autonomous people. Also, there often is a very high emphasis inside organizations on task considerations, sometimes at the expense of human considerations. The main challenge that we believe HRD practitioners need to confront the organization with is to correct the blind spot that so many managers have about the impact of change on the individual worker.

An additional strategy available to HRD practitioners is to expand their knowledge and skills into the areas of HRD that they are not now conversant with or credible in. This requires retraining and study, but it adds to the repertoire of services that the HRD practitioner can offer to the organization.

As a part of the training function of the organization, the HRD practitioner can develop management courses on the knowledge and skills needed to engage in the various HRD functions that may be present or planned for in the organization. Courses in how to conduct a performance review or assessment center, coaching, counseling, etc., can allow managers full participation in human resource development and can also help them to see HRD as an organizational priority.

Another entry strategy for HRD practitioners is to invite themselves into the planning processes for the start up of new aspects of the organization. If a new plant is to be planned, the HRD practitioner can offer to join the planning team as a process consultant—a technical expert on the development of human resources.

## Careers in HRD

It is clear that training and organization development are here to stay as recognizable, supported activities within a wide array of organizations. Since more and more management publications and popular magazines have referred to human resource development in the past few years, it is clear that HRD is becoming visible within a variety of organizations and that top management is becoming more sensitive to the need for HRD as part of corporate planning and problem solving. This opens the way for new steps in the career ladders of group facilitators within organizations. A number of organizations have now created vice-presidential slots for human resource development, opening a new avenue of growth and development for professional people within this area. This field is continuing to emerge rapidly, and it is incumbent on practitioners not only to pay attention to the kinds of services they are able to provide to organizations, but also to be acutely aware of the HRD functions that can be brought into the organization through outside consultants; these efforts can help the organization make HRD a continuing priority in its overall system development.

*John E. Jones, Ph.D., is the senior vice president for research and development for University Associates, Inc., San Diego, California, and vice president for academic affairs of the UA graduate school. Dr. Jones is co-editor of* Group & Organization Studies *and of the Pfeiffer and Jones Series in Human Relations Training. He consults internationally with educational, industrial, and community organizations and specializes in team development, group training, intergroup relations, organization development, and counseling.*

# AN ADLERIAN PRIMER

## Daniel G. Eckstein

Whatever their theoretical orientations, group facilitators probably know and use concepts pioneered by Alfred Adler and the school of psychology he founded, Individual Psychology. Adler believed in a humanistic and holistic psychology and in the social determinants of behavior. This was a break with Freudian theory and a step toward the development of social psychology.

Adler is considered to be a pioneer in the group counseling movement (Gazda, 1975). He was the first psychiatrist known to use collective counseling in a formal and systematic manner. As early as 1922, Adler was counseling children in front of an audience of adults who actively participated. In these clinics, participant parents gave one another support and Adler found that discussing a child's difficulties in front of a group objectified the problems and helped the child to recognize them as social rather than private affairs.

Exponents of Adler, led by Rudolph Dreikurs, have developed his understanding of human behavior into a theoretical approach to counseling. This approach is summarized here.

## THEORY

Adlerian theory, as suggested by Dinkmeyer, Pew, and Dinkmeyer (1979), is characterized by the following major premises.

### All Behavior Has Social Meaning

Adler disagreed with Freud's assumption that human behavior is motivated by sexual instinct. Adler's assumption was that human behavior is motivated by *social* urges and that humans are inherently social beings. He substituted an interpersonal social-relationship mode for the intrapersonal id-ego-superego personality structure of Freud.

Adler developed a belief in high social interest as "the ironclad logic of social living." Social interest creates an attitude toward life, characterized by an individual's willingness to cooperate with others for the common good and "specific awareness of the universal interrelatedness of all human beings."

Adler theorized "tasks" of living encountered by everyone in the process of individual development: love, friendship, and work. Two more life tasks—self-concept and the spiritual or existential search for meaning—were added by Mosak in conjunction with Dreikurs (1977).

A crucial Adlerian concern was how individuals found their places within their first social group, the family, and in later social groups, i.e., schools, friendships, vocational and love relationships, throughout life. Adler felt that an individual with high self-esteem and high social interest will move toward the group in an encouraging manner. Conversely, a person suffering from self-doubts or inadequacies, or who has few concerns for the rights and needs of others, will move away from the community in a discouragingly dependent or mutually independent manner.

### The Human Personality Has Unity and Definite Patterns

The Adlerian seeks a unified understanding of the "total person" through synthesis of the physical, emotional, intellectual, and spiritual dimensions of human personality. For example, Adler (1938, p. 205) notes that to deny the total context of a personality is like "picking single notes out of a melody to examine them for their significance, their meaning. A better understanding of this coherence is shown by Gestalt psychology which uses their metaphor as frequently as we do. The only difference is that we are not satisfied with the 'Gestalt' or as we prefer to say with the 'whole,' when we refer to the notes of the melody. We are satisfied only when we have recognized in the melody the originator and his attitudes as well, for example, Bach and Bach's style of life."

Style of life is the key term in Adler's personality theory. He used it to describe self, personality, a personal problem-solving method, an attitude toward life, a line of movement, a pattern, a technique, the system by which an individual functions. A life style is formed early in childhood and it is unique; no two people develop the same style. Dreikurs (1953, p. 44) noted that life style is "comparable to a characteristic theme in a piece of music. It brings the rhythm of recurrence into our lives."

### Behavior Is a Function of Our Subjective Perceptions

Adlerians take a position similar to that of other phenomenological disciplines in their concept of perception: An individual defines a personal reality through subjective experience, perceiving and learning what is accommodated by his or her life style. Adler called this a "private logic."

### All Behavior Is Purposeful

Adler maintained that all behavior is purposeful and goal directed, although the individual may not always be consciously aware of having such motives. He observed that the children of deaf parents would "throw" a temper tantrum utilizing all the typical facial and bodily gestures but without making a sound. It was obvious that screaming was of no consequence to deaf parents. Adler concluded that a person does not "lose" his or her temper, but rather "throws" it away for such purposes as putting others into his or her service, punishing others, demanding attention, displaying frustrations and inadequacies, etc. By seeking to discover the payoff or purpose of behavior, group leaders can more readily understand dysfunctional behavior displayed by group members.

Related to the Adlerians' belief that people engage in behavior that is most effective in meeting their purposes is a concern with *use*, as in "What does one do with ability?," rather than with *possession*, as in "What skills does one have?"

### The Striving for Significance Explains Motivation

Adler is probably best known for the concepts of "inferiority complex" and "strivings for success." His premise was simply that as a result of its initial helplessness, an infant feels inferior and strives to overcome a feeling of incompletion by developing to a higher level. Feeling inferior and compensating for that feeling becomes the dynamic principle of motivation, moving an individual from one level of development to another. The striving continues throughout life as what Adler called "the great upward drive" toward perfection. Overcompensation for feelings of inferiority was another Adlerian concept.

Adler coined the term "masculine protest" to indicate the cultural problems involved where men dominated or were deemed superior to women. Dreikurs (1946) further explains conceptualization within children by noting, "The phantom of masculine superiority intimidates boys by imposing on them an obligation which they can never expect to fulfill and invites girls to rebel against their secondary role." He also spoke of the fallacy of glamor and chivalry, noting they were merely indications of superior and inferior interrelationships. Adlerian writings on "cooperation between the sexes" can be found in Ansbacher and Ansbacher (1978).

An inferiority complex results when special difficulties of incapability, constant discouragement from others, or faulty self-evaluations relative to one's own feelings of worth are put in the path of normal development.

Adlerians ask, "How is the person seeking to be known?" Dreikurs (1953) envisioned a "vertical versus the horizontal plane." Persons operating on the vertical plane continually measure themselves as either "better than" or "worse than" others on every dimension, resulting in interpersonal relationships that are either "one up" or "one down." A much more useful interpersonal orientation is illustrated by the "horizontal" plane whereby each person is recognized by his or her different and unique attributes.

## GOALS OF ADLERIAN COUNSELING

Adlerian counseling is characterized by the following four developmental phases.

### The Relationship

An Adlerian counselor initially seeks to establish an equal relationship, a collaborative effort between two or more active partners who are working toward mutually agreeable goals. This kind of relationship can be developed and maintained only by the mutual trust and respect of the counselor and the client or the group members.

Carkhuff (1980) said that such a relationship is built during the facilitation phase of counseling, which is characterized by the following behaviors:

- *Unconditional Positive Regard.* There are no conditions placed on the relationship such as: "You would be O.K., if you would only . . . "
- *Genuineness.* The counselor and client are two equals—real people—not a "healthy" therapist and a "sick" patient.
- *Empathy.* The counselor accurately perceives the feelings, thoughts, and attitudes of the client, including the client's "feeling tone" toward the environment.
- *Self-Disclosure.* Relevant personal information is freely volunteered.
- *Concreteness.* The counselor and client talk about specific concerns rather than vague abstractions.

People who are experiencing interpersonal conflicts may have difficulty in forming close relationships. This makes the counseling process an important first step for the client toward social living. It also makes the counseling relationship an ongoing task because the counselor must continue to earn the confidence of the client.

The reality of the relationship between the client and the counselor can threaten the client's self-esteem or methods of relating to people. Shulman (1973) noted that the client's fear of disapproval—of being exposed and found defective—may interfere with the counseling relationship. He listed the following defenses used by clients to "defeat" the counselor or to "save" their self-esteem:

1. Externalization: *The fault lies outside me,* including:
   - Cynicism: *Life is at fault.*
   - Inadequacy: *I am just an innocent victim.*
   - Rebellion: *I cannot afford to submit to life.*
   - Projection: *It is all their fault.*
2. Blind Spots: *If I don't look at it, it will go away.*
3. Excessive Self-Control: *I will not let anything upset me.*
4. Arbitrary Rightness: *My mind is made up; don't confuse me with facts.*

5. Elusiveness and Confusion: *Don't pin me down.*
6. Contribution and Self-Disparagement: *I am always wrong.*
7. Suffering as Manipulation: *I suffer to control others.*

All such defenses have the potential for destroying the counselor-client relationship.

## Psychological Investigation

After establishing trust and agreeing on their future goals and methods, the counselor and client move next into psychological investigation (Eckstein, Baruth, & Mahrer, 1978). This phase of Adlerian counseling is a discussion of the client's subjective and objective situations:

- The *subjective situation* includes the client's feelings and concerns—complaints, problems, and symptoms.
- The *objective situation* carries the investigation to how the client is functioning in such basic areas as work, relationships, and moral-ethical beliefs. The relationships discussed may be with friends, with the opposite sex, or with a deity.

Having established the subjective and objective situation, the counselor links both sets of information by asking the client what Dreikurs (1953) called The Question: "What would be different if you had all these problems or concerns solved?" The client's answer to such a question helps explain the purpose or payoff for complaints and emotional stresses. It also indicates in what area the person is experiencing difficulty and where or on whom the problem is centered.

At this point the counselor is ready to conduct a "life-style investigation" and to administer other psychometric tests, such as interest, achievement, aptitude, and personality inventories that are deemed helpful. The person's family atmosphere provides clues as to how his or her place in the initial social group was achieved. Early recollections represent subjective personal conclusions, "filtered" by the child from external, environmental circumstances. Such recollections coincide with the individual's current outlook. The family atmosphere of the client and his or her early recollections are analyzed for crucial attitudes concerning "Life is . . . , Others are . . . , I am . . . ."

## Interpretation

When the counselor and the client are in the interpretation phase of counseling, they share their basic attitudes about life, self, and others. The consistent emphasis in their dialog is on goals and purposes, rather than on causes or why people act the way they do.

During interpretation, the counselor is concerned with increasing the client's awareness of his or her:

1. Life style;
2. Current psychological movement and its direction;
3. Goals, purposes, and intentions; and
4. Private logic and how it works.

Their discussion of the client's private logic includes its implications for the client's present and future activities. They also confront the discrepancies between the words that are expressed and the actions that are taken and between the ideal goals that are stated and the real goals that are sought. The client begins to experience insight into his or her true intentions—what is really desired—by examining the specific means he or she employs and the ends, or goals, they produce. This examination of the client's life style allows the counselor to specifically refer to self-defeating ideas that are dysfunctional in the person's life.

According to Dinkmeyer, Pew, and Dinkmeyer (1979), an Adlerian systematic summary would include identification of the following:

1. The individual's problems and feelings of deficiency;
2. Directions taken by the individual to overcome the perceived deficiency;

3. The relationship between such direction and cooperative social interest;
4. Specific areas of difficulty the individual experiences with life tasks;
5. How the individual is avoiding the resolution of problems;
6. How the individual manages to feel superior while avoiding confrontation of problems; and
7. Contributing influences from the individual's past history.

Such an interpretive summary should also use support and encouragement to identify the individual's strengths and assets. Adler disapproved of the "red-pencil mentality" of a therapist who constantly analyzes a client's deficits and liabilities. "We build on strengths, not on weaknesses," was the reminder that Adler continually gave to his counselor trainees.

## Reorientation

In the final phase of Adlerian counseling, reorientation, the counselor and client work together to consider alternative beliefs, behaviors, and attitudes—a change in the client's life style. Specific reference is made to the "subjective" concerns stated by the client during the life-style investigation. A particular Adlerian technique involves what Nikelly (1971) described as "stroke and spit tactics." "Stroking" is synonymous with encouragement, caring, and other "powerful invitations" directed from the counselor to the client. An example of an encouragement workshop is included later in the article.

While providing encouragement to the client, reorientation also consists of what Adler called "spitting in the soup." A bowl of soup will not be enticing to a soup lover if someone contaminates it with spittle. Similarly, the counselor uses the life-style summary of the individual's goals and private logic to reveal faulty beliefs and self-defeating behavior. Once these are acknowledged in the counseling dialog, the client is consciously aware of them. Although the individual may continue to engage in the self-defeating behaviors, they probably will not be as pleasurable as before—they have been contaminated.

### Faulty Cognitions

Utilizing the "basic mistakes" of Adler, the "irrational beliefs" of Ellis (1973), and the "cognitive deficiencies" of Beck (1970), Kern et al. (1978) compiled the following list of faulty cognitions:

1. *Casual Inference.* Making an unjustifiable jump in logic by drawing a conclusion from evidence that is either insufficient or actually contrary to the conclusion reached.

2. *Blowup.* Tending to exaggerate or magnify the meaning of an event out of proportion to the actual situation; generating a general rule from a single incident. ("I made a mess of my relationship with Ellen. I guess you could consider me a real social bust.")

3. *All-or-Nothing Thinking.* Thinking in extremes; allowing only two possibilities— good or bad, right or wrong, always or never. ("People never have a good time with me.")

4. *Responsibility Projection.* Failing to assume responsibility for one's emotional state ("This course is causing me to have a nervous breakdown!") or for one's personal worth.("If my parents had only made me study in high school, I'd have been able to qualify for college.")

5. *Perfectionistic Thinking.* Making idealistic demands on oneself. ("I made a D on that test; I'm so stupid!")

6. *Value-Tainted Thinking.* Couching a statement in such terms as "good," "bad," " worthless," "should," "ought," or "must." ("I must get into medical school or I won't be able to look my father in the eye.")

7. *Self-Depreciation.* Focusing on punitive self-statements rather than task orientation. ("I hate myself for not being able to break this habit.")

## Correcting Faulty Thinking

Once clients discover the illogical aspect of their thinking, they generally are motivated to make changes in their personal private logic that will render it more functional. According to Kern et al. (1978, pp. 21-22), the correction of self-defeating, private logic includes the following steps:

1. Asking the client to describe only the facts of the actual situation that gave rise to an expression of the faulty thinking ("I made a 78 on my freshman composition exam") and to omit the self-defeating statement (". . . and I know I'm just going to flunk out of college"). In this way, the reality of the situation is separated from the individual's personal conclusion.

2. Asking the client to generate alternative explanations for the situation that triggered the illogical conclusion. The student making the 78 on the composition exam could have concluded, "I made a high C when I'm used to making A's, and this discrepancy is disappointing. I guess I'll just have to study much harder if I am to meet my expectations."

The client is told to avoid being the direct object or the subject of a passive verb. In the case of responsibility projection, the personal statement is to be reconstructed in such a way that the client becomes the subject of an active verb. For example, the statement "My roommate makes me so mad when she doesn't hang up her clothes " could become: "When my roommate doesn't hang up her clothes, I become very angry because I'm telling myself that she should meet my expectations and something's wrong with me since I can't get her to do better. Clearly, my roommate is not doing it to me—I'm doing it to myself!"

3. Asking the client to design a positive course of action based on the more reasonable of his or her alternative explanations. This technique is used to assist clients to recognize the poor fit between many of their fictions and reality and to practice a more responsible kind of self-talk.

## ADLERIAN COUNSELING SKILLS

Counseling skills used by Adlerians include active listening, goal alignment ("Is this the person you want to be?"), reflection of feelings and empathic understanding, confrontation, interpretation and encouragement, and the following steps:

### Paradoxical Intention

There is a technique that was called "prescribing the symptom" by Adler, "antisuggestion" by Dreikurs, and "paradoxical intention" by Frankl (1971). It is a technique in which clients are encouraged to emphasize their symptoms or develop them even more. For example, a person who is afraid of losing consciousness may be asked to try "passing out." Bringing humor into the situation, the counselor adds, "Come on now, pass out all over the place." When people discover that they cannot intentionally do what they had feared would happen to them, they are often able to laugh at the situation. The counselor then may attempt to assure such persons that "since it is impossible to pass out here on purpose, why should you pass out any other place?" Frankl said such an intervention "takes the wind out of the sails" of the fear.

### Acting "As If"

When a client says, "If only I could . . . ," the counselor suggests that the client pretend or "act as if" it were possible to be that way. Mosak and Dreikurs (1973, p. 60) suggested that "We show him that all acting is not phony pretense, that he is being asked to try on a role as one might try on a suit. It doesn't change the person wearing the suit, but sometimes with a handsome suit of clothes, he may feel differently and perhaps behave differently, in which case he becomes a different person."

### Catching Oneself

As individuals become aware of their purposeful goals, they are encouraged to "catch themselves" engaging in any behavior they want to change. Initially, it may be after the fact when they think, "There I go again." Eventually, however, they are able to anticipate, and thereby alter, the undesirable behavior.

## Creating Movement

Introducing the element of surprise by doing the unexpected can help encourage clients to consider a change in behavior or attitude, although judicious use of the technique by the counselor is advised. In the following example, the counselor momentarily assumes the client's faulty logic:

Sam: Whenever I join groups, it is always the same—I reach out in a trusting manner, and then someone always hurts me by being insensitive. I'm leaving this group.

Counselor: Yes, all groups are that way. I suggest a safer, nonthreatening place for you.

Such an intervention would obviously be inappropriate if stated in a sarcastic manner. However, if the counselor briefly mirrors or agrees with such faulty either/or overgeneralizations as well as the "I can't handle being hurt" feelings, then perhaps the client can recognize the mistaken belief more easily.

## Goal Setting and Commitment

Whatever the theoretical approach, an essential task of counseling relates to behavior and attitude change. Each counseling session should conclude with specific homework assignments concerned with observable behaviors. McKay (1976) suggested that a "change card" be written on an index card with the following instructions on one side:

This week I will . . . (be specific, remember, "think small"). I can sabotage my commitment by . . . (your own special means). I will evaluate my commitment on . . . (time and day).

The reverse side of the card is used by the client to chart daily progress. The client is advised by the counselor to focus this evaluation on what is accomplished and not to dwell on mistakes. If things did not go as well as you would like, analyze possible reasons: Did I expect too much of myself? Did I sabotage my commitment? How? Make a new commitment based on your discovery. (p.16)

## SPECIFIC APPLICATIONS FOR GROUP LEADERS

In an excellent chapter on group counseling and psychotherapy, Dinkmeyer, Pew, and Dinkmeyer (1979) extended Adlerian theory of behavior to the therapeutic group:

1. All behavior has social meaning; therefore, all transactions among group members have a social direction and a social intention.

2. All behavior can best be understood in holistic terms; therefore, group members should be encouraged to become aware of one another's life styles.

3. With their recognition that all behavior is purposeful, group members discover that while words may be deceiving, a person's behavior reveals direction and intention. A group member may express a desire to change, but the other members soon learn to pay attention and respond more to what that person actually does.

4. The group can serve as a microcosm, aiding members in discovering how they find a place in this group and all other groups.

5. Positive psychological development is based on each individual's capacity to belong to the group, to make a commitment, to engage in the give-and-take of life, and to extend his or her social interest.

6. Because each group member is responding on the basis of a personal phenomenological field, the members should be encouraged to understand how their subjective perceptions influence their feelings and behavior.

## Group-Leader Competencies

Specific competencies needed by group leaders include the "core conditions of helping" of Carkhuff (warmth, genuineness, positive regard, etc.) and the following skills listed by Dinkmeyer, Pew, and Dinkmeyer (1979):

- Structuring the group and communicating its purpose
- Utilizing interaction exercises and programs effectively
- Universalizing
- Dealing with the here-and-now interaction
- Linking
- Confronting
- Blocking
- Encouraging and focusing on assets and positive feedback
- Facilitating participation by confronting nonverbal clues
- Facilitating "I" messages
- Paraphrasing and clarifying to stimulate reality testing
- Offering feedback
- Formulating tentative hypotheses
- Setting tasks and getting commitment
- Capping and summarizing

## ADLERIAN GROUP APPROACHES AND RESOURCES

Adlerians stress that all behavior has social implications. It is, therefore, only logical that groups characterize the essence of their psychology. Several representative group approaches are identified and briefly described here, along with Adlerian workshop designs that reflect important contributions to the profession.

### Parent Education and Family Therapy

Books offering the Adlerian approach are in heavy demand for parent education and family therapy (e.g., Dreikurs & Soltz, 1964). A noteworthy characteristic of such parent meetings is that by using an accompanying study guide, lay (nonpsychologist) parents can rotate as discussion-group leaders. Churches and parent-teacher associations have shown much enthusiasm in sponsoring such groups. Other widely used books include: Dinkmeyer and McKay (1973), Corsini and Painter (1975), and a structured group experience by Dinkmeyer and McKay (1976).

One of the first steps in parent education is learning to understand the four goals of a child's misbehavior that Dreikurs (1957) defined as: undue attention, power, revenge, and display of inadequacy. When undue attention is the goal, the child is saying "I only count when you pay attention to me." Parents usually feel frustrated or annoyed by such an "ever-present child." When corrected or scolded the child may stop temporarily, but then resumes the behavior later for the same purpose—to get the parent involved. Specific methods of change include suggesting to the parents that they ignore the misbehavior, do the unexpected, or give attention at pleasant times.

When mistakenly seeking the goal of power, a child is saying "I am significant only when I am dominating others." Parents generally react to this with anger, revealing their feelings to the child with raised voice, clenched jaw, or sharp language ("I'll make you do it! You won't get away with that!"). In such a power struggle, parental reprimands merely intensify the child's actions. It may be suggested to parents that they should try to extricate themselves; to act, not talk; to be friendly and establish equality; to redirect the child's efforts into more constructive channels.

Revenge is one of the most discouraging mistaken goals of children. Basically the child's life stance is "I can't be liked and I don't have power, but my significance comes from my abusing others as much as I have been abused." Parents who feel hurt or angry may react with "How could you do this to me?" When disciplined by the parent, such a child may try to get even or display behaviors that put him or her in even more disfavor. Suggested corrective measures include winning the child by avoiding retaliations, realizing that such discouragement takes time and effort to overcome, and maintaining order with minimal restraint.

Children who say, "I can't do it right so I won't try to do anything at all," are displaying inadequacy. Their parents may report a feeling of despair, saying, "I've tried everything, so I give up." Specific suggestions for improving such a condition are given in the principles of encouragement, described later in the sample workshop design.

Helping parents to become aware of a child's mistaken goals and to learn how they can transform such misbehavior is an important first step in family counseling when it is coupled with additional family constellation information. Dinkmeyer and McKay (1976) suggest transforming a child's mistaken approaches into the following goals of positive behavior: "I belong by contributing. I can decide and be responsible for my behavior. I am interested in cooperating. I can decide to withdraw from conflict."

## Teacher Consultation

Attitudes toward discipline are changing, as reflected in the language used by teachers. Baruth and Eckstein (1976) stated that the traditional language of power (control, direct, punish, threaten, setting limits, policing, enforcing, laying down the law, being tough, reprimanding, scolding, ordering, or demanding) is being replaced by a new problem-solving vocabulary (conflict resolution, influencing, confronting, collaboration, cooperation, joint decision making, working out contracts with students, obtaining mutual agreements, winning students over, or agreeing to disagree). Baruth and Eckstein offered information on developing techniques for rectifying misbehavior, improving the classroom atmosphere, and utilizing classroom meetings to solve problems.

The approach suggested by Dinkmeyer and Carlson (1973) utilizes group process ("C" group consultations) and focuses on the following techniques:

- *Consultation* that is provided and received by all the group members.
- *Collaboration* on the concerns of the group members, who work together as equals.
- *Cooperation* among members, so that encouragement can be offered and received.
- *Clarification* of the concepts under discussion, as well as of the members' belief systems and feelings.
- *Confrontation* of the purposes, attitudes, beliefs, and feelings that interfere with the successful modification of the parent-child relationship. If change is to occur, confrontation of old, useless beliefs must take place. A norm of confrontation—not to prove who is right but to share discrepancies and observations—is established by the group leader at the beginning of the group.
- *Confidentiality* that assures the members that what they say in confidence will be shared only by the group.
- *Commitment* to the tasks confronting each member that goes beyond reading the assignment and discussing it at the next meeting of the group.
- *Change*, as the purpose of involvement in the group, is assessed by each member in specific terms that evaluate both the goals and the rate of change.

Dinkmeyer (1970) is also used by many elementary school systems. His kit contains a variety of experiential activities, including: role playing, puppetry, group discussion, and problem situations, plus music and art activities, and suggested reading lists.

## Marriage Counseling

Investigating, interpreting, and summarizing the life styles of a husband and wife can increase their interpersonal understanding. Dreikurs (1946) suggested four principles of conflict resolution that are useful in marriage counseling: (1) showing mutual respect, (2) pinpointing the issue, (3) reaching a new agreement, and (4) participating in decision making. Additional marital counseling strategies and resources are available in Dinkmeyer, Pew, and Dinkmeyer (1979).

## REPRESENTATIVE ADLERIAN GROUP DESIGNS

### Early Recollections

Two Adlerian contributions that are significant for group facilitators are (1) the influence of birth order and family constellation on personality and (2) the relation of early recollections (ER) to interpersonal and intrapersonal conflicts. Eckstein (1980) notes the following uses for ER in group settings:

1. The sharing of early recollections can be included as an option in a group program of relatively nonthreatening introductory activities. Subgroups of two or three persons can become better acquainted by sharing spontaneous ER caricatures of themselves, a "life-line," descriptive adjectives, superlatives, or other demographic information.

2. Early recollections can provide useful data regarding values, conflicts, and behavioral goals for growth for participants to use in subsequent group sessions.

3. Because of their simplicity and the brief amount of time needed for analyzing them, early recollections can also be used for mass investigation of a total group. For instance, when coupled with data from such instruments as the inclusion-control-affection paradigm of FIRO-B (Schutz, 1966), facilitators may vary intervention styles and workshop design according to the particular individual and/or group climate. For example, rigid structured activities could receive resistance from group participants who have a low desire for control, as measured by the FIRO-B. Early recollections can provide an additional "climate-sensing" source of data for facilitators.

4. Early recollections can serve as indicators of therapeutic growth and the positive consequences of group counseling. A crucial Adlerian theoretical notion regarding ERs is that during the course of therapy either an entirely new set of memories will be recalled by the client, or an objective recollection will be accompanied by different subjective personal reaction (Dreikurs, 1967; Eckstein, 1976; Nikelly, 1971). Thus, pre/post ERs (recorded before and after counseling) can supplement other psychometric and impressionistic data in validating the personal growth of participants.

Eckstein (1980) integrates ERs and guided imagery as a means of integrating intrapersonal exploration. A group leader instructs participants to close their eyes, relax, and imagine the following:

> Go back in your life to a particularly pleasant or positive moment. How does it feel? What is happening? Who else is there? Now let that image fade away and go back in your life to an unpleasant or negative experience. How does it feel? What is happening? What makes the memory different from the first one? If you could change this event, what would you do? Now give yourself the ability to make the change. How does it feel? How are you different? Now let that image fade away and with your eyes closed, reflect on the memory of this experience for you. Now come back to this room. Open your eyes and silently write down your impressions. (pp. 80-90)

Participants are then invited to each select a partner and share any parts of their fantasy they choose to disclose. Total group discussion, processing, and application conclude the exercise and often lead to individual sharing and intensive counseling/therapy. Possible therapeutic consequences of this activity for participants include: implications for the present and future, identification of unfinished business with oneself or with significant others, recognition of irrational self-defeating attitudes, plus growth and healing.

## Encouragement Lab

O'Connell (1975) described the procedure used in a typical one-day encouragement lab as follows:

1. *Mixing.* The group participants are instructed to mill about nonverbally, select partners, and arrange themselves in two groups.
2. *Thinking about methods by which you can encourage others.* The facilitator has the group members relax and imagine acts of encouragement and possible dangers of encouraging.
3. *Stopping, looking and listening to one another.* The members form dyads. A interviews B on how B wants to be encouraged and what fears B has concerning such encouragement. B later interviews A on the same theme. Then the As move to the center of the room and the Bs observe. The As talk about their partners' views of encouragement. Later, the Bs give feedback on whether the As were correct. The process is reversed, with the Bs moving to the center.
4. *Clarify content, guess at feelings.* The Bs interview the As to rate them on self-esteem and social interest. Each B has already rated himself or herself independently. The facilitator calls time periodically to have the Bs paraphrase the As' content and guess at their feelings. The members describe difficulties they had in following the task. They share their ratings, discuss the evidence used and the reasons for differences between the raters. Then the process is reversed with A interviewing B.
5. *Lecturette on how to lower self-esteem and social interest.* The facilitator describes behavioral signs and their purposes and presents a lecturette on the three Cs of interdependence:

   All persons are *constricted* in that no one creates an optimal self-esteem and social interest. We are all *creative* in maintaining our life styles by making old inferences in new situations. We all *cooperate* in reinforcing behaviors and attitudes, even though we would like to think of ourselves as independent when successful or at the mercy of fate when we fail.
6. *Natural high.* Each participant projects the self-esteem and social interest he or she will have one year from now and rates them. A interviews B, and later B interviews A to find out what evidence the partner used to constrict the self at a future time. Interview questions include: How does the partner select and arrange the constricting environment? How can the partner move to prevent constriction?
7. *Practice in reinforcement.* The facilitator role plays types of constricted individuals, creatively searching for reinforcement of the constriction. The members of one group try to encourage one another while another group watches and later gives feedback. All groups have a chance for action.
8. *Sense of humor.* The facilitator in each group writes a list of highly stressful situations, and the group selects one. Through psychodramatic techniques, the facilitator illustrates feelings and behaviors that make a situation stressful for an individual. Other members model humorous responses to the situation that make the scene relatively nonstressful.

Frank Walton (1975) describes an adolescent minilife group workshop that is based on an unpublished model developed by Bob Powers.

## SUMMARY

Adlerian psychology is given much practical usage by group facilitators who represent varied humanistic theoretical orientations. O'Connell (1976) refers to such contemporary theorists as Viktor Frankl, Colin Wilson, Ernest Becker, Ira Progoff, Rollo May, and Werner Erhard, as characterized by a "yes, but" attitude toward Adlerian principles. Although all these "friends" acknowledge the use of many of Adler's ideas in their own systems, they add qualifying statements to their similarities.

Current Adlerian psychology is experiencing a rapid growth by attracting related practitioners who are interested in the useful contributions of Adlerian theory and practice. The North American Society of Adlerian Psychology (NASAP) coordinates activities in the United States and Canada. Additional information, membership forms, and book orders for all Adlerian publications referenced in this article may be obtained from the North American Society of Adlerian Psychology, 159 N. Dearborn Street, Chicago, Illinois 60601 or the International Association of Individual Psychology, c/o Dr. Marvin Nelson, 8 Valley View Terrace, Suffern, New York 10901.

### REFERENCES

Adler, A. Nochmals—Die Einheit der Neurosen. *International Journal of Individual Psychology*, 1930, *8*, 201-216.

Ansbacher, H., & Ansbacher, R. *Cooperation between the sexes: Writings on women love and marriage, sexuality and its disorders.* Garden City, NY: Doubleday, 1978.

Baruth, L., & Eckstein, D. *The ABC's of classroom discipline.* Dubuque, IA: Kendall Hunt, 1976.

Baruth, L., & Eckstein, D. *Life style: Theory, practice, and research.* Dubuque, IA: Kendall Hunt, 1978.

Beck, A. Cognitive therapy: Nature and relation to behavior therapy. *Behavior Therapy*, 1970, *1*, 184-200.

Carkhuff, R. *The art of helping IV.* Amherst, MA: Human Resource Development Press, 1980.

Combs, A. Counseling as a learning process. *Journal of Counseling Psychology*, 1954, *1*(1), 31-36.

Corsini, R., & Painter, G. *The practical parent: The ABC's of child discipline.* New York: Harper & Row, 1975.

Dinkmeyer, D. *Developing understanding of self and others (DUSO).* Circle Pines, MN: American Guidance Service, 1970.

Dinkmeyer, D., & Carlson, J. *Counseling: Facilitating human potential and change processes.* Columbus, OH: Merrill, 1973.

Dinkmeyer, D., & McKay, G. *Raising a responsible child.* New York: Simon & Schuster, 1973.

Dinkmeyer, D., & McKay, G. *Systematic training for effective parenting (STEP).* Circle Pines, MN: American Guidance Service, 1976.

Dinkmeyer, D., Pew, W., & Dinkmeyer, D. *Adlerian counseling and psychotherapy.* Monterey, CA: Brooks-Cole, 1979.

Dreikurs, R. *The challenge of marriage.* New York: Hawthorn, 1946.

Dreikurs, R. *Fundamentals of Adlerian psychology.* Chicago: Alfred Adler Institute, 1953.

Dreikurs, R. *Psychology in the classroom.* New York: Harper & Row, 1957.

Dreikurs, R. *Psychodynamics, psychotherapy & counseling.* Chicago: Alfred Adler Institute, 1967.

Dreikurs, R., & Soltz, V. *Children: The challenge.* New York: Hawthorn, 1964.

Eckstein, D. Early recollection changes after counseling: A case study. *Journal of Individual Psychology*, 1976, *32*(2), 212-223.

Eckstein, D., Baruth, L., & Mahrer, D. *Life style: What it is and how to do it.* Dubuque, IA: Kendall Hunt, 1978.

Eckstein, D. The use of early recollections in group counseling. *Journal of Specialists in Group Work*, 1980, *5*(2), 87-92.

Ellis, A. *Humanistic psychotherapy: The national emotive approach.* New York: Julian Press, 1973.

Frankl, V. *The doctor and the soul.* New York: Bantam, 1971.

Gazda, G. *Basic approaches to group psychotherapy and group counseling.* Springfield, IL.: Charles C Thomas, 1975.

Kern, et al. *A case for Adlerian counseling.* Chicago: Alfred Adler Institute, 1978.

McKay, G. *The basics of encouragement.* Coral Springs, FL: CMTI Press, 1976.

Mosak, H., Early recollections as a projective technique. *Journal of Projective Techniques*, 1958, *22*, 302-311.

Mosak, H. *On purpose.* Chicago: Alfred Adler Institute, 1977.

Mosak, H., & Dreikurs, R. Adlerian psychotherapy. In R. Corsini (Ed.), *Current psychotherapies.* Itasca, IL.: F.E. Peacock, 1973.

Nikelly, A. (Ed.). *Techniques for behavior change.* Springfield, IL: Charles C Thomas, 1971.

O'Connel, W. *Action therapy and Adlerian theory.* Chicago: Alfred Adler Institute, 1975.

O'Connel, W. The "friends of Adler" phenomenon. *Journal of Individual Psychology*, 1976, *32*(1), 5-17.

Pfeiffer, J.W. & Jones, J.E. (Eds.). *A handbook of structured experiences for human relations training* (Vols. I-VIII). San Diego, CA: University Associates, 1974-1981.

Reiner, C. Some words of encouragement. In *Study group leader's manual*. Chicago: Alfred Adler Institute, 1967.

Schutz, W. *Fundamental interpersonal relations orientation-behavior*. Palo Alto, CA: Consulting Psychologists Press, 1966.

Shulman, B. Confrontation techniques in Adlerian psychotherapy. In B. Shulman (Ed.), *Contributions to individual psychology*. Chicago: Alfred Adler Institute, 1973.

Walton, F. Group workshop with adolescents. *The Individual Psychologist*, 1975, *12*(1), 26-28.

***Daniel G. Eckstein, Ph.D.**, is assistant professor of psychology at the School of Human Behavior, United States International University, and serves as director of the university's counseling clinic. He is co-author of* Life Style: What It Is and How To Do It, Life Style: Theory, Practice, and Research, *and* The ABC's of Classroom Discipline. *His current professional interests include laboratory education, human relations training, life-style assessment, and living/dying/grieving.*

# AN OVERVIEW OF TEN MANAGEMENT AND ORGANIZATIONAL THEORISTS

## Marshall Sashkin

> What is called for is a complete mental revolution on the part of workers and on the part of managers, such that both take their eyes off the division of profit and together turn toward increasing the size of the profit, until it becomes so large that it is unnecessary to quarrel over how it shall be divided.[1]

The above statement is paraphrased from one of the ten management and organizational theorists who will be discussed in this paper. Although the comment may sound idealistic, even humanistic, it is derived from the writing of Frederick Taylor, the father of "scientific management" and a man whom one would never describe as a "humanist" after even a casual inspection of his words and deeds. Most texts cover the details of various management theories reasonably well, explaining the nature of Taylor's "scientific management," and Fayol's "basic functions" of management, defining Weber's elements of bureaucracy, and so on. However, it is possible to really understand what a theory is "all about" only if one has some understanding of the individual who created it. So, although it is not possible to fully describe or explore the creative, complex people who developed the theories and approaches discussed in this brief article, it is possible—and should be interesting—to look at what they said, how they behaved (or are reported to have behaved), and the consistency (or lack of it) between each individual's thoughts and actions. The latter, according to Argyris (1976), tells much about the person. This comparison will be made in the context of the historical periods in which these various individuals lived and worked and will focus on the periods of their greatest influence. (Table 1 shows the chronological progression of these influences.)

**Table 1. Periods of Greatest Influence of Ten Management and Organizational Theorists**

| Theorist(s) | Period of Greatest Influence |
|---|---|
| Historical Management | pre-1900 |
| Frederick W. Taylor | 1890-1915 |
| Henri Fayol | 1890-1920 |
| Max Weber | 1885-1920 |
| Elton Mayo | 1910-1940 |
| Fritz Roethlisberger and W.J. Dickson | 1925-1955 |
| Douglas McGregor | 1945-1965 |
| Rensis Likert | 1955-1975 |
| Fred Emery and Eric Trist | 1965-Present |

[1]See "Hearings Before Special Committee of the House of Representatives . . . " in reference list.

## Historical Management Theory (Pre-1900)

Ancient organizations were considerably more simple than those in which we live and work today. The archetype is the tribe, ruled by a religious leader-authority figure who is obeyed by all. Such a system becomes unwieldy when two conditions occur: (a) the group size increases beyond a dozen or so and (b) the work to be done becomes more complicated than the most primitive of tasks (foraging for food, setting up shelters, etc.). Thus, in a very old text, the Bible, we find a clear description of organizational change. Moses found that he could not cope with being the only leader of the Israelites; the job was too complex, and he simply did not have the time to give instructions to every single person. So he named a group of leaders, each of whom was responsible for ten persons. For every ten "leaders of tens," there was a leader of tens of tens, or hundreds. Thus, an early hierarchy was developed.

Of course, the hierarchical structure that is characteristic of most organizations is even older than the one developed by Moses, but it is important to note that hierarchies taller than Moses' were rare in the ancient world. For example, the Roman armies, and others, usually contained captains who led anywhere from a few dozen to a few hundred men. The captains reported to a general, who was often the head of the army. Sometimes a very large—or very sophisticated—force might include sub-captains (lieutenants) or "junior" generals who reported to the chief general, but even then the hierarchy would be relatively flat, a characteristic of most organizations throughout history. During the past few centuries, and even in the last century, a typical small factory was organized like a feudal estate. Figure 1 depicts this similarity.

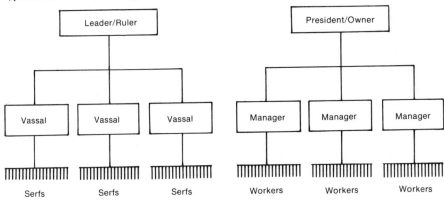

A: TRADITIONAL FEUDAL STRUCTURE
(circa 1500 A.D.)

B: TRADITIONAL ORGANIZATION STRUCTURE
(circa 1875 A.D.)

**Figure 1. Traditional Structures**

As the world changed, the traditional form of organizational hierarchy began to malfunction because of problems that it was not designed to handle. It could not accommodate the complex interdependencies with which organizations were confronted as technology advanced. Well before 1900, it was clear that most organizations could not operate effectively within this framework. It was around the turn of the century that three men developed modifications of the traditional structure in an effort to aid organizational functioning. This paper will present these three men in an artificial order, since they were truly contemporaries and the extent to which they influenced each other is not known.

## Frederick W. Taylor: Individually Centered Structure

The author of the statement that is paraphrased at the beginning of this article was a complex and, frequently, contradictory person. He believed that by applying his precepts for the scientific analysis and design of jobs, labor and management cooperatively could create a profit large enough to provide ample remuneration for both the workers and the manufacturer. In contrast, Taylor's own description of a worker, in an experiment to increase efficiency, is: "One of the very first requirements for a man who is fit to handle pig-iron . . . is that he shall be so stupid . . . that he more nearly resembles in his mental make-up the ox than any other type" (Hearings, 1912). In instructing this man, Taylor told him, "If you are a high-priced man, you will do exactly as [you are told] . . . from morning till night. When [told] to pick up a pig and walk, you pick it up and you walk. . . . When [told] to sit down and rest, you sit down. . . . And what's more, no back talk" (Taylor, 1911, p. 46). Finally, returning to the issue of the profit so large that there would be no need to argue over its division between labor and management, Upton Sinclair, a popular "expose" writer of the time, noted that Taylor "gave about 61 percent increase in wages, and got 362 percent increase in work" (Copley, 1923, p. 30).

Aside from this view of how to divide increased profits fairly, it is clear that Taylor and his followers went overboard in fractionating jobs by time and motion study. Taylor's approach, however, was for many years the defining characteristic of modern industrial work, and many industries still use time-and-motion-study methods to design jobs. It was years before people began to realize the tremendous psychological damage that was done to hundreds of thousands of workers by carrying these methods to an extreme. Ultimately, Taylor's approach led down a dead-end path.

Although Taylor's success was not in dealing with large-scale organizational structures, he did have some interesting, and quite radical, ideas. He would have done away with the principle of chain of command, or one worker/one boss. In his design, shown in Figure 2, each worker was supervised by a number of "functional foremen" who were expert teacher/trainers rather than the traditional overseers. Taylor's idea of the functional foreman failed; it was never fully implemented and was soon forgotten for two reasons: it threatened management/supervisory notions of control, and it was a far more complex design than was warranted by the nature of jobs at the time (1890-1910).

Years later, a somewhat changed version of Taylor's ideal structure would be known as a "matrix" organization (Davis & Lawrence, 1977). Even so, these organizations differ substantially from Taylor's model because jobs are typically complex and technically demanding rather than fractionated and technically simple.

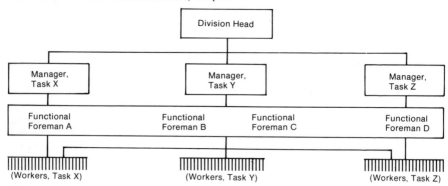

**Figure 2. Taylor's Ideal Structure**

Taylor's statements, then, sounded progressive but were not. He was enough of an influence, however, that Congress investigated him as a possible communist subversive. (This was at the time of the successful Russian revolution, when "red scares" were common in the U.S.) Taylor talked his way out of this, too, and continued, in his very successful career, to train the next generation of "time-study men."

In France, a contemporary of Taylor was also working on codification of management theory and was aware of Taylor's work. We will examine his achievements next.

## Henri Fayol: Organizationally Centered Structure

We describe Fayol as being concerned with the structure of the organization—large-scale structure—as opposed to a focus on task design or small-scale structure. But more than this, Fayol was a pragmatist. As head of a French steel-and-coal mining organization for thirty years, he developed a set of fourteen principles that he felt covered most managerial situations. It is not clear just how absolute Fayol meant to be about his principles—whether he intended them to be guidelines or powerful and stable laws. In one essay he wrote, "I became convinced that social phenomena are, like physical phenomena, subject to natural laws independent of our will" (Fayol, 1978). Yet, in his 1916 papers on general and industrial management he wrote, "There is nothing rigid or absolute in management affairs . . . seldom do we . . . apply the same principle twice in identical conditions. . . . Therefore principles are flexible and capable [of] adaptation" (Fayol, 1949, p. 19). As can be seen, later theorists who advocated absolute principles could appeal to Fayol—just as could those who favored more situationally flexible approaches. It was primarily the former type of theorist, however, who followed Fayol's lead in defining law-like principles.

Aside from creating the first set of principles of organization, Fayol added one small note to the traditional theory of organization, a note that was actually the first step toward major change in our view of organizational structure. In a traditional structure (Figure 1B) a worker at any level had only one primary interaction—with his or her supervisor. Fayol called this the "scalar" principle; in the military it is commonly referred to as "chain of command." Fayol, however, modified this principle significantly with still another principle, that of the "gangplank," which is illustrated in Figure 3 with the more recent label "Fayol's Bridge."

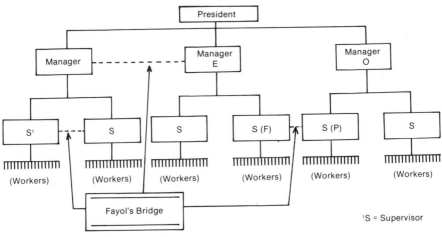

**Figure 3. Fayol's Modification of the Traditional Structure**

Fayol explains it thusly: "Imagine that department F has to be put in contact with department P . . . it is much simpler and quicker to go directly from F to P by making use of a 'gangplank' and that is what is most often done. The scalar principle will be safeguarded if managers E and O have authorized their respective subordinates F and P to deal directly" (Fayol, 1949, p. 35). This may seem ridiculously simple, but was revolutionary when Fayol was writing, at the beginning of the century.

Fayol was, in a pragmatic way, becoming aware of the increasing need for coordination in organizations, a need brought about by continuing technological development and one that could not be satisfied by traditional organizational structure. Fayol was, however, no radical; in fact, he strongly opposed Taylor's revision of the traditional structure as an unacceptable violation of the principle of chain of command.

Fayol's principles had a strong and lasting impact on the development of management thought in Europe and in England. His effect on American management was indirect, because his book did not appear in an easily obtainable English-language edition until 1949. Nevertheless, his work encouraged others to add more principles until, by the 1930s, some authors had developed hundreds of "principles of management."

Like his gangplank idea, Fayol's principles were generally sensible if sometimes a bit fuzzy. Unfortunately, later authors did not always have his depth of managerial experience, and their principles often were meaningless lists of trivia. In fact, management theory generally was the product of scholars and academics (such as Max Weber), rather than the result of contributions from managers.

## Max Weber: Organizationally and Societally Centered Structure

Weber was far more successful than Taylor in his approach to the analysis of organizational arrangements. Most social scientists would agree that Weber was a genius in his field. His name is most closely associated with "bureaucracy" (although he was also a great religious scholar), but bureaucracy was not his invention.

What Weber (1947) did was first codify (describe) and then slightly modify a system of organization as old as history. A complex, fairly efficient, and very stable bureaucracy has been the basis of the Chinese civilization for over 3000 years. Weber examined and analyzed in detail it and other bureaucratic systems that seemed to have been effective in terms of organizational survival and goal attainment, including the Catholic church and the Prussian army. Weber's analysis of the bureaucratic form, shown in Figure 4, was the first clear, detailed statement of organizational structure.

There were two modifications of the traditional structure in Weber's presentation. The first was the notion of authority based on a rational-legal system, rather than on tradition (e.g., hereditary rule) or force. In Weber's day, many (if not most) organizations—including business and industrial firms—assumed controls over workers that seem unbelievable today. These included not merely ten-, twelve-, or fourteen-hour working days, but also how the employees' free time might be spent and the assumption of absolute obedience to superiors, however irrational or nonwork related their orders. The concept of rational-legal authority prescribes clearly defined limits over what may and may not be required of workers. The second thing Weber defined was organizational arrangement as a hierarchy of *offices* rather than of individuals. That is, each "office" carries specified duties along with the legal authority to carry out those duties—no more and no less. The effect of this was twofold: first, the basis of authority—rational and legal—was emphasized and control over workers was limited to behavior specifically related to the work; second, the activities of the manager—duties, responsibilities, etc.—were clearly defined, thus making it possible to choose persons for specific jobs on the basis of their competence and skills.

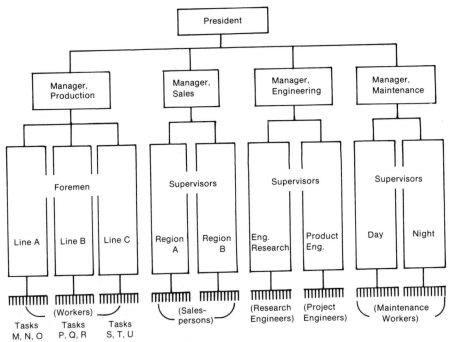

**Figure 4. Basic Bureaucratic Structure (Weber)**

Note that each position is defined as to specific tasks, duties, authority, and responsibility of the position (or "office"). Characteristics (skills, etc.) of persons necessary for each position are specified and any person with these characteristics may be hired to fill the position.

Although today people often react negatively to the term "bureaucracy," when reading Weber, one is aware that bureaucracy was a great invention. Weber (1946) says, for example, "The decisive reason for the advance of bureaucratic organization has always been its purely technical superiority over any other form of organization" (1946, p. 214). He also writes that bureaucracy "is superior to any other form in precision, in stability, in the stringency of its discipline, and in its reliability . . . [it] is formally capable of application to all kinds of administrative tasks" (1946, p. 214). If this sounds autocratic, one may be reassured by the fact that Weber also said, "The progress of bureaucratization . . . is a parallel phenomenon of democracy" (1946, p. 225). "This results from the characteristic principle of bureaucracy: the abstract regularity of the execution of authority, which is a result of the demand for 'equality before the law' in the personal and functional sense [1946, p. 224]. . . . Bureaucracy . . . strives . . . for a 'right to the office' by the establishment of a regular disciplinary procedure and by removal of the completely arbitrary disposition of the 'chief' over the subordinate [1946, p. 242]. . . . The march of bureaucracy has destroyed structures of domination [such as patriarchialism, feudalism, and charismatic authority] which had no rational character" (1946, p. 244). Thus bureaucracy had two great advantages in Weber's view. First, it was the most efficient and effective form of organization and, second, it was the most humane form of organization.

Weber was more overtly unhappy as a person than Taylor. Plagued with a variety of physical ailments, he was also neurotic and suffered from a number of psychological symptoms.

His fascination with rigidly disciplined bureaucratic organizations (e.g., the army and the church) was probably not unrelated to his various psychological problems. Even so, his contributions—which were not limited to defining and delineating bureaucracy—were monumental.

In summary, Weber made organizations rational, just as Taylor made specific tasks rational. Although many organizations had endured and functioned in similar ways for centuries, Weber made a large contribution, observing with acute detail and clarity the organizational form that was so functional for survival and identifying modern modifications to that form that took into account the increasing complexity of organizations in an increasingly technologically sophisticated world.

## Elton Mayo: Societally Centered Human Interaction

It is not possible to understand the human relations movement of the 1930s, 1940s, and 1950s without recognizing that the now-discredited evidence of superiority (in terms of productivity and quality) was never much more than an excuse for what is really a philosophical position. Elton Mayo, a great social philosopher of the 1920s and 1930s, was the major force behind the human relations school. Although Mayo was not one of those who wrote much about the "Hawthorne Studies" (see Carey, 1967; Dickson & Roethlisberger, 1966; Landesberger, 1958; and Shepard, 1971), he was directly involved in that research, and the results seemed to him to offer clear evidence for his philosophy.

Mayo was particularly opposed to the scientific management so forcefully advocated by Taylor. In fact, Mayo's philosophy was partly shaped as a response to Taylor's ideas. Mayo wrote, "as a system, Taylorism effects much in the way of economy of labor; its chief defect is that workmen are not asked to collaborate in effecting such economies" (p. 60). "No social system can be considered satisfactory which deprives the great majority of mankind of every vestige of autonomy. No society is civilized in which the many [work] in the interests of the few. When 'work' signifies intelligent collaboration in the achievement of a social purpose, 'industrial unrest' will cease to be" (1919, p. 63). It is interesting to note that this was written in 1919, before the Hawthorne Studies began and before the term "human relations" was invented. It is also important to recognize that Mayo was not arguing against efficiency or productivity; he is speaking, basically, about how management ought to deal with people in the work environment.

Mayo served as the faculty member, at Harvard, responsible for the industrial psychology experiments at Western Electric's Hawthorne plant near Chicago. It was these studies that led to the term human relations and the subsequent movement. Mayo himself, however, concentrated on larger social issues, as is indicated by the titles of his last books, e.g., *The Human Problems of an Industrial Civilization* (1933). Mayo's student, Fritz Roethlisberger, was more directly involved in the Hawthorne Studies and in creating the human relations movement.

## Fritz Roethlisberger and W.J. Dickson: Individually Centered Human Interaction

The Hawthorne Studies (Roethlisberger & Dickson, 1936) have been analyzed and reanalyzed, attacked and defended for over forty years (Carey, 1967; Landesberger, 1958; Shepard, 1971). What was so controversial was not the research findings but their philosophical interpretations. In the guise of scholarly debate and critique, people argued about the worth, importance, and correctness of the human relations approach based on Mayo's values.

A brief review of this historically important research program is worthwhile. In the late 1920s, industrial psychologists were actively applying Taylor's time-study methods as well as analyzing work conditions to determine how human work capacities varied with the physical environment (light, heat, noise, ventilation, etc.). At Western Electric's Hawthorne plant, a special test area was set up. Workers and supervisors were selected to participate in the study, in which work behavior was measured as physical conditions varied. At first everything seemed reasonable, e.g., illumination levels were increased and production increased. However, when the level of light was decreased, production continued to increase, until the workers were producing more than ever under conditions equivalent to bright moonlight. At this point the engineers gave up, and a new research team from Harvard was brought in. Roethlisberger was on-site head, working with the company's personnel-department liaison, W.J. Dickson. What soon became evident was that social relationships in the test area were having a great influence on worker productivity. One view is that the supervisor, who had been chosen because of his excellent reputation, had developed a strongly loyal work group with high morale, and that these workers, who also had been screened, worked hard to satisfy him, even under adverse conditions. Thus, the importance of human relations was demonstrated. A less sanguine view is that the workers responded to the special treatment they were being given by working hard to please the researchers, even when conditions were poor. This explanation, commonly referred to as the Hawthorne effect, was thought to be true during the 1950s and 1960s, when a strong backlash swept toward the human relations movement. The truth is somewhere in between. Katz and Kahn (1966) observed that the Hawthorne workers had the best supervisor, were given special privileges, and formed a cohesive team. These factors, they argued, go far beyond the effects possible from just special attention, although special attention does have effects.

The importance of the Hawthorne Studies is the demonstration that social factors have strong impacts on work behavior. This is true whether one believes that the social factors were the special attention given the workers or the quality of supervision and group interaction they experienced. Roethlisberger put it this way: "People like to feel important and have their work recognized as important. . . . They like to work in an atmosphere of approval. They like to be praised rather than blamed. . . .They like to feel independent in their relations to their supervisors. . . .They like to be consulted about and participate in actions that will personally affect them. In short, employees, like most people, want to be treated as belonging to and being an integral part of some group" (1950).

Mayo saw that in society the extended family was becoming the nuclear family, with consequent loss of family-group identification for many. He proposed to substitute a new work group for the old family group. Mayo and Roethlisberger conceived an organization along the lines illustrated in Figure 5. Every work unit became self-regulating. The development of positive work relationships (indicated by the work units in Figure 5) was seen as beneficial to workers in that they regained a sense of group identification lost to them as their families became smaller (parents and children, not including grandparents, aunts, uncles, etc., as had been true in the last century). Management benefited because, when treated properly (the human relations approach), the members of these groups would support high production goals, solve problems, and help one another as needed. The prescription was simply to allow small groups of workers maximum freedom in controlling their own work. Within the groups, workers would establish their own patterns of coordination. By recognizing and supporting this informal organization, management theoretically could gain the support and cooperation of workers, leading to greater productivity and more efficient job performance.

Over time these human relations ideas gained a fair degree of acceptance among managers, although there was also considerable resistance. Many managers feared loss of control or power, which was not an unrealistic concern. The rather laissez-faire, undirected approach prescribed conceivably could generate some anxiety even in a liberal manager.

By the mid-1950s it was clear that productivity and efficiency were not attainable through the simple solutions generated by the human relations advocates (see Sales, 1966). The Hawthorne Studies actually foretold this, and later parts of the study showed that groups of workers acted to regulate their output, limiting it to no more than a certain average amount per day even though they could have easily produced at far higher levels. This finding was verified in

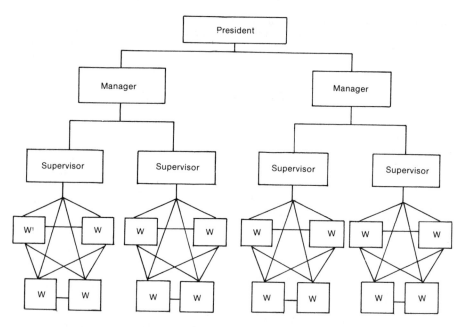

**Figure 5. Roethlisberger and Dickson's Human Relations Model**

other studies. Still further research showed that very unhappy workers could be highly productive, while very satisfied workers in cohesive work groups could be quite unproductive. The relationships among satisfaction, group morale, and productivity turned out to be much more complicated than Mayo and his colleagues had expected.

Eventually, managers—and not just academic researchers—realized this fact. Perhaps the disillusionment of some accounts for the subsequent backlash, illustrated by articles in the *Harvard Business Review* titled "What Price Human Relations?" (McNair, 1957) and "The Case for Benevolent Autocracy" (McMurray, 1958). In any case, human relations has become a ritual term, a thing that all believe in with no particular action implications (other than generally treating workers with common courtesy).

Although the human relations approach idealized by Mayo and by Roethlisberger and Dickson ultimately failed, it did provide the basis for the continued development of the behavioral-science theories of organization, which we now will examine.

## Douglas McGregor: Individually Centered Behavioral Science

The influence of the human relations movement provided support for behavioral scientists in business schools. One of the first and best known was Douglas McGregor, a psychologist who served to link a psychological view of human motivation to a theory of management. In doing this he coined the terms "Theory X" and "Theory Y." The former represents traditional assumptions about human motivation, some of which are that people are lazy and work only because they have to and that workers must be controlled and led. Theory Y, in contrast, asserts that workers are responsible and want to be involved more in their work (such that their own needs are met as the organization's are). McGregor said, "The essential task of management is to arrange the organizational conditions and methods of operation so that people can achieve their own goals best by directing their own efforts toward organizational objectives" (1957, p. 26).

McGregor based his approach on the motivation theory of Abraham Maslow (1943). This theory suggests that human needs can be categorized as survival, security, social, esteem, and self-development (or growth). As one type of need is basically fulfilled, the individual progresses toward higher needs (survival is primary, growth is most advanced). This suggests that if management can design work to fulfill the higher needs of workers, the workers' motives can be directed toward organizational, as well as individual, goals. (This assumes, reasonably enough, that for most workers the survival needs are met, and, for the majority, so are the security needs.)

One implication of this approach is that managers must diagnose individual workers' needs and offer opportunities for those needs to be satisfied. If this is so, effective management would seem to be rather impractical. However, while the range of specific individual needs is great, the basic categories of need are few in number. Furthermore, when workers are involved in defining their own needs, goals, and potential rewards, the task of creating appropriate organizational conditions seems more feasible.

McGregor's great gift was in taking some fairly complex ideas and expressing them in a clear, yet not oversimplified manner. He was able to explain the failure of human relations— and of autocracy—and offer a possible alternative: Theory Y. In 1954, he said, "There are big differences in the kinds of opportunities that can be provided for people to obtain need satisfaction. It is relatively easy to provide means (chiefly in the form of money) for need satisfaction—at least until the supply is exhausted. You cannot, however, provide people with a sense of achievement, or with knowledge, or with prestige. You can provide *opportunities* for them to obtain these satisfactions through efforts directed toward organization goals. What is even more important, the *supply of such opportunities*—unlike the supply of money—*is unlimited*" (1966, pp. 44-45).

McGregor developed a philosophy of how to manage individual workers, based on the best knowledge available about human motivation. Although he presented this philosophy in sugar-coated capsule form—Theory Y—he recognized that it would not be so simple to implement. People's expectations, which were based on past treatment, would have to be radically changed, and such change comes slowly. In 1957 McGregor wrote, "It is no more possible to create an organization today which will be a fully effective application of this theory than it was to build an atomic power plant in 1945" (1966, p. 24).

A major part of McGregor's implementation problem, however, was that his theory was not an *organizational* theory, but a theory of how individual managers might better manage. McGregor neglected to consider the organizational framework needed to support such management behavior. We will look next at a theorist who did develop such a framework.

### Rensis Likert: Organizationally Centered Behavioral Science

In the work of Likert (1961, 1967), one finds the most complete and sophisticated theory of organization based on behavioral science. It developed out of research conducted during the twenty-five years that Likert was director of the Institute for Social Research at the University of Michigan. Likert's theory is clearly prescriptive; he argues that his approach describes effective organizations and that if it is implemented, the organization will be effective.

Likert can be seen, in one sense, as expanding McGregor's two alternatives to four systems. System 1 is much like an extreme Theory X-organization: rigid, autocratic, and exploitative of workers. System 2 represents benevolent autocracy or paternalism. System 3 is called "consultative" management. Workers are involved to a degree in making decisions, but all real power remains with the managers. System 4 is participative management; all workers are involved in decisions that concern them.

In Likert's words, System 4 has three key elements: "(1) the use by the manager of the principle of supportive relationships, (2) his use of group decision making and group methods of supervision, and (3) his high performance goals for the organization" (1967, p. 47). The principle of supportive relationships states that "the leadership and other processes of the organization must be such as to ensure a maximum probability that in all interactions and in all relationships within the organization, each member, in the light of his background, values, desires, and expectations, will view the experience as supportive and one which builds and maintains his sense of personal worth and importance" (1967, p. 47). These statements mean several things. First, supervision is seen as a group—not a one-to-one, superior-to-subordinate—activity. Second, the group is delegated as much authority as possible; decisions are group decisions, not orders from above. Third, the supervisor or manager is seen as a "link-pin." That is, he is the head of one group but a member of another group (at the next level up), as illustrated in Figure 6. Thus, he serves as an important communication link between the two levels.

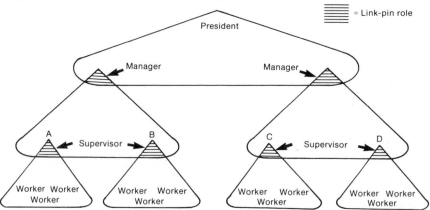

**Figure 6. Likert's Overlapping Group/Link-Pin Model**

Managers and supervisors are "link-pins," that is, members of two groups. Their function is to act as coordinative "linkers" (information transmitters) between the two groups.

Likert incorporates some of the earlier organizational theories in System 4. He is the only modern behavioral scientist to speak of a "principle" of management. In content this principle owes much to the human relations school but also, in a very general way, incorporates Maslow's needs of esteem and growth. The group methods that Likert mentions also derive from Mayo and reflect Maslow's social-need category. Likert's notion of performance goals as well as the basic structure he follows are derived from Weber's theory of bureaucracy. Although the organization shown in Figure 6 may look unusual at first glance, the only modification to the traditional bureaucratic form is that authority is shared at one level below that shown in Figure 4. Instead of the manager making a decision, the decision is made by the manager in collaboration with the manager's subordinates. This is an important change, just as Fayol's Bridge was an important change, but like the bridge, it is a modification, not a radical restructuring. Likert even has his own version of Fayol's Bridge; this is shown in Figure 7. Since coordination has continued to become complex since Fayol's time, Likert uses an ad hoc group for this purpose, selecting relevant individuals from each of the units that need to coordinate activities.

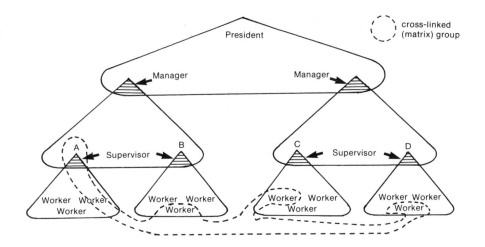

**Figure 7. Likert's Combined Behavioral/Matrix Model**

Likert should not be underestimated. He has developed what appears (after much study and trial) to be a workable organizational form for implementing the basic human relations approach and for putting Theory Y into practice.

Likert believes that most managers can learn to operate under his theory: "Data . . . show that managers who seek to do so can readily learn better systems of management" (1967, p. 190). He also argues for the utility of sound behavioral science research: "Most organizations today base their standard operating procedures and practices on classical organizational theories. These theories rely on key assumptions; . . . until recently, the shifting sands of practitioner judgment were the major if not the only source of knowledge about how to organize and run an enterprise. Now, research on leadership, management, and organization, undertaken by social scientists, provides a more stable body of knowledge . . . .The art of management can be based on verifiable information derived from rigorous, quantitative research" (1967, p.1). Likert's position is well stated in the opening lines of his book, *The Human Organization* (1967): "All the activities of any enterprise are initiated and determined by the persons who make up that institution. Plants, offices, computers, automated equipment, and all else that a modern firm uses are unproductive except for human effort and direction . . . . Every aspect of a firm's activities is determined by the competence, motivation, and general effectiveness of its human organization" (p. 1).

This last statement highlights what many consider to be the major flaw in Likert's approach: the conspicuous absence of anything reminiscent of Taylor or Taylorism. Although Taylor could be rejected for a number of reasons, Likert's reason is unusual. He believes that Taylor's basic concept of job technology is irrelevant to organizational effectiveness. At a professional meeting in 1978, Likert was asked why his theory contained no meaningful consideration of the specific characteristics of jobs (design, technology, etc.) or of the motivations of individuals. He replied to the effect that these factors are organizationally irrelevant.

Most current organizational theorists disagree strongly with this view. Some, like Charles Perrow (1972), an organizational sociologist, go so far as to assert the opposite, that technology determines everything and that human variables are essentially irrelevant. Most, however, take a more balanced view, seeing the technical and social aspects of organizations as interdependent.

The best current example of such an approach derives from work at the Tavistock Institute for Human Relations (England), which began in the 1940s and continues today. Many names are associated with this approach; this paper will discuss the writings of the two Tavistock members who are most known in the United States.

## Fred Emery and Eric Trist: A Comprehensive Behavioral Science Theory

Emery and Trist (1960) are the two names most familiarly attached to the theory called "sociotechnical systems," or, simply, STS (see Pasmore & Sherwood, 1978). This approach was developed in the 1950s and 1960s at the Tavistock Institute. The STS approach has actually involved over a dozen behavioral scientists, including (in alphabetical order) Kenneth Bamforth (Trist & Bamforth, 1951), Wilfred Bion (1961), Wilfred Brown (1960), P.G. Herbst (1974), Elliot Jaques (1951), Eric Miller (1967), A.K. Rice (1958), Einer Thorsrud (Emery & Thorsrud, 1976), and A.T.M. Wilson, among others. The most clear statements of STS as an organized theory have, however, been presented by Emery and Trist, both together and independently.

The STS concept started at the bottom of a coal mine. Trist and a former student, Bamforth (Trist & Bamforth, 1951), were studying the use of new work methods in the mining industry. What they found, however, was that under certain conditions that made the new methods impractical, workers had solved the problem by going all the way back to the small-group team mining that had been abandoned at the time of semi-mechanization in the 1940s (see Trist, Higgin, Morray, & Pollock, 1963). The team approach not only solved the technical problems, but it fit better with the needs of the miners (e.g., for strong social contacts when faced with a very dangerous task). Trist said, "After going down into the coal mine this time, I came up a different man. I was certain that the things I observed were of major significance" (1980, p. 151). The concept was brilliantly simple: the technological system used in an organization must fit or mesh properly with the social system if the organization is to operate effectively.

In the mid-1950s another British researcher, working independently of the Tavistock group, confirmed this notion. Joan Woodward's (1965) intent was to test some of the basic principles of management by checking to see whether more profitable firms did, in fact, follow the principles more closely than less profitable firms. Her answer was a strong "no." There was no relation at all between effectiveness and adherence to management principles. This seemed odd, because some principles were considered common sense, such as the proper "span of control" or average number of workers to be supervised by a first-line supervisor.

Woodward re-examined her data and found a pattern. All the measures seemed to differ by industry—in fact, by type of technology (which was crudely categorized as production of individual units, mass production, and continuous-process production). Examples of the first would be the manufacture of locomotives, of hand-knit sweaters, or of one-of-a-kind, high-technology items. The second type is the traditional assembly-line operation. The third represents high-technology products that are manufactured in a continuous process, such as oil or chemicals. Each basic technology type did differ, on the average, in number of levels of hierarchy, span of control, ratio of managers to nonmanagers, and a number of other variables. This showed that the principles did not seem to be universal but, rather, were modified depending on an organization's technology. But what of effectiveness? Woodward then showed that the more effective organizations consistently were characterized at about the average or mean value on each measure. In other words, there seemed to be a best method of organizing to fit each type of technology. Firms that stayed close to this best approach for their technical system were most effective. Firms that had too many or too few levels of hierarchy, too wide or too narrow a span of control, or too small or too large a manager/worker ratio *for their type of technology* were least profitable. The support of Woodward's findings for the STS approach is striking, especially when one realizes that Woodward worked totally independently and was unaware of the Tavistock STS approach. In fact, that approach was most clearly stated at just about the time that Woodward was publishing her findings in 1958, so Trist and Emery could not have been influenced by her work either.

The STS approach does not prescribe one particular organizational form, so there is no one diagram to illustrate it. It is based on the participative involvement of workers in semiautonomous groups and is like Likert's System 4 in this respect. How these groups are set up, their sizes, and the formal structural arrangements in the organization—all these things may vary widely from Likert's modified bureaucratic format.

STS theory does incorporate modern behavioral science as derived from human relations theory and industrial/organizational psychology. Katz and Kahn (1966) comment that the STS approach assumes three basic human work needs: (a) a need for closure, for finishing a whole task; (b) a need for autonomy or control of one's own behavior as a mature adult; and (c) a need for some level of interpersonal contact at work, not as a diversion or tangential to work activity but as a basic part of task activities. It is easy to see how these concepts relate to the human relations approach, to McGregor's Theory Y, and to Likert's group-based approach.

Where STS goes well beyond any of the earlier theoretical approaches is in incorporating technology as a major determinant of how the system should be socially organized. This, of course, directly contradicts Likert's views of organizations while incorporating the key points of his and many earlier theories—as well as parts of some less well-known sociological theories of organization that we have not mentioned, such as Thompson's (1967) and Perrow's (1970). Finally, STS theory incorporates a concern with organizational environments and the effects of the environment on organizations. Likert's and all of the earlier theories totally ignored this dynamic interaction.

Only Paul Lawrence and Jay Lorsch (1969), professors at Harvard, attempted to examine organizations in terms of the demands of their environments. They suggest that more traditional structures (Figure 4) are appropriate when the environment is quite stable in terms of technological complexity and change, market demand, and low internal organizational specialization of tasks and functions. When environments are very unstable (rapid, uncertain changes in the above factors and high internal specialization), more complex devices are needed to coordinate organizational activities. These devices include temporary cross-link teams (as defined by Likert), liaison roles, and even departments whose task is simply to coordinate among other departments.

STS theory, however, deals with this issue through Emery and Trist's (1965) concept of "causal texture" of the environment. They define four types of environment, the first two being subdivisions of the stable environment defined by Lawrence and Lorsch; the second two being unstable. The "type-four" environment is called "turbulent," uncontrollably reactive, almost unpredictable. Trist notes, "We . . . hit on the word 'turbulence' when I was describing how I [once] became airsick" (1980, p. 162).

Unlike the various older approaches, STS theory does not pretend to offer a cure for all organizational ills. In fact, Trist comments that "environmental turbulence has become such a strong dynamic that I'm a pessimistic optimist. I'm scared as hell about what will happen on a large scale during the next few decades. We may well be faced with wholesale unemployment as technological advances continue to replace workers. The 'management of decline' may become a new approach as resources are exhausted and various aspects of our economy wind down. Our focus has been on micro processes, yet we must try to do something at macro levels, at the large-scale system level" (1980, p. 166). Trist's comments seem about as pessimistic as an organizational theorist's can be.

## Overview

At this point it should be clear why this paper has labeled each theorist according to the primary social system level dealt with and the primary orientation taken. From the narrow, structural, individual-behavior focus of traditional theory (Taylor, 1911), there has been steady development in organizational theory. It has passed through a concern with small groups (Mayo, 1919; Roethlisberger & Dickson, 1936), with organizations (Likert, 1961; McGregor, 1957), and finally with all these factors in the context of a broad, social-system approach.

The aim of this paper has been to show how organizational theorists have built on one another's ideas and how, even when one individual or group vehemently disagreed with another, the basic ideas of both were usually incorporated into a new approach. By looking at the theorists as people and not just inanimate sources of ideas, and by examining the social-historical contexts in which they lived, one can see even more clearly how this "thesis-antithesis-synthesis" process has worked. One sees in Likert not merely his new ideas (such as the organizational link-pin concept) but also the reflection of the times he lived in, the days of principles of management and the Hawthorne Studies. In McGregor's work we can find new ideas about management philosophy, and also old ideas about human motivation that were developed in the 1930s and 1940s (and are not unrelated to Mayo's ideas about human needs). And in the sociotechnical systems approach we see the most recent generation of fully developed organizational theory, incorporating much of what came before, accepting and rejecting or correcting earlier elements, and going beyond the prior theories.

Who will become the dominant theorists of the upcoming generation is not clear; even less clear is the possible nature of the theories yet to come. Management and organizational theory has come a long way, from the turn-of-the-century world of Taylor to the world of supersonic aircraft and potential nuclear holocaust. Still, there is no indication that the earlier forms are totally superseded by later developments. Many organizations remain faithful to Weber's bureaucratic model, and there are even a few that still adhere to the traditional structural model. Good arguments can be made that such organizations will continue to decrease in number, but it is unlikely that all will ever disappear, simply because circumstances do exist that make such structural forms not only possible but desirable. In all probability, the world is diverse enough that such circumstances will continue to exist. Nor would it be correct to conclude that the more recently developed structural forms are best in any absolute sense; there is no way of knowing what will succeed them, although it would be reasonable to assume that whatever theories follow will be hierarchical in nature and—to some degree—bureaucratic in orientation.

## REFERENCES

Argyris, C. *Increasing leadership effectiveness.* New York: John Wiley, 1976.

Bion, W.R. *Experiences in groups.* New York: Basic Books, 1961.

Brown, W. *Exploration in management.* London: Heinemann, 1960.

Carey, A. The Hawthorne studies: A radical criticism. *American Sociological Review,* 1967, *32,* 403-416.

Copley, F.B. *Frederick W. Taylor: Father of scientific management.* New York: Harper & Row, 1923.

Davis, S.M., & Lawrence, P.R. *Matrix.* Reading, MA: Addison-Wesley, 1977.

Dickson, W.J., & Roethlisberger, F.J. *Counseling in an organization: A sequel to the Hawthorne researches.* Boston, MA: Division of Research, Graduate School of Business Administration, Harvard University, 1966.

Emery, F.E., & Thorsrud, E. *Democracy at work.* Leiden, The Netherlands: Martinus Nijhoff, 1976.

Emery, F.E., & Trist, E.L. *Socio-technical systems.* Oxford, England: Pergamon Press, 1960.

Emery, F.E., & Trist, E.L. The causal texture of organizational environments. *Human Relations,* 1965, *18,* 21-32.

Fayol, H. *L' incapacite industrielle de l'état: Les P.T.T.* Paris: Dunod, 1921.

Fayol, H. *General and industrial management.* Translated from the French by Constance Storrs. London: Pitman, 1949.

Fayol, H. *L' éveil de esprit publique.* Quoted in Ernest Dale, *Management: Theory and practice* (4th ed.). New York: McGraw-Hill, 1978.

Hearings Before Special Committee of the House of Representatives to Investigate the Taylor and Other Systems of Shop Management Under Authority of House Resolution 90. Washington, DC: U.S. Government Printing Office, 1912, 1388-1389.

Herbst, P.G. *Socio-technical design.* London: Tavistock, 1974.

Jaques, E. *The changing culture of a factory.* London: Tavistock, 1951.

Katz, D., & Kahn, R. *The social psychology of organizations.* New York: John Wiley, 1966 (rev. ed., 1978).

Landesberger, H.J. *Hawthorne revisited.* Ithaca, NY: Cornell University Press, 1958.

Lawrence, P.R., & Lorsch, J.W. *Organization and environment: Managing differentiation and integration.* Homewood, IL: Richard D. Irwin, 1969.

Likert, R. *New patterns of management.* New York: McGraw-Hill, 1961.

Likert, R. *The human organization.* New York: McGraw-Hill, 1967.

Maslow, A.H. A theory of human motivation. *Psychological Review,* 1943, *50,* 370-396.

Mayo, E. *Democracy and freedom: An essay in social logic.* Melbourne, Australia: Macmillan, 1919.

Mayo, E. *The human problems of an industrial civilization.* Cambridge, MA: Harvard University Press, 1933.

McGregor, D. The human side of enterprise. In *Adventure in thought and action,* Proceedings of the Fifth Anniversary Convocation of the School of Industrial Management, Massachusetts Institute of Technology, Cambridge, Massachusetts, April 9, 1957.

McGregor, D.M. The human side of enterprise. *The Management Review,* 1957, *46*(11), 26.

McGregor, D.M. A philosophy of management. In W.G. Bennis & E.H. Schein (Eds.), with the collaboration of C. McGregor, *Leadership and motivation: Essays of Douglas McGregor.* Cambridge, MA: M.I.T. Press, 1966.

McMurray, R.N. The case for benevolent autocracy. *Harvard Business Review,* 1958, *36*(1), 82-90.

McNair, M.P. What price human relations? *Harvard Business Review,* 1957, *35*(2), 15-39.

Miller, E.J., & Rice, A.K. *Systems of organization.* London: Tavistock, 1967.

Pasmore, W.A., & Sherwood, J.J. *Sociotechnical systems: A sourcebook.* San Diego, CA: University Associates, 1978.

Rice, A.K. *Productivity and social organization: The Ahmedabad experiment.* London: Tavistock, 1958.

Perrow, C. *Organizational analysis: A sociological view.* Monterey, CA: Brooks/Cole, 1970.

Perrow, C. *Complex organizations: A critical essay.* Glenview, IL: Scott, Foresman, 1972.

Roethlisberger, F.J. The human equation in employee productivity (Speech before the personnel group of the National Retail Dry Goods Association, 1950).

Roethlisberger, F.J., & Dickson, W.J. *Management and the worker.* Cambridge, MA: Harvard University Press, 1936.

Sales, S.M. Supervisory style and productivity: Review and theory. *Personnel Psychology,* 1966, *19,* 275-286.

Shepard, J.M. On Alex Carey's radical criticism of the Hawthorne studies. *Academy of Management Journal,* 1971, *14,* 23-31.

Taylor, F.W. *Scientific management.* New York: Harper, 1911.

Thompson, J.D. *Organizations in action.* New York: McGraw-Hill, 1967.

Trist, E.L. Interview: Eric Trist, British interdisciplinarian. *Group & Organization Studies,* 1980, *5*(2), 144-166.

Trist, E.L., & Bamforth, K.W. Some social and psychological consequences of the longwall method of coal-getting. *Human Relations,* 1951, *4,* 3-38.

Trist, E.L., Higgin, G.A., Murray, H., & Pollock, A.B. *Organizational choice: Capabilities of groups at the coal face under changing technologies: The loss, re-discovery and transformation of a work tradition.* London: Tavistock, 1963.

Weber, M. *From Max Weber: Essays in sociology* (H.H. Gerth & C. Wright Mills, eds. & trans.). New York: Oxford University Press, 1946.

Weber, M. *The theory of social and economic organizations* (A.M. Henderson & T. Parsons, trans., & T. Parsons, ed.). New York: The Free Press, 1947.

Woodward, J. *Industrial organization: Theory and practice.* London: Oxford University Press, 1965.

## SUGGESTED READINGS

The following are books by the most recent crop of organizational theorists. They provide limits and guidelines for the future development of organizational theory.

Child, J. (Ed.). *Man and organization: The search for exploration and social relevance.* New York: Halstead-Wiley, 1973.

Galbraith, J.R. *Designing complex organizations.* Reading, MA: Addison-Wesley, 1973.

Khandwalla, P.N. *The design of organizations.* New York: Harcourt Brace Jovanovich, 1977.

Mintzberg, H. *The structuring of organizations.* Englewood Cliffs, NJ: Prentice-Hall, 1979.

Pfeffer, J. *Organization design.* Arlington Heights, IL: AHM Publishing, 1978.

Weick, K.E., Jr. *The social psychology of organizing* (rev. ed.). Reading, MA: Addison-Wesley, 1980.

**Marshall Sashkin, Ph.D.,** *is a professor of industrial and organizational psychology at the University of Maryland, College Park, Maryland. He is also senior editorial associate for University Associates, Inc., San Diego, California, and is a co-editor of* Group & Organization Studies. *Dr. Sashkin has served on the faculties of several universities and has published a book and numerous journal articles. He has also consulted to governmental agencies, mental health institutions, industrial firms, and school systems.*

# A METHOD FOR STRUCTURED NATURALISTIC OBSERVATION OF ORGANIZATIONAL BEHAVIOR

Dennis N.T. Perkins, David A. Nadler, and Martin D. Hanlon

## INTRODUCTION

### Observation in Organizational Assessment

Groups and organizations are characterized by cycles of events (Katz & Kahn, 1978), and each cycle is made up of episodes or sequences of behavior. Any one sequence is jointly determined by factors in the individual members as well as factors in the social environment (Porter, Lawler, & Hackman, 1975). Because individuals develop and execute patterns of behavior over time, the total behavior in the organization is dynamic and complex.

This complexity is difficult to measure, and many methods of data collection for organizational research are simply not adequate for capturing the stream of behavioral phenomena. For example, perceptually based measures such as interviews and questionnaires provide *post hoc* information; that is, something may be assumed to cause a behavior merely because it occurred prior to the behavior. In addition, past events and behaviors are modified by the perceptual filters of individuals who are reporting or responding (Staw, 1975). Attempts to measure behavior through the use of secondary data sources, such as measures of productivity, absenteeism records, and turnover statistics (see Macy & Mirvis, 1976), also present problems. Each type of data indicates only a specific piece of behavior taken out of its social context. Finally, the data-collection processes themselves frequently are fraught with error.

An alternative approach to gathering data about behavior in organizations is the use of observational methods. Observational methods were used frequently in the study of organizational behavior in the past, but other data-collection technologies methods (particularly survey methods) eventually superseded them. Observational methods, however, still provide a unique perspective, since the data-gathering instrument is the observer himself. A trained and perceptive observer is capable of collecting and integrating more data about complex and dynamic sequences of behavior than can be gathered through any other research method. Thus, the disadvantages of observation as a data-collection method may be balanced by its value within the context of a multiple-methods approach.

### Advantages and Disadvantages of Observation

A distinct advantage of observation as a data-collection method (see Nadler, 1977) is that the data gathering occurs *in situ*, in the actual presence of the behavior. Observation also allows the behavior (either continuous behavior or behavior measured at selected points in time) to be analyzed over a period of time. In addition, the observer can interpret the behavior of organizational members within the context of the social structure and climate of the organization. Finally, observation is adaptive; the focus of the observer's investigation can be shifted to take into account changes in the functioning of the organization. Unpredicted events or unanticipated consequences of organizational changes can be integrated into the observational model.

Although the scope and flexibility of observational methods constitute major strengths, the characteristics of the method also lead to problems. The totalistic nature of observation means that the observer is faced with many choices. There are critical questions of sampling: Which events should be observed? What locations within the organization should be given the most attention? What types of behavior should be recorded? The observer also must be continually aware of the fact that his or her presence in the organization may alter the situation being observed in subtle but important ways. Finally, observation is an active process; because the observer must make frequent choices about what to observe and how to integrate incoming data, no two observers will report the same data about the functioning of an organization. One of the major aims of this paper is to describe how some of these sources of bias can be overcome without sacrificing the unique advantages of observational methods.

## Organization of This Paper

This paper presents one approach to the observation of behavior for assessment purposes in complex organizations. This approach is called *structured naturalistic observation*. It is naturalistic in that it does not predetermine the phenomena to which the observer will attend. Rather, the observer is placed in the presence of a stream of behavior in a natural setting and is guided only by general frameworks. At the same time, the approach is structured in that specific procedures are used to record observations and to store the resultant data.

In the first part of this paper, the basic rationale for structured naturalistic observation will be presented. Next, the specific instruments and procedures of the method will be described and discussed. Some perspectives on how the technology might be implemented in the field will follow. Sample observations, coding schemes, and additional instruments will be included in an appendix.

## THE RATIONALE FOR STRUCTURED NATURALISTIC OBSERVATION

### Approaches to Observation

The history of observational methods in the social sciences reflects a diversity of contexts, theoretical developments, and applications. Observation as a research method evolved more or less independently in different disciplines as a set of techniques for dealing with particular research problems. This absence of a common heritage is the cause of some of the more intractable problems of observational research, which lacks both a widely accepted and consistent terminology and the degree of codification of procedures that is characteristic of other research methods.

The observational methods that have been used in the study of organizational behavior draw from three disciplines in particular: psychology, anthropology, and sociology (see Hanlon [1979], Heyns & Lippitt [1954], and Weick [1968] for reviews of pertinent literature). Methods adapted from psychology have been used primarily for the observation of behavior of individuals or small groups (see, for example, Argyris [1962] and Bales [1950, 1971] ). Typically, these approaches have focused on microbehavior, i.e., specific and discrete instances of behavior that can be reliably observed, coded, and counted. Patterns of behavior are then inferred from analysis and aggregation of the pieces of data.

Another source of observational methodology has been anthropology. The organizational literature (for example, Sayles, 1964, and Whyte, 1955) reflects this tradition. The researcher is immersed in the subject and observes activity ranging from micro to macrolevel phenomena. The objective is to identify patterns of behavior in order to develop explanatory frameworks that can be used to understand those patterns.

Perhaps the most extensive contribution to the theory and methods of observational research in complex organizations has come from the discipline of sociology. The difficult issues of validity in observation-based research have received considerable attention (e.g., McCall & Simmons, 1969) in this field, and the recent literature includes several useful attempts to provide "how-to-do-it" knowledge of observational methods (Bogdan & Taylor, 1975; Schatzman & Strauss, 1973). The methodological and ethical dilemmas inherent in the role of the observer have been extensively described (Erikson, 1967; Gold, 1958; Miller, 1952; Scott, 1963), and sociological researchers using observational methods have made extremely important contributions to the scientific understanding of complex organizations (for example, Blau, 1955; Gouldner, 1963). At the present time, however, there is no long-range study of the use of observation-based methods in organizational research.

## Bias and Structure in Observational Methods

Although organizational researchers have used a wide range of observational strategies that are based on different disciplinary traditions, most of these strategies share certain characteristics. Most basically, the observer is the principal data-gathering instrument. Although other instruments or procedures may be used, it is the observer who sees the events and records them.

As was mentioned earlier, the use of the observer and the choices that the observer makes while collecting data constitute both the major strengths and the most critical weaknesses of observational methods. Because the observer can make choices about what, when, and whom to observe, the method is adaptive and flexible. It is, therefore, well suited to the observation of dynamic phenomena or streams of behavior over time. Because the observer, through the choices that he or she makes, selectively perceives patterns in behavior and feeds back these interpretations into the ongoing collection of data, the strengths of the method also are potential sources of bias. Thus the choices made constitute potential threats to the validity and reliability of the data collected.

One way of dealing with the potential bias is to structure the actions of the observer, thereby reducing the number and extent of choices to be made. Two dimensions of observation can most easily be structured. First, the focus or content of the observational activity itself can be structured, since it is possible to specify the particular classes and types of behavior to be observed. An example is Bales' (1950) scheme, which defines and identifies specific types of interaction to be observed. Second, the method of recording the observational data can be structured. The specific notations, coding schemes, etc., can be specified, to guide the observer in recording data. An example of this approach is the standardized job-observation techniques developed by Jenkins and Nadler (Jenkins, Nadler, Lawler, & Cammann, 1975; Nadler & Jenkins, 1978), in which fixed, finite response categories are used to rate job characteristics.

One can think of the range of observational methods and structure in terms of a two-dimensional space. One dimension represents the degree to which the content of the observation is structured. The other dimension represents the degree to which the method of recording is structured. Other points in the space represent different degrees of structure of each type.

The fundamental structural trade-off is one of validity and reliability as opposed to flexibility and adaptiveness. As the method becomes more structured, the choices available to the observer decrease—as do opportunities for bias or error. At the same time, reduction of choice mitigates the capacity of the method to be adaptive and integrative.

Within this context, structured naturalistic observation involves relatively unstructured content (to preserve the adaptiveness of the method) but a relatively structured recording process (to create a measure of comparability and consistency in the observational data). It reflects one trade-off of degrees of structure and is just one of many combinations that are possible.

## INSTRUMENTS FOR STRUCTURED NATURALISTIC OBSERVATION

Structured naturalistic observation assumes a relatively skilled observer who is familiar with concepts and patterns of organizational behavior. The observer is not highly limited in terms of *what* to observe, but a specific structure is provided for *communicating* what has been observed. This structure is necessary if the observational record is to be made up of comparable data in a retrievable form.

The issue here is how to structure the communication of what has been observed. Typically, if one were to observe a series of activities involving people and report what was seen, the report would include various kinds of information. It is likely that it would mention specific activities or behaviors that occurred. These would be tangible and discrete occurrences, and it would be possible to verify whether or not they did occur as described, especially if several observers were present or if the sequence were videotaped. On the other hand, the report would probably be more than a listing of tangible events. It might include attempts by the observer to make sense of what was seen, to identify patterns, to determine causes and effects, and so on. Of course, these would be speculative. The observational record also might reflect the feelings that the observer had while watching the activity or behavior. If, for example, the observer found one of the people being observed to be personally distasteful, it could influence how that person's behavior is described or explained. The observer, therefore, communicates some perceptions of tangible events, some interpretations of what those events mean, and some feelings he or she experienced during the period of observation. The problem is that these are frequently interwoven, and it is difficult to evaluate the different types of information.

Theory related to interpersonal communication and behavior deals with a similar problem in the observation of how individuals communicate information to each other (Argyris, 1962, 1974). One approach to improving the effectiveness of communication is to separate out the different types of data, perceptions, interpretations, and feelings and to label them clearly. Similarly, in the naturalistic observation method, the purpose of the instrumentation is to structure the recording (and thus communication) of data so as to separate out and label the different kinds of information communicated by the observer.

### The General Observation Form

The core of the observational method is the general observation form (see Figure 1), which includes five categories for recording observations as well as space for various identifying and coding information. The first category is *overview of the event*, a relatively brief summary of the major activities, behaviors, occurrences, etc., that happened during the observation period. Although usually fairly short, it includes enough information so that someone analyzing a series of observations could decide whether to read further or to go on to another recorded observation. Thus, this overview is functionally similar to a table of contents.

The second category is *detailed observations*. This section is the central component of the observation instrument and is intended to provide the first level of information (perceptions). It is a detailed record of what occurred during the observation period and usually is in chronological order. Here it is important to limit the information to that which is factual, i.e., tangible, discrete events that could be verified by other observers or by visual record. It is important to avoid interpretation or causal attribution in this section. The ultimate test of the adequacy of the data in this section might be to ask the observer if he or she would be willing to show the section to the individuals being observed for purposes of verification. If the detailed observations are free of interpretation or observer affect, the information could—in theory—be shown to those involved and verified without concern about misinterpretation.

Site _____ Setting _____

Observer _____ Event _____

Date & Time _____ Variables _____

_____

(Title of Observation)

Overview of the Event:

Detailed Observations:

Interpretations:

Observer Feelings:

Attachments:

**Figure 1. General Observation Form**

The third section of the observation form is for *interpretations*. Here the observer is called on to make statements that attempt to make sense of the specific activities and behaviors that have been observed. These are, in fact, propositions or hypotheses that cannot be verified immediately but that can guide future data collection by observation as well as data collection by other methods. Interpretations might include attempts to identify patterns of behavior, attributions concerning the causes of behavior or the factors that motivate the behavior, speculation about the nature and meaning of events, and so on. Ideally, interpretations should be propositions, that is, they should be tentative, and, thus, testable. They might therefore be recorded as questions or hypotheses.

The fourth section, *observer feelings*, concerns the personal reactions of the observer to the events that have been observed. They are the observer's specific affective reactions to what is going on. These reactions tend to influence how choices are made about what behavior to observe and how interpretations are developed. Two purposes are achieved by making these feelings explicit. First, the observer may become more aware of the feelings he or she has and thus more able to correct for their potential bias. Second, others who are using the observational record can consider the observer's feelings in qualifying the data.

The final category is *attachments*. Frequently the observer has access to supporting documents or other information relevant to the behavior or activity being observed. The range of possible attachments is large, and could include meeting agendas, critical memos, correspondence, membership lists, other observational instruments used during the event, handouts from meetings, maps, floor plans, or sketches. These should be physically attached to the observation to which they are relevant.

The observer might write a tentative outline or overview before the activity and then make detailed notes during the period of observation. Separate sheets would be used to record interpretations and observer feelings during the observation itself, with these sheets becoming the last pages of the observation report. Observers often have found it useful to type up the observations as soon as possible after the actual observation period, and the information is then put into the order specified on the form. For an observation of one or two hours, the written observation form could be from five to ten typewritten pages.

An alternative to this method involves a somewhat different version of the same observation form (see figure 2). The same information is provided, but the form is set up so that detailed observation, interpretations, and feelings can be recorded concurrently as they happen, rather than sequentially. This form does not have a section for an overview but does provide for variable coding next to the different observations. All the subsequent material on coding and use of instruments can be applied to either form.

## Coding and Identification of Observations

A major problem in the use of observational data is analysis. If data are to be used for analytic purposes, they need to be identified (labeled and coded) on the general information form so that they can be retrieved and so that specific observations can be related to variables in a conceptual or analytic framework. This approach is best used when some conceptual framework is employed to guide the observations; however, it can be used with an inductive approach in which categories and variables for observation are developed from the data during the course of the study.

A variety of identification and coding data are possible. First, each observation is given a descriptive *title*. This title, while brief, should include enough information so that the observation is easily identified. For example, an observation might be entitled, "Fourth Meeting of the Executive Committee, NPH Project," with the date indicated elsewhere. As will be seen later, the title is an important element of the data-retrieval process.

The observation form also includes space for other identifying data that are relatively simple and straightforward. The *site* refers to the project or organization in which the observation is conducted. *Observer* obviously refers to the name of the person doing the observation and recording the data, while *date & time* refers to the specific day and time period when the behaviors and/or activities were observed.

The final three types of information are the basic elements of the observation storage and retrieval system. In this system, there are three classes of codes. The basic structure of these codes can be established before the observation is begun, although codes may be changed as the study progresses.

The first level of coding is based on the concept that all observations occur within one of several unique *settings* within a research site. A setting often is *geographical*—analogous to a physical location. For example, behavior observed in a manufacturing plant could be set within different departments such as plating, finishing, and packing. On the other hand, another setting in the same plant might be within the top management team, and that group might meet and interact in several geographical locations. This is a *functional* setting. In some cases, settings may overlap, and consistent practices must be established concerning the coding of a specific observation. (The appendix to this article contains a sample set of codes.)

Site _____        Setting _____

Observer _____        Event _____

Date & Time _____        Page _____ of This Observation

_____
(Title of Observation)

| Time | Detailed Observations | Interpretations | Feelings | Variable Code |
|------|----------------------|-----------------|----------|---------------|
|      |                      |                 |          |               |

Figure 2. Alternative General Observation Form

Within each setting, it is possible to observe a number of different *events*. Events are major classes of behavior or activity that occur in the setting. For example, an observation of the management team of the plant might be comprised of events that occur frequently, such as weekly staff meetings or monthly performance reviews. In most cases, there will be observations of events that do not fit into any pattern, and these typically are labeled "ongoing behavior."

The detailed observations and interpretations noted on the general observation form also can be coded in another way. This third level of coding involves labeling the observations in terms of the variables to which the behaviors or activities observed are relevant. For example, the monthly staff meetings of the top-management group might be coded for "leadership style" or for "conflict resolution" or for "decision making." Variables for coding can be obtained from different sources. In some cases a specific list of variables derived from a conceptual or theoretical framework might be used (a sample list of variables is contained in the appendix). In other cases, classes of variables might be developed as the observation proceeds. For example, specific themes that emerge repeatedly in observations might be identified and then used to code existing, subsequent, and prior observations.

When combined with the basic identification data (title, site, observer, and date/time), this three-level scheme (setting, event, and other variables) enables full identification and retrieval of observations. Each observation thus becomes a unique piece of data within the larger data set.

### Storage and Retrieval of Observational Data

The three-level coding scheme forms the basis of a storage/retrieval/analysis system. Specific observation forms and attachments are stored in notebooks that are created for each setting; within the setting, observations are inserted chronologically. Thus, by knowing the setting and approximate date of an observation, one can locate it relatively easily.

Numerous observations are accumulated over time. In a typical observation project of a year or so, several hundred observation forms might be filed, and it would become increasingly difficult to find a specific observation containing a piece of needed data. An aid to retrieval and analysis therefore is needed. One approach is to use an observation log sheet. Each time an observation is placed in a setting notebook, it is also logged on this sheet. For each observation, the key identification data are provided, including the date of the observation, its entry number (a consecutive number to identify each log entry), the title of the observation, the name of the observer, and the codes for setting, event, and variables. The log form usually is stored in a master notebook, along with the various codes and variable lists; it is the basic tool for retrieval or analysis of the observations.

To use the manufacturing plant example again, if one wanted to obtain a chronological record of all of the staff meetings of the management team, one could simply scan the event column on the log and note all observations of that event (staff meetings) within the top-management-team setting. Similarly, if one wanted to identify elements of conflict, the variable codes would indicate observations in which "conflict" was noted. The date and setting columns also make it easy to locate the observation in a notebook.

### Supplemental Instruments

The observation forms, categories of observation, coding scheme, and log sheet are the core of the structured naturalistic observation method. It is these elements that structure the observation and recording of data so that the data are comparable, retrievable, and in a form that facilitates analysis. In practice, however, other instruments also are used frequently. It can be valuable to make use of other observational technologies in combination with this basic approach; in fact, the instrumentation is designed to be flexible enough to permit integration with other types of observation and naturalistic data collection. The specific choice of supplemental instruments will depend on the expertise of the researcher, the goals of the research, and the variables to be investigated. A few instruments that have been used in combination with naturalistic observation have been included in the appendix in order to provide a sense of the range of techniques that can be used.

## OBSERVATION IN PRACTICE: DESIGN ISSUES

Guidance in the practice of structured naturalistic observation tends to fall at the ends of a continuum: at one end the researcher is counseled to "observe key events" or to "be perceptive"; at the other end, the researcher is given instruction in the mechanics of note taking, the specifics of filing systems, and so forth. "Mid-range" guidance is difficult to provide, since the precise context of observation is unknown and appropriate methodology must, of necessity, be tailored to the research setting. Experience has yielded a few generalizations that seem to be applicable to many organizational settings, however, and these are discussed below.

### Characteristics of Observers

Some individuals obviously are more facile than others in negotiating organizational environments. Although many observational skills can be taught, individuals with demonstrated ability to establish rapport with others—particularly with those who are not familiar with the style and argot of the social scientist—seem to perform exceptionally well as observers. For example, an individual who demonstrates the ability to deal with the various members of a research program—colleagues, support personnel, computer personnel, and so forth—will likely be successful in other interpersonal functions; and a person who experiences frequent personality conflicts in an academic setting is not likely to deal with others successfully in the outside world.

This is not to say that observers need to be "like" the members of the organizations they study. Neither must they conform rigidly to the norms of the research site. In fact, tolerable differences may elicit data that would not appear otherwise, i.e., variations in the phenomena observed. One study, for example, was conducted by two observers: a Philippine female and a white American male (Perkins, Nieva, & Lawler, in press). The two observers found systematic variation in observed events: the Philippine woman found that her identity produced a "novelty effect," which made her nonthreatening and promoted respondent candor. At the same time, however, she observed no instance of racial prejudice, although that behavior was readily visible to the white observer.

### Training Observers

If an individual has the basic skills needed to negotiate entry into an organizational setting, two additional hints may further smooth the entry process and improve the validity of the observation. These are as follows:

1. *Attire.* Observers should not attempt to "blend" into the organizational environment by adopting extremes in dress, e.g., overalls or three-piece suits. Unless the role is one of "observer as participant" (Junker, 1960), it will be obvious that the researcher is not a true member of the organization. It is important, however, that the observer maintain *credibility* as a member of a respectable scientific enterprise. This implies that the observers would, ideally, wear such clothing as members of the organization would *expect* an observer to wear. Of course, the clothing also should be appropriate to the observer's age and social status. These guidelines would vary for an investment banker and a drill-press operator or for a graduate student and a senior professor. The objective, of course, is to create as little disturbance as possible and to minimize the reaction to the observation.

2. *Reliability.* It is entirely possible that an individual may be skilled at establishing rapport and be able to enter the organization unobtrusively. The observer's ability to reliably observe behavioral phenomena is another matter, however. Observer reliability can be tested prior to entry by conducting simultaneous observation of exemplary events. For example, it may be instructive to have potential observers use the general observation form (Figure 1) to record the "stream of behavior" (Barker, 1968) that occurs in a research-planning meeting. Divergence in recording can be used as discussion material, both to improve the reliability of observation and to identify potential sources of invalidity, e.g., do the data recorded in the "events" column represent valid evidence for the inferences made in the "hypothesis" space?

Observer rating scales (Guilford, 1954) or attitudinal surveys (e.g., the Michigan Organizational Assessment Package) also can be used to improve observer reliability. Instruments such as Likert's (Likert, 1967) Profile of Organizational Characteristics can be completed by two or more observers after a period of study, and points of disagreement can be used to identify systematic biases in perception. Agreement on global rating scales does not, of course, imply or assure agreement on the component events in an observation. Disagreement, however, does suggest the possibility of divergent frames of reference or possible misinterpretation of research constructs.

## Sampling

In an organizational setting, conclusions reached by an observer may be affected by systematic variance in perception or by sampling, i.e., the data collected may vary as a result of the passage of time, the particular individuals or events observed, the physical locations studied, and so forth. The problem for the observer is to determine when to observe, whom to observe, and in which locations to observe in order to obtain the most valuable information. One solution is to sample exhaustively and observe everything, but the defects of this strategy are obvious; limitations on observer time, scheduling constraints, and problems of accessibility generally render this approach unfeasible. The solution must ultimately depend on specific organizational properties and research objectives. However, experience suggests that certain priorities are common to many organizational-research situations. In general, it is important that any sampling design be free of systematic biases that could distort the research findings. As obvious as this may sound, it is easier than one might expect to incorporate an "elite bias" (Sieber, 1973)—because some individuals are engaging or articulate—or a "setting bias"—in which certain locations are oversampled because of accessibility, convenience, and/or comfort. When this occurs, the temptation to generalize to other instances is almost unavoidable, since more appropriate data are nonexistent.

## Exemplary Observation Strategies

Assuming some form of representative observation, it is possible to identify various "levels of effort" that characterize the researcher's involvement in the setting under study (see Nieva, Fichman, & Perkins, 1975). Three such levels will be described here, although the intensity of any observation clearly can be seen as a continuum, with an unlimited number of hypothetical positions.

### Level I: Site Orientation

The most basic level of involvement requires that the researcher establish sufficient contact to become familiar with key staff, obtain a rudimentary understanding of the organization's technology, and be able to compile a chronology of the major events that occurred during the course of the research. At this level of effort, recording will be so sporadic as to preclude meaningful analysis of the activities actually observed, so no attempt should be made to maintain detailed notes on observations. In most cases this sort of impressionistic observation will be useful only in conjunction with some other form of data collection such as attitudinal surveys. This level of involvement does, however, permit the collection of archival data such as memoranda, minutes of staff meetings, and other records that will be helpful in establishing an accurate chronology of events. The primary objective at this basic level of research is to develop a "sense" of the organizational environment and to preclude the errors that might occur were other analyses to be conducted with no first-hand knowledge of the setting.

## Level II: Basic Observation

The minimum level of effort that could be labeled "structured naturalistic observation" would include the previous research activities as well as the following:

- Observation of key organizational events of direct relevance to the research, e.g., meetings to discuss the progress of organizational change programs, the administration of research instruments, etc.
- Observation of other regularly occurring meetings that could identify issues for further exploration, provide a baseline for understanding the development of the setting, or generally help the observer to develop a picture of the organization.
- Observation of interventions (e.g., activities of change agents) that are designed to alter the structure and processes of the setting.
- Unstructured or semistructured interviews with key informants. Although there are dangers in cultivating relationships with a limited sample of individuals, some organizational members undoubtedly will be able to provide more relevant data than others. Moreover, it is likely that the same individuals will be more comfortable and articulate in sharing their perceptions. Hypotheses developed through these sources must, however, be corroborated through more representative sampling, because these special informants, by definition, will have biased perspectives of the organization.

If this second level of observation is chosen, the time sampling becomes important. There are no hard and fast rules about how frequently the observer should visit the setting, but a key consideration is the reaction that can be expected. The observer should, as much as possible, avoid disturbing the organizational ambience. After the initial entry phase, the observer should enter the setting frequently enough that a handshake or other formal greeting is considered unnecessary. In other words, the arrival of the observer should not be an "event" that calls attention to his or her presence, thereby altering the behavior of members of the organization.

## Level III: Intensive Participant Observation

In the most intensive level of involvement, the observer may assume an anthropological role, living and working within the setting. This modality has the advantage of minimizing reactions and it enables the observer to perform analyses that otherwise would be impossible. This level of activity might also include the following:

- Structured interviews, which can be used to corroborate findings developed through other sources and which permit multi-trait/multi-method checks on the research methodology.
- Structured job observation such as that proposed by Jenkins et al. (1975). This would be particularly appropriate in studies designed to assess the impact of job-enlargement interventions.
- Structured group observation (e.g., Bales, 1971; Gibbard & Hartman, 1973), the results of which will be amenable to time-series analysis, thereby strengthening the design of studies involving single cases.

- Combined questionnaire and interview formats in which respondents first complete survey instruments and then participate in open-ended discussions that provide opportunities to clarify and elaborate on their questionnaire responses. The information generated can be used in later analyses of quantitative data; for example, critical misunderstandings about questionnaire items could be uncovered by this process.

This level of effort enables the observer to seek out and develop rapport with individuals who would be reluctant to speak candidly with researchers engaged in straight data-collection efforts. Such individuals may be suspicious of the purpose of the research or simply intimidated by the presence of an outsider. Yet, a balanced, valid picture of the setting would include the views of these individuals.

The observer who becomes part of the setting must be aware of the danger of co-optation. As Perkins, Nieva, and Lawler (in press) observe, personal relationships may eclipse professional identity. The problem is similar to that faced by anthropologists in their studies of other cultures: How much intimacy is necessary to obtain valid information and at what point does one lose the capacity to be a critical observer?

Once again, there are no simple solutions to the dilemma, but certain precautions can be taken. Observations and conclusions can, for example, be corroborated with those of other researchers who enter the organization; this mechanism is particularly effective if observers have different characteristics, such as race or sex, that could cause them to draw different conclusions or to elicit dissimilar reactions from members of the setting. Further, the inferences drawn by observers can be subjected to the scrutiny of an "external critic" (Sarason, 1972), for example, a researcher who is familiar with the study but not directly associated with the data-gathering effort. Observers also should be aware that the likelihood of identification with the organization to be studied will increase with the level of involvement that is selected.

## CONCLUSION

The methods and instruments suggested in this paper are illustrative of a structured naturalistic approach to the observation of organizational behavior. Obviously, the researcher would want to choose an integrated "set" of techniques that can provide a valid picture of the organization under study. Although this discussion has suggested examples, the final design should be based on a contingency approach to the evaluative task (Perkins, 1977). That is, one should attempt to establish a "fit" between the objectives of the research and the specific instruments and methods employed. Such a design must include considerations of observer selection and training, sampling, instrumentation, and the appropriate level of observer involvement in the setting and behavior under investigation.

### REFERENCES

Argyris, C. *Interpersonal competence and organizational effectiveness.* Homewood, IL: Irwin-Dorsey, 1962.

Argyris, C. *Behind the front page.* San Francisco: Jossey-Bass, 1974.

Bales, R.F. *Interaction process analysis.* Reading, MA: Addison-Wesley, 1950.

Bales, R.F. *Personality and interpersonal behavior.* New York: Holt, Rinehart and Winston, 1971.

Barker, R.G. *Ecological psychology.* Stanford, CA: Stanford University Press, 1968.

Blau, P.M. *The dynamics of bureaucracy.* Chicago: The University of Chicago Press, 1955.

Bogdan, R., & Taylor, S.J. *Introduction to qualitative research methods.* New York: John Wiley, 1975.

Erikson, K.T. A comment on disguised observation in sociology. *Social Problems,* 1967, *14*(4), 366-373.

Gibbard, G.S., & Hartman, J.J. Relationship patterns in self-analytic groups. *Behavioral Science,* 1973, *18*(5), 335-353.

Gold, R.L. Roles in sociological field observations. *Social Forces,* 1958, *36*(3), 217-223.

Gouldner, A.W. *Patterns of industrial bureaucracy.* New York: The Free Press, 1954.

Guilford, J.P. *Psychometric methods* (2nd ed.). New York: McGraw-Hill, 1954.

Hanlon, M.D. Observational methods in organizational assessment. In E.E. Lawler, D.A. Nadler, & C. Cammann (Eds.), *Oganizational assessment: Perspectives on the measurement of organizational behavior and the quality of working life.* New York: John Wiley, 1980.

Heyns, R.W., & Lippitt, R. Systematic observational techniques. In G. Lindzey (Ed.), *Handbook of social psychology.* Reading, MA: Addison-Wesley, 1954.

Jenkins, G.D., Nadler, D.A., Lawler, E.E., & Cammann, C. Standardized observations: An approach to measuring the nature of jobs. *Journal of Applied Psychology,* 1975, *60*(2), 171-181.

Junker, B.H. *Fieldwork.* Chicago: University of Chicago Press, 1960.

Katz, D., & Kahn, R.L. *The social psychology of organizations* (2nd ed.). New York: John Wiley, 1978.

Likert, R. *The human organization: Its management and value.* New York: McGraw-Hill, 1967.

Macy, B.A., & Mirvis, P.H. A methodology for assessment of quality of work life and organizational effectiveness in behavioral economic terms. *Administrative Science Quarterly,* 1976, *21*(2), 212-226.

McCall, G., & Simmons, J. *Issues in participant observation.* Reading, MA: Addison-Wesley, 1969.

Miller, S.M. The participant observer and "over-rapport." *American Sociological Review,* 1952, *17*(1), 97-99.

Nadler, D.A. *Feedback and organization development: Using data-based methods.* Reading, MA: Addison-Wesley, 1977.

Nadler, D.A., & Jenkins, C.D., Jr. A method of standardized observation of the psychological characteristics of jobs. *Michigan organizational assessment package.* Ann Arbor, MI: Institute for Social Research, 1978.

Nieva, R., Fichman, M., & Perkins, D.N.T. Unstructured observation. In D.A. Nadler (Ed.), *Michigan organizational assessment package: Progress report II.* Ann Arbor, MI: Institute for Social Research, 1975.

Perkins, D.N.T. Evaluating social interventions: A conceptual schema. *Evaluation Quarterly,* 1977, *1*(4), 639-656.

Perkins, D.N.T., Nieva, V.F., & Lawler, E.E. *Quality of work life in new settings.* New York: John Wiley, in press.

Porter, L.W., Lawler, E.E., & Hackman, J.R. *Behavior in organizations.* New York: McGraw-Hill, 1975.

Sarason, S.B. *The creation of settings and the future societies.* San Francisco: Jossey-Bass, 1972.

Sayles, L.R. *Managerial behavior: Administration in complex organizations.* New York: McGraw-Hill, 1964.

Scott, W.R. Field work in a formal organization: Some dilemmas in the role of observer. *Human Organization,* 1963, *22*(2), 162-168.

Schatzman, L., & Strauss, A.L. *Field research: Strategies for a national sociology.* Englewood Cliffs, NJ: Prentice-Hall, 1973.

Sieber, S.D. The integration of fieldwork and survey methods. *American Journal of Sociology,* 1973, *78*(6), 1335-1359.

Staw, B.M. Attribution of the "causes" of performance: A general alternative interpretation of cross-sectional research on organizations. *Organizational Behavior and Human Performance,* 1975, *13*(3), 414-432.

Weick, K.E. Systematic observational methods. In G. Lindzey & E. Aronson (Eds.), *The handbook of social psychology* (Vol. 2). Reading, MA: Addison-Wesley, 1968.

Whyte, W.F. *Money and motivation: An analysis of incentives in industry.* New York: Harper & Row, 1955.

**Dennis N.T. Perkins, Ph.D.,** *is an assistant professor in the School of Organization and Management and Department of Psychology at Yale University, New Haven, Connecticut. His teaching and research interests are in the areas of human motivation, self-assessment and careers, community psychology, social ecology, evaluation, research, and new organizations. He has consulted with organizations in both the public and private sectors and is the author of a forthcoming book on new organizations.*

**David A. Nadler, Ph.D.,** *is an associate professor in the organizational behavior area of the Graduate School of Business, Columbia University, New York, New York. His specialties include organizational change, feedback and group performance, and organizational design. Dr. Nadler has worked extensively as a consultant on problems of organizational behavior, management, organizational design, and planned organizational change. He is the author of numerous articles and book chapters and has co-authored or edited five books.*

**Martin D. Hanlon, Ph.D.,** *is an assistant professor in the Department of Urban Studies, Queens College of the City University of New York. His research interests include the quality of working life in organizations, mental health aspects of work and unemployment, and measuring the effectiveness of health care and human service organizations.*

# APPENDIX

A sample of a completed general observation form, a sample list of setting and event codes, a table of sample variables, a supplemental orientation interview, and a supplemental group behavior observation form are included here to illustrate the range of instrumentation that can be used in structured naturalistic observation.

## SAMPLE GENERAL OBSERVATION FORM

Site:   Columbia National Bank        Setting:   Top Management

Observer:   Mary B.                   Event:   Project Committee Meeting

Date & Time:   1/16/76, 11:30 a.m.    Variables:   Evaluation, Project Opposition

21st Meeting of NPH Project Committee

(Title of Observation)

*Overview of Event:*   Meeting was held to review progress of the project, to find out how initial meetings with the new consultants and branch staff had gone, to review evaluation procedures, and to meet with a representative of the consulting team. See attached agenda.

*Detailed Observations:*

1. Meeting called to order at 11:30 by Cassis. Also in attendance are Norton, Flinton, Orlinoff, Burns, and Pote. Cassis reviews agenda.

2. Cassis calls on Flinton to give progress report on the project to date. Flinton gives report, including the following: "We are making good progress, although it may seem slow to you. We have finished the interviews in the different branches; unfortunately, this took much longer than we expected because it was difficult to get cooperation in some branches. In other branches we obtained cooperation but it was difficult to find people free during working hours, and many did not want to stay and be interviewed on their own time."

3. Norton replies: "What do you think all this means? Do you have any sense that the problems that you are having may be significant in terms of the project?"

4. Flinton: "No. I don't think it says anything about the project; I think it is just one of those things that we run into when doing something like this."

5. Others, including Pote and Burns, raise questions about the progress to date.

*Interpretations:*

1. Why did the project run into so many problems? Is this important?
2. Flinton seems to be very defensive. Why? What does this mean?
3. Norton appears to be leading a group that is trying to "gun down" the project.

*Observer Feelings:*

I was angry at Flinton for being defensive. I felt frustrated.

*Attachments:*

Meeting agenda

# SAMPLE SETTING AND EVENT CODES[1]

*Setting: Surgical Unit #1*

*Event categories:*

| | |
|---|---|
| 1. Staff conferences | All formal staff meetings of the unit, with or without consultants |
| 2. Doctors' orientation | Monthly orientation meetings as well as all other formal project activities directly involving and based around unit house staff, doctors, and questionnaire administration |
| 3. Random observations | Limited to observations listed on random observation schedule |
| 4. Unscheduled observations | Unscheduled observations, brief visits to the unit |
| 5. Research activities | Descriptions of questionnaire administration, formal interviews with unit staff, personnel rosters |
| 6. Other | Residual category |

*Setting: Surgical Unit #2*

*Event categories:*

| | |
|---|---|
| 1. Random observations | As above |
| 2. Unscheduled observations | As above |
| 3. Research activities | As above |
| 4. Other | As above |

*Setting: Nursing-Service Administration*

*Event categories:*

| | |
|---|---|
| 1. Surgery Administrator—Surgery #1 supervisors | All meetings involving the assistant director of nursing for surgery and the SCN's and CS's of Surgical Unit #1 |
| 2. Surgery Administrator—Leadership group | All meetings involving the surgery administrator and supervisory staff under her direction, within and outside surgery pavilion |
| 3. Surgery Administrator—Consultants | All consultant work with the surgery administrator in which other hospital staff are not participants |
| 4. Director of nursing | All consultant activities involving the director of nursing and special projects within the nursing department initiated by consultants and the director of nursing |
| 5. Other | Residual category |

*Setting: Project Steering Committee*

*Event categories:*

| | |
|---|---|
| 1. Steering committee meetings | Regular meetings, meetings of subcommittee, and meetings of work groups |
| 2. Interviews | Interviews with steering-committee members and "one-on-one" meetings |
| 3. Other | Residual category |

---

[1]Adapted from an observational study of a change project in a hospital. Identifying information has been changed.

**SAMPLE VARIABLES FOR CODING OF OBSERVATIONS**[2]

| Task | Individuals | Organizational Arrangements | Informal Organization |
|---|---|---|---|
| *Organizational tasks* | *Response capabilities* | *Subunits* | *Small-group functioning* |
| complexity | intelligence | grouping of tasks | norms |
| predictability | skills and abilities | and roles | informal goals |
| required interdependence | experience | unit composition | communication |
| | training | unit design | patterns |
| | | formal leadership | cohesiveness |
| | | in the unit | informal group |
| | | physical arrangements | structure |
| *Subunit and individual tasks* | *Psychological differences* | *Coordination and control* | *Intergroup relations* |
| complexity | need strength | goals | conflict/cooperation |
| predictability | attitudes | plans | information flow |
| required interdependence | perceptual biases | hierarchy | perceptions |
| dence | expectations | reward systems | |
| autonomy | differences in | personnel systems | *Organizational level* |
| feedback | background | control systems | |
| task variety | | integrator roles | |
| task identity | | and groups | networks, cliques, |
| task meaningfulness | | | and coalitions |
| task skill demands | | | conflicting-interest |
| | | | groups |
| | | | distribution of |
| | | | power |
| | | | ideology and values |

---

[2]Adapted from D.A. Nadler & M.L. Tushman, A diagnostic model for organizational behavior. In J.R. Hackman, E.E. Lawler, & L.W. Porter (Eds.), *Perspectives on behavior in organizations.* New York: McGraw-Hill, 1977.

# SUPPLEMENTAL ORIENTATION INTERVIEW

*Instructions:* This interview guide is designed to be used for preliminary data collection in an organization and as a prelude to observation. Included are a list of open-ended questions that can be used to conduct an interview that could last from twenty minutes to two hours. Such an interview usually will be used after the researchers have entered the organization and made introductory presentations to the employees. The questions are to be used as a general guide, rather than as a script that must be adhered to. In most sections of the interview, a beginning question is followed by one or more questions designed to follow-up on the main question and to probe for additional information. These follow-up questions are optional.

**Introduction to Interviewee**

Hello, my name is ——————————. I was here not long ago to describe a project that I am working on in this organization. (*Review basic goals of specific research program and answer any questions that the interviewee may have about the project before proceeding further.*)

As I mentioned the last time I was here, one of the first things that I have to do is to learn about this organization and what it is like to work here. One way of doing this is to interview some of the people who work here. I have asked to speak to people working at different levels and in different work units. Specific individuals were picked at random, essentially like picking a name out of a hat. Your name was picked as one of the people to be interviewed from this unit.

What I would like to do is to spend about an hour today talking with you about your job, this organization, and how things are around here. I have a set of questions that I will be asking you. Everyone who is interviewed will be asked basically the same questions. Some of these questions will seem a little vague, but please answer the questions based on what you think they mean. If you don't know the answer or don't feel like talking about a topic, let me know and we will move on to the next set of questions.

During this interview, I would like you to be as open and frank as you can. The contents of this interview are *strictly confidential.* No one except you and me will ever know specifically what was said here. I will, of course, be using the information you give me as part of the research data about this organization, but all the information will be summarized and no sources will be given. No person's individual comments will be seen, and no information will be presented in a way that might allow someone to figure out who said it. Before we start, do you have any questions? (*Pause for questions.*)

As we proceed, I would like to make some notes so that I can remember what you have said. Do you mind my taking notes? (*Pause for answer.*)

Interviewee ————————————————————————————————

Date of Interview ————————————————————————————————

Location of Interview ————————————————————————————————

Interviewer ————————————————————————————————

**Questions**

    I.  The Person and His/Her Job

        A.  What is your job title here in this organization?

        B.  If you had to describe your job to someone who is not familiar with this kind of work, how would you describe what you do?

        C.  When did you first start to work in this job?

        D.  How long have you worked for this organization?

        E.  What other jobs have you had in this organization?

II. The Work

A. *Main question:* How does the work get done in this unit (department, organization, etc.)?

B. *Follow-up probe questions:*
1. How does your job fit into the way the work is done?
2. With whom do you have to talk in order to get your work done?
3. What kinds of communication (such as reports, memos, instructions, etc.) do you receive or send out as part of your job?
4. What are the major problems in getting the work done here?

III. Groups

A. *Main question:* What are some of the groups that exist here (both formal and informal)?

B. *Follow-up probe questions:*
1. What kinds of people belong to these groups?
2. How do these groups contribute to getting the work done?
3. How do these groups get along with each other?
4. Do you feel as if you are a part of any group?
5. How are decisions made in your group?
6. If you worked particularly well, how would the members of your group feel about you?

IV. Supervision

A. *Main question:* Who is your supervisor (the person who directs your work, gives you assignments, evaluates you, etc.)?

B. *Follow-up probe questions:*
1. How frequently do you communicate with your supervisor?
2. What kinds of things does your supervisor do to help you with your job?
3. In general, how much "say" do you have in the decisions that your supervisor makes?
4. In general, how well do you get along with your supervisor?

V. Structure

A. *Main question:* How is this work unit organized and how does it fit into the total organization?

B. *Follow-up probe questions:*
1. Describe or draw an organizational chart of this particular work unit.
2. What kinds of planning, budget, or information systems exist here?
3. What other work units does your unit have to relate to or deal with?
4. What kinds of problems arise between different work units? How are they usually dealt with?
5. What is the structure of the total organization (or appropriate larger organizational unit)?
6. Who really controls what goes on in this organization?
7. What are the key informal groups that make things happen in this organization?

VI. Rewards

A. *Main question:* If you do your job well, will you be rewarded for it (by pay, promotion, praise, etc.)?

B. *Follow-up probe questions:*
1. How is pay determined in this organization?
2. How are promotions made in this organization?

VII. Satisfaction

A. *Main question:* In general, how satisfied are you with working here?

B. *Follow-up probe questions:*
1. About what things are you most dissatisfied?
2. About what things do you feel most satisfied at work?

VIII. Problems and Changes

A. *Main question:* If you could make any change you wanted to in this organization (within reason), what would you change and why?

B. *Follow-up probe questions:*
   1. What do you think are the major problems in this organization?
   2. What do you think are the major strengths of this organization?
   3. What do you think is blocking changes that are needed here?

IX. Union Activity (Optional; should be asked earlier in the interview if used.)

A. *Main question:* What is the situation here between management and the union(s)?

B. *Follow-up probe questions:*
   1. Are you a union member? If so, what union?
   2. What do you think of labor-management relations here?
   3. How does the union affect the way you do your job?

## Summary

I have asked you a number of questions about yourself and the organization. Are there other things that I should know if I want to understand what goes on around here? (*Pause for answer.*)

We have spent some time answering my questions. Do you have any questions that you would like to ask me? (*Pause for answer.*)

Thank you very much for your help. The information you have provided will be very valuable as we begin trying to understand this organization. I appreciate your cooperation.

# GROUP-BEHAVIOR OBSERVATION SHEET

Observer _____     Setting _____

Date _____     Event _____

Time _____     Variables _____

Name of group/meeting: _____

Purpose of meeting: _____

*Instructions:* This form is designed to help the observer to structure his or her observation of what happens in a group meeting. The form should be filled out as soon after the meeting as possible.

For each area of observation, read the question and check the number of the response that is most appropriate. As you answer the questions, be sure to think only of the group that you have just observed and, in particular, be careful to think in terms of *this* current meeting of the group. Many of the questions ask about things that "group members" do. Answer these questions, in terms of how the group members behaved *in general*.

## A. Group Identity

1. Do members have a sense of group identity?

   No, members have little
   or no sense of themselves           (1) (2) (3) (4) (5) (6) (7)
   as a group

   Yes, members are
   very aware of themselves
   as being a group.

2. Is the membership of the group clear?

   No, it is unclear who is
   a member of the group and           (1) (2) (3) (4) (5) (6) (7)
   who is not.

   Yes, it is very
   clear who the
   group members are.

3. Do most members seem to feel that they really are part of the group?

   No, most members do
   not feel that they are part         (1) (2) (3) (4) (5) (6) (7)
   of the group.

   Yes, most members
   do feel that they are part of
   the group.

4. Do group members appear to be involved in the activities of the group?

   No, most members do not
   seem to care what happens           (1) (2) (3) (4) (5) (6) (7)
   within the group.

   Yes, most members
   are very concerned
   about the group's activities.

## B. Group Goals

5. How clear are the goals of the group?

   None of the members have
   a clear idea of the group's         (1) (2) (3) (4) (5) (6) (7)
   goals.

   All the members clearly
   understand the group's
   goals.

6. Does the group know exactly what needs to be done?

   No, the group is not
   sure what it is supposed            (1) (2) (3) (4) (5) (6) (7)
   to do.

   Yes, the group knows
   exactly what it is
   supposed to do.

7. Is there general agreement on the goals of the group?

No, some people
have very different      (1) (2) (3) (4) (5) (6) (7)      Yes, everyone agrees about
goals for the group.      the goals of the group.

## C. Group Roles

8. Is it clear what roles different members have?

No, there is much confusion      Yes, everyone knows
about who is supposed to do      (1) (2) (3) (4) (5) (6) (7)      exactly what he or she and
what.      others are supposed to do.

## D. Patterns of Member Participation and Communication

9. How even is participation by members?

Uneven; a small number      Even; members
of people do all the      (1) (2) (3) (4) (5) (6) (7)      participate equally.
talking.

10. To whom do most people direct their comments?

Most members direct      All members seem
their comments to one      (1) (2) (3) (4) (5) (6) (7)      to be talking to
person or a few people.      each other.

11. Are the opinions of all members listened to?

No; some members'      Yes; all members
inputs are ignored.      (1) (2) (3) (4) (5) (6) (7)      seem to be listened
to by others.

## E. Openness of Communication

12. How open are group members in expressing their feelings in the group?

Group members are very      Group members are
closed, guarded, and do not      (1) (2) (3) (4) (5) (6) (7)      very open and express
express feelings.      their feelings freely.

13. How supportive are group members toward each other?

Members are not supportive.      (1) (2) (3) (4) (5) (6) (7)      Members are very
supportive.

14. Are group members willing to confront each other or to respond negatively to the comments of others?

No; group members do      Yes; group members are
not confront each      (1) (2) (3) (4) (5) (6) (7)      very confrontive.
other.

15. How well do members receive negative comments?

Poorly; people seem to be      Very well; people seem to
threatened by negative      (1) (2) (3) (4) (5) (6) (7)      listen to, value, and make
comments and react defensively.      use of negative comments.

## F. Problem Solving

16. Does the group define problems before starting to work on them?

No; the group jumps into      Yes; the group clearly
problem solving without clearly      (1) (2) (3) (4) (5) (6) (7)      defines the nature and
defining what the problem is.      scope of the problem before
starting work.

17. Are multiple solutions generated for problems?

No; the group tends to use
the first solution that comes      (1) (2) (3) (4) (5) (6) (7)
along and stops looking for
other solutions.

Yes; the group attempts
to explore a whole range of
solutions before deciding
on a course of action.

## G. Conflict Within the Group

18. How much conflict is there within the group?

Little conflict is apparent.      (1) (2) (3) (4) (5) (6) (7)

Much conflict is apparent
among members.

19. How openly are conflicts expressed?

Not at all; the conflicts
are often hidden and the      (1) (2) (3) (4) (5) (6) (7)
real issues are not dealt
with.

Very openly; the real
issues emerge and the
nature of the conflict
is "above board."

20. In general, how is conflict dealt with?

    (1) forcing (person with power wins)
    (2) smoothing (denial of the conflict)
    (3) withdrawal (by one side or member)
    (4) confrontation (those in conflict directly work it out)
    (5) arbitration (a third party decides)
    (6) other

## H. Leadership Within the Group

21. Are leadership roles and assignments clear?

No; it is not clear who
is supposed to do what,      (1) (2) (3) (4) (5) (6) (7)
who is in charge, etc.

Yes; it is very clear
who has responsibility
and leadership.

22. How much is leadership shared?

Little; one person performs
all leadership functions.      (1) (2) (3) (4) (5) (6) (7)

Much; each person performs
different leadership
functions as appropriate.

23. How would you characterize the "style" of the formal group leaders?

Very directive      (1) (2) (3) (4) (5) (6) (7)

Very participative

24. How effectively were the task-leadership functions performed?

Not at all      (1) (2) (3) (4) (5) (6) (7)

Effectively

25. How effectively were the maintenance-leadership functions performed?

Not at all      (1) (2) (3) (4) (5) (6) (7)

Effectively

## I. Decision Making Within the Group

26. Are needed decisions generally made?

No; frequently important
questions are not answered      (1) (2) (3) (4) (5) (6) (7)
or issues are not resolved.

Yes; the group always
makes a decision when
it has to.

27. How much do group members participate in decision making?

Very little; a few people
make the decisions and      (1) (2) (3) (4) (5) (6) (7)
others are not involved.

A great deal; the whole
group is involved in
making most decisions.

28. How are decisions usually made?

        (1) consensus
        (2) one person makes them for the larger group
        (3) a small group makes them for the larger group
        (4) open voting
        (5) secret ballot
        (6) other

## J. Overall Group Effectiveness

29. How would you rate the group along the following dimensions?

| | Ineffective | | | | | | Effective |
|---|---|---|---|---|---|---|---|
| a. problem solving | (1) | (2) | (3) | (4) | (5) | (6) | (7) |
| b. decision making | (1) | (2) | (3) | (4) | (5) | (6) | (7) |
| c. getting the work done | (1) | (2) | (3) | (4) | (5) | (6) | (7) |
| d. making use of members' skills, abilities, resources | (1) | (2) | (3) | (4) | (5) | (6) | (7) |
| e. meeting individual needs | (1) | (2) | (3) | (4) | (5) | (6) | (7) |

## K. Ratings of Group "Climate"

30. Indicate the general tone or climate of the group meeting.

| | | | | | | | | |
|---|---|---|---|---|---|---|---|---|
| Happy | (1) | (2) | (3) | (4) | (5) | (6) | (7) | Sad |
| Anxious | (1) | (2) | (3) | (4) | (5) | (6) | (7) | Calm |
| Clear | (1) | (2) | (3) | (4) | (5) | (6) | (7) | Confused |
| Proud | (1) | (2) | (3) | (4) | (5) | (6) | (7) | Ashamed |
| Angry | (1) | (2) | (3) | (4) | (5) | (6) | (7) | Friendly |
| Frustrated | (1) | (2) | (3) | (4) | (5) | (6) | (7) | Satisfied |
| Energetic | (1) | (2) | (3) | (4) | (5) | (6) | (7) | Lazy |
| Strong | (1) | (2) | (3) | (4) | (5) | (6) | (7) | Weak |
| Restless | (1) | (2) | (3) | (4) | (5) | (6) | (7) | Content |
| Involved | (1) | (2) | (3) | (4) | (5) | (6) | (7) | Apathetic |

## L. Specific Information About the Group Meeting

31. Who assumed leadership in the group and in what ways?

32. What major conflicts emerged in the group?

33. What subgroups seemed to be forming and working, and around what issues?

34. Where is this group in its overall development (growth)?

35. Other comments relevant to the group:

# INTRODUCTION TO THE
# RESOURCES SECTION

We all are familiar with the knowledge explosion, the fact that the amount of new knowledge produced increases dramatically each year. This continuing expansion of the information base both hard and soft sciences presents two major problems. First there is the issue of turning theory into practice, of gaining acceptance for and adoption of innovations that are based on new knowledge. This can be easy, as in the case of television, but sometimes user acceptance is difficult to obtain, as in the case of automobile seat belts.

Rogers (1971) has identified several variables that affect the adoption of an innovation. One is the extent to which the innovation is (or seems to be) better, more useful, easier to use, etc., than the thing it displaces. For example, television had an obvious *relative advantage* when compared to radio.

A second factor identified by Rogers is *compatibility*: the degree to which the innovation is in harmony with existing standards, practices, norms, and beliefs. For most Americans, television seemed as compatible with their values and beliefs as radio. (Only forty years later did people realize the extent to which television has affected these values and beliefs.)

A third factor is *complexity*. To continue the previous example, color televisions were not accepted as quickly as the initial black-and-white televisions because their relative advantages were not so great and because their technical complexity made them more difficult to operate and more costly to repair.

The easier it is to try out an innovation without final commitment, the more widespread the innovation is likely to become (assuming that it meets the previous criteria). *Trialability* is Roger's fourth variable.

Finally, *visibility*, the extent to which the innovation can be seen in use—and to which *users* can be seen—affects adoption. Those who recall the beginnings of television may remember that some people purchased and installed antennas, even though they had no television sets, in order to appear to be keeping up with the new standards. Color television, in contrast, had no additional, publicly visible aspect; therefore, it was not necessary to turn in one's old television set for a new color set unless one could afford to do so.

In reviewing these five factors, it becomes clear that television, as an innovation, met almost all the requirements for public acceptance, while the further refinement of color television did not. Thus, color television required a great marketing effort by the manufacturers and the television industry before it received widespread acceptance.

The second major issue in accepting innovation based on new knowledge is the user's problem in evaluating the innovation and the information that is given about it. This is especially serious when the user is not an expert and is relatively unqualified to judge the technical merit of research knowledge or of a specific device based on that knowledge. Obviously, some expert, technical advice is quite desirable, but the five factors identified by Rogers also can provide the user of a resource or the adopter of an innovation with some standards by which to evaluate that resource or innovation.

1. *Relative Advantage*: Is it better than what is currently done or available? How much better?

2. *Compatibility*: Is it consistent with accepted or other practices on products, or is it *preferable* to what is currently available or done?

3. *Complexity*: How difficult or complicated is it to use this resource or innovation effectively or to engage in this practice?

4. *Trialability*: Can it be tried out before a final decision or commitment is made?

5. *Visibility*: Is it obvious that one is using this resource or innovation? Is visibility (or nonvisibility) important or desirable in this case?

These questions can be applied to a practice, such as a new method of performance appraisal or a new managerial style, as well as to a physical innovation such as a new machine for the production department. Although not fully adequate for evaluating a particular resource or innovation, these standards can be very helpful as *part* of an evaluation and decison-making process.

Users might even try to evaluate the four resources in this section in terms of the previous criteria. Our hope is that every *Annual* user will rate some of them quite positively. Some (if not all) of the following resources should at least prove compatible with the practices, beliefs, and needs of every *Annual* user.

**Reference**

Rogers, E.M., with Shoemaker, F.F. *Communication of innovation*. New York: The Free Press, 1971.

# FACILITATING SIMULATION GAMES

## Myron R. Chartier

Experiential-learning methods are widely used as major training interventions by human relations facilitators. According to Gaw (1979, p. 147), "experiential learning provides activities that have the potential to involve the whole person in the educational process." As experiential, communication devices, simulations potentially have the ability to convey a gestaltic awareness of a referent reality. Social-simulation games, which involve participants interactively in a simulated environment and create within them an awareness and understanding of social systems, are dynamic, operating models of human realities.

The purpose of this article is to provide the human relations facilitator with an overview of this highly involving technology. Three aspects are explored: viewing simulation games as simulated social systems, facilitating simulation games, and designing such games. The primary emphasis is on facilitation.

## GAMES AS SIMULATED SOCIAL SYSTEMS

Simulations are attempts to simulate social realities (e.g., marital dyads, decision-making groups, organizations, neighborhoods, cities, nations, or groups of nations). Many behavioral scientists view such entities from a social-systems perspective (Katz & Kahn, 1978; Olsen, 1968). Any scientific attempt to understand a social organism as a system involves the observer in theoretical model building. Because of the complexity of social reality, critical variables must be identified and extracted from the whole. Such processes, however, tend to oversimplify social reality in order to make it comprehensible.

### Definition of a Social System

A system is a bounded set of components standing in transactive relationship to each other. In a social system the whole is more than the sum of its parts. A simulation seeks to operationalize the transactive relationships of a social system so that its functions and processes may be observed and experienced. For example, "The Marriage Game" has to be comprehended in terms of two sets of elements: those in the society at large and those in the individuals making marital decisions. This game posits that marital interactions take place between persons who live in a world of external social facts, many of which have been internalized, affecting conceptions and values (Greenblat, 1975).

### Primary Components of Social Systems

Simulations seek to place the following primary components of social systems into an actual transactive relationship:

1. *People.* People make a system "social" rather than "mechanical." The ways people or groups of people interact with respect to the other basic components define the nature of a system with respect to kind (e.g., a family, a classroom, or a decision-making group) and quality (i.e., salubrious or pathogenic).

2. *Goals.* Because goals draw people together for interaction, social systems are purposeful. People develop social systems to accomplish their purposes, but goals vary in different social systems.

3. *Tasks.* To accomplish their goals, people have to perform certain tasks. Each social system has its task requirements, and they vary widely among social organisms.

4. *Structure.* In order to perform task requirements, social structure is necessary. This component is intermeshed with the other six. For example, the nature of the goals, the demands of the tasks, and the characteristics of people have a fundamental influence upon structure.

5. *Resources.* Resources are needed to perform tasks and accomplish goals. These include people and their varied abilities, finances, time, space, and facilities.

6. *Values.* This component varies with the type of social system (e.g., loyalty in families, profit in businesses).

7. *Constraints.* The limits of a social system are defined by its firm (but alterable) constraints. These tenacious forces provide an ordered consistency in social systems.

## THE NATURE OF SOCIAL SYSTEMS

Any one component by itself would fail to create a social unit, and changing any one component would redefine the system. The various elements acting upon each other create a social system.

Social systems are open systems—that is, they receive inputs from the environment, process them, and send outputs back to the environment. However, they are also bounded systems, because they have boundaries that filter the inputs and outputs. Social units are in constant transactive relationships with their environments. In that sense they are adaptive; "they possess the ability to react to their environments in a way that is favorable . . . to the continued operation of the system" (Hall & Fagen, 1975, p. 61).

Figure 1 is a verbal-graphic model of a social system. It portrays the various components and their transactive processes in relationship to each other and to the environment.

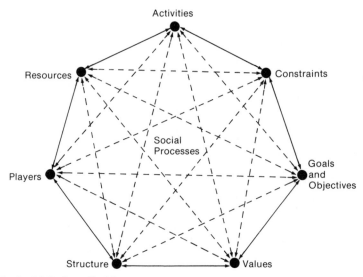

**Figure 1. The Social-Systems Model**

# FACILITATING SIMULATION GAMES

Human relations facilitators who want participants to experience the complexity of a social system with its constant interplay of variables will find simulations a suitable technology. The games are available for the four major areas of activity in human relations—individual, group, organization, and community (Jones & Pfeiffer, 1975)—with a focus on personal growth as well as leadership, organization, and community development (Horn & Cleaves, 1980).

## Evaluating Simulation Games

Most of the game manuals explain the theoretical model and state the principal objectives. After reading the rules and actually playing the game, the facilitator may discover other training values or conclude that the stated objectives have been exaggerated or that important concepts are oversimplified or neglected. The evaluation should also consider the abilities and interests of the potential participants, because simulations vary in subject matter, complexity, and sophistication.

The novice facilitator should use simple games to prevent frustration or disenchantment with games. However, the game must be difficult enough to challenge the participants. The room space and physical equipment required must also be considered. Some evaluation questions are provided in the appendix to this article to help in making decisions about the worth and suitability of a game in relation to training objectives, the abilities of the participants, and needed facilities.

## Preparing the Facilitator

The key to a successful game experience is thorough preparation. The facilitator must discover what is being simulated and how the designer is attempting to bring these processes into operation through game play. This information is often included in the instructional materials that accompany the games.

As the facilitator studies the prepared materials, he or she should try to understand the interrelationships among the game components, which parallel the elements within a social-systems model (see Figure 1).

### Players

The first component consists of the *players*. Answers to the following questions will provide needed information: Are individuals or teams used? Do the players assume a role as in role-playing games? How should roles be assigned? What is the optimum/minimum number of people who can play the game? Can the game be played by an odd number of players or must the number be even?

### Goals and Objectives

The next component includes both *goals* and *objectives* and should provide answers to the following questions: What are the goals of the simulated processes? What educational/training objectives does the game provide for the players? Is the game structured to communicate concepts and their utilization, or is it structured to involve people in new feelings, attitudes, and/or behaviors? The goals and objectives may be the same or quite distinct. Goals may relate to the simulated processes, whereas objectives may be related to training.

### Activities

*Activities* in a simulation game are related to the task requirements of a social system. Relevant questions include the following: In what specific tasks does the game involve players? Is there a sequence of activities? If so, what? Is the game played in cycles? How are the game activities related to the educational/training objectives? What is required from the players? How much time is needed?

## Structure

Simulation games and social systems require *structure*, which raises the following questions: What space and furniture arrangements are needed to create the simulated social dynamics? Is more than one room required? If players must move around, how much space is needed? Does the game require individuals or teams in special locations? Will the room accommodate the noise level of the activities?

## Resources

The *resources* component consists of the game materials, which can range from sheets of paper (explaining profiles or scenarios for role playing) to game boards, poker chips, chance cards, score sheets, etc. The facilitator needs to know what these materials are and should find answers to the following questions: How are they related to each other? With which rules do they function? How are they related to the game activities? How much time is needed to set up materials for game play? Are there enough materials for the present purposes? What other resources and equipment are needed?

## Values

Simulations—like social systems—have *values*. Some game instructions specify values, but others require the facilitator to discern the values by examining the other game components. The values may become apparent after the game is in progress.

## Constraints

The *constraints* in a simulation game are its rules and procedures. A detailed study of the game rules will reveal how the game will function as a social system. Failure to understand the game rules and procedures can short-circuit the social dynamics of the entire experience, or even cause them to fail.

After the rules and procedures are understood, the facilitator needs to decide how these will be communicated to the players. Manuals for participants, which are sometimes included with the game, are usually quite brief, because participants are rarely told all the details in advance; they learn the details as they participate. Some games are marketed with sound filmstrips that give a general overview and brief explanation of the game rules, and others require the facilitator to instruct the players orally or to provide a summary of the rules in print.

### Facilitator's Role

The facilitator must understand his or her *role* in the game, because he or she is responsible for the enactment of a simulated social system through game play. The primary functions of the facilitator are understanding and interpreting game rules, answering players' questions, encouraging participation and experimentation, helping players cope with uncertainty, and helping the participants to discuss and evaluate their experience.

After the game components and the facilitator's role are understood, defects and errors should be removed before the simulation is formally introduced in a training event. Several options are available:

1. Without actually playing a simulation game, a person can acquire a feel for it by playing the various roles and performing the activities.

2. Some simulation games need to be played in advance with several participants. These same participants could be assigned to major roles in the actual simulation or scattered among the teams so that they could help the slower participants.

3. A select number of persons could be assigned the task of learning the rules, introducing the game to a group, and supervising the play. The facilitator would then be free to help participants integrate the game experience with selected training objectives by planning a postgame discussion and related activities.

Any of these options will decrease confusion and increase the positive training experience.

## Preparing the Players

After the facilitator is thoroughly prepared, he or she must prepare the players by assigning roles, deciding on the number of players, and introducing the simulation.

### Assigning Roles

In simulations with a role-playing component, there may be little differentiation between roles (for instance, all may play the role of managers) or roles may vary in the degree of activity and aggressiveness required (for example, a small number may play management roles while the rest play workers). In the latter case the problem of casting arises. Casting practices vary from choosing numbers out of a hat to asking for volunteers, assigning roles arbitrarily, or deliberately assigning leadership roles to those who are natural leaders in the group.

Teams for a simulation should be heterogeneously grouped rather than homogeneously (Chartier, 1973). Participants' satisfaction with and performance in the game are maximized when competing teams have similar potential in game competition. Team role playing may be useful with slow or easily discouraged participants. Allowing a couple to play a single role decreases frustration at setbacks and provides the security of a teammate for decisions. Team efforts also accommodate more participants and may be especially advantageous with large groups.

Some games can be played more than once so that participants have an opportunity to play different roles and gain a better understanding of the simulated process. When multiple role playing is possible, it needs to be planned and encouraged.

### Deciding Number of Players

The facilitator's manual usually indicates an optimum number of players. When groups become too large, participants lose interest, and training effectiveness is decreased because participants learn rules less efficiently, interact less, participate less actively, and make fewer moves (Chartier, 1973). With some games a large group can be divided into several subgroups, each playing separately and using a set of game materials.

### Introducing the Game

The introduction will depend partly on the intended use of the game and on the training objectives. The facilitator must communicate two points: First, the participants need to understand the purpose of the game. If they have never played a simulation, the briefing could include a definition of "simulation," a comparison of simulation games with other games (such as charades), and an overview of the content and value of the game. Second, the briefing should include a clear, concise statement of how the game operates. The physical layout and game materials should be discussed. Rules need to be explained and, in some cases, demonstrated. A broad overview of the roles is useful. Knowledge of these factors helps to eliminate uncertainty. Overexplaining, however, will dampen the trainees' enthusiasm. Specific questions can be handled as they arise in the course of play.

The quality of this pregame briefing is likely to affect the participants' predisposition toward the game experience, their enjoyment of the game, and their acquisition of knowledge during the game. The facilitator needs to display enthusiasm and confidence in order to present the learning experience as attractively as possible.

## Facilitating the Game

The primary task of the facilitator is to help the simulation function smoothly. He or she should circulate in the room to answer those questions related to the *rules* of the game. The participants should discover for themselves the points of game strategy, the values of game play, and the things to be learned from participation. The facilitator may ask the participants questions unrelated to the game in order to help them arrive at their own solutions. If the facilitator forgets a rule or if a rule is not discussed in the facilitator's manual, one can be created on the spot. If materials become misplaced, the facilitator's improvisation can save the game. Active participation on the part of players should be encouraged. The extent of participation by players is directly related to the degree of learning from and satisfaction with the game experience (Chartier, 1973). The facilitator can be many things—a referee, an enabler, a coordinator, a scorekeeper, a timekeeper, and/or an observer—depending on the  game, and must be imaginative and flexible.

Generally, it is unwise for someone to facilitate a game and participate in it at the same time, because facilitators who keep changing their own roles are likely to play the roles partially and poorly. If there is little to do but watch the action of the game, a facilitator may choose to participate as a player. If this is done, however, this person has relinquished the role of facilitator and has turned the control of game flow and the postgame discussion over to the group. There is nothing wrong with this, but one must be clear about what has been done and act accordingly. A person either facilitates the game or participates, but *not both.*

## Discussing the Game Experience

People find the learning experience associated with games more satisfying if play is stopped periodically for group discussions (Chartier, 1972). After each discussion, participants can resume play and try alternate strategies or reinforce concepts learned during the game or in the group discussion. Although the facilitator's manual may suggest how a discussion needs to be handled, the questions depend on the facilitator's purpose.

Although there is no universal way to structure the group discussion, some suggestions may prove helpful. Since simulation games tend to generate a high level of interaction, participants need to discuss what happened during the game and how they feel about it. The facilitator is the key to the quality of the discussion. Participants often like to talk about a game in personal terms—"Who did what to whom?"—before going on to more substantive matters. This aspect of the discussion can be an important experience in gaining insights into interpersonal relationships. Because the interaction between participants is obviously genuine, it gives individuals an opportunity to express how they feel about how they were treated by others during the experience. This discussion should be cordial, and the basic worth of participants should never be questioned.

The facilitator should also lead the group in a discussion of the game model. This discussion gives the participants an opportunity to verbalize their understanding of the general principles underlying the simulation and to question or elaborate on the understanding of the others. During this phase the facilitator may—if appropriate—identify the winning teams or individuals and discuss the winning strategies.

A facilitator can use the participants' experiences in the game as a takeoff point for discussing the reality that has been simulated. This discussion process has at least two training payoffs: (1) It prompts participants to explicate their beliefs about the social reality being simulated and (2) it provides an opportunity for the facilitator to confront participants with alternative ways of viewing the referent reality.

The facilitator should encourage participants to be explicit about their experience with and in the game and to examine this experience in relation to their views of real social systems. A leading question could be "How do you think the game (or some aspect of it) compares with the real world?" If the participants claim the real world is different, then the next logical questions are "How do you think reality is different?" and "Why is reality different?" Other ideas for discussing insights from simulation games can be found in Gaw (1979).

## Possible Postgame Activities

One of the fundamental values of games is their ability to stimulate interest and conversation. The creative facilitator will take advantage of this and link it to other training experiences. The opportunities for interlinkage are limited only by a person's own perceptions. Listed below are a few suggestions:

1. After a group has played and discussed a simulation game, it may be motivated to pursue other activities related to the theme. For example, after playing "Dignity" a group may want to visit a ghetto and discuss life in a ghetto with the people who live there.

2. After playing a game the participants may want to change some of the game components or construct a new game. In "Generation Gap," for example, participants may like to change the issues for discussion between the parent and the teenager. They may include issues from their daily conversation or religious values and ideas. The teenagers may want to play it with their own parents.

3. Someone might be assigned to observe and report on the participants' behavior during a game. After playing "Starpower"—which tends to bring out unjust, fascistic, or racist behavior in the squares—a group may become interested in a study of human nature.

## DESIGNING SIMULATION GAMES

If a game that fits the training objectives cannot be located, a facilitator may design one. The designing process includes identifying training objectives, describing the social system, structuring the game, and writing the rules.

*Identifying Training Objectives.* Knowing what needs to be accomplished with a training event is the first step in designing a simulation. The most difficult task is to decide what aspects of a given social system to leave out and which to include. The game will be easier to design if the training objectives are clear, precise, and specific.

*Describing the Social System.* The social system needs to be selected, carefully analyzed, and described with respect to its systemic components (players, goals and objectives, activities, structure, resources, values, and constraints). The analysis should define the social system by identifying the characteristics of the components, the interlinkages of the elements and their properties, and the operational processes of the diverse units with respect to the whole system.

*Structuring the Game.* After the conceptual model of a social system has been explicated, the facilitator is ready to develop a simulation game based on these elements. The structuring process involves designing, testing, redesigning, retesting, etc., until the product is satisfactory. The designer should remember that "game design is not only not a science, it is hardly a craft, but rather an 'art' in the sense that we have no explicit rules to transmit" (Boocock & Schild, 1968, p. 266).

The designer begins by creating a rough game format that seeks correspondence between the simulation and a given social reality. Decisions are necessary on the ways that the primary components will interact with each other. As each component is placed in the game its interface with other components needs careful consideration, because the matching of each component with the others will determine the success or failure of the game. The degree of likeness in form between the game components and the social-system components will determine whether or not the participants experience the simulated reality intended.

*Writing the Rules.* Easily understood game rules are as important as the game structure.

According to Livingston and Stoll (1973, p. 30), answers to the following questions will help the participants to understand the rules:

1. What social reality does the game simulate?
2. What is the purpose of the game?
3. What does each of the game materials represent?
4. How is the game set up for playing?
5. What is the order of game play?
6. What do the participants do during each step?
7. How might a participant play a typical round of the game?
8. How does the simulation end?

As the game is put into play, problems will appear that could not be anticipated. It is important to note the successful features of the game design as well as those that failed. In observing the game play, the designer should check for both *playability* and *realism*.

A simulation game is playable if it functions well as a game. Participants must desire to play it, and they must be able to engage themselves in it. It must be interesting, enjoyable, and easily learned. The game must also be manageable.

Realism involves three questions: (1) Does the game accurately represent those aspects of the real-life social system that it is intended to simulate?, (2) Does it include the most critical aspects of the real situation and simulate them in sufficient detail?, and (3) Does it provide a feeling of being in a real social situation? After the prototype has been tested for playability and realism, the necessary adjustments should be made. Each component needs to be examined to determine if changes are required. Then careful attention should be given to rewriting the rules before testing the game again. Although further revisions may be necessary, participants can learn from an unfinished version of a game. Indeed, they may learn as much from suggesting revisions as from playing it in its final form.

## CONCLUSION

Simulations are one of the most involving technologies available to the human relations facilitator. Social simulations are based on social systems and potentially can communicate holistic awareness and understandings. Facilitating such games requires careful preparation, skillful administration, and effective discussion. Designing simulation games requires theoretical model building of a social system, constructing a game based on the model, and a process of testing and redesigning.

## RESOURCES FOR SIMULATIONS

### Professional Associations

**American Educational Research Association**
Charles M. Plummer
The Evaluation Center
Western Michigan University
Kalamazoo, MI 49008

**International Simulation and Gaming Association (ISAGA)**
Secretariat for Europe (General Secretary)
Dr. J.H.G. Klabbers
University of Nijmegen, Department of Psychology
Social Systems Research Group
P.O. Box 9104
6500 HE Nijmegen
The Netherlands

U.S. National ISAGA Representative
Richard Duke
321 Parklake
Ann Arbor, MI 48103

**National Gaming Council**
Clark Rogers
3R24 Forbes Quad.
Graduate School of Public and International Affairs
University of Pittsburgh
Pittsburgh, PA 15260

**North American Simulation
and Gaming Association (NASAGA)**
W. Thomas Nichols
NASAGA Secretary/Treasurer
International Studies Institute
Westminister College
New Wilmington, PA 16142

**Simulation and Gaming Association (SAGA)**
Michael Raymond
4833 Greentree Road
Lebanon, Ohio 45320
or
456 Jamesway Drive
Eaton, OH 45320

**Society for Academic Gaming and Simulation
in Education and Training (SAGSET)**
David Walker
Centre for Extension Studies
Loughborough University of Technology
Loughborough, Leics  LE11 3TU
England

**Urban Gaming/Simulation Conference**
School of Education
The University of Michigan
Ann Arbor, MI 48109

## Bibliographies

Belch, J. (Ed.). *Contemporary games: A directory and bibliography describing play situations or simulations, Vol. 2: Bibliography.* Detroit, MI: Gale Research, 1974.

Greenblat, C. Gaming and simulation in the social sciences. *Simulation & Games,* 1972, *3,* 477-491.

Ruben, B.D. Games and simulations: Materials, sources, and learning concepts. In J.W. Pfeiffer & J.E. Jones (Eds.), *The 1972 annual handbook for group facilitators.* San Diego, CA: University Associates, 1972.

Stadsklev, R. *Handbook of simulation gaming in social education (Part 2: Directory of noncomputer materials)* (2nd ed.). University, AL: Institute of Higher Education Research and Services, 1979.

## Directories

Belch, J. (Ed.). *Contemporary games: A directory and bibliography describing play situations or simulations, Vol. 1: Directory.* Detroit, MI: Gale Research, 1973.

Horn, R.E., & Cleaves, A. *The guide to simulations/games for education and training* (4th ed.). Beverly Hills, CA: Sage, 1980.

Stadsklev, R. *Handbook of simulation gaming in social education (Part 2: Directory of noncomputer materials)* (2nd ed.). University, AL: Institute of Higher Education Research and Services, 1979.

## General Works

Duke, R.D. *Gaming: The future's language.* New York: Halsted, 1974.

Dukes, R.L., & Seidner, C.J. (Eds.). *Learning with simulations and games.* Beverly Hills, CA: Sage, 1978.

Greenblat, C.S., & Duke, R.D. *Gaming-simulation: Rationale, design, and applications.* New York: Halsted, 1975.

Inbar, M., & Stoll, C.S. *Simulation and gaming in social science.* New York: The Free Press, 1972.

Lehmann, J., & Portele, G. (Hrsg.). *Simulationsspiele in der erziehung.* Weinheim, Federal Republic of Germany: Beltz Verlag, 1976.

Livingston, S.A., & Stoll, C.S. *Simulation games: An introduction for the social studies teacher.* New York: The Free Press, 1973.

Stadsklev, R. *Handbook of simulation games in social education (Part 1: Textbook).* University, AL: Institute of Higher Education Research and Services, 1975.

Tansey, P.J. (Ed.). *Educational aspects of simulation.* London: McGraw-Hill, 1971.

Taylor, J., & Walford, R. *Learning and the simulation game.* Beverly Hills, CA: Sage, 1978.

## Journals

*Journal of Experiential Learning and Simulation*
Elsevier North-Holland, Inc.
52 Vanderbilt Avenue
New York, NY 10017
(Subscription Rate: $17.50/year)

*Simulation/Games for Learning*
The Secretary
SAGSET
Centre for Extension Studies
Loughborough University of Technology
Loughborough, Leics. LE11 3TU
England
(Subscription Rate: 8 £/year)

*Simages*
W. Thomas Nichols
NASAGA Treasurer
Box 100
Westminister College
New Wilmington, PA 16142
(Subscription included in NASAGA dues: $25/year)

*Simgames*
Champlain Regional College
Lennoxville Campus
Lennoxville, Quebec J1M 2A1
Canada
(Subscription Rate: $2.50/year)

*Simulation & Games: An International Journal*
  *of Theory, Design, and Research*
Sage Publications, Inc.
275 South Beverly Drive
Beverly Hills, CA 90212
(Subscription Rate: $15/year)

## Sources for Simulation Games

Many simulation games have to be purchased on an individual basis, and some are listed in the directories identified above. Cited below are selected books containing simulation games useful to human relations facilitators.

Duke, R.D., & Greenblat, C.S. *Game-generating games*. Beverly Hills, CA: Sage, 1979.

Pfeiffer, J.W., & Jones, J.E. (Eds.). *The annual handbook for group facilitators (1972-1981)*. San Diego, CA: University Associates, 1972-1981.

Pfeiffer, J.W., & Jones, J.E. (Eds.). *A handbook of structured experiences for human relations training*. (Vols. I-VIII). San Diego, CA: University Associates, 1974-1981.

Ruben, B.D. *Human communication handbook: Simulations and games* (Vol. 2). Rochelle Park, NJ: Hayden Book, 1978.

Ruben, B.D., & Budd, R.W. *Human communication handbook: Simulations and games*. (Vol. 1). Rochelle Park, NJ: Hayden Book, 1975.

## REFERENCES

Boocock, S.S., & Schild, E.O. (Eds.). *Simulation games in learning*. Beverly Hills, CA: Sage, 1968.

Chartier, M.R. Learning effect: An experimental study of a simulation game and instrumented discussion. *Simulation & Games*, 1972, 3, 203-218.

Chartier, M.R. *Simulation games as learning devices: A summary of empirical findings and their implication for the utitlization of games in instruction*. Covina, CA: American Baptist Seminary of the West, 1973. (ERIC Document Reproduction Service No. ED 101 384)

Gaw, B.A. Processing questions: An aid to completing the learning cycle. In J.E. Jones & J.W. Pfeiffer (Eds.), *The 1979 annual handbook for group facilitators*. San Diego, CA: University Associates, 1979.

Greenblat, C.S. From theory to model to gaming-simulation: A case study and validity test. In C.S. Greenblat & R.D. Duke (Eds.), *Gaming-simulation: Rationale, design, and applications*. New York: Halsted Press, 1975.

Hall, A.D., & Fagen, R.E. Definition of system. In B.D. Ruben & J.Y. Kim (Eds.), *General systems theory and human communication*. Rochelle Park, NJ: Hayden Book, 1975.

Horn, R.E., & Cleaves, A. (Eds.). *The guide to simulations/games for education and training* (4th ed.). Beverly Hills, CA: Sage, 1980.

Jones, J.E., & Pfeiffer, J.W. Introduction to the theory and practice section. In J.E. Jones & J.W. Pfeiffer (Eds.), *The 1975 annual handbook for group facilitators*. San Diego, CA: University Associates, 1975.

Katz, D., & Kahn, R.L. *The social psychology of organizations* (2nd ed.). New York: John Wiley, 1978.

Livingston, S.A., & Stoll, C.S. *Simulation games: An introduction for the social studies teacher*. New York: The Free Press, 1973.

Olsen, M.E. *The process of social organization*. New York: Holt, Rinehart and Winston, 1968.

*Myron R. Chartier, Ph.D.*, *is professor of ministry and director of doctoral programs at the Eastern Baptist Theological Seminary, Philadelphia, Pennsylvania. He is engaged in relating the behavioral sciences to the theology and practice of ministry. Dr. Chartier's background is in interpersonal, group, and organizational communication as it relates to theory, research, and methodological application.*

# APPENDIX

## Questions for Evaluating Simulation Games

A facilitator may find the following questions helpful in selecting a simulation game:

1. What is the name of the game?
2. What social system and processes does the game simulate?
3. What are the instructional/training objectives of the game?
4. For what age group(s) is this game best suited?
5. How many players can this game accommodate? Is there a minimum or maximum?
6. What abilities do the players need?
7. Are mathematical skills required? How difficult are these procedures?
8. How complicated are the player activities? How difficult are the rules and procedures?
9. How clear are the instructions? Can anyone follow them?
10. Does the game provide a summary of the rules for the players? Would players need a copy of them?
11. How much space is needed? Will a room that accommodates noise be needed?
12. What equipment is needed?
13. How much time (minimum/maximum) is needed to play and discuss the game?
14. How much preparation time will a facilitator need?
15. In what educational/training context(s) could a facilitator use this simulation game?
16. Can the game be modified? How easily?
17. What is the cost of the game?
18. Do the game experience and the possible learnings justify the cost, the facilitator's preparation time, and the participants' learning time?
19. To what degree does the game adequately simulate a real social situation?
20. In what sense would the simulation game provide a valuable learning/training experience?

# PERIODICALS IN ORGANIZATION DEVELOPMENT AND RELATED FIELDS

## Steven M. Rosenthal and L. Paul Church

The field of organization development is rapidly expanding, and therefore so is what we know and need to know as practitioners. The field is also highly eclectic. We are informed by theories, models, and world views drawn from diverse disciplines, systems, and cultures. This diversity creates a problem for those who would like to know more: Where to look? This listing of periodical resources should prove a useful starting place for those beginning that quest.

**AAUW JOURNAL**
American Association of University Women
2401 Virginia Avenue, N.W.
Washington, DC 20037
7/yr. (Nonmembers $4)
Devoted entirely to educational, community, and cultural affairs.

**THE ACADEMY OF MANAGEMENT JOURNAL**
Dr. D.D. Warrick
Academy of Management, OD Newsletter
College of Business
University of Colorado
Colorado Springs, CO 80907
Scholarly publication (research, theory, and administration).

**THE ACADEMY OF MANAGEMENT REVIEW**
Dennis F. Ray, Business Manager
P.O. Drawer KZ
Mississippi State University
Mississippi State, MS 39762
Quarterly (1 year, $24; 2 years, $44; 3 years, $60)
Articles in the fields of management, history, management education and development, organizational behavior, business policy, production operations, management, organization and management theory, personnel, human resources, social issues in management, etc.

**ADMINISTRATION SCIENCE QUARTERLY**
Karl E. Weick
Graduate School of Business
& Public Administration
Cornell University
Ithaca, NY 14853

Quarterly ($22; individuals $14)
Scholarly journal; (administrative studies, theoretical models, analysis, and research).

**ADMINISTRATION AND SOCIETY**
Sage Publications
P.O. Box 5024
Beverly Hills, CA 90210
($16.50)
Seeks to further the understanding of public and human-service organizations. Publishes empirically oriented research reports and theoretically specific articles.

**ADULT LEADERSHIP**
Adult Educational Association of the USA
810 18th Street, N.W.
Washington, DC 20006
Monthly (Nonmembers $18)
Emphasis on how-to-do-it directed to adult educators and community leaders.

**ADVANCED MANAGEMENT JOURNAL**
Geyer-McAllister Publications
51 Madison Avenue
New York, NY 10010
Monthly ($12)
Systems magazine for administrative executives; focus on long-range planning, zero-based budgeting, participative management, etc.

**THE AFFECTIVE EDUCATOR**
Harold Stonehouse
Department of Geology
Michigan State University
East Lansing, MI 48824

Researched and compiled for the OD Network's Spring 1980 conference held in Boston, Massachusetts.

($5; institutions $25)
Newsletter of the Michigan Affective Education Association.

**AFFIRMATIVE ACTION REGISTER**
Warren H. Green
8356 Olive Boulevard
St. Louis, MO 63132
Monthly ($15; free to qualified libraries, agencies and organizations)
Displays ads of equal opportunity employers and describes job openings throughout the nation.

**AHP NEWSLETTER**
Association for Humanistic Psychology
325 9th Street
San Francisco, CA 94108
(Free to members)
Information on humanizing education.

**AMERICAN ACADEMY OF POLITICAL AND SOCIAL SCIENCE ANNUALS**
AAPSS
3937 Chestnut Street
Philadelphia, PA 19104
Bimonthly ($18)

**AMERICAN BEHAVIORAL SCIENTIST**
Sage Publications
275 S. Beverly Drive
Beverly Hills, CA 90212
Bimonthy ($18; institutions $33)
Articles in the areas of human geography and economics.

**AMERICAN ECONOMIC REVIEW**
Rending Fells
1313 21st Avenue, South
Nashville, TN 37212
6/yr. ($39.35)
Prestigious economics journal; articles on decision making, theory of the firm, management history, etc.

**AMERICAN JOURNAL OF SOCIOLOGY**
University of Chicago Press
5801 Ellis Avenue
Chicago, IL 60637
Bimonthly ($27)
Articles on organizational career mobility, age and employment, and images and industry.

**AMERICAN MANAGEMENT ASSOCIATIONS MANAGEMENT REVIEW**
American Management Association
AMACOM Division
135 West 50th Street
New York, NY 10020
($19.50 for members and employees of member companies only)

**AMERICAN SOCIOLOGICAL REVIEW**
American Sociological Association
1722 N. Street, N.W.
Washington, DC 20036
Bimonthly ($30)
Articles on organizations, culture diffusion, human ecology and industrial organization; includes ads, jobs, schools, and books relating to the field; lists conferences.

**ASSIGNMENTS IN MANAGEMENT**
Personnel Journal, Inc.
Box 2440
Costa Mesa, CA 92627
Monthly
Guide to supervisory action.

**BEHAVIORAL SCIENCE RESEARCH**
Human Relations Area Files, Inc.
Box 2015
Yale Station
New Haven, CT 06520
Quarterly ($8; institutions $12)

**BROTHER: A FORUM FOR MEN AGAINST SEXISM**
Brother
P.O. Box 4387
Berkeley, CA 94704
Irregular publication ($5; institutions $15)
Men respond to the women's movement.

**BUREAU OF SOCIAL SCIENCE NEWSLETTER**
Bureau of Social Science Research, Inc.
1990 M Street, N.W.
Washington, DC 20036
Quarterly (Free)

**BUSINESS: THE MAGAZINE OF MANAGERIAL THOUGHT AND ACTION**
Georgia State University
College of Business Administration
Public Services Division
University Plaza
Atlanta, GA 30303
Bimonthly ($10)

**BUSINESS QUARTERLY**
Doreen Sanders
School of Business Administration
University of Western Ontario
London, Ontario
N6A 3K7, Canada
Quarterly ($12)
Technical magazine primarily for executives and middle management; articles dealing with theory and practical business problems.

## BUSINESS AND SOCIETY REVIEW
Warren, Gorham and Lamont, Inc.
870 7th Avenue
New York, NY 10019
Quarterly ($38)
Business ethics.

## CALIFORNIA MANAGEMENT REVIEW
University of California, Berkeley
School of Business Administration
350 Barrows Hall
Berkeley, CA 94726
Quarterly ($12)
West Coast version of the *Harvard Business Review;* of interest to academics and active managers; wide range of topics from marketing to personnel management.

## COMPENSATION REVIEW
American Management Association
P.O. Box 319
Saranac Lake, NY 12983
Quarterly ($17; nonmembers $20)
Directed toward company personnel managers.

## CONFLUENT EDUCATION JOURNAL
Confluent Education Journal
P.O. Box 30128
Santa Barbara, CA 93105
($8)
Articles on confluent education, integrating affective and cognitive teaching, research, curricula, lesson plans, and book reviews; recommended for classroom teachers.

## CONFLUENT EDUCATION NEWSLETTER
Confluent Education Newsletter
Box 219
Minedosa, Manitoba, Canada

## CONSULTANTS NEWS
Kennedy & Kennedy, Inc.
Templeton Road
Fitzwilliam, NH 03447
Monthly ($56)

## CORNELL JOURNAL OF SOCIAL RELATIONS
Cornell University
Department of Sociology
Ithaca, NY 14850
Semiannual ($2; institutions $7)

## CREATIVE MANAGEMENT
Business Research Publications, Inc.
87 Terminal Drive
Plainview, NY 11803
Monthly ($36 + $1.80 postage)
Information on practical in-use principles of good management, organization, control, planning, training, communication, and performance evaluations.

## DAWNPOINT
Association for Humanistic Psychology
325 9th Street
San Francisco, CA 94103
Semiannual (1 year, $5; 2 years, $8)
Articles on humanistic psychology.

## DECISION LINE
American Institute for Decision Sciences
University Plaza
Atlanta, GA 30303
Quarterly ($7.50)

## EFFECTIVE MANAGER
Warren, Gorham and Lamont, Inc.
210 South Street
Boston, MA 02111
Monthly ($42)

## ENVIRONMENT AND BEHAVIOR
Gary Winkel
Sage Publications, Inc.
275 S. Beverly Drive
Beverly Hills, CA 90212
Quarterly ($15; institutions $30)
Study, design, and control of physical environment and its interaction with human behavioral systems.

## ESSENTIA
Bob Samples and Associates
P.O. Box 129
Tiburon, CA 94920
(Free)
Newsletter; sample article: "The Metaphoric Mind."

## ETHNICITY: AN INTERDISCIPLINARY JOURNAL OF THE STUDY OF ETHNIC RELATIONS
Academic Press, Inc.
111 5th Avenue
New York, NY 10003
Quarterly ($32)
Group interaction.

## EVALUATION AND PROGRAM PLANNING: AN INTERNATIONAL JOURNAL
Pergamon Press, Inc.
Maxwell House
Fairmead Park
Elmsford, NY 10523

## EVALUATION QUARTERLY (JOURNAL OF SOCIAL RESEARCH)
Sage Publications
275 S. Beverly Drive
Beverly Hills, CA 90212
Quarterly ($15; institutions $30)

## EXCHANGE: THE ORGANIZATIONAL BEHAVIOR TEACHING JOURNAL- A JOURNAL OF TEACHING THEORY AND TECHNIQUE

The Organizational Behavior Teaching Society: Exchange: TOBTJ
Bureau of Business Research and Services
Box U-41Br
Storrs, CT 06268
Quarterly ($7.50)
Devoted to exploring various techniques and theories of teaching organizational behavior in schools of business, public administration, and education, departments of psychology and sociology, and public and private organizations.

## FMA BULLETIN (formerly SFMA BULLETIN)

Fulfillment Management Association
c/o Dorothea E. Forier, President
224 W. 57th Street
3rd Floor
New York, NY 10019
($35)

## FORTUNE

Robert Lubar
Time, Inc.
Time-Life Building
New York, NY 10020
($20)
Business and general interest topics.

## THE FUTURIST

Edward Cornish
World Future Society
4916 St. Elmo Avenue
Washington, DC 20014
Bimonthly ($18)
What to expect of the future; objective reports by reputable scientists, social scientists, educators, and political scientists.

## THE GRANTSMANSHIP CENTER NEWS

The Grantsmanship Center
1031 S. Grand Avenue
Los Angeles, CA 90015
(1 year, $20; 2 years, $36)
Information on funding and management; feature articles, regular departments (includes job openings across country), federal grant deadlines, etc.

## GROUP & ORGANIZATION STUDIES: THE INTERNATIONAL JOURNAL FOR GROUP FACILITATORS

University Associates
8517 Production Avenue
P.O. Box 26240
San Diego, CA 92126

Quarterly ($24; institutions $30)
Designed to bridge the gap between research and practice for group facilitators, educators, and consultants.

## GROUP PSYCHOTHERAPY, PSYCHODRAMA & SOCIOMETRY

Z.T. Moreno
Beacon House, Inc.
259 Wolcoll Avenue
Beacon, NY 12508
Semiannual ($14)
Articles dealing with method, technique, group therapy, role playing, transactional analysis, and sociometrics.

## HARVARD BUSINESS REVIEW

Ralph F. Lewis
Harvard University
Graduate School of Business Administration
Soldiers Field Road
Boston, MA 02163
Bimonthly ($18)
Trends, predictions, and developments in all phases of business.

## H.R.A.F. NEWSLETTER

Human Relations Area Files, Inc.
Box 2015
Yale Station
New Haven, CT 06520
Quarterly (Free)

## HUMAN BEHAVIOR

Human Behavior
Subscription Department
P.O. Box 2810
Boulder, CO 80302
Monthly ($14)
News magazine of the social and behavioral sciences; reports cover learning, therapy, family, sex, minorities, etc.

## HUMAN COMMUNICATION RESEARCH

James C. McCroskey
International Communications Association
Balcones Research Center
10100 Burnet Road
Austin, TX 78758
Quarterly ($15)
Broad focus on behavioral sciences; emphasizes process and results of communication.

## HUMAN ORGANIZATION

Deward C. Walker, Jr.
University of Colorado
Institute of Behavioral Science
Boulder, CO 80302
Quarterly ($8; institutions $18; students $6)

Reports research and explores human behavior in community contexts; anthropological theory and method in the study of urban and modernizing societies.

## HUMAN RELATIONS: A JOURNAL OF STUDIES TOWARDS THE INTEGRATION OF THE SOCIAL SCIENCES
Tavistock Institute of Human Relations
Plenum Press
227 W. 17th Street
New York, NY 10011
Monthly ($85)
Articles primarily devoted to psychological and social aspects of group process, systems, interpersonal relations, and interactions.

## HUMAN RESOURCE MANAGEMENT
Graduate School of Business Administration
University of Michigan
Monroe & Tappan Streets
Ann Arbor, MI 48109
Quarterly ($8)

## HUMANISTIC EDUCATORS NETWORK
National Humanistic Education Center
Upper Jay, NY 12987
($10)
New techniques, materials, book reviews, articles, interviews, and listings of events in the area of humanistic education.

## HUMANITIES
Sara D. Toney
National Endowment for the Humanities
806 15th Street, N.W.
Washington, DC 20506
Bimonthly (Free)
Vehicle of the National Endowment for the Humanities.

## HUMBOLDT JOURNAL OF SOCIAL RELATIONS
Humboldt State University
Department of Sociology
54 Library Street
Arcata, CA 95521
Semiannual ($5; institutions $12)
Contemporary American problems and issues; sociology, welfare, geography, political science, economics, and psychology.

## INTERFACE JOURNAL: ALTERNATIVES IN HIGHER EDUCATION
Interface
P.O. Box 970
Utica, NY 13505
($6)
Articles on alternative approaches to higher education.

## INTERFACES
Institute of Management Sciences
146 Westminister Street
Providence, RI 02903
Quarterly ($18)

## INTERNATIONAL ECONOMIC REVIEW
Department of Economics
McNeil Building CR
University of Pennsylvania
Philadelphia, PA 19174
3/yr.

## INTERNATIONAL JOURNAL OF PUBLIC ADMINISTRATION
Marcel Dekkes Journals
P.O. Box 11305
Church Street Station
New York, NY 10249

## INTERNATIONAL SOCIAL SCIENCE JOURNAL
UniPub.
P.O. Box 433
Murray Hill Station
New York, NY 10016
Quarterly ($14)
Each issue concentrates on a topical problem. Notes on new journals, news of international conferences, update on services and references from UNESCO.

## INTERNATIONAL STUDIES OF MANAGEMENT AND ORGANIZATIONS
M.E. Sharp, Inc.
901 N. Broadway
White Plains, NY 10603
Quarterly ($25; institutions $90)

## THE JOURNAL OF APPLIED BEHAVIORAL SCIENCE
Journal of Applied Behavioral Science
NTL Institute
P.O. Box 9155
Arlington, VA 22209
Quarterly ($19)
Recent articles have included the areas of small groups, research, organizational problem solving, etc.

## JOURNAL OF APPLIED MANAGEMENT
Journal of Applied Management, Inc.
1200 Mt. Diablo Boulevard
Suite 312
Walnut Creek, CA 94596
Bimonthly ($32)

## JOURNAL OF CONSULTING
## AND CLINICAL PSYCHOLOGISTS
American Psychological Association, Inc.
1200 17th Street, N.W.
Washington, DC 20036
Bimonthly ($40)
Has covered Gestalt therapy and interpersonal relations.

## JOURNAL OF CREATIVE BEHAVIOR
Creative Education Foundation
State University College
1300 Elmwood Avenue
Buffalo, NY 14222
($9)
Articles, research, reports, and book reviews related to creativity and education.

## JOURNAL OF ECONOMIC THEORY
Academic Press
111 5th Avenue
New York, NY 10003
Bimonthly ($53)

## JOURNAL OF EXPERIMENTAL
## SOCIAL PSYCHOLOGY
Academic Press
111 5th Avenue
New York, NY 10003
By and for psychologists working in the field of social interactions.

## JOURNAL OF FINANCIAL
## AND QUANTITATIVE ANALYSIS
Western Finance Association
University of Washington
Graduate School of Business Administration
127 Mackenzie Hall
Seattle, WA 98195

## JOURNAL OF HUMANISTIC EDUCATION
Journal of Humanistic Education
West Georgia College
Carrollton, GA 30017
Annually ($2.50; institutions $5)

## JOURNAL OF HUMANISTIC PSYCHOLOGY
Thomas Greening
Association for Humanistic Psychology
325 9th Street
San Francisco, CA 94103
Quarterly ($10)
Topics include encounter, self-transcendence, search for meaning, and being motivation.

## JOURNAL OF MANAGEMENT
Auburn University
School of Business
Department of Management
Auburn, AL 36830
($15)

## JOURNAL OF MENTAL IMAGERY
Brandon House
P.O. Box 240
Bronx, NY 10471
($15; institutions $20; students $12)
Sample articles: "Eidetics: An Overview" and "Imagery and Verbal Behavior"

## JOURNAL OF OCCUPATIONAL BEHAVIOR
Subscription Department
John Wiley & Sons, Inc.
605 3rd Avenue
New York, NY 10016
Quarterly (Institutions $30)
An international journal of social science research on human behavior in the work place and on related social change for those concerned with occupational behavior and management.

## JOURNAL OF ORGANIZATIONAL
## COMMUNICATION
International Association
of Business Communications
870 Market Street
Suite 928
San Francisco, CA 94102
($8)

## JOURNAL OF PERSONALITY
## AND SOCIAL PSYCHOLOGY
Subscription Section
American Psychological Association
1200 17th Street, N.W.
Washington, DC 20036
Monthly ($60)
Articles on groups and behavior.

## JOURNAL OF PSYCHOLOGY
Journal Press
Box 543
2 Commercial Street
Provincetown, MA 02657
3/yr. ($54)

Articles on organizational effectiveness, leadership, supervision, employees, achievement motivation, and conformity.

## JOURNAL OF SOCIAL PSYCHOLOGY
Box 543
2 Commercial Street
Provincetown, MA 02657
Bimonthly ($45)
Articles on achievement motivation, conformity, helping behavior, interpersonal relations, and leadership.

## JOURNAL OF TRANSPERSONAL PSYCHOLOGY

Journal of Transpersonal Psychology
P.O. Box 4437
Stanford, CA 94305
($15)

Articles on values, unititive consciousness, peak experiences, ecstasy, mystical experience, B values, essence, bliss, awe, wonder, self-actualization, ultimate meaning, transcendence of the self, spirit, oneness, cosmic play, synergy, etc.

## LEADERSHIP AND ORGANIZATIONAL DEVELOPMENT

Leadership and Organizational Development
Dr. Andrew Kukabadse, Editor
Cranfield School of Management
Cranfield, Bedfordshire, MK43 OAL, England

## LEARNING MAGAZINE

1255 Portland Place
Boulder, CO 80302
($8)

Major magazine in education.

## THE LINK: SOCIAL SCIENCE EDUCATION CONSORTIUM NEWSLETTER

The Link
855 Broadway
Boulder, CO 80302
($5)

Broad range of social sciences in the classroom.

## MANAGE

National Management Association
2210 Arbor Boulevard
Dayton, OH 45439

## MANAGEMENT DEVELOPMENT GUIDE

American Management Associations
135 W. 50th Street
New York, NY 10020

Subscriptions: Box 319, Saranac Lake, NY 12983
Semiannual ($3.75 per copy)

## MANAGEMENT HORIZONS

Management Horizons
Kansas State University
College of Business Administration
Manhattan, KS 66502
Monthly (Free)

## MANAGEMENT RESEARCH

Stephen R. Michael
School of Business Administration
SBA 357
University of Massachusetts
Amherst, MA 01003
Bimonthly ($15; institutions $25)
Abstracts of books and articles from journals.

## MANAGEMENT REVIEW

Management Review
P.O. Box 319
Saranac Lake, NY 12983
Monthly ($18)

Quick overview of current management literature; condenses and/or reviews articles from major business magazines.

## MANAGEMENT SCIENCE

Institute of Management Sciences
146 West Minister Street
Providence, RI 02903
Monthly ($40)

For managers who wish to apply mathematical and scientific methods to management and decision making.

## MANAGEMENT WORLD
## (formerly AMS MANAGEMENT BULLETIN)

Jim Bruno
Administrative Management Society
Willow Grove, PA 19090
Monthly (Nonmembers $12)

Short articles, latest developments, disciplines of administration and management.

## MBA

MBA Communications, Inc.
730 3rd Avenue
New York, NY 10017
($11/yr; free to qualified personnel)

Directed primarily toward students and younger professionals; articles include issues in management, business, societal problems, salary, openings, and promotional prospects.

## MEDIA AND METHODS

Media and Methods
134 N. 13th Street
Philadelphia, PA 19107
($6)

Articles on humanizing learning process; especially interesting for those who use films in teaching.

## NEWSFRONT: MANAGEMENT TRENDS MAGAZINE

Year, Inc.
Box 380
Petaluma, CA 94952
Bimonthly ($6)

## NORTHEAST TRAINING NEWS:
## A MONTHLY NEWSPAPER
## FOR THE TRAINING PROFESSIONAL

Circulation Manager
NE Training News
176 Federal Street
Boston, MA 02110

(Free to qualified personnel within covered area; nonqualified personnel or those outside area $18) Seminars, training aids, idea exchange, and classified ads.

## OD PRACTITIONER:
## (A PUBLICATION OF THE OD NETWORK)
OD Practitioner
1011 Park Avenue
Plainfield, NJ 07060
Quarterly (Nonsubscription basis for members; single copies $3)

## ORGANIZATIONAL AND ADMINISTRATIVE SCIENCES
Kent State University
Comparative Administrative Research Institution
Graduate School of Business Administration
Kent, OH 44242
Quarterly ($12)

## ORGANIZATIONAL BEHAVIOR
## AND HUMAN PERFORMANCE
American Psychological Association
1200 17th Street, N.W.
Washington, DC 20036
Articles with conceptual models relative to organizational structures and processes.

## ORGANIZATIONAL DYNAMICS:
## A QUARTERLY REVIEW
## OF ORGANIZATIONAL BEHAVIOR
## FOR PROFESSIONAL MANAGERS
American Management Associations
Subscription Services
Box 319
Saranac Lake, NY 12983
Quarterly ($18 nonmembers; $14 members; $9 students)
Articles on problems of higher management.

## OPERATIONS RESEARCH
George L. Nemhauser
Operations Research Society of America
428 E. Preston Street
Baltimore, MD 21202
Bimonthly ($40)
Mathematically oriented research tool.

## PEOPLE AND BUSINESS:
## THE EFFECTIVE MANAGER
Warren, Gorham and Lamont, Inc.
210 South Street
Boston, MA 02111
Monthly ($36)

## PERFORMANCE IMPROVEMENT
## MAGAZINE

Performance Improvement
Publishing Company
500 Main Street
Box 128
Ridgefield, CT 06877
Monthly ($36)

## PERSONNEL
American Management Association
Subscription Service
P.O. Box 319
Saranac Lake, NY 12983
Career trends, executive action, human resource management, supervision, social response to business, etc.; authors include management consultants.

## PERSONNEL ADMINISTRATION
Catherine D. Bower
American Society
for Personnel Administration
19 Church Street
Berea, OH 44017
9/yr. ($12)
Covers most aspects of personnel in business, government, and education; especially interesting to the professional administrator.

## PERSONNEL AND GUIDANCE JOURNAL
Derald Wing Sue
American Personnel
and Guidance Association
1607 New Hampshire Avenue
Washington, DC 20009
Monthly, Sept.-June (Nonmembers $20)
Of interest to the practicing counselor in school, college, or agencies.

## PERSONNEL JOURNAL: THE MAGAZINE
## OF INDUSTRIAL RELATIONS
## AND PERSONNEL MANAGEMENT
Arthur C. Croft
The Personnel Journal, Inc.
P.O. Box 1510
Santa Monica, CA 90406
Monthly ($16)
Covers most aspects of personnel management.

## PERSONNEL PSYCHOLOGY
Milton D. Hakel
Personnel Psychology, Inc.
P.O. Box 6965
College Station
Durham, NC 27708
Quarterly ($18)
Primarily for industrial psychologists; of interest also to counselors and anyone involved in personnel.

## PSYCHOLOGICAL REPORTS
Box 9229
Missoula, MT 59807
Bimonthly ($96.20)
Has published articles on supervisors, achievement motivation, employee attitudes, interviewing, and interviews.

## PUBLIC MANAGEMENT
International City Management Association
1140 Connecticut Avenue, N.W.
Washington, DC 20036
Monthly ($10)
Articles on group relations training and leadership training; wide range of management issues; of special interest to urban government management.

## PUBLIC PERSONNEL MANAGEMENT
John W. Moore
International Personnel
Management Association
1313 E. 60th Street
Chicago, IL 60637
Bimonthly ($15)
Directed at personnel managers on all levels of government.

## RESEARCH MANAGEMENT
Henry R. Clauser
Industrial Research Institute
100 Park Avenue
New York, NY 10017
Bimonthly ($27)
Aims to improve communication between research and other corporate activities.

## RESEARCH REPORTS
## IN THE SOCIAL SCIENCES
Research Reports in the Social Sciences
University of Notre Dame
Notre Dame, IN 46556
Semiannual

## SEMINARS
Seminars
Langdon Hall
525 N. Lake Street
Madison, WI 53703
3/yr. ($40)
Directory of continuing and professional education programs.

## SEX ROLES
Phyllis A. Katz
Plenum Publishing Corporation
227 W. 17th Street
New York, NY 10011
Quarterly ($14; institutions $35)

Sex-role stereotypes, attitudes, and effects; by women professors, sociologists, psychologists, and educators.

## SLOAN MANAGEMENT REVIEW
Gay Van Ausdall
Sloan Management Review
Alfred P. Sloan School of Management
Massachusetts Institute of Technology
Cambridge, MA 02139
Subscriptions: 50 Memorial Drive
3/yr. ($14)
Exchange of information between academic and business worlds.

## SMALL GROUP BEHAVIOR:
## INTERNATIONAL JOURNAL OF THERAPY,
## COUNSELING AND TRAINING
Sage Publications, Inc.
P.O. Box 5024
Beverly Hills, CA 90210
Research and theory relating to small groups.

## SOCIAL CHANGE
NTL Institute
P.O. Box 9155
Rosslyn Station
Arlington, VA 22209
Quarterly ($5)

## SOCIAL PSYCHOLOGY QUARTERLY
American Sociological Association
1722 N Street, N.W.
Washington, DC 20036
Quarterly ($14)
Articles on behavior, achievement motivation, nonverbal communication, and group problem solving.

## SOCIAL RESEARCH: INTERNATIONAL
## JOURNAL OF POLITICAL
## AND SOCIAL SCIENCE
New School for Social Research
65 5th Avenue
New York, NY 10003
Quarterly ($12; institutions $20)

## SOCIAL SCIENCE
Pi Gamma Mu
National Social Science Honor Society
Toledo University
Toledo, OH 43606
Quarterly ($4)

## SOCIAL SCIENCE JOURNAL
Western Social Science Association
Colorado State University
Social Science Building
Fort Collins, CO 80523
3/yr. ($9)

Review of American studies, anthropology, economics, political science, and sociology.

**SUCCESS ORIENTATION:**
**THE MANAGEMENT NEWSLETTER**
**FOR SUPERVISORS, SALESMEN,**
**AND PERSONAL DEVELOPMENT**
Success Publications, Inc.
3121 Maple Drive, N.E.
Suite 1
Atlanta, GA 30305
Monthly ($39)

**SUPERVISORY MANAGEMENT**
Supervisory Management
P.O. Box 319
Saranac Lake, NY 12983
Monthly ($12; nonmembers $16)
An American Management Association publication.

**TECHNOLOGY AND CULTURE**
Society for the History of Technology
University of Chicago Press
5801 Ellis Avenue
Chicago, IL 60637
Quarterly ($15; institutions $30)
A study of the development of technology and its relation to the society and its culture.

**TODAY'S MANAGER**
Penton-IPC
Penton Plaza
Chester Avenue
Cleveland, OH 44114
Monthly ($12)

**TODAY'S PROFESSIONAL**
Today's Professional, Inc.
3030 W. 6th Street
Los Angeles, CA 90020
Monthly ($12)

**TRAINING AND DEVELOPMENT JOURNAL**
Subscription Department
American Society for Training
and Development
P.O. Box 5307
Madison, WI 53705
(Nonmembers $20; single copy $3)
Official magazine of the American Society for Training and Development; training aids, articles, and classified ads.

**TRAINING MAGAZINE OF MANPOWER**
**AND MANAGEMENT DEVELOPMENT**
Lakewood Publications, Inc.
731 Hennepin Avenue
Minneapolis, MN 55403
Monthly ($12)

**TRAINING MANAGEMENT**
**AND MOTIVATION**
North American Publishing Company
401 N. Broad Street
Philadelphia, PA 19108

**TRAINING WORLD: THE MAGAZINE**
**FOR TRAINING PROFESSIONALS**
Training World
80 N. Broadway
Hicksville, NY 11801
Bimonthly ($10)

*Steven M. Rosenthal* is an associate consultant for R.S.I., Inc., a Deerfield, Massachusetts, firm specializing in organization development, management training, and strategic planning. He also is an organization development consultant and specializes in the areas of sociotechnical systems, career planning, stress management, and management training. Mr. Rosenthal has taught MBA courses in organizational behavior at Suffolk University, Boston, Massachusetts, and at the University of Massachusetts, Amherst, Massachusetts. His background is in industrial engineering, public management, and organizational behavior.

*L. Paul Church* is currently completing requirements for a degree in sociology at Boston University. He also is a staff assistant for the Industrial Relations Section, Sloan School of Management, Massachusetts Institute of Technology, and has been a staff assistant for the Office of Personnel Development, M.I.T. Mr. Church has been active in planning and research for OD Network conferences and has served as program coordinator for the Scanlon Plan conference at M.I.T.

# ANNOTATED BIBLIOGRAPHY ON POWER IN ORGANIZATIONS

## Mark Smith and Howard L. Fromkin

Economists, psychologists, sociologists, political scientists, and others have attempted to explain the phenomenon of power. Partially because it has had so much attention, no single definition exists. One possible general statement is that the exercise of power involves causing someone to do something different from what he or she intended.

This annotated bibliography includes selections from most of the research disciplines that have examined power. The emphasis in on interpersonal and organizational power, with a number of articles focusing on the problems of definition and application. Section I looks at various theoretical approaches to power; Sections II and III examine the interpersonal and organizational bases of power; Section IV includes some of the literature on power, organization development, and change; and Section V focuses on some of the wider environmental issues, especially as seen by economists. The sections are somewhat arbitrary, and many of the articles could have appeared under several headings.

## SECTION I. THEORETICAL VIEWS OF POWER

This section presents various theoretical approaches to power. It illustrates the problems of definition and method faced by various theoretical disciplines.

### Political Theories

Bachrach, P., & Baratz, M.S. Two faces of power. *American Political Science Review*, 1962, *56*, 947-952.

> Two definitions of power are presented: (1) Power is (or comes from) participation in public decision making. Therefore, one studies power by observing behavior in decision-making situations. (2) Power is (or comes from) removing issues from public decision making. Therefore, one studies power by observing how some issues are prevented from entering the decision-making arena.

Bell, D.V. *Power, influence and authority: An essay in political linguistics.* New York: Oxford University Press, 1975.

> Bell tries to use language to distinguish between power, influence, and authority: "Power" involves a threat or promise. Therefore, it assumes that the individual has a choice, that some object is valued by the individual, and that control over that object is possible. For example, the typical power sentence is "If you do A, I'll do B." In contrast, "influence" is not based on sanctions, and it assumes knowledge of but not control of the objects valued by the individual. For example, a typical sentence might be "If you do X, Y will happen." "Authority" is command; therefore, no choice is offered to the listener. It is based on beliefs that are held as valid by the person who accepts authority.

Bierstedt, R. An analysis of social power. *American Sociological Review*, 1950, *15*, 730-738.

> Bierstedt tries to make the following distinctions: (1) Influence is persuasive; power is coercive. (2) Power is hidden force; force is exercized power; authority is institutionalized power. (3) Power stems from numbers of people in a group, the social organization of a group, or the resources available to a group.

Dahl, R.A. *Modern political analysis*. Englewood Cliffs, NJ: Prentice-Hall, 1963.

In Chapter 1, "The Nature of Politics," Dahl argues that a political system is a pattern of human relationships that involves power, will, and authority and that politics is necessary because of the division of labor. He also states that the resulting specialization requires coordination; therefore it is a coordinator with power, and position in politics is the equivalent of property in economics.

Dubin, R. A theory of conflict and power in union management relations. *Industrial and Labor Relations Review*, 1960, *13*(4), 501-518.

The author presents three ways of describing power: (1) power in numbers or organization, (2) power to control or influence, and (3) power in a social relationship. He lists the key measures of power in an organization as (1) who performs the most *important* functions and (2) who performs functions *exclusively* as opposed to *sharing* them.

Etzioni, A. *A comparative analysis of complex organizations* (2nd ed.). New York: The Free Press, 1975 (especially pp. 4-20).

Etzioni focuses on three types of power: coercive (based on physical threat), remunerative (based on rewards), and normative (based on feelings and beliefs). He also emphasizes three types of involvement or responses to power: alienated (highly negative), calculated (mildly negative or positive), and moral (highly positive). Together, they give a nine-fold classification of power in organizations.

Frey, F. Comment: On issues and non-issues in the study of power. *American Political Science Review*, 1971, *65*, 1081-1101.

In studying power, according to Frey, one is presented with the following difficulties: (1) The choice of issues affects the distribution of power, so one can study power only on an issue-by-issue basis; (2) the most powerful methods for studying power (reconstructing decisions and in-depth interviews) are very expensive; and (3) to study nondecisions or nonevents, one must introduce questions of what might have happened that did not happen, which are normative rather than strictly empirical issues.

White, D.M. Power and intention. *American Political Science Review*, 1971, *65*, 749-759.

The author presents hypothetical political situations to demonstrate that acts can be called "powerful" without the actors intending the particular effects. He concludes that such examples show "that a precise and exhaustive conceptual analysis of power is impossible."

Wolfinger, R.E. Nondecisions and the study of local politics. *American Political Science Review*, 1971, *65*, 1063-1080.

Wolfinger discusses the concept of power as preventing certain problems from even being discussed (the nondecisions of Bachrach and Baratz). He concludes that the term "nondecisions" is too general.

## Exchange Theories

Bacharach, S.B., & Lawler, E.J. The perception of power. *Social Forces*, 1976, *55*, 123-134.

The authors argue that the basic tenet of exchange theory is that the value attributed to outcomes and the scarcity of alternative outcomes provide the foundation for social relationships. People tend to maintain relationships in which the outcomes received are highly valued and not available in alternative relationships.

Blau, P. *Exchange and power in social life*. New York: John Wiley, 1964.

Neoclassical economic exchange theory is applied to social interaction. Blau argues that power emerges when A wants something ("X") that B has and must comply with B's wishes in order to receive it. For example, if A (1) cannot give something else in exchange for X, (2) cannot obtain X elsewhere, (3) cannot take X by force, and (4) cannot do without X, then A must comply.

Cook, K.S. Exchange and power in networks of interorganizational relations. *Sociological Quarterly*, 1977, *18*, 62-68.

Exchange theory is presented as similar to neoclassical economic theory. Power is conceptualized as relative power over resources.

Cotton, C.C. Measurement of power-balancing styles and some of their correlates. *Administrative Science Quarterly*, 1976, *21*(2).

Power-dependence theory is applied in a university. The four power-balancing styles (exchange for X, reduce need for X, find alternative sources for X, take X by force) are correlated with biographical data of subjects in the study.

Emerson, R.M. Power-dependence relationships. *American Sociological Review*, 1962, *27*, 31-41.

Emerson makes the following observations: Power of A over B is a function of B's dependency on A. To reduce A's power, B has two options: to withdraw or to form a coalition with allies. Forming a coalition usually leads to a status hierarchy to maintain the coalition and continue to keep A's power at bay.

Jacobs, D. Dependency and vulnerability: An exchange approach to the study of organizations. *Administrative Science Quarterly*, 1974, *19*, 45-59.

Exchange and dependency theories are extended to a market structure framework. According to the author, organizations are dependent on their environments for acquiring inputs, labor forces, capital, and production factors and for disposing of their products. He suggests that "organizational behavior can be represented in part as a rank-weighted average of the organization's five areas of dependence on its environment."

## Problems in Studying Power

Ball, T.P. Power, causality and explanation. *Polity*, 1976, *8*, 189-214.

The problem of defining power is analyzed. Ball argues that the key mistake most people make is perceiving power as "A's behavior causing B to do something." Instead, he argues, power is a function of some ability a person has in a particular situation.

Baumgartner, T., Buckley, W., & Burns, T. Metapower and relational control in social life. *Social Sciences Information*, 1975, *14*(6), 49-78.

The authors state that metapower focuses not on interpersonal behavior, but on the possibilities for action in a situation, the interaction payoffs in the situation, or the prevailing beliefs of the actors involved.

Crozier, M. The problem of power. *Social Research*, 1973, *40*(2), 211-228.

The author's main points are (1) A's power over B corresponds to A's capacity to impose on B terms of exchange that are favorable to A; (2) no power analysis can be separated from the institutional framework in which it develops; (3) each participant in a system wields power over other members insofar as he occupies a strategically favorable position regarding the problems on which the success of the system depends, but he is limited by the rules of the game, which restrict the use of his advantages; (4) organization members are constantly negotiating to enforce the rules (limit others' power) and break the rules (expand their own power); and (5) power has a "necessary" element (i.e., accomplishes things in the face of uncertainty) and a "moral" element (notions of equity and fair play in the face of dependence).

Grimes, A.J. Authority, power, influence, and social control. *Academy of Management Review*, 1978, *3*, 724-735.

Power and authority are viewed as opposite ends of a continuum of social control: Authority is exercised in the service of goals held by a majority, and power is exercised in the service of privately held goals. How minorities attempt to influence authorities is viewed as dictated by their level of trust. The article attempts to synthesize the difficult concepts of power, influence, and authority.

Habermas, J. Hannah Arendt's communications concept of power. *Social Research*, 1977, *44*, 3-24.

The author argues that power comes from being in a group. Leaders may use power, he claims, but groups produce it. He concludes that leaders often feel impotent because they do not produce power directly.

Kiessler, K. Power and participation in two school environments. *International Studies of Management and Organization*, 1977-1978, *7*, 33-46.

The author attempted a field study of hierarchical-versus-equalized power on decision making in two school settings in Germany. He found by accident that the setting explained more differences than the kind of power distribution used. He concludes that this points to the importance of *specific* context in the study of power.

Liebert, R., & Immerschein, A. The three faces of power. In R. Liebert & A. Immerschein (Eds.), *Power, paradigms and community research*. Beverly Hills, CA: Sage, 1977.

Three traditions in the study of power are identified: "Social facts" theories, which focus on social structure, "social behavior" theories, which look at what people do, and "social definition" theories, which examine how people interpret and experience power.

Lukes, S. *Power: A radical view*. London: Macmillan Press, 1974.

Methodologies of studying power are contrasted: the pluralist approach to studying decision making (Dahl), the nondecisions of Bachrach and Baratz, and the author's view, which includes latent conflict and the subjective-versus-"real" interests of those involved.

March, J.G. The power of power. In D. Easton (Ed.), *Varieties of political theory*. Englewood Cliffs, NJ: Prentice-Hall, 1966.

March compares the basic empirical models used for analyzing power to discover which models can make "effective use" of the concept. He concludes that power is probably a useful concept for many short-run situations involving the direct confrontations of committed and activated participants but that it is probably not a useful concept for many long-run situations involving high degrees of complexity and limited ability to process information.

Martin, R. *The sociology of power*. London: Routledge & Kegan Paul, 1977.

This book on power in society, as seen by a sociologist, gives two main explanatory theories: systems theory and social-action theory.

McLelland, D. The two faces of power. *Journal of International Affairs*, 1970, *24*, 29-47.

The author makes the following argument: The "personal" face of power is characterized by "If I win, you lose." A person with this power drive tends to treat people as pawns. The "socialized" face of power is characterized by a concern for group goals and enabling people to reach them. A person with this power drive wants to exercise influence *for* others.

Murnigham, J.K. Models of coalition behavior: Game theoretic, social psychological, and political perspectives. *Psychological Bulletin*, 1978, *85*, 1130-1153.

In this review of the three major approaches to coalition behavior, power is not considered directly, but implied in the area of the dominance of some coalitions over others.

Nagel, J.H. *The descriptive analysis of power*. New Haven, CT: Yale University Press, 1975.

The author equates power and causality and demonstrates how path analysis can be used to study power.

Tedeschi, J.T., Barry, R.S., & Banana, T.V. *Conflict, power & games*. Chicago: Aldine, 1973.

This academic work on the use of experimental games to study power and conflict is a good review of the field of experimental games.

## SECTION II. THE INTERPERSONAL BASES OF POWER

This category is the most extensive theoretical and heuristic treatment of power. Authors in this tradition have attempted to categorize the types of power in order to assess which are most effective in which situations.

Backman, G.G., Bowers, D., & Marcus, P. Bases of supervisory power: A comparative study in five organizational settings. In A.S. Tannenbaum (Ed.), *Control in organizations*. New York: McGraw-Hill, 1968.

The authors found that the most effective supervisors relied mainly on legitimate and expert power rather than reward and coercive power.

French, J.R.P., Jr. A formal theory of social power. *Psychology Review*, 1956, *63*, 181-194.

"The power of A over B (with respect to a given opinion) is equal to the maximum force which A can induce on B minus the maximum resisting force which B can mobilize in the opposite direction."

With regard to the above quotation, numerous studies have examined the relative effectiveness of different types of power and have concluded that reward power is more effective than coercive power in most situations. Relevant articles are the following:

Brigante, T.R. Adolescent evaluations of rewarding, neutral, and punishing power figures. *Journal of Personality*, 1958, *26*, 435-450.

French, J.R.P., Jr., Morrison, H.W., & Levinger, G. Coercive power and forces affecting conformity. *Journal of Applied Social Psychology*, 1960, *61*, 93-101.

Zipf, S.G. Resistance and conformity under reward and punishment. *Journal of Abnormal Social Psychology*, 1960, *61*, 102-109.

French, J.R.P., Jr., & Raven, B. The bases of social power. In D. Cartwright & A. Zander (Eds.), *Group conflict in organizations*. New York: Basic Books, 1964.

The author examines how power, personality, and other variables mediate the effect of participation on productivity.

French, R.P., & Raven, B. The bases of social power. In D. Cartwright & A. Zander (Eds.), *Group Dynamics*. New York: Harper & Row, 1960.

The five bases of power are listed as (1) reward power (based on one's perception that another can prescribe rewards), (2) coercive power (based on one's perception that another can prescribe punishment), (3) legitimate power (based on one's perception that another has a legitimate right to prescribe behavior), (4) referent power (based on one person's identification with another), and (5) expert power (based on one's belief that another has some special expertise).

Goodstadt, B., & Kipnis, D. Situational influences on the use of power. *Journal of Applied Psychology*, 1970, *54*, 201-207.

In a laboratory study using university students, problems of discipline evoked the use of coercive power by supervisors, whereas problems of ineptness evoked expert power. When supervisors were overseeing larger numbers of workers (eight or more), they spent less time with problem workers and gave fewer pay raises to satisfactory workers.

Jamieson, D. W. & Thomas, K.W. Power and conflict in the student-teacher relationship. *Journal of Applied Behavioral Science*, 1974, *10*, 321-336.

A social-power inventory based on French and Raven's six types of power (coercive, legitimate, expert, information, reward, and referent) is used to assess how students at different stages of training (high school, undergraduate, and graduate) perceive the power base of their teachers. Coercive and legitimate power dominated the high-school and undergraduate levels, with information and expert power more important in graduate school.

Kahn, R.L. Field studies of power in organizations. In R.L. Kahn & E. Boulding (Eds.), *Power and conflict in organizations*. New York: Basic Books, 1964.

The Control Graph is a survey method that asks people at different organizational levels how much power they have. This article shows its use in different studies.

Kipnis, D., Castell, P., Gergen, M., & Mauch, D. Metamorphic effects of power. *Journal of Applied Psychology*, 1976, *61*, 127-135.

The authors found that the use of power tended to lead to the power holders' devaluation of the less powerful and to increase the power holder's belief that he or she "caused" the performance of the other. Power holders also tended to keep physically distant from the less powerful.

Korda, M. *Power: How to get it, how to use it*. New York: Random House, 1965.

Examples of the use of individual power are given.

Mulder, M. *The daily power game*. Leiden, Netherlands: Martinus Nijhoft Social Sciences Division, 1977.

The core propositions in the author's "power-distance" theory are the following: (1) The mere exercise of power will give satisfaction; (2) the more powerful individual will strive to maintain or to increase the power to the less powerful person; (3) the greater the distance from the less powerful person, the stronger the striving to increase it; (4) individuals will strive to reduce the power distance between themselves and more powerful persons; and (5) the smaller the distance from the more powerful person, the stronger the tendency to reduce it.

O'Day, R. Rituals of intimidation: Reactions to reform. *Journal of Applied Behavioral Science*, 1974, *10*, 373-386.

Four tactics often used by power holders to inhibit protest are described: In ascending order of severity, power holders may first try to nullify a reformer's voice, then isolate him, then defame his character, and finally expel him. One section deals with the psychological tactics of defamation.

Patchen, M. The locus and basis of influence in organizational decisions. *Organizational Behavior and Human Performance*, 1974, *11*, 195-221.

The author presents an exhaustive treatment of the six types of social power.

Schein, V.E. Individual power and political behaviors in organizations: An inadequately explored reality. *Academy of Management Review*, 1977, *2(1)*, 64-71.

A conceptual scheme is proposed that aligns the bases of an individual's power with the intent of the power holder to pursue either organizational or personal goals. The means of exhibiting power is viewed as a function of the individual's power base and his or her intent. Two short examples are provided.

Sorensen, P.F., Jr., & Barum, B.H. The measurement of intraorganizational power: The application of the Control Graph to organization development. *Group & Organization Studies*, 1977, *2(1)*, 61-74.

This is a review of work from the past twenty years with the Control Graph, including the evolution of Control-Graph studies, its relationship to other perspectives of organizations, and an overview of study findings.

## SECTION III. THE STRUCTURALISTS AND INTERGROUP POWER

An organization is composed of subunits (e.g., production and marketing). Authors who take a structuralistic approach examine under what conditions certain subunits have the most power. Subunits are also composed of leaders and members, so other authors explore how information control and selective perception affect power-oriented decision making. These authors emphasize that organizational coalitions—as opposed to subunits—are the most important groups to study.

Bougon, M. Cognition in organizations: An analysis of the Utrecht Jazz Orchestra. *Administrative Science Quarterly*, 1977, *22(4)*, 606-639.

This research represents Weick's approach to organization analysis based on a study of participants' "cause maps." It begins by ranking the variables of the average cause map and then, using these ranks, unfolding the map into a content-free "etiograph." The intent is to develop a model of how different organizational participants view change within the organization.

Butler, R.J., Hickson, D., Wilson, D., & Axelsson, R. Organizational power, politicking and paralysis. *Organization and Administrative Sciences*, 1977-1978, *8*, 45-59.

An organization is viewed as a coalition of internal interest units (i.e., subunits with differing goals and methods) and external interest units (e.g., labor pools, banks, regulatory agencies, and competitors). Other observations by the authors include the following: The potential use of power by any of these interest units is shaped by its setting, the "rules of the game," including values acquired over time. When power shifts to external interest units, the organization becomes paralyzed. When power shifts to internal interest units, the organization becomes politicized.

Hickson, D.J., Hinings, C.R., Lee, C.A., Schneck, R.E., & Pennings, J.M. A strategic contingencies theory of intraorganizational power. *Administrative Science Quarterly*, 1971, *16*, 216-229.

Recognizing that organizations consist of interdependent subunits, all of which are trying to cope with uncertainty, the authors suggest that the relative power of any one subunit will be a function of the degree to which (1) it is centrally connected to other subunits, (2) it copes with uncertainty for other units, and (3) other resources can be substituted for the subunits' skills and behavior.

Hinings, C.R., Hickson, D.J., Pennings, J.M., & Schneck, R.E. Structural conditions of intra-organizational power. *Administrative Science Quarterly*, 1974, *19*, 22-44.

The authors examine subunits in seven firms. Results suggest coping with uncertainty is the key variable in gaining power, but they also sugggest two different routes.

Kotter, J.P. Power, success and organizational effectiveness. *Organizational Dynamics*, 1978, *6*, 27-40.

A power/dependence analysis is presented for assessing how a manager uses power to manage the dependencies inherent in his or her job. The author finds that the more dependent managers are on other people and subunits to accomplish the job, the more they will engage in power-oriented behavior.

Mechanic, D. Sources of power of lower participants in complex organizations. *Administrative Science Quarterly*, 1962, *7*, 349-362.

According to the research, the most effective way for lower participants to achieve power is to obtain, maintain, and control access to persons, information, and organizational resources. Factors affecting access were length of time spent in the organization, the effort exerted in a given area, personal attractiveness, the centrality of one's work, and expert knowledge. The article is theoretical, not empirical.

Perrow, C. Departmental power and perspectives in industrial firms. In M. Zald (Ed.), *Power in organizations*. Nashville, TN: Vanderbilt University Press, 1970.

In a series of studies, subgroups within organizations tended to minimize the amount of power they said they had, to maximize the amount they said they should have, to see their middle and lower management groups as more powerful than others saw them, and to minimize the extent to which they should be justly criticized.

Pettigrew, A. Information control as a power source. *Sociology*, 1972, *6*, 187-204.

A study of a capital budgeting decision shows how control over information can act as a power source. Regarding his theoretical orientation to power, the author states, "The basic units of analysis (in studying power) are not individual persons or groups, but actors operating from one or more structural positions within a specific social system. The resources which form the base of an actor's power are assumed to be differentially located by structural position, and in this sense the transferability of power across system boundaries is regarded as problematic."

Pettigrew, A. *The politics of organizational decision-making*. London: Tavistock Press, 1973.

This is the book form of the above article. The author looks at information and the processing of political demands. Some key insights are as follows: (1) The processing of demands and the generation of support are the principal components of the general political structure through which power may be wielded. (2) Knowledge is not power per se. Neither accurate perception nor careful action will benefit the power aspirant very much unless he or she has access to key political figures. (3) The weapons of power contests are the resources that individuals possess, control, and manipulate and the ties of dependency they can form with relevant others.

Pettigrew, A. Strategic formulation as a political process. *International Studies of Management and Organization*, 1979, *7*(2), 78-87.

The author's views include the following: Strategy formulation is a process of mobilizing political power in favor of demands on the resource-sharing system of the organization. A key factor regarding demands is the question of legitimacy. The meaning of demands is managed through the use of language and values to legitimize some demands and discount others.

Pettigrew, A. Towards a political theory of organizational intervention. *Human Relations*, 1975, *28*, 191-208.

The author makes the following assertions: An organization is a political system, and any change effort is political and involves the redistribution of power. Internal consultants are usually ineffective when they fail to have a strategy for dealing with the political realities of the client organization and when they fail to present a united political front to the client organization. A consultant's sources of power are expertise, control over information, political access and sensitivity, assessed stature (i.e., how others perceive the consultant), and group support by fellow consultants within the consulting team.

Pfeffer, J., & Salanick, G.R. *The external control of organizations.* New York: Harper & Row, 1978.

It is proposed that organizations are dependent on their environments for needed resources but that the organization's response to its environment is not a rational mapping of the environmental dependencies. According to the authors, subunits have differential access to information, different power bases, and, therefore, different "maps" of the environment and different abilities to enforce on others their defintions and priorities.

Pfeffer, J., Salanick, G.R., & Leblebici, H. The effect of uncertainty on the use of social influence in organizational decision-making. *Administrative Science Quarterly,* 1976, *21,* 227-245.

The authors found that in uncertain situations, decision makers rely on particularistic criteria (idiosyncratic to the people immediately involved) rather than universalistic criteria (in which large numbers of people would agree). The use of particularistic criteria was also pronounced when resources were scarce.

Pondy, L.R. The other-hand clapping: An information-processing approach to organizational power. In T.H. Hamner & S.B. Bacharach (Eds.), *Reward systems and power distribution.* Ithaca, NY: Cornell University School of Industrial and Labor Relations, 1977.

In complement to the resource-control theories of power (i.e., the strategic-contingencies model), Pondy looks at the effects of the informational environment of the organization on the distribution and exercise of power. He suggests that examining (1) the frequency with which different group members may be interrupted, (2) the notion of evoking preprogrammed behavior in others, (3) organizational members' subjective theories of who has power, and (4) the effects of common or disparate languages or jargon would be useful in understanding power in organizations.

Ranson, S., Hinings, R., & Greenwood, R. The structuring of organizational structure. *Administrative Science Quarterly,* 1980, *25*(1), 1-17.

The authors view an organization as an instrument of power that intrinsically embodies relations of inequality, dependence, and compliance. An aspect of power examined by the authors is that organizational power holders attempt to structure organizational interactions so that a power holder's view of events is dominant prior to any decision making.

Roos, L.L., Jr., & Hall, R. Influence diagrams and organizational power. *Administrative Science Quarterly,* 1980, *25*(1), 57-71.

The authors give a practical example of Weick's theories of "influence diagrams" to model the contingent power relationships in a hospital extended-care unit.

Salanick, G.R., & Pfeffer, J. The bases and uses of power in organizational decision-making: The case of a university. *Administrative Science Quarterly,* 1974, *19,* 453-473.

The most general findings are (1) subunits that provide scarce resources to the organization gain power and (2) those subunits are in turn rewarded with scarce resources by the organization.

Thompson, J.D. *Organizations in action.* New York: McGraw-Hill, 1967.

This book contains a series of propositions about politics and power regarding people who have discretion in jobs that are interdependent: (1) Individuals in highly discretionary jobs seek to maintain power equal to or greater than their dependencies; (2) if power is less than dependency, people seek a coalition; and (3) the more sources of uncertainty or contingency for the organization, the more bases for power and the larger the number of political positions in the organization.

Weick, K. *The social psychology of organizing.* Reading, MA: Addison-Wesley, 1979.

The author examines the ways individuals construct different "maps" of the organization from selective information, their own beliefs, and preprogrammed behavior. These maps become the basis for "influence diagrams," which model the power relationships in an organization.

## SECTION IV. POWER, ORGANIZATION DEVELOPMENT, AND CHANGE

The literature on organization development (OD) tends to be based on case studies and practical examples. It encompasses everything from power equalization to office politics.

Alinsky, S. *Rules for radicals*. New York: Random House, 1971.

> In this primer on how to gain community power, Alinsky makes a distinction between power as the ability to act and power as control. In the chapter on power tactics, he states, "Power is not only what you have but what the enemy thinks you have."

Barthol, R.P. The placebo organization. *California Management Review*, 1978, *20*(4), 26-40.

> The author argues that rewards in many organizations vary directly with the number of people supervised and therefore supervisors resist change toward more efficiency because that would reduce the numbers they supervise and thereby reduce their own prestige and rewards. The author offers a humorous solution.

Beckhard, R. *Organization development: Strategies and models*. Reading, MA: Addison-Wesley, 1969.

> This is a short introduction to OD and an example of earlier OD writing, in which planning was conceived as a substitute for an active consideration of power in organizations.

Boulding, K. A pure theory of conflict applied to organizations. In R.L. Kahn & E. Boulding (Eds.), *Power and conflict in organizations*. New York: Basic Books, 1964.

> According to the author, the use of power in organizations inevitably leads to conflict. He lists four aspects of every conflict: (1) a minimum of two parties, (2) the field of conflict, (3) the dynamics of conflict, and (4) the management of conflict. He states that the hierarchical structure of an organization can be viewed as a device for the resolution of conflicts of the level below.

Chester, P., & Goodman, E.J. *Women, money and power*. New York: William Morrow, 1976.

> The authors list thirteen major forms of power. "Seven are almost totally controlled by men and are fluid or interchangeable with each other (Physical, Technological, Scientific, Military and Consumer Power; the Power of Organized Religions and Secular Institutions). Two powers may be controlled equally by women and men and are also interchangeable (Social Position and Influence). Three forms of power are almost exclusively female and are noninterchangeable or nonfluid spheres of power (Beauty, Sexuality and Motherhood). Money, the thirteenth power, can buy and control the other twelve powers."

Crowfoot, J.E., & Chesler, M.A. Contemporary perspectives on planned social change: A comparison. *Journal of Applied Behavioral Science*, 1974, *10*, 278-301.

> The authors look at the bases of power for social change coming from three value frameworks: the professional/technical, the political, and the counter cultural. A chart summarizes the differences.

Dubrin, A. *Fundamentals of organizational behavior*. New York: Pergamon Press, 1978.

> In the chapter entitled "Political Manoeuvring in Organizations," the author states that political manoeuvring is caused by (1) competition for power, itself a scarce resource; (2) basic distrust of top management's ability to measure performance objectively; and (3) increased mobility among managers, which means one often moves on before the results of his or her performance are in. The article provides a checklist of some strategies for office politics.

Duke, J.T. *Conflict and power in social life*. Salt Lake City, UT: Brigham Young University Press, 1976.

> In Chapter 12 ("A Summary of Conflict Theory") power is viewed as control over wealth and over deference shown by others. All societies, the author claims, show rank hierarchies in terms of power. Conflict is seen as inevitable, with the resolution of inevitable conflict depending upon power differences. Duke argues that power is most effective when hidden and based upon multiple sources and that the elite operate to legitimate and hide their power.

French, W.L., & Bell, C.H., Jr. *Organization development*. Englewood Cliffs, NJ: Prentice-Hall, 1973.

> This book presents an overview of OD and, by implication, a particular view of power in change agentry.

Frost, P.J., & Hayes, D. *An exploration in two cultures of political behavior in organizations*. Presented at the Conference on Cross-Cultural Studies in Organizational Functioning, Hawaii, September 1977.

The authors view power as the property of a social relationship: A is powerful if A can get B to do something B would not ordinarily do. Relative power is viewed as a function of B's dependence on A for resources that A controls. Politics is viewed as a struggle for power and a struggle to limit, resist, and/or escape from power.

Frost, P.J., Mitchell, V.F., & Nord, W.R. *Organizational reality: Reports from the firing line.* Pacific Palisades, CA: Goodyear, 1978.

This is a collection of slices of organizational life, some dealing with power.

Gandz, J., & Murray, V.V. *Politics at work: The view from inside.* Unpublished manuscript, York University School of Management, Toronto, Ontario, Canada, 1978.

The authors hold that office power and political behavior are intertwined. They define politics as concerned with influencing the criteria by which decisions are made and observe that "The higher up the corporate ladder, the higher his income, the more variety in one's work, the more feedback received and the more personally satisfied one is with one's work, the less an individual is likely to feel that 'politics' is a necessary part of his job."

Haire, M. The concept of power, and the concept of man. In G. Strother (Ed.), *Social science approaches to business behavior.* Homewood, IL: Dorsey Press, 1962.

The author presents a chart of the change in the source of authority in the corporation over time. He presents a critique of classical organization theory and argues that power and authority are being increasingly internalized within the organization. "The final source of authority will be the work group . . . Control will come from the individual's commitment to the general goals and activities of the organization."

Heller, F.A., Dreuth, P., Koopman, P., & Veljko, R. A longitudinal study in participative decision-making. *Human Relations,* 1977, *30*(7), 567-587.

The framework and method of a three-country comparative study on the process of participative decision making are described. Research methods, models, and instruments are developed in the context of a longitudinal design. The major hypotheses relate to the situationally determined relation between power decentralization, skill utilization, and effectiveness.

Jay, A. *Management and Machiavelli.* New York: Holt, Rinehart and Winston, 1967.

The author applies the amorality of Machiavelli to management. His aim is to find management principles that "work" by examining political examples of the past.

Kahn, S.I. *How people get power: Organizing oppressed communities for action.* New York: McGraw-Hill, 1970.

Like Alinsky's book, this one deals with the practicalities of gaining community power when faced with opposition. The examples from communities can be translated to the organizational setting.

Kanter, R.M. *Men and women of the corporation.* New York: Basic Books, 1977.

Chapter 7, "Power," is a review of many issues concerning power and organization. A distinction is made between power as mastery or autonomy and power as control or domination. Politics and power are seen as a way of reducing a huge, impersonal organization to manageable size. "Power issues occupy center stage not because individuals are greedy for more, but because some people are incapacitated without it."

Kanter, R.M., & Stein, B.A. (Eds.). *Life in organizations.* New York: Basic Books, 1979.

Case studies of power in organizations are presented. Section one is titled "Life at the Top: The Struggle for Power."

King, D.C., & Glidewell, J.C. Power. In J.W. Pfeiffer & J.E. Jones (Eds.), *The 1976 annual handbook for group facilitators.* San Diego, CA: University Associates, 1976.

This simplified approach to power gives a brief overview. According to the authors, power arises from the meeting of one person's needs and another person's ability to meet those needs, and factors affecting the stability of a power relationship are unfulfilled needs, unutilized means, alternate resources, "do-without" time, and reciprocity. Sources of power (similar to but extending those of

French and Raven) and a way of characterizing the system in which a power relationship exists (based on Oshry) are presented.

Kotter, J.P. Power, dependence and effective management. *Harvard Business Review*, 1977, *55*, 125-136.

The author suggests some ways to establish power: (1) Create a sense of obligation in others, (2) build a reputation as an expert, (3) foster unconscious identifications with yourself, (4) foster others' dependence on you by acquiring resources others want or influencing others' perception of your resources, and (5) acquire formal authority.

Lammers, C.J. Power and participation in decision-making in formal organizations. *American Journal of Sociology*, 1967, *73*, 201-216.

Using economic analogies, the author disputes that power is a fixed amount in any organization and that an inevitable conflict of interest exists between power holders and power seekers. Instead, he suggests that granting power to lower participants in the organization may boost overall productivity, thereby increasing the organization's total power in its product market. European co-management experiments are used as evidence.

Lawrence, P.R., Kolodny, H.F., & Davis, S.W. The human side of the matrix. *Organizational Dynamics*, 1977, *6*(1), 43-61.

The authors argue that a mature management matrix involves a radically different structure for the organization that in turn requires different behaviors at key levels of management. The changes in power, pressures, and perceptions that follow from these new management roles are discussed.

March, J., & Simon, H. *Organizations*. New York: John Wiley, 1958.

According to the chapter entitled "Conflict in Organizations," power derives from the division of labor and individuals' feeling the need for joint decision making. The authors state that the more that individuals mutually depend on a resource and the greater the interdependence of the timing of their activities, the more they will feel the need for joint decision making.

Martin, N., & Sims, J. Power tactics. *Harvard Business Review*, 1956, *34*, 25-29.

The authors offer an unusual focus of power upon the subordinate, not the superior. They suggest that the ultimate source of power is in the group. Ways to enhance one's power are listed.

Mayes, B.T., & Allen, R.W. Toward a definition of organizational politics. *Academy of Management Review*, 1977, *2*, 672-678.

The authors claim that "Organizational politics is the management of influence to obtain ends not sanctioned by the organization or to obtain sanctioned ends through nonsanctioned influence means."

McCall, M. *Power, authority and influence: The hazards of carrying a sword.* (Tech. Rep. No. 10). Greensboro, NC: Center for Effective Leadership, 1978.

The author argues that power is a product of relations in systems, involving people-to-people networks and the interface between the organization and the environment. He lists power as deriving from (1) one's location in the division of labor (e.g., those units most able to cope with the organization's critical problems and uncertainties acquire power), (2) one's resources (e.g., scarce resources create dependence, leading to power over other subunits and individuals), and (3) timing (e.g, people who can influence the timing of events acquire power). The author further states that efforts by power holders to preserve the existing power distribution disrupt the smooth exchange of power between subunits as they attempt to solve problems posed by the environment.

McMurray, R. Power and the ambitious executive. *Harvard Business Review*, 1973, *51*, 140-145.

The author claims that power is essential for authority, discipline, and system functioning. Ways for executives to use power are listed.

Mowday, R.T. The exercise of upward influence in organizations. *Administrative Science Quarterly*. 1978, *23*(1), 137-156.

A study of selected aspects (intrinsic motivation, instrumental motivation, and self-perceptions of power) of the exercise of influence by elementary school principals is examined.

Mulder, M. Power equalization through participation? *Administrative Science Quarterly*, 1971, *16*, 31-38.

The author cites European research on co-determination and a laboratory experiment to confirm his hypothesis that when large differences in expert power exist between members of a system, participation will *increase*, not *decrease*, power differences.

Olmosk, K.E. Seven pure strategies of change. In J.W. Pfeiffer & J.E. Jones (Eds.), *The 1972 annual handbook for group facilitators*. San Diego, CA: University Associates, 1972.

Seven models of change are compared on criteria such as their basic assumptions, who they include, chronic problems, questions avoided, etc. Assumptions about power (who has it, who does not, and why) are embedded in each model.

Oshry, B. *Controlling the contexts of consciousness*. Boston, MA: Power and Systems Training Inc., 1976.

Oshry, B. *Notes on the power and systems perspective*. Boston, MA: Power and Systems Training, Inc., 1976.

Oshry, B. *Organic power*. Boston, MA: Power and Systems Training Inc., 1976.

Oshry, B. *Organizational spasms: When a stable organization meets an unstable environment*. Boston, MA: Power and Systems Training Inc., 1978.

Oshry, B. *Power and position*. Boston, MA: Power and Systems Training Inc., 1977.

Oshry, B. Power and the power lab. In W.W. Burke (Ed.), *New technologies in organization development: 1*. San Diego, CA: University Associates, 1975.

Oshry, B. *Taking a look at yourself: Self-in-system sensitizers*. Boston, MA: Power and Systems Training Inc., 1978.

Oshry is an OD practitioner who has developed the "power lab" as a simulation to examine individual and group behavior in power-laden situations. A sample quote is "Power is acting *as if* you can make happen what you want to have happen, knowing that you *cannot*, and working with *whatever does* happen."

Pages, M., & Descendre, D. [Research on the phenomenon of power within large industrial organizations.] *Sociologie et Societes*, 1977, *9*(2), 122-147. (In French.)

This research project had two objectives: (1) to elaborate a theory of power within organizations and (2) to identify the specific characteristics of power in the ultramodern organization, of which the prototype is the multinational. Power is described as a system with four categories: economic, political, ideological, and psychological.

Parshall, L. Balance of power: A cooperation/competition activity. In J.W. Pfeiffer & J.E. Jones (Eds.), *The 1978 annual handbook for group facilitators*. San Diego, CA: University Associates, 1978.

This is a simulation game to explore the effects of cooperation, competition, and leader power on decision making in groups.

Ritti, R., & Funkhouser, G.R. *The ropes to skip and the ropes to know*. Columbus, OH: Grid, 1977.

The authors give a series of anecdotal examples of organizational life, some of which deal with the use of power.

Sashkin, M. Models and roles of change agents. In J.W. Pfeiffer & J.E. Jones (Eds.), *The 1974 annual handbook for group facilitators*. San Diego, CA: University Associates, 1974.

This article compares six models of organizational change and the associated roles and tasks required of the change agent. Power is ignored as a variable, although it is implicit in each model of change.

Schmidt, S.M., & Kochan, T.A. Interorganizational relationships: Patterns and motivations. *Administrative Science Quarterly*, 1977, *22*(2), 220-234.

Two competing approaches—exchange and power-dependency—are integrated. Propositions are developed from these two approaches for explaining variations in the frequency of interaction and the nature of interactions between pairs of organizations in an interorganizational set. Special emphasis is given to the nature of interactions in an asymmetrical relationship. The propositions were tested with data on interactions between twenty-three community organizations and local offices of the U.S. Training and Employment Service. Results suggest that interorganizational relationships should be conceptualized as a mixed-motive situation in which each organization behaves in accordance with its own self-interests.

Strauss, G. Some notes on power equalization. In H.J. Leavitt (Ed.), *The social science of organization.* Englewood Cliffs, NJ: Prentice-Hall, 1963.

The author notes that power equalization has been a consistent theme of the OD human relations school and that individuals are seen as self-actualizing and expansive although organizations desire to program individual behavior and reduce discretion. He examines the value assumptions behind this approach (finding many questionable) and notes that the human relations people ignore the "organizational economics" of the issue.

Swingle, P.G. *The management of power.* Toronto, Ontario, Canada: John Wiley, 1976.

The central theme of this wide-ranging book about power, conflict, and violence seems to be that power is inevitably centralized in a bureaucracy and that leaders inevitably become isolated. Similarly, conflict is proposed as inevitable, and therefore to create change (and changeable institutions), one has to design overlapping centers of decision-making authority.

Twomey, D.F. The effects of power properties on conflict resolution. *Academy of Management Review,* 1978, *3,* 144-150.

The author presents a classification scheme of conflict resolution strategies based on an individual's power and dependence.

Winn, A. Change agents, scapegoats, power and love. *Group Process,* 1973, 5(2), 153-160.

The author discusses high turnover among internal consultants serving as change agents in OD efforts. The suggested reasons for presumed limited effectiveness of internal change agents include (1) staff positions of low status with no legitimate power; (2) dependency feelings, in the event of success, that evoke feelings of hostility and rejection; (3) "scapegoating" to preserve intragroup relations among senior managers; (4) status incongruity that creates anxiety and prevents the development of social confidence; (5) line managers' feelings of ambivalence toward organization development; and (6) the untenable belief that the internal resource person can function as a true "third party." It is concluded that although the *external* consultant has a better chance for a sustained relationship with a client system, the same forces operate to ensure limited tenure for *any* OD consultant.

Witte, E. Power and innovation: A two-center theory. *International Studies of Management and Organization,* 1977-1978, 7, 47-70.

Through a study of the introduction of computers in West German firms, the author argues that resistance to innovation comprises barriers of will and barriers of know-how and that innovation succeeds best when there is a personal relationship between someone with expert power (to break barriers of know-how) and someone with legitimate power (to break barriers of will).

Zalesnik, A. Power and politics in organizational life. *Harvard Business Review,* 1970, *48*(3), 47-60.

The author, a psychoanalyst, argues that everybody has an initial "capitalization" of power based on (1) the formal authority invested in the position, (2) the authority vested in one's expertise and reputation for competence, and (3) the attractiveness of one's personality. The following "life dramas" occur, he claims, in all organizational life: (1) the need to consolidate power around a central figure to whom others make emotional attachments, (2) the guilt that follows displacing the parental figure, (3) paranoia (believing those who oppose you are evil), and (4) ritual ceremonies (performing activities that give the illusion of solving problems, e.g., calling a meeting).

Zaltman, G., Kotler, P., & Kaufman, I. *Creating social change.* New York: Holt, Rinehart and Winston, 1972.

In Section III, "Power Strategies," eight articles deal with the use of various kinds of power in social-change situations.

## SECTION V. POWER AND THE ECONOMISTS

The neoclassical economists believe market competition eliminates problems of power. Those economists who focus on market structure and internal labor markets regard power as a central variable. The Marxists focus on power as a tool of class domination.

Alchian, A., & Demsetz, H. Production, information costs and economic organization. In E.G. Furnbotn & S. Pejovich (Eds.), *The economics of property rights.* Cambridge, MA: Ballinger, 1974.

> The authors acknowledge that power could emerge in the firm because team production makes it impossible to measure an individual's marginal productivity, and therefore it is impossible to give an individual an accurate marginal income in relation to his or her work. Although team production requires supervisors who oversee and manage all individuals' labor time, potentially leading to questions of power and control, in this neoclassical economic view, problems of power do *not* emerge because market competition prevents them.

Coleman, J.S. Notes on the study of power. In R. Liebert & A. Immerschein (Eds.), *Power, paradigms and community research.* Beverly Hills, CA: Sage, 1977.

> Classical economic theory is applied to the analysis of the power of an organization in its product, capital, and labor markets.

Dubois, J. Power and reform within the firm. *International Studies of Management and Organization,* 1977-1978, *7,* 7-15.

> Dubois argues that the struggle for power no longer is placed inside the firm; instead, the economy has become global, and the new governing classes pursue technical and economic efficiency globally, with the firm being only one tool. Dubois claims that power belongs to those who define what is rational and desirable; although participation, codetermination, and autonomous work groups may equalize the power balance within the firm, the larger question of power to decide what is rational and desirable goes unanswered.

Friedman, M. *Capitalism and freedom.* Chicago: University of Chicago Press, 1962.

> The essence of economic power, Friedman argues, is in choice—e.g., not buying one product and buying another—because choosing prevents domination by power.

Hayek, F.A. The price system as a mechanism for using knowledge. *American Economics Review,* 1945, *35*(4), 519-530.

> Hayek looks at the power of information. He argues that capitalism gains its strength by placing decision-making power in the hands of individuals, who know intimately what the people around them need and want.

Hirsch, F. *Social limits to growth.* Cambridge, MA: Harvard University Press, 1978.

> According to Hirsch, economic power (i.e., command over resources) is a function not just of how much money one has, but where one's income stands relative to others' incomes. Other concepts addressed by the book include the following: As specialization of labor and the service-based economy increase, personal productivity and pay are more subjectively assessed; workers are judged increasingly on personal attributes, e.g., their ability to "get along"; and conflicts of interest and power concerns become more common as groups bargain about their wages and benefit packages *relative* to those of others.

Lindblom, C.E. *Politics and markets.* New York: Basic Books, 1977.

> In this overview of power in markets and governmental systems, Lindblom claims that the power of the state rests in its authority (i.e., its routinized permission to control and do things denied to others), that authority exists when people permit someone else to make decisions for them for some category of acts, and that economic power is based on property—the authority to control assets. In a market-based economy, Lindblom argues, the market controls relations *between* groups; within groups, power, authority, and persuasion are the means of control.

Nord, W. A Marxist critique of humanist psychology. *Journal of Humanistic Psychology,* 1977, *17*(1), 75-83.

Nord holds that humanistic goals cannot be achieved without major changes in economic organization and the distribution of power.

Scitovsky, T. *The joyless economy*. London: Oxford University Press, 1976.

Scitovsky examines the power of economists to shape behavior. He argues that the subject of economics is whatever passes through markets and that markets in turn represent a pressure to conform, because they consist of one person's receiving a benefit *only if* someone likes or needs what is offered. He claims that economic power in modern capitalism resides with the rich and the crowd: The rich have the dollars individually to command the goods they want, and the crowd has the aggregate buying power.

Weierman, K. *The evolution of labor market structure*. Paper presented at the annual meeting of the Atlantic Economic Society, Salsbury, England, May 1979.

Weierman traces the development of the economic theory of the treatment of labor within the firm. He observes that (1) it is more efficient to hire permanent laborers and to work by teams than to pay workers by individual contracts; (2) long-term employment disrupts the relationship between marginal productivity and wages, because pay is attached to jobs and roles, not individual workers; and (3) training provided within the organization increases specialization and the need for teamwork, placing less emphasis on marginal productivity and more on power relations within the firm.

Weierman, K. *Worker participation, worker incentives and efficiency of the firm*. Paper presented at the spring meeting of the Atlantic Economic Society, Freeport, Bahamas, February 1980.

The author extends the analysis of internal labor markets, in which workers immobilize themselves to some degree and risk exploitation, because they may not receive marginal pay equivalent to their marginal productivity. With job-specific skills and market uncertainty, power accrues to those who have knowledge—according to the author—i.e., to supervisors (who are party to every contract and therefore show people how to work together) and experts (people whose knowledge makes them indispensable and mobile).

Williamson, O.E., Wachter, M.L., & Harris, M. Understanding the employment relation: The analysis of idiosyncratic exchange. *Bell Journal of Economics*, 1975, *6*(1), 250-278.

In this analysis of why neoclassical microeconomic theory cannot account for power in organizations, the authors argue the following points: During employment, workers acquire significant task-specific skills and knowledge, which are sources of power to them in bargaining with employers. Employers cannot pursue a contracting approach with their workers, because the contract for future performance cannot be specified clearly enough. Consequently, a small-numbers bargaining situation arises, which is short-circuited by the development of *internal* labor markets which are characterized by (1) the attachment of wages to jobs, not individuals; (2) internal promotion ladders that encourage cooperation; and (3) collective agreements, which foster *group* interests and informal organization.

**Mark Smith** *is a doctoral student in organizational psychology at York University, Toronto, Canada. His special interests are in organizational design and development, especially in the nonprofit sector. Mr. Smith also is a fellow of the Gestalt Institute of Toronto.*

**Howard L. Fromkin, Ph.D.,** *is executive vice president of Fromkin Van Horn Limited, a Toronto-based consulting firm. He was previously a professor of psychology at York University and professor and chairman of the Department of Administrative Sciences, Krannert Graduate School of Management, Purdue University. Dr. Fromkin has co-authored four books and numerous professional articles and has consulted internationally with a variety of organizations. His major interests are organizational effectiveness, assessment and diagnosis, consultation processes, and conflict management.*

# A BIBLIOGRAPHY OF SMALL-GROUP TRAINING, 1976-1979

## W. Brendan Reddy and Kathy M. Lippert

This bibliography is a compilation of experiential small-group literature published from January 1976 through December 1979.[1] Although the authors have attempted to be comprehensive and complete, some articles may not be included because of oversight or inaccessibility.

The bibliography is divided into eight sections, arranged alphabetically: Books, Client Systems, Evaluation and Outcome, Models and Theory, Research, Reviews and Surveys, Standards, Ethics, and Values, and Techniques. Appropriate subunits and authors appear alphabetically under each section. When articles were applicable to more than one category, the authors chose the section that seemed most appropriate.

## BOOKS

Back, K.W. *In search for community: Encounter groups and social change.* Boulder, CO: Westview, 1978.

Blumberg, A., & Golembiewski, R.T. *Learning and change in groups.* Baltimore, MD: Penguin, 1976.

Morris, K.T., & Cinnamon, K.M. *Controversial issues in human relations training groups.* Springfield, IL: Charles C Thomas, 1976.

Pfeiffer, J.W. & Jones, J.E. (Eds.). *The annual handbook for group facilitators (1976-1979).* San Diego, CA: University Associates, 1976-1979.

Pfeiffer, J.W., & Jones, J.E. (Eds.). *A handbook of structured experiences for human relations training* (Vols. IV-VII). San Diego, CA: University Associates, 1974-1979.

Rogers, C. *On personal power: Inner strength and its revolutionary impact.* New York: Delacorte Press, 1977.

Rosenbaum, M., & Snadowsky, A. *The intensive group experience: A guide.* New York: The Free Press, 1976.

Sampson, E.E., & Marthas, M.S. *Group process for the health professions.* New York: John Wiley, 1977.

Shapiro, J.L. *Methods of group psychotherapy and encounter: A tradition of innovation.* Itasca, IL: Peacock, 1978.

Zander, A. *Groups at work.* San Francisco, CA: Jossey-Bass, 1977.

## CLIENT SYSTEMS

Bailey, A.E. The effects of human relations training upon facilitative communication of prospective teachers (Doctoral dissertation, 1976). *Dissertation Abstracts International,* 1976, *36,* 5032.

Bennett, R.M., Rosser, R.S., & Hope, L.H. Effects of human relations training on preservice teachers' attitudes toward human nature. *Psychological Reports,* 1977, *40*(3), 1287-1290.

Bledsoe, J.C., & Layser, G.R. Effects of human relations training with houseparents on attainment of group facilitation skills. *Psychological Reports,* 1977, *40*(3), 787-791.

---

[1]For a compilation of previous literature published, see W.B. Reddy, A Bibliography of Small-Group Training, 1973-1974, in J.E. Jones and J.W. Pfeiffer (Eds.), *The 1975 Annual Handbook for Group Facilitators.* San Diego, CA: University Associates, 1975, and W. B. Reddy and K. Lippert, A Bibliography of Small-Group Training, 1974-1976, in J.E. Jones and J.W. Pfeiffer (Eds.), *The 1977 Annual Handbook for Group Facilitators.* San Diego, CA: University Associates, 1977.

Bloom, S. A study of the impact of sensitivity training on the elderly. *Interpersonal Development*, 1976, *6*, 150-152.

Casey, C.N. The effects of a human relations training model upon ninth grade students (Doctoral dissertation, 1976). *Dissertation Abstracts International*, 1976, *36*, 11-A.

Charles, N.A. A study of the effects of human resource training on selected groups of military personnel over a three-year period (Doctoral dissertation, 1979). *Dissertation Abstracts International*, 1979, *39*, 11-B.

Chishom, A.J. Some effects of systematic human relations training on offenders' ability to demonstrate helping skills (Doctoral dissertation, 1977). *Dissertation Abstracts International*, 1977. (University Microfilms No. 77-4108)

Covey, S.R. Effects of human relations training on the social, emotional and moral development of students, with emphasis on human relations training based upon religious principles (Doctoral dissertation, 1977). *Dissertation Abstracts International*, 1977, *37*, 9-A.

Crisler, J.R., & Long, E.G. The effects of human relations training upon the self concept of severely disabled persons. *Journal of Applied Rehabilitation Counseling*, 1978, *9*(2), 50-52.

Davis, E.D., Sturgis, D.K., & Braswell, M.C. Effects of systematic human relations training on inmate participants. *Rehabilitation Counseling Bulletin*, 1976, *20*(2), 105-109.

Eaton, R.R. Human relations training: A study of communication skills for high school students (Doctoral dissertation, 1977). *Dissertation Abstracts International*, 1977, *37*.

Emener, W.G., & Pankowski, J.M. In-service training for rehabilitation secretaries. *Rehabilitation Counseling Bulletin*, 1978, *21*(4), 339-342.

Evans, D.R., Uhlemann, M.R., & Hearn, M.T. Microcounseling and sensitivity training with hotline workers. *Journal of Community Psychology*, 1978, *6*(2), 139-146.

Follingstead, D.R., Robinson, E.A., & Pugh, M. Effects of consciousness-raising groups on measures of feminism, self-esteem, and social desirability. *Journal of Counseling Psychology*, 1977, *24*(3), 223-230.

Hall, E. Human relations training in a comprehensive school. *British Journal of Guidance and Counseling*, 1977, *5*(2), 207-214.

Hardley, G.K. An analysis of the changes in reported self-evaluations by self-selected high school students in human relations training courses and the changes in self-esteem behaviors as reported by the students' teacher-advisor (Doctoral dissertation, 1977). *Dissertation Abstracts International*, 1977, *37*, 9-A.

Heitzmann, D. Forgotten facilitators—Human-relations training for support personnel. *Personnel and Guidance Journal*, 1979, *57*, 543-544.

Herlihy, B.J. An experiential approach to human relations training for prospective teachers (Doctoral dissertation, 1979). *Dissertation Abstracts International*, 1979, *39*,8-A.

Herron, L. The effects of early human relations training on the attitudes of students from two selected high schools (Doctoral dissertation, 1976). *Dissertation Abstracts International*, 1976, *37*, 5-A.

Hume, K.R. The effects of training in human relations and program development skills on the staff of a state psychiatric hospital (Doctoral dissertation, 1977). *Dissertation Abstracts International*, 1977, *38*, 4-B.

Kautz, E. Can agencies train for racial awareness. *Child Welfare*, 1976, *55*(8), 547-551.

Kegan, D.L. Perceived effects of sensitivity training: Samples of police officers, college students, and a group dynamics class. *Small Group Behavior*, 1976, *7*(2), 131-146.

King, M. Changes in self-acceptance of college students associated with the encounter model class. *Small Group Behavior*, 1976, *7*(3), 376-384.

Kutter, P., Laimbock, A., & Roth, J.K. Psychoanalytic sensitivity training in college. *Gruppendynamik Forschund Und Praxis*, 1979, *10*, 176-186.

Lett, W.R., & Williams, A.J. Extending human relations work with teachers. *Australian Psychologist*, 1976, *11*(2), 159-168.

Lewin, M.M. The effects of twenty hours of systematic human relations training on the classroom behavior of experienced self-selected elementary school teachers (Doctoral dissertation, 1976). *Dissertation Abstracts International*, 1976, *36*, 11-A.

Maxwell, M.A. The efficacy of human relations training for adolescents (Doctoral dissertation, 1978). *Dissertation Abstracts International*, 1978. (University Microfilms No. 7812281)

McCurdy, B., Ciucevich, M.T., & Walker, B.A. Human-relations training with seventh grade boys identified as behavior problems. *School Counselor*, 1977, *24*(4), 248-252.

McCurdy, M.E. Human relations training with a church related population. *Journal of Psychology and Theology*, 1976, *4*(4), 291-299.

McGuane, D.R. The effects of modified marathon and traditional human relations on student self-concept (Doctoral dissertation, 1978). *Dissertation Abstracts International*, 1978, *38*, 4550-A.

Milton, F.T. A comparison of the effects of intensive developmental human relations training and a performance based curriculum in human relations on the counseling skills of professional counselor trainees (Doctoral dissertation, 1976). *Dissertation Abstracts International*, 1976, *38*, 5-A.

Moracco, J., & Bushwar, A.G. The effect of human relations training on dogmatic attitudes of educational administration students. *Journal of Experimental Education*, 1976, *44*(4), 32-34.

Moreland, J.R. A humanistic approach to facilitating college students learning about sex roles. *Counseling Psychologist*, 1976, *6*(3), 61-64.

Morrison, M.H. A human relations approach to problem solving. *Gerontologist*, 1976, *16*(2), 185-186.

Pacoe, L.V., Naar, R., Guyett, I.P., & Wells, R. Training medical students in interpersonal relationship skills. *Journal of Medical Education*, 1976, *51*(9), 743-750.

Quirk, M.P. Training in human relations for dormitory resident assistants. *Psychological Reports*, 1976, *39*(1), 123-129.

Redman, G.L. Study of the relationship of teacher empathy for minority persons and inservice human relations training. *Journal of Educational Research*, 1977, *70*(4), 205-210.

Rosenblum, J.J. The effects on interpersonal growth and group leadership skills of a training for trainers workshop (Doctoral dissertation, 1977). *Dissertation Abstracts International*, 1977, *38*.

Rosser, R.S. Effects of human relations training on secondary preservice teacher philosophy of human nature and belief about disadvantaged students (Doctoral dissertation, 1978). *Dissertation Abstracts International*, 1978, *38*.

Runyon, H.L., & Cohen, L.A. Effects of systematic human-relations training on freshman dental students. *Journal of the American Dental Association*, 1979, *98*, 196-201.

Sachs, R.H. The use of a group contract to facilitate interpersonal growth in undergraduates (Doctoral dissertation, 1978). *Dissertation Abstracts International*, 1978, *38*.

Sadler, O.W., Seyden, T., Howe, B., & Kaminsky, T. An evaluation of groups for parents: A standardized format encompassing both behavior modification and humanistic methods. *Journal of Community Psychology*, 1976, *4*(2), 157-163.

Sigan, J., Barveman, S., Pilon, R., & Baker, P. Effects of teacher-led, curriculum integrated sensitivity training in a large high school. *Journal of Educational Research*, 1976, *70*(1), 3-9.

Smith, P.R., & Futch, J.I. A human relations training program for recreation leaders. *Therapeutic Recreation Journal*, 1978, *12*(1), 33-39.

Steinberg, R.A. The encounter group movement and the tradition of Christian enthusiasm and mysticism (Doctoral dissertation, 1976). *Dissertation Abstracts International*, 1976, *36*.

Taintor, Z. Group sensitivity training for psychiatric residents. *Journal of Psychiatric Education*, 1977, *9*(1), 93-99.

Thompson, L.H. A comparative analysis of the impact of human relations training and rational behavior training on interpersonal relations of community action agency staff (Doctoral dissertation, 1978). *Dissertation Abstracts International*, 1978, *39*.

Vega, F. The effect of human and intergroup relations education on the race/sex attitudes of education majors (Doctoral dissertation, 1978). *Dissertation Abstracts International*, 1978, *39*.

Winger, L.J. Programmed interpersonal relations training for high school students (Doctoral dissertation, 1978). *Dissertation Abstracts International*, 1978, *38*, 8-B.

Wittmer, J., Lanier, J.E., & Parker, M. Race relations training with correctional officers. *Personnel and Guidance Journal*, 1976, *54*(6), 302-306.

Woodburn, L.T. The effects of human relations training on institutional environment (Doctoral dissertation, 1977). *Dissertation Abstracts International,* 1977, *37.*

## EVALUATION AND OUTCOME

Beach, L. A note on self-reported long-term effects of encounter groups. *Interpersonal Development,* 1976, *6*(2), 65-67.

De Julio, S., Lambert, M., & Bentley, J. Personal satisfaction as a criterion for evaluating group success. *Psychological Reports,* 1977, *40*(2), 409-410.

Epps, J., & Sikes, W.W. Personal growth groups: Who joins and who benefits. *Group & Organization Studies,* 1977, *2*(1), 88-100.

Green, J. Changes in interpersonal perception associated with an encounter-group experience. *Australian Psychologist,* 1979, 14, 197.

Hipple, J.L. Effects of differential human relations laboratory designs on personal growth. *Small Group Behavior,* 1976, *7*(4), 407-422.

Katz, S.I., & Schwebel, A.I. The transfer of laboratory training: Some issues explored. *Small Group Behavior,* 1976, *7*(3), 271-286.

Lukas, G., Blaiwes, A.S., & Weller, D. *Evaluation of human relations training programs.* Naval Training and Equipment Center, 1977. (No. 75-C-0076-1)

Madden, F.M. The effect of human relations training on group leaders' decisions and members' satisfaction (Doctoral dissertation, 1977). *Dissertation Abstracts International,* 1977, *38.*

Miglionico, L.R. The relative efficacy of Gestalt and human relations training group treatment (Doctoral dissertation, 1979). *Dissertation Abstracts International,* 1979, *39.*

Nykodym, N., & Simonetti, J.L. An evaluation of structured experiences: How effective is experience-based learning? *Group & Organization Studies,* 1978, *3,* 489-496.

Purce, T.L. A study of long-term and short-term human relations training (Doctoral dissertation, 1978). *Dissertation Abstracts International,* 1978, *36.*

Sechrest, L., & Olbrisch, M.E. Special considerations in conducting evaluations of encounter groups. *Professional Psychology,* 1977, *8*(4), 516-525.

Shadish, W.R., & Zarle, T. Validation of an encounter-group measure. *Small Group Behavior,* 1979, *10,* 101-112.

Smith, P.B. Social influence processes and the outcome of sensitivity training. *Journal of Personality and Social Psychology,* 1976, *34*(6), 1087-1094.

Smith, P.B. Changes in relationships after sensitivity training. *Small Group Behavior,* 1979, *10,* 414-430.

Therrien, M., & Fischer, J. Written indicators of empathy in human-relations training: A validational study. *Counselor Education and Supervision,* 1978, *17*(4), 272-277.

Toukmanian, S.G., Capelle, R.G., & Rennie, D.L. Counsellor trainee awareness of evaluative criteria: A neglected variable. *Canadian Counsellor,* 1978, *12*(3), 177-183.

## MODELS AND THEORY

Babad, E.Y., Tzur, A., Oppenheimer, B.T., & Shaltiel, A. An all-purpose model for group work. *Human Relations,* 1977, *30*(4), 389-401.

Becvar, R.J. Paradoxical double binds in human relations training. *Counselor Education and Supervision,* 1978, *18*(1), 36-44.

Benjafield, J., Pomeroy, E., & Jordan, D. Encounter groups: A return to the fundamental. *Psychotherapy: Theory, Research, and Practice,* 1976, *13*(4), 387-389.

Blake, R.R., & Mouton, J.S. A comparison of spread and change strategies in two applied behavioral science movements. *Group & Organization Studies,* 1977, *2*(1), 25-32.

Brice, R.H. The relation of structured exercises to process and outcome variables in sensitivity training (Doctoral dissertation, 1978). *Dissertation Abstracts International,* 1978, *38,* 9-B.

Cash, R.W., & Vellema, D.K. Conceptual versus competency approach in human relations training programs. *Personnel and Guidance Journal,* 1979, *58,* 91-94.

Farrell, M.P. Patterns in the development of self-analytic groups. *Journal of Applied Behavioral Science,* 1976, *12*(4), 523-542.

Goodstein, L.D., Goldstein, J.J., Dorta, C.V., & Goodman, M.A. Measurement of self-disclosure in encounter groups: A methodological study. *Journal of Counseling Psychology,* 1976, *23*(2), 142-146.

Lorber, N.M. The group as a medium for change. *Psychology,* 1976, *13*(1), 30-32.

Mangha, I. Definitions, interactions, and disengagement: Notes towards a theory of intervention processes in T-groups. *Small Group Behavior,* 1977, *8*(4), 487-510.

Roe, J.E. The relationship of two process measurement systems in encounter groups (Doctoral dissertation, 1977). *Dissertation Abstracts International,* 1977, *38.*

Sage, R.E. A comparison between two different approaches to teaching counseling skills: A modified human relations training model vs. a traditional approach (Doctoral dissertation, 1977). *Dissertation Abstracts International,* 1977, *37.*

Tausch, R. Facilitative dimensions in interpersonal relations: Verifying the theoretical assumptions of Carl Rogers in school, family education, client-centered therapy, and encounter groups. *College Student Journal,* 1978, *12*(1), 2-11.

Tosi, D.J., & Eshbaugh, E.M. A cognitive-experiential approach to the interpersonal and intrapersonal development of counselors and therapists. *Journal of Clinical Psychology,* 1978, *34*(2), 494-500.

Widok, W. What is a sensitivity group: What is a balint group. *Psychotherapie und Medizinishe Psychologie,* 1977, *27*(5), 189-193.

## RESEARCH

### General

Bugen, L.A. Expectation profiles: Members expect more than they get while leaders give more than they expect. *Small Group Behavior,* 1978, *9,* 115-123.

Casteel, T.D. Degree of life crisis and general adaptive capability in a human relations lab population (Doctoral dissertation, 1976). *Dissertation Abstracts International,* 1976, *37.*

Chase, C. No joking matter: A study of laughter in sensitivity training groups (Doctoral dissertation, 1979). *Dissertation Abstracts International,* 1979, *39,* 8-B.

Curran, J.P., Gilbert, F.F., & Little, L.M. A comparison between behavioral replication training and sensitivity training approaches to heterosexual dating anxiety. *Journal of Counseling Psychology,* 1976, *23*(3), 190-196.

Das, A. The relationship between active involvement in the T-group and self reports of personal growth. *Pupil Personnel Services Journal,* 1976, *5*(1), 16-19.

Dauphinais, S., & Leitner, D.W. Effect of birth order, sex, and family size on affiliation with encounter groups. *Psychological Reports,* 1978, *42,* 673-674.

De Julio, S., Bentley, J., & Cockayne, T. Pregroup norm setting effects on encounter group interaction. *Small Group Behavior,* 1979, *10,* 368-388.

Dies, R.R., & Greeberg, B. Effects of physical contact in an encounter group context. *Journal of Consulting and Clinical Psychology,* 1976, *44*(3), 400-405.

Hardy, R.C., & Flatter, C.H. Human relations training and task-orientation of individuals. *Perceptual and Motor Skills,* 1977, *44*(3), 1123-1129.

Holeman, R., & Seiler, G. Effects of sensitivity training and transcendental meditation on perception of others. *Perceptual and Motor Skills,* 1979, *49,* 270.

Horowitz, R.S. An investigation of the relationship between an intensive small group experience and changes in interpersonal attitudes, behavior, and self-actualization (Doctoral dissertation, 1978). *Dissertation Abstracts International,* 1978, *38.*

Hurley, J.R. Two prepotent interpersonal dimensions and the effects of trainers on T-groups. *Small Group Behavior,* 1976, *7*(1), 77-98.

Johnson, D.L., & Hanson, P.G. Locus of control and behavior in treatment groups. *Journal of Personality Assessment,* 1979, *43*(2), 177-183.

Lundgren, D.C. Developmental trends in the emergence of interpersonal issues in T-groups. *Small Group Behavior*, 1977, *8*(2), 179-200.

Lundgren, D., & Knight, D.J. Sequential stages of development in sensitivity training groups. *Journal of Applied Behavioral Science*, 1978, *14*(2), 204-222.

Magyar, C.W., & Apostal, R.A. Interpersonal growth contracts and leader experience: Their effects in encounter groups. *Small Group Behavior*, 1977, *8*(3), 381-392.

McCanne, L. Dimensions of participant goals, expectations, and perceptions in small group experiences. *Journal of Applied Behavioral Science*, 1977, *13*, 533-542.

Meade, C.J. Human relations training and interpersonal process recall: An empirical investigation (Doctoral dissertation, 1979). *Dissertation Abstracts International*, 1979, *39*.

Miller, F.D. The problem of transfer of training in learning groups: Group cohesion as an end in itself. *Small Group Behavior*, 1976, 7(2), 221-236.

Mumma, F.S. The relevance of identity statuses in the development of a T-group: I & II (Doctoral dissertation, 1978). *Dissertation Abstracts International*, 1978, *39*.

Nieto, C.E. Effects of an interpersonal relations training microlab on the level of discrimination in training. *Revista De Psicologia, Universidad De Monterrey*, 1977, *5*(1), 26-342.

Reinken, M.L. The relationship between learning styles and laboratory design in human relations training (Doctoral dissertation, 1978). *Dissertation Abstracts International*, 1978, *38*.

Scamman, M.H. Dogmatism and human relations training: An experimental analysis (Doctoral dissertation, 1976). *Dissertation Abstracts International*, 1976, *37*, 1-A.

Shadish, W.R. The development, reliability, and validity of the interpersonal relations scale: The measurement of intimate behavior with special application to encounter group outcome (Doctoral dissertation, 1978). *Dissertation Abstracts International*, 1978, *39*.

Shapiro, J.B. Direct versus vicarious experiencing in a primarily nonverbal personal growth group microlab (Doctoral dissertation, 1976). *Dissertation Abstracts International*, 1976, *36*.

Slaney, R.B. Perceptions of alternative roles for the facilitative conditions. *Journal of Counseling Psychology*, 1977, *24*(2), 169-172.

Smith, P.B. Sources of influence in the sensitivity training laboratory. *Small Group Behavior*, 1976, 7(3), 331-348.

Speierer, G.W., & Weidelt, J. Development and place of anxiety and stress in client centered encounter groups. *Zeitschrift Für Klinsche Psychologie and Psychotherapie*, 1979, *27*, 135-145.

Street, P.A. Towards an aesthetic and affective analysis of extralinguistic processes in the encounter group using a musical analogue (Doctoral dissertation, 1978). *Dissertation Abstracts International*, 1978, *38*.

Sturgies, C.H. An examination of the relationship between locus of control, sociometric choice, individual performance and group effectiveness in human relations training (Doctoral dissertation, 1978). *Dissertation Abstracts International*, 1978, *38*.

Tindall, J. Time limited and time extended encounter groups: Descriptive stage development. *Small Group Behavior*, 1979, *10*, 402-413.

## Composition

Bugen, L.A. Composition and orientation effects on group cohesion. *Psychological Reports*, 1977, *40*, 175-182.

Dyson, J.W., Godwin, P.H.B., & Hazelwood, L.A. Group composition, leadership orientation, and decisional outcomes. *Small Group Behavior*, 1976, 7, 114-128.

Melnick, J., & Woods, M. Analysis of group composition research and theory for psychotherapeutic and growth-oriented groups. *Journal of Applied Behavioral Science*, 1977, *12*(4), 493-512.

Patterson, M.L., & Schaeffer, R.E. Effects of size and sex composition on interaction distance, participation, and satisfaction in small groups. *Small Group Behavior*, 1977, *8*, 433-442.

Ruhe, J., & Eatman, J. Effects of racial composition on small work groups. *Small Group Behavior*, 1977, *8*, 479-486.

Stava, L.J., & Bednar, R.R. Process and outcome in encounter groups: The effects of group composition. *Small Group Behavior*, 1979, *10*, 200-213.

## Feedback

Burke, J.J. Feedback in groups: Effect of valence, sequence, preceding activity, rating method, and sex on credibility of feedback (Doctoral dissertation, 1977). *Dissertation Abstracts International*, 1977, *33*, 3-B.

Harris, B. The effects of cohesiveness and sequences of positive and negative feedback on acceptance of feedback in personal growth groups (Doctoral dissertation, 1976). *Dissertation Abstracts International*, 1976, *36*, 12-B.

Lundgren, D.C., & Schaeffer, C. Feedback processes in sensitivity training groups. *Human Relations*, 1976, *29*(8), 763-782.

## Participants

Dies, R.R. Encounter group volunteering: Implications for research and practice. *Small Group Behavior*, 1978, *9*, 23-42.

Grossman, D.E. Member activity and change in behavior and attitude in T-groups (Doctoral dissertation, 1976). *Dissertation Abstracts International*, 1976, *37*, 4-B.

Morrison, T.L., & Thomas, M.D. Participants' perceptions of themselves and leaders in two kinds of group experience. *Journal of Social Psychology*, 1976, *98*(1), 103-110.

Vestre, N.D., Greene, R.L., & Marks, M.W. Psychological adjustment of persons seeking sensitivity group experience. *Psychological Reports*, 1978, *42*, 1295-1298.

## Self-Actualization

Butler, R.R. Self-actualizing: Myth or reality. *Group & Organization Studies*, 1977, *2*(2), 228-233.

Cate, R.M. Review of D.W. Johnsons' reaching out: Interpersonal effectiveness and self-actualization. *The Family Coordinator*, 1977, *26*, 196-197.

Cooper, C.L., & Kobayashi, K. Changes in self-actualization as a result of sensitivity training in England and Japan. *Small Group Behavior*, 1976, *7*(4), 387-396.

Reddy, W.B., & Beers, T. Sensitivity training . . . and the healthy become self-actualized. *Small Group Behavior*, 1977, *8*(4), 525-532.

Ritter, K.Y. Growth groups and the Personal Orientation Inventory. *Group & Organization Studies*, 1977, *2*(2), 234-241.

## Self-Concept

Bean, B.W., & Houston, B.K. Self-concept and self-disclosure in encounter groups. *Small Group Behavior*, 1978, *9*(4), 549-554.

Finando, S.J., Croteau, J.M., Sanz, D., & Woodson, R. The effects of group type on changes of self-concept. *Small Group Behavior*, 1977, *8*, 123-134.

Klemke, L.W. Sociological perspectives on self-concept changes in sensitivity training groups. *Small Group Behavior*, 1977, *8*(2), 135-146.

## Structure

Bednar, R.L., & Battersby, C.P. The effects of specific cognitive structure on early group development. *Journal of Applied Behavioral Science*, 1976, *12*(4), 513-522.

Crews, C.Y., & Melnick, J. Use of initial and delayed structure in facilitating group development. *Journal of Counseling Psychology*, 1976, *23*(2), 92-98.

Lee, F., & Bednar, R.L. Effects of group structure and risk-taking disposition on group behavior, attitudes, and atmosphere. *Journal of Counseling Psychology*, 1977, *24*, 191-200.

Shaw, M.E., & Harkey, B. Some effects of congruency of member characteristics and group structure upon group behavior. *Journal of Personality and Social Psychology*, 1976, *34*, 412-418.

## Trainer Behavior

Biberman, G. Trainer behavior in a T-group setting: A survey of current practice (Doctoral dissertation, 1978). *Dissertation Abstracts International*, 1978, *39*, 2-A, 768-769.

Deaver, D.L. Effects of group leader modeling and prompting feedback on member feedback, consensus, and cohesiveness (Doctoral dissertation, 1976). *Dissertation Abstracts International*, 1976, *36*.

Enright, M.F. The effects of leadership style on development and productivity in encounter groups (Doctoral dissertation, 1978). *Dissertation Abstracts International*, 1978.

Hansen, W.D. Impact of leader verbal communication style on T-groups (Doctoral dissertation, 1978). *Dissertation Abstracts International*, 1978. (University Microfilms No. 822830)

Kavanaugh, R.R. Categories of group interaction: The effects of leader and goal variables on the development of intimacy in T-groups (Doctoral dissertation, 1977). *Dissertation Abstracts International*, 1977, *38*.

Lundgren, D.C., & Knight, D.J. Trainer style and member attitudes toward trainer and group in T-groups. *Small Group Behavior*, 1977, *8*(1), 47-64.

Moss, C.J. Effects of leader behavior in personal growth groups: Self-disclosure and experiencing (Doctoral dissertation, 1976). *Dissertation Abstracts International*, 1976, *36*.

O'Day, R. Individual training styles: An empirically derived typology. *Small Group Behavior*, 1976, *7*(2), 147-182.

Oliverson, L.R. Identification of dimensions of leadership and leader behavior and cohesion in encounter groups (Doctoral dissertation, 1977). *Dissertation Abstracts International*, 1977. (University Microfilms No. 76-16760)

## REVIEWS AND SURVEYS

Back, K.W., & Harris, R.N. In search for community encounter groups and social change. *Contemporary Sociology: A Journal of Reviews*, 1979, *8*, 764-765.

Hunsaker, P.L. T-groups for MBA's: A state-of-the-art survey. *Group & Organization Studies*, 1978, *3*(3), 356-364.

Klee, J.B. A reflection on encounter groups. *Interpersonal Development*, 1976, *6*(1), 62-64.

Levine, N., & Cooper, C.L. T-groups: Twenty years on a prophecy. *Human Relations*, 1976, *29*(1), 1-23.

Lieberman, M.A. Change induction in small groups. *Annual Review of Psychology*, 1976, *27*, 217-250.

Russell, E.W. Encounter groups: First facts? A reexamination. *Catalog of Selected Documents in Psychology*, 1977, *7*.

Russell, E.W. Critique of a study on encounter groups. The facts about "Encounter Groups: First Facts." *Journal of Clinical Psychology*, 1978, *34*(1), 130-137.

What's happened to small group research? M. Lakin (Ed.), Special issue. *The Journal of Applied Behavioral Science*, 1979, *15*, 265-432.

## STANDARDS, ETHICS, AND VALUES

Bennett, F.D. Encounter groups: Growth or addiction? *Journal of Humanistic Psychology*, 1976, *16*, 59-70.

Braaten, L.J. Some ethical dilemmas in sensitivity training, encounter groups, and related activities. *Scandinavian Journal of Psychology*, 1979, *20*, 89-91.

Cooper, C.L. Taking the terror out of T-groups. *Personnel Management*, 1977, *9*(1), 22-26.

Friedman, M. Aiming at the self: The paradox of encounter and the human potential movement. *Journal of Humanistic Psychology*, 1976, *16*(2), 5-34.

Galinsky, M.J., & Schepler, J.H. Warning: Groups may be dangerous. *Social Work*, 1977, *22*, 89-95.

Hartley, D., Roback, H.B., & Arbramowitz, S.I. Deterioration effects in encounter groups. *American Psychologist*, 1976, *31*(3), 247-255.

Lieberman, M.A., & Gardner, J.R. Institutional alternatives to psychotherapy: A study of growth center users. *Archives of General Psychiatry*, 1976, *33*(2), 157-162.

Parker, R.S. Ethical and professional considerations concerning high risk groups. *Journal of Clinical Issues in Psychology*, 1976, *7*(1), 4-19.

## TECHNIQUES

Babad, E.Y., Birnbaum, M., & Benne, K.D. The C-group approach to laboratory learning. *Group & Organization Studies*, 1978, *3*(2), 168-184.

Daugelli, A.R., Meyer, R.J., & Conter, K.R. The effects of leaderless encounter group experiences on helping skills training. *Counselor Education and Supervision*, 1977, *17*(2), 92-97.

Friedman, S.B., Ellenhorn, L.J., & Snortum, J.R. A comparison of four warm-up techniques for initiating encounter groups. *Journal of Counseling Psychology*, 1976, *23*(6), 514-519.

Hallenstein, C.B. Comparison of short term group dynamic training methods on the development of group decision making ability (Doctoral dissertation, 1978). *Dissertation Abstracts International*, 1978, *38*, 9-B.

Harrison, R. Self-directed learning: A radical approach to educational design. *Simulations and Games*, 1977, *8*(1), 73-94.

Harrison, R. How to design and conduct self-directed learning experiences. *Group & Organization Studies*, 1978, *3*(2), 149-167.

Ortiz, G.C. The effect of relaxation and relaxation focusing on moods and openness in a human relations training program (Doctoral dissertation, 1977). *Dissertation Abstracts International*, 1977, *37*.

Sheridan, E.P., & Mehhus, G.E. A programmed personal growth laboratory. *Psychological Reports*, 1977, *41*(1), 143-150.

Uhlemann, M.R., Lea, G.W., & Stone, G.L. Effect of instructions and modeling on trainees low in interpersonal-communication skills. *Journal of Counseling Psychology*, 1976, *23*, 509-513.

**W. Brendan Reddy, Ph.D.,** *is a professor of psychology and the director of the Community Psychology Institute in the Department of Psychology, University of Cincinnati, Cincinnati, Ohio. Dr. Reddy's interests are in research and teaching and in organization and community consultation.*

**Kathy M. Lippert** *is a consultant in private practice in Cincinnati, Ohio. A professional member of NTL Institute, Ms. Lippert's interests are in organizational behavior, affirmative action, and research.*

# CONTRIBUTORS

Cassandra E. Amesley
Instructor in Women Studies
University of Washington, GN-45
Seattle, Washington 98195
  (206) 543-6900

Michael A. Berger, Ph.D.
Assistant Professor of Education
Human Development Counseling
  and Coordination
Peabody College
Vanderbilt University
P.O. Box 322
Nashville, Tennessee 37203
  (615) 327-8401

Walton C. Boshear
President
Solutions
Box 1389
Rancho Santa Fe, California 92067
  (714) 756-4895

Lt. Col. Frank Burns
Office of Chief of Staff
Attn: DACS-DME
Hdq. Department of the Army
Washington, D.C. 20310
  (202) 695-1825

Myron R. Chartier, Ph.D.
Director of Doctoral Programs
Professor of Ministry
The Eastern Baptist Theological Seminary
City and Lancaster Avenues
Philadelphia, Pennsylvania 19151
  (215) 896-5000

Rich Cherry, Ph.D.
Director, International Quality of Work Life
General Motors Corporation
3044 West Grand Boulevard (6-229)
Detroit, Michigan 48202
  (313) 556-2260

L. Paul Church
Staff Assistant
Industrial Relations Section
Sloan School of Management
Massachusetts Institute of Technology
Cambridge, Massachusetts 02139
  (617) 253-2653

Gary W. Combs, Ph.D.
Associate Professor of Administration
Public Administration Program
Sangamon State University
Springfield, Illinois 62708
  (217) 786-6310

Walter J. Cox
Principal Training Officer
Department of Personnel Services
Leeds City Council
"Linghithe," 6 Kenworthy Rise
Holt Park, Adel
Leeds LS16 7QW
West Yorkshire, England
  (England) 0532-610381

Bob Crosby
President
Concern for Corporate Fitness
W. 1614 Riverside
Spokane, Washington 99201
  (509) 747-8016

Drew P. Danko
Senior Administrator of Personnel
  and Organizational Research
General Motors Corporation
3044 West Grand Boulevard
Detroit, Michigan 48202
  (313) 556-3220

Daniel G. Eckstein, Ph.D.
Director, Counseling Clinic, and
  Assistant Professor of Psychology
School of Human Behavior
U.S. International University
10455 Pomerado Road
San Diego, California 92131
  (714) 271-4300

James V. Fee, Ph.D.
Professor
Mass Media-Communication
University of Akron
Akron, Ohio 44325
  (216) 375-7954

**Howard L. Fromkin, Ph.D.**
Executive Vice President
Fromkin Van Horn Limited
1 Yonge Street, Suite 2205
Toronto, Ontario, Canada M5E 1ES
  (416) 862-7050

**Major Robert L. Gragg**
HQ #DARCOM
5001 Eisenhower
Attn: DRXMM-OE
Alexandria, Virginia 22333
(202) 274-8532

**Martin D. Hanlon, Ph.D.**
Assistant Professor
Department of Urban Studies
Queens College City University of New York
Flushing, New York 11367
  (212) 520-7510

**John E. Jones, Ph.D.**
Senior Vice President for Research
  and Development
University Associates, Inc.
8517 Production Avenue
P.O. Box 26240
San Diego, California 92126
  (714) 578-5900

**William W. Kibler**
Manager, Training and Development
R.J. Reynolds Tobacco Company
401 N. Main Street
Winston-Salem, North Carolina 27102
  (919) 777-6910

**Aharon Kuperman, Ph.D.**
Coordinator of Teachers' Workshop in
  Creativity and Design
Bezalel, Academy of Arts and Design
10 Shmuel Hanagid
Jerusalem, Israel 94592
  Israel (02) 225-111

**L. Phillip K. Le Gras**
Assistant Professor
Military Leadership and Management Department
The Royal Military College of Canada
Kingston, Ontario, Canada K7L 2W3
  (613) 545-7408

**Kathy M. Lippert**
Consultant
1611 Braintree Drive
Cincinnati, Ohio 45230
  (513) 231-0286

**Bruce A. McDonald, Ed.D.**
Curriculum Materials Developer
  and Assistant Professor
Department of Vocational Education Studies
Southern Illinois University at Carbondale
Carbondale, Illinois 62901
  (618) 453-3321

**Thomas J. Mulhern, Ph.D.**
Director, Education and Training
Letchworth Village Developmental Center
Lincoln Building
Thiells, New York 10984
  (914) 947-1000

**David A. Nadler, Ph.D.**
Associate Professor of Organizational Behavior
Graduate School of Business
Columbia University
716 Uris Hall
New York, New York 10027
  (212) 280-3494

**David R. Nicoll, Ph.D.**
Organization Consultant and
  Co-Director, Confluent Systems
Kaiser-Permanente Medical Care Program
4647 Zion Avenue
San Diego, California 92120
  (714) 563-2333

**Stella Lybrand Norman**
Family Systems Specialist
Crossroads South County Office
6301 Richmond Highway
Alexandria, Virginia 22306
  (703) 960-9554

**Albert B. Palmer, Ph.D.**
Professor of Psychology
Department of Psychology
University of Toledo
Toledo, Ohio 43606
  (419) 537-2715

**Maureen A. Parashkevov**
MH Staff Development Specialist III
Education and Training Department
Letchworth Village Developmental Center
Lincoln Building
Thiells, New York 10984
(914) 947-1000

**Udai Pareek, Ph.D.**
Larsen & Toubro Professor of
   Organizational Behavior
Indian Institute of Management
Ahmedabad 380015
Gujarat, India
(India) (307) 450041

**Hugh Pates, Ph.D.**
Counseling Psychologist
University of California at San Diego
Senior Consultant
University Associates, Inc.
6186 Stetson Place
San Diego, California 92122
(714) 453-0645

**Dennis N.T. Perkins, Ph.D.**
Assistant Professor
School of Organization and Management
Department of Psychology
Yale University
135 Prospect, Box 1A
New Haven, Connecticut 06520
(203) 432-3832

**Lawrence C. Porter, Ed.D.**
Senior Consultant
University Associates, Inc.
401 Wayne Avenue
Oakland, California 94606
(415) 834-2444

**W. Brendan Reddy, Ph.D.**
Director and Professor
Community Psychology Institute
University of Cincinnati
336 Dyer Hall
Cincinnati, Ohio 45221
(513) 475-5981

**Steven M. Rosenthal**
Associate Consultant
R.S.I., Inc.
386 Commercial Street, #5F
Boston, Massachusetts 02109
(617) 720-1281

**Martin B. Ross, Dr., Ph.**
Assistant Professor and
   Associate Director
Program in Health Services Management
School of Public Health
University of California, Los Angeles
Partner, Pointer-Ross and Associates
905 Hilgard Avenue
Los Angeles, California 90024
(213) 825-5773

**Marshall Sashkin, Ph.D.**
Senior Editorial Associate
University Associates, Inc.
Professor of Industrial and
   Organizational Psychology
University College
University of Maryland
College Park, Maryland 20742
(301) 454-4931

**John J. Scherer**
Associate Director
Whitworth/LIOS Graduate Center
   for Applied Studies
Whitworth College
Executive Vice President
Concern for Corporate Fitness
W. 1614 Riverside
Spokane, Washington 99201
(509) 747-8016

**Henry P. Sims, Jr., Ph.D.**
Associate Professor of Organizational Behavior
College of Business Administration
The Pennsylvania State University
609 Business Administration Building
University Park, Pennsylvania 16802
(814) 234-1856

**Mark Smith**
Department of Psychology
York University
4500 Keele Street
Downsview, Ontario, Canada M3J 1P3
(416) 967-0873

**Michele Stimac, Ed.D.**
Professor and Doctoral Program
   Counselor
Graduate School of Education
Pepperdine University
8035 South Vermont Avenue
Los Angeles, California 90044
(213) 971-7817

**Joseph P. Stokes, Ph.D.**
Assistant Professor of Psychology
University of Illinois at Chicago Circle
P.O. Box 4348
Chicago, Illinois 60680
  (312) 996-4462

**Raymond C. Tait**
R.F.D. 1, Box 71A
Sperryville, Virginia 22740
  (703) 987-8342